T0190042

Lecture Notes in Computer Science 13415

More information about this series at https://link.springer.com/bookseries/558

Mario Trapp · Erwin Schoitsch ·
Jérémie Guiochet · Friedemann Bitsch (Eds.)

Computer Safety, Reliability, and Security

SAFECOMP 2022 Workshops

DECSoS, DepDevOps, SASSUR, SENSEI, USDAI, and WAISE
Munich, Germany, September 6–9, 2022
Proceedings

Springer

Editors
Mario Trapp
Fraunhofer IKS
Munich, Germany

Erwin Schoitsch [iD]
Austrian Institute of Technology
Vienna, Austria

Jérémie Guiochet
LAAS-CNRS
University of Toulouse
Toulouse, France

Friedemann Bitsch [iD]
Thales Deutschland GmbH
Ditzingen, Germany

ISSN 0302-9743   ISSN 1611-3349 (electronic)
Lecture Notes in Computer Science
ISBN 978-3-031-14861-3   ISBN 978-3-031-14862-0 (eBook)
https://doi.org/10.1007/978-3-031-14862-0

This Springer imprint is published by the registered company Springer Nature Switzerland AG
The registered company address is: Gewerbestrasse 11, 6330 Cham, Switzerland

Preface

The SAFECOMP workshops preceding the SAFECOMP conference have become more attractive since they started generating their own proceedings in the Springer LNCS series (LNCS vol. 13415, the book in your hands, accompanies the main conference proceedings published in LNCS vol. 13414). This meant adhering to Springer's guidelines, i.e., the International Program Committee of each workshop had to make sure that at least three independent reviewers reviewed the papers carefully. The selection criteria differed from those of the main conference since authors were encouraged to submit workshop papers on work in progress or controversial topics. In total, 23 regular papers (out of 27) were accepted for the SAFECOMP 2022 workshops. There were a few invited papers and talks, which were not all included in the proceedings. All workshops had an introduction written by the chairs. The workshops were organized as online or hybrid events because of uncertainties around COVID-19.

This year, eight workshops had been proposed, one was cancelled, one (DepDevOps) was integrated with DECSoS, and one (ARCH 2022) arranged its own proceedings outside this volume:

- DECSoS 2022 – 17th Workshop on Dependable Smart Embedded and Cyber-Physical Systems and Systems-of-Systems, chaired by Erwin Schoitsch and Amund Skavhaug.
- DepDevOps 2022 – 3rd International Workshop on Dependable Development-Operation Continuum Methods for Dependable Cyber-Physical Systems, chaired by Miren Illarramendi, Aitor Arrieta, and Irune Agirre.
- SASSUR 2022 – 9th International Workshop on Next Generation of System Assurance Approaches for Critical Systems, chaired by Jose Luis de la Vara, Alejandra Ruiz, and Antonio Kung.
- SENSEI 2022 – 1st International Workshop on Security and Safety Interactions, chaired by Christina Kolb, Milan Lopuhaä-Zwakenberg, and Elena Troubitsyna.
- USDAI 2022 – 3rd International Workshop on Underpinnings for Safe Distributed AI, chaired by Morten Larsen, Merijn van Tooren, Alain Sears, and Daniel Reti.
- WAISE 2022 – 5th International Workshop on Artificial Intelligence Safety Engineering, chaired by Orlando Avila-García, Mauricio Castillo-Effen, Chih-Hong Cheng, Zakaria Chihani, and Simos Gerasimou.

The workshops provided a truly international platform for academia and industry.

It was a pleasure to work with the SAFECOMP conference chairs Mario Trapp and Francesca Saglietti, the general workshop co-chair Jeremie Guiochet, the publication chair Friedemann Bitsch, the workshop chairs, the Program Committees, the local organization team, and the authors. Thank you all for your cooperation and excellent work!

September 2022   Erwin Schoitsch

Organization

EWICS TC7 Chair

Francesca Saglietti   University of Erlangen-Nuremberg, Germany

Conference Chairs

Mario Trapp   Fraunhofer Institute for Cognitive Systems, Germany
Francesca Saglietti   University of Erlangen-Nuremberg, Germany

General Workshop Co-chairs

Erwin Schoitsch   AIT Austrian Institute of Technology, Austria
Jérémie Guiochet   LAAS-CNRS, France

Publication Chair

Friedemann Bitsch   Thales Deutschland GmbH, Germany

Industry Chair

Simon Fürst   BMW, Germany

Local Organization Chair

Simon Burton   Fraunhofer Institute for Cognitive Systems, Germany

Local Organization Committee

Martin Simon   Fraunhofer Institute for Cognitive Systems, Germany
Eva von Wardenburg   Fraunhofer Institute for Cognitive Systems, Germany

Workshop Chairs

DECSoS 2022

Erwin Schoitsch   AIT Austrian Institute of Technology, Austria
Amund Skavhaug   Norwegian University of Science and Technology, Norway

DepDevOps 2022

Miren Illarramendi   Mondragon University, Spain

Aitor Arrieta   Mondragon University, Spain
Irune Agirre   Ikerlan Research Centre, Spain

SASSUR 2022

Jose Luis de la Vara   Universidad de Castilla-La Mancha, Spain
Alejandra Ruiz   TECNALIA R&I, Spain
Antonio Kung   Trialog, France

SENSEI2022

Christina Kolb   Independent Scholar, The Netherlands
Milan Lopuhaä-Zwakenberg   University of Twente, The Netherlands
Elena Troubitsyna   KTH Royal Institute of Technology, Sweden

USDAI 2022

Morten Larsen   AnyWi Technologies, The Netherlands
Merijn van Tooren   Almende, The Netherlands
Alain Sears   Leiden University, The Netherlands
Daniel Reti   DFKI, Germany

WAISE 2022

Orlando Avila-García   ARQUIMEA Research Center, Spain
Mauricio Castillo-Effen   Lockheed Martin, USA
Chih-Hong Cheng   Fraunhofer Institute for Cognitive Systems, Germany
Zakaria Chihani   CEA-List, France
Simos Gerasimou   University of York, UK

Supporting Institutions

European Workshop on
Industrial Computer Systems
Technical Committee 7 on
Reliability, Safety and Security

Fraunhofer Institute for
Cognitive Systems

Technical University of Munich

Austrian Institute of Technology

Laboratory for Analysis and
Architecture of Systems, CNRS

Thales Deutschland GmbH

Lecture Notes in Computer Science
(LNCS),
Springer Science + Business Media

Gesellschaft für Informatik (GI)

Informationstechnische Gesellschaft
(ITG) im VDE

Technical Group ENCRESS
in GI and ITG

Austrian Computer Society

Electronic Components and Systems
for European Leadership – Austria now:
Electronics and Software Based
Systems (ESBS) Austria

European Research Consortium for
Informatics and Mathematics

Verband österreichischer
Software Industrie

Contents

5th International Workshop on Artificial Intelligence Safety Engineering (WAISE 2022)

17th International ERCIM/EWICS/ARTEMIS Workshop on Dependable Smart Embedded Cyber-Physical Systems and Systems-of-Systems (DECSoS 2022)

17th International Workshop on Dependable Smart Cyber-Physical Systems and Systems-of-Systems (DECSoS 2022)

European Research and Innovation Projects in the Field of Dependable Cyber-Physical Systems and Systems-of-Systems (supported by EWICS TC7, ERCIM and Horizon2020/ECSEL JU projects' work)

Erwin Schoitsch[1], and Amund Skavhaug[2]

[1] Center for Digital Safety and Security, AIT Austrian Institute of Technology GmbH, Vienna, Austria
Erwin.Schoitsch@ait.ac.at
[2] Department of Mechanical and Industrial Engineering, NTNU (The Norwegian University of Science and Technology), Trondheim, Norway
Amund.Skavhaug@ntnu.no

1 Introduction

The DECSoS workshop at SAFECOMP follows already its own tradition since 2006. In the past, it focussed on the conventional type of "dependable embedded systems", covering all dependability aspects as defined by Avizienis, Lapries, Kopetz, Voges and others in IFIP WG 10.4. To put more emphasis on the relationship to physics, mechatronics and the notion of interaction with an unpredictable environment, massive deployment and highly interconnected systems of different type, the terminology changed to "cyber-physical systems" (CPS) and "Systems-of-Systems" (SoS). The new megatrend IoT ("Internet of Things") as super-infrastructure for CPS as things added a new dimension with enormous challenges. "Intelligence" as a new ability of systems and components leads to a new paradigm, "Smart Systems", with embedded AI (Artificial Intelligence) inside. Collaboration and co-operation of these systems with each other and humans, and the interplay of safety, cybersecurity, privacy, and reliability, together with cognitive decision making, are leading to new challenges in verification, validation and certification/qualification, as these systems operate in an unpredictable environment and are open, adaptive and even (partly) autonomous. Examples are e.g., the smart power grid, highly automated transport systems, advanced manufacturing systems ("Industry 4.0"), mobile co-operating autonomous vehicles and robotic systems, smart health care, and smart buildings up to smart cities. The conventional properties "Safety" and "Cybersecurity" are no longer sufficient to describe requirements on system behaviour – "trustworthiness" is the new term.

Society depends more and more on CPS and SoS - thus it is important to consider trustworthiness (dependability (safety, reliability, availability, security, maintainability, etc.), privacy, resilience, robustness and sustainability), together with ethical aspects in a holistic manner. These are targeted research areas in Horizon 2020 and public-private partnerships such as the ECSEL JU (Joint Under-taking) (Electronic Components and Systems for European Leadership), which integrated the former ARTEMIS (Advanced Research and Technology for Embedded Intelligent Systems), ENIAC and EPoSS efforts as "private partners". The public part are the EC and the national public authorities of the participating member states. Funding comes from the EC and the national public authorities ("tri-partite funding": EC, member states, project partners). Besides ECSEL, other JTIs (Joint Technology Initiatives), who organize their own research & innovation agenda and manage their work as separate legal entities according to Article 187 of the Lisbon Treaty, are: Innovative Medicines Initiative (IMI), Fuel Cells and Hydrogen (FCH), Clean Sky, Bio-Based Industries, Shift2Rail, Single European Sky Air Traffic Management Research (SESAR).

Besides these Joint Undertakings there are many other so-called contractual PPPs, where funding is completely from the EC (via the Horizon 2020 program), but the work program and strategy are developed together with a private partner association, e.g. Robotics cPPP SPARC with euRobotics as private partner. Others are e.g. Factories of the Future (FoF), Energy-efficient Buildings (EeB), Sustainable Process Industry (SPIRE), European Green Vehicles Initiative (EGVI), Photonics, High Performance Computing (HPC), Advanced 5G Networks for the Future Internet (5G), the Big Data Value PPP and the cPPP for Cybersecurity Industrial Research and Innovation.

The period of Horizon 2020 Programme and the current PPPs ended with the last EU budget period. The landscape of PPPs was updated in the context of the next EC Research Programme "HORIZON Europe" (2021–2027), where re-organized JUs have been established (e.g. ECS-KDT (Electronic Components and Systems, Key Digital Technologies) as ECSEL successor), including additional key themes like photonics and software, advanced computing technologies, bio-sensors and flexible electronics, besides new PPPs. Due to the COVID-19 crises and other negotiations within the EC, the new Programmes were delayed, e.g., the first Call for KDT started December 2021, the first new projects will be decided June 2022.

But this will not be the end of the story – the climate crises and the Ukraine war have demonstrated the vulnerability of European economy. The European Commission reacted by the "Green Deal" and measures to mitigate the energy and chip respectively other resources' shortness. KDT JU as research programme will be extended and become the "Chips Joint Undertaking" to ensure European digital sovereignty and make us "future fit". Billions will be invested in course of the European Chips Act with the aim of jointly creating a state-of-the-art European chip ecosystem from production to security of supply, so developing a new arena for groundbreaking European technologies, while remaining true to the policy objectives for digital transformation and the Green Deal. The concept of running tripartite joint undertakings allows - better than other similar entities - to establish an extremely fruitful cooperation with Participating States, European Commission and Industry, stated Doris Vierbauch, Chair of the Public Authorities Board of the KDT JU, in the corresponding KDT JU and EC press release.

2 ECSEL and KDT JU: The European Cyber-Physical Systems Initiative

Some ECSEL Projects which have "co-hosted" the Workshop, in supporting partners by funding their research, have been finished Autumn last year (delayed by the Covid-19 crisis which influenced negatively full achievements of some of the co-operative demonstrators because it was not possible to work together at the demonstrators' locations) (see reports in last year's Springer Safecomp 2021 Workshop Proceedings, LNCS 12853). This year, the last series of H2020/ECSEL projects has started, and recent H2020/ECSEL and nationally funded projects are "co-hosting" scientifically the DECSoS Workshop via contributions from supported partners, some of the reports covering contributions from more than one project such achieving synergetic effects. Of course, the organizations of the authors have to be recognized as supporter of the work presented. Some examples are (see also acknowledgements in the papers):

- FRACTAL: A Cognitive Fractal and Secure EDGE based on a unique Open-Safe-Reliable-Low Power Hardware Platform Node, under grant agreement No. 877056, Electronic Component Systems for European Leadership Joint undertaking (ECSEL JU).
- VALUE3S: Verification and Validation of Automated Systems' Safety and Security, a framework to reduce time and cost needed to verify and validate automated systems (H2020-ECSEL grant agreement no. 876852).
- iRel4.0: Intelligent Reliability 4.0, improving reliability of electronic components and systems by reducing failure rates along the entire value chain (H2020-ECSEL grant agreement no. 876659).
- SECREDAS ("Product Security for Cross Domain Reliable Dependable Automated Systems"), (https://www.ecsel.eu/projects/secredas), contributing to ECSEL Lighthouse Cluster "Mobility.E").
- Erasmus+ Call 2020 Round 1 KA203 Programme of the European Union under the agreement 2020-1-CZ01- KA203-078494.

National Programmes funding DECSoS projects, were for example:

- SMARTEST2, a project supported by the German Federal Ministry of Economic Affairs and Energy (BMWi) (project no. 1501600C).
- GTÜ Gesellschaft für Technische Überwachung mbH, Stuttgart, Germany.
- LIDER Programme, National Centre for Research and Development, Poland.
- COMET K2 Competence Centers for Excellent Technologies from the Austrian Federal Ministry for Climate Action (BMK), the Austrian Federal Ministry for Digital and Economic Affairs (BMDW), the Province of Styria and the Styrian Business Promotion Agency (SFG) (Virtual Vehicle Research GmbH).
- ADEX Autonomous-Driving Examiner, (Austrian Research Promotion Agency, Programme "ICT for the Future", Grant Agreement 880811). ADEX aims at developing a trustworthy examiner for controllers of self-driving vehicles. The project will adopt a scenario-based approach, combining techniques from artificial intelligence and traffic accident analysis to generate concrete challenging scenarios. Following a human-centered iterative design approach the developed automated

verification and testing methodology will be transparent and user understandable. The project results will be evaluated both in virtual (simulation) and physical environments. Project outcomes will help to significantly increase the trust of design engineers and regulatory bodies in autonomous-driving controllers.
- Other national funding programmes from Poland, Czech Republic, and in context of the "tri-partite" funding of ECSEL projects from Austria, Belgium, Czech Republic, Finland, France, Germany, Hungary, Italy, Latvia, Lithuania, The Netherlands, Norway, Poland, Portugal, Romania, Sweden, Spain, Switzerland, and sometimes even from outside Europe (e.g., Tunisia, India).

Results of these projects are partially reported in presentations at the DECSoS-Workshop. Some presentations refer to work done within companies or institutes, not referring to particular public project funding.

Other important ECSEL projects in the context of DECSoS are the two large ECSEL "Lighthouse" projects for Mobility.E and for Industry4.E, which aim at providing synergies by cooperation with a group of related European projects in their area of interest:

- iDev40 ("Integrated Development 4.0", https://www.ecsel.eu/projects/idev40), contributing to ECSEL Lighthouse Cluster "Industry4.E" (project no. 783163).
- AI4CSM (Automotive Intelligence for Connected, Shared Mobility, https://www.ait.ac.at/en/research-topics/dependable-systems-engineering/projects/ai4csm; https://ai4csm.automotive.oth-aw.de/) (project no. 101007326-2. Electric, Connected, Automated and Shared Mobility build together the European approach to mitigate climate change and environmental degradation in the transport and mobility domain, thus fulfilling goals of the European Green Deal, the European implementation of the UN SDG (Sustainable Development Goals). Functional architectures, embedded intelligence and functional virtualization for connected and shared mobility developing and using advanced electronic components, trustworthy AI for decision making, systems for advanced perception, efficient propulsion and batteries, advanced connectivity, new integration and platform concepts, are developed and implemented in use cases (demonstrators). Demonstrators on system-integration-level include:

  - Smart, connected and shared mobility for urban areas,
  - Electric vehicle development on AI-inside based components and functions (fault detection, analysis and mitigation, highly automated driving, AI enabled perception and sensor fusion platforms etc.),
  - Particular aspects are the evaluation of the achievements with respect to the "Green Deal" (climate neutrality, zero pollution, sustainable transport, transition towards circular economy), of the ethical/societal aspects of decision making, and standardization activities.

- Comp4Drones (Framework of key enabling technologies for safe and autonomous drones' applications, https://artemis-ia.eu/project/180-COMP4DRONES.html; started October 2019) (project no. 826610).

This list is of course not complete, it considers only projects which provided contributions to the work and papers of the authors and co-authors directly or indirectly via the work within their organizations and companies. Short descriptions of the projects, partners, structure and technical goals and objectives are described on the project- and the ECSEL websites, see also the Acknowledgement at the end of this introduction and https://www.ecsel.eu/projects.

3   This Year's Workshop

The workshop DECSoS 2022 provides some insight into an interesting set of topics to enable fruitful discussions. The mixture of topics is hopefully well balanced, with a specific focus on (highly) automated driving (cybersecurity & safety, regulations, sensors and platforms), on critical systems development, validation and applications. Presentations are mainly based on ECSEL, Horizon 2020, and nationally funded projects mentioned above, and on industrial experiences of partners' companies and universities. In the following explanations the projects are mentioned, which at least partially funded the work presented.

Additionally, the DepDevOps workshop had contributions fitting well into the DECSoS scope and was therefore joining DECSoS as "DepDevOps Session".

The session starts with an introduction and overview to the DECSoS Workshop, setting the scene for European Research and Innovation and co-hosting projects and organizations ERCIM, EWICS and ECSEL (Austria).

The first session on "**Safety and Automated Driving Systems**" comprises two presentations:

(1) **Triggering Conditions Analysis and Use Case for Validation of ADAS/ADS Functions,** by *Víctor J. Expósito Jiménez, Helmut Martin, Christian Schwarzl, Georg Macher, and Eugen Brenner.*
    More advanced components have opened new trends which have to be covered from the safety perspective. This includes not only specifications and requirements but also scenarios taking into account uncertainties from the environment. SotiF (Safety of the intended functionality) appears to ensure system safety in case of technological shortcomings or misuse by users. The potential triggering conditions which lead to failures are a key issue to be identified.

(2) **A Statistical View on Automated Driving System Safety Architectures,** by *Rainer Faller and Krystian Radlak.*
    To meet a tolerable risk level is key for automated driving functions, considering safety architectures, sensor performance and the possible safety-related driving and traffic scenarios. Diverse redundancy is costly, but the analysis discussed in this paper shows evidence, that two-channel diversity may not be sufficient. Correlation of failures between sensor measurements has to be better understood, and extension of the architecture by a warning system may improve the situation.

The second session is the Joint DECSoS - DepDevOps Session, which integrates the DepDevOps workshop into DECSoS because of similar topics. It covers "**Tools and Methods**" aspects with three papers:

(1) **Watch: A Validation Framework and Language for Tool Qualification**, *by Luiz Cordeiro, Christian Becker, Markus Pielmeier and Julian Amann.*
ISO 26262:2018 is one of the most important standards for functional safety within the automotive domain. One crucial aspect of the standard is software tool qualification. The goal of software tool qualification is to ensure that none of the used software tools (compilers, code generators, etc.) is introducing a safety-related malfunctional behavior. Therefore, for each tool a so-called tool confidence level (TCL) is determined. *Watch* is a software validation framework and domain-specific language to support tool qualification for automotive functional safety. It helps to identify all used tools within our toolchain, ensures that the correct version of a tool has been used, and allows us to define in a formal way how a tool can be used within our environment. Furthermore, it offers the possibility to formulate qualification toolkits.

(2) **Criteria for the Analysis of Gaps and Limitations of V&V Methods for Safety- and Security-Critical Systems**, *by Enrico Ferrari, Rupert Schlick, Jose Luis de la Vara, Peter Folkesson and Behrooz Sangchoolie.*
As society increasingly relies on safety- and security- critical systems, the need for confirming their dependability becomes essential. Adequate V&V (verification and validation) methods must be employed. It is important to analyze their possible gaps and limitations, such as scalability issues. However, and as we have experienced, common, explicitly defined criteria are seldom used for such analyses. This results in analyses that consider different aspects and to a different extent, hindering their comparison and thus the comparison of the V&V methods. As a solution, we present a set of criteria for the analysis of gaps and limitations of V&V methods for safety- and security-critical systems. They agreed upon the use of nine criteria: functionality, accuracy, scalability, deployment, learning curve, automation, reference environment, cost, and standards.

(3) **A Guided Search for Races Based on Data Flow Patterns**, *by Andreas Neubaum, Loui Al Sardy, Marc Spisländer, Francesca Saglietti and Sara Kretschmer.*
The increasing impact of potential cyber-attacks on the behavior of automated processes is evident. They are frequently based on existing software vulnerabilities which may be intentionally exploited via knowledge or trial. This asks for efficient verification techniques designed to explicitly address the detection of exploitable vulnerabilities of predefined type before allowing for operation. The project SMARTEST2 pursues the goal of developing intelligent techniques for a more systematic identification of vulnerabilities of predefined type. A strategy for searching for exploitable races is derived, implemented and evaluated.

The first afternoon session is dedicated to "**Dependable Sensors and Platforms for Highly Automated/Autonomous Systems**", with three papers:

(1) **Building a Test Bed for the Periodical Technical Inspection of Sensors Perceiving the Environment in Autonomous Vehicles,** *by Felix Müller, Philipp Nenninger and Eric Sax.*
For autonomous vehicles, the environmental perception plays a key part in its ability to navigate the public roads. At the same time, the sensors used for the

perception are very likely to differ between individual vehicles over their lifespan due to maintenance and environmental differences as well as different incidents, that might impact their functionality. The periodical technical inspection of road vehicles is an established tool to ensure the technical capabilities of vehicles. This concept must be advanced further because of the higher impact in case of autonomous vehicles. The focus here is on sensor performance for environmental perception of the surroundings of the vehicle. A test bed for evaluation of the vehicles' roadworthiness is presented.

(2) **Testing and verification of the deep neural networks against sparse pixel defects,** *by Michal Szczepankiewicz, Krystian Radlak, Karolina Szepankiewicz, Adam Popowicz, and Pawel Zawistowski.*

Deep neural networks can produce outstanding results when applied to image recognition tasks but are susceptible to image defects and modifications. Substantial degradation of the image can be detected by automatic or interactive prevention techniques. However, sparse pixel defects may have a significant impact on the dependability especially of autonomous driving vehicles, but may not be detected by a human. This work introduces a novel sparse adversarial attack generation method and introduces a novel framework for sparse adversarial attack generation, which can be integrated into the safety-critical systems development process.

(3) **Observing the impact of multicore execution platform for TSP systems under schedulability, security and safety constraints,** *by Ill-ham Atchadam, Laurent Lemarchand, Frank Singhoff, and Hai Nam Tran.*

Multicore execution platforms are becoming popular in avionic systems. Time and Space Partitioning (TSP), which consists of isolating applications within partitions, is a well-known means to assign avionic applications to computing units according to security, schedulability, and safety constraints. Partitioning of avionic applications over such execution platforms while considering these constraints is explained, proposing a design space exploration approach using a multi-objective meta-heuristic, that provides trade-offs between schedulability and security while considering safety.

The last session **"Automotive Security and Regulations"** includes two presentations on security assessment and regression analysis in context of vehicle regulations:

(1) **Security Assessment Prospects as part of Vehicle Regulations**, *by Mona Gierl, Reiner Kriesten, and Eric Sax.*

The World Forum for the harmonization of vehicle regulations works continuously on keeping the regulations up to date considering current technological innovations and scientific progress. With the advances in automotive connectivity, cybersecurity engineering is becoming mandatory for connected cars. Thus, present roadworthiness assessments must be extended with adequate security assessment methods. The current state of the type-approval and periodic technical inspection regulations for passenger cars are presented. Further, the UN R155 Cybersecurity Regulation [1] and the ISO/SAE 21434 [2] are analyzed.

(2) **UNECE Threat List Case Study: Prediction of Cyber Risks in the Automotive Domain Using Regression Analysis,** *by Abdelkader Magdy Shaaban, Sebastian Chlup, and Christoph Schmittner.*
Automobile manufacturers should ensure their vehicle's cybersecurity, considering the UNECE regulation for road vehicle approval. Estimating risk severity is critical in this domain for specifying appropriate security mechanisms to address existing cyber risks. Accurate risk evaluation needs to consider multiple factors of likelihood and impact, which indicate the probability of risk occurrence and its severity. However, establishing a relationship amongst multiple factors of impact and likelihood remains a challenging problem. In this work, machine learning regression analysis to create correlations between various independent factors of likelihood and impact for predicting dependent variables are proposed that indicate the assessment of cyber risk severities. The UNECE threat list is used as a case study to show how machine learning regression approaches may help predict realistic cyber risk estimations in the automotive domain. The effectiveness of regression analysis for evaluating cyber risks in the automotive sector is demonstrated.

As chairpersons of the DECSoS workshop, we want to thank all authors and contributors who submitted their work, Friedemann Bitsch, the SAFECOMP Publication Chair, the SAFECOMP conference chairs Mario Trapp and Francesca Saglietti, my general workshop co-chair Jeremie Guiochet and the members of the International Program Committee who enabled a fair evaluation through reviews and considerable improvements in many cases. We want to express our thanks to the SAFECOMP organizers, who provided us the opportunity to organize the workshop at SAFECOMP 2022 as a hybrid event, because of the still existing uncertainties of the CoVID-19 situation. Particularly we want to thank the EC and national public funding authorities who made the work in the research projects possible. We do not want to forget the continued support of our companies and organizations, of ERCIM, the European Research Consortium for Informatics and Mathematics with its Working Group on Dependable Embedded Software-intensive Systems, and EWICS, the creator and main sponsor of SAFECOMP, with its chair Francesca Saglietti and the sub- groups, who always helped us to learn from their networks.

We hope that all participants will benefit from the workshop, enjoy the conference and will join us again in the future!

Acknowledgements. Part of the work presented in the workshop received funding from the EC (H2020/ECSEL Joint Undertaking) and the partners National Funding Authorities ("tri-partite") through the projects SECREDAS (nr. 783119), iDev40 (nr. 783163), AfarCloud (nr. 783221), Comp4Drones (nr. 826610), ARROWHEAD Tools (nr. 826452), VALUE3S (nr. 876852), iRel40 (nr. 876659) and AI4CSM (nr. 101007326). Other EC funded projects are e.g., in Horizon 2020 the Erasmus+ project 2020-1-CZ01- KA203-078494. Some projects received national funding, e.g., SMARTEST2 from the German Federal Ministry for Economic Affairs and Energy (BMWi) (nr. 1501600C), ADEX "ICT for Future" (FFG, BMK Austria) (no. 880811), the COMET K2 Program (BMK Austria, Styria). This list does not claim to be complete, for further details check the acknowledgements in the papers.

International Program Committee 2022

Triggering Conditions Analysis and Use Case for Validation of ADAS/ADS Functions

Víctor J. Expósito Jiménez[1]([✉]) [ID], Helmut Martin[1], Christian Schwarzl[1], Georg Macher[2] [ID], and Eugen Brenner[2]

[1] Virtual Vehicle Research GmbH, Inffeldgasse 21a, 8010 Graz, Austria
{victor.expositojimenez,helmut.martin,christian.schwarzl}@v2c2.at
[2] Graz University of Technology, Rechbauerstraße 12, 8010 Graz, Austria
{georg.macher,brenner}@tugraz.at

Abstract. Safety in the automotive domain is a well-known topic, which has been in constant development in the past years. The complexity of new systems that add more advanced components in each function has opened new trends that have to be covered from the safety perspective. In this case, not only specifications and requirements have to be covered but also scenarios, which cover all relevant information of the vehicle environment. Many of them are not yet still sufficient defined or considered. In this context, Safety of the Intended Functionality (SOTIF) appears to ensure the system when it might fail because of technological shortcomings or misuses by users.

An identification of the plausibly insufficiencies of ADAS/ADS functions has to be done to discover the potential triggering conditions that can lead to these unknown scenarios, which might effect a hazardous behaviour. The main goal of this publication is the definition of an use case to identify these triggering conditions that have been applied to the collision avoidance function implemented in our self-developed mobile Hardware-in-Loop (HiL) platform.

Keywords: Triggering conditions · SOTIF · ADAS · Automated Driving Systems

1 Introduction

The validation of the Advanced Driver-Assistance Systems (ADAS)/Automated Driving Systems (ADS) has been a topic for numerous research works due to the complexity of functions that have been exponentially growing over the years, since there are more components and software included in each function and their relationships between them (e.g. AI algorithms,...) are getting more challenging . Reported public cases [1,2] with human deaths have occurred in the last years, which have given an unreliable picture of the current status of the automated driven cars to the public view. Many standards have been developed to provide

M. Trapp et al. (Eds.): SAFECOMP 2022 Workshops, LNCS 13415, pp. 11–22, 2022.
https://doi.org/10.1007/978-3-031-14862-0_1

a common framework and to overcome these accidents as much a possible in the future in which all aspects related to system dependability have to be covered. The dependability of a function can be split into three main parts according to the origin of the hazard. Functional Safety hazards, effected by malfunctions based on hardware and systematics faults, are covered in the ISO26262 [3]. Cybersecurity is covered in the ISO/SAE 21434 [4], which is focused on external threads. The ISO21448, Safety of the Intended Functionality (SOTIF) [5], standard is being developed to cover the gap that has been added due to the new requirements and safety standards that ADAS/AD functions developments have to face. With more functions dependent on complex sensors and algorithms, more unknown scenarios could occur in which the function is not designed for. The main goal of the SOTIF standard is to minimize the unknown hazardous scenarios due to technical shortcomings or misuses, specially the ones that can lead to hazardous situations. Many researches [6,7] have been trying to reuse and link part of the processes described in the ISO26262 into the SOTIF standard, such as Hazard Analysis and Risk Assessment (HARA) or System-Theoretic Process Analysis (STPA). Another important point for SOTIF is the identification of the limitation of each technology used for automated driving [8], which gives more knowledge in order to identify and understand the cause of these unknown scenarios. To make the steps more explicit for the safety argumentation, the UL4600 [9] provides a checklist of necessary elements to ensure that a function is safe in all aspects.

The complexity of covering all possible variations and scenarios that can occur, make validation of ADAS/AD functions a hard task and there are different approaches to face this goal. For example, the validation approach based only on real driven miles data would be unpractical and the cost of the process would be unacceptable [10]. Another way to support this task would be through simulations. During the last years, new environment simulators specifically designed for this domain, such as CARLA [11] or SVL Simulator [12], have been developed. The main issue with this kind of validation is the creation of the realistic high-fidelity sensor models, which are highly complex to develop and also need huge computational resources and high-performance machines [13] as well as the generation of scenarios [14] to cover all possible scenario variations. Authors in [15] also include machine learning approaches to get the conclusion that the lack of meaningful trained data makes this approach not ready to fully cover the whole SOTIF argumentation yet. On the other hand, to avoid the issues previously commented, the authors in [16] present an approach purely statistical, which could provide a quantitative argument of functions validation. Since some concepts could be reused in our research, in this case, the direction of our research is focused on the decomposition of the function to identify the triggering conditions according to the function design.

One of the main step of a SOTIF analysis is the definition of the Operation Design Domain (ODD), according to the standards such as ISO21448 or UL4600. An ODD can be defined as the intended behavior within defined environmental condition that the function has been designed to work on. The definition of the

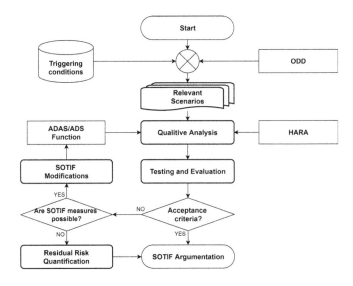

Fig. 1. Flowchart of the proposed triggering conditions methodology

ODD must include all necessary parameters, which make the definition meaningful such as constraints to road conditions. There are different approaches for the definition of a ODD, from the described in the PEGASUS project [17] in which the ODD definition is split into six different layers according to the functionality of the parameters to the description given in the SAKURA project [18] or the provided by ASAM in ASAM OpenODD [19]. The authors in [20] present an overview of available approaches for the most common ODD definition. These approaches provide us with the necessary taxonomy to give the basis to create a triggering conditions list. This publication gives an overview of triggering conditions in automated driving [21], but in our approach, it is based on scenario level and not the system as it is described.

The structure of the paper at hand is as follows: our approach is explained in the next section. Section 2 goes through all blocks of the proposed use case and its implementation in the collision avoidance function of our Hardware-in-Loop (HiL) platform. Finally, Sect. 3 shows the conclusions and the future outlook of our research.

2   Use Case and Methodology

The proposed methodology is shown in Fig. 1 in which the used blocks and their relationships are depicted. The main goal of this publication is to show the key ideas and process of our use case to give the elements to provide a SOTIF argumentation. This is described as a brief basis and further description will be given in following research work as a more mature methodology.

2.1   ADAS/ADS Function Description

In this first block, the function and its functionality as well as relevant technical aspects are given in order to be able to know the behaviour of the function. The use case example in this publication is the collision avoidance function implemented in our self-developed mobile Hardware-in-Loop (HiL) platform called SPIDER [22,23]. A collision avoidance function could work in two ways, as an Automatic Emergency Brake (AEB) or providing an alternative way/evasive maneuver to reach the target location. For simplicity, only the AEB is implemented at this moment on the robot and it will be used in the analysis in this paper. The function uses four 16-lines lidar sensors located at each corner (Front-Left, Front-Right, Back-Left, Back-Right) to provide redundancy where each point is seen, at least, by two sensors and leave the centre of the robot for different flexible setups in the future as Fig. 2 shows. The data from the lidars are fused to generate an occupancy grid, which shows the objects surrounding the robot and sends the activation signal to start the emergency brake in case one object enters within the delimited zone as the danger zone. According to the SAE J3016 Standard [24], it is a Level 4 function since the dynamic driving task fallback has no human interaction.

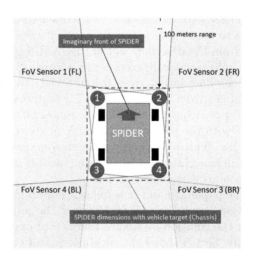

Fig. 2. Hardware setup of the collision avoidance function on the HiL Platform (Field of View - FoV, Front Left - FL, Front Right - FR, Back Right - BR, Back Left - BL)

To guarantee that there is no collision on the nominal scenario, the Responsibility-Sensitive Safety (RSS) [25] model was implemented as the minimum distance before the emergency brake is activated, which formula was adapted for our use case. RSS model was chosen since it provides a proven [26] safe distance according to our robot parameters. Ego vehicle is defined as the main actor of interest in the scenario, sometimes is also refereed as Vehicle Under

Test (VUT). On the other hand, the target vehicle is considered as an element of the scenario and its behaviour is described in the scenario definition. The assumption of zero speed of the vehicle located at front of the ego vehicle(target vehicle) was set to zero due to the ODD is only taking into account static objects. Therefore, the RSS equation of the used function is given as follows:

$$d_{min} = \left[v_r\rho + \frac{1}{2}a_{max,accel}\rho^2 + \frac{(v_r + \rho a_{max,accel})^2}{2a_{min,brake}} \right]_+$$

$$[x]_+ := max\{x, 0\}. \tag{2.1}$$

- d_{min}: Minimum distance to ensure that there is no crash with the obstacle.
- v_r: Current velocity of the SPIDER (m/s)
- ρ : Response time in seconds.
- $a_{max,accel}$: Maximum acceleration of the robot (m/s^2).
- $a_{max,brake}$: Minimum braking acceleration of the robot (m/s^2).

2.2 Operational Design Domain

The defined ODD for our use case is a simple one-way road as shown in Fig. 3 in which there is a static object located at the end of the road within the intended driving path of the robot vehicle. In the definition of this ODD, clear weather conditions as well as dry asphalt are assumed, but these conditions would be modified as a part of the test scenarios in the following sections to identify the triggering conditions of the function. The ego-vehicle, our robot, drives with constant velocity towards the object.

- D_{object}: Distance between the static object and the robot.
- D_{rss}: Distance calculated by using the RSS equation from (2.1).
- D_{ρ}: The distance that the robot travels until it perceives the object, makes a decision, and sends an actuation signal.
- D_{act}: The distance between the robot activates the actuation process and it is finished.
- D_{brake} the distance necessary to brake the robot until velocity is zero. $D_{brake} = D_{act} + D_{\rho}$. In nominal situations, $D_{brake} = D_{rss}$.
- $D_{perception}$: the perception range of the sensors. $D_{perception}$ should be longer than D_{object} and D_{brake}.
- μ: the friction factor of the road.

According to the technical parameters of the function (v_r: 50 km/h, ρ: 1 s, $a_{max,accel}$: 2.0 m/s^2, and $a_{max,brake}$: 5.0 m/s^2), and the used RSS model, is assumed that the maximum RSS minimum distance (D_{rss}) will always be smaller than the range of the perception sensors ($D_{rss,max} < D_{perception}$).

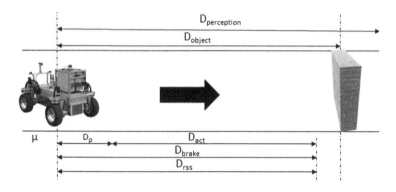

Fig. 3. Operational design domain (ODD) for the selected use case

2.3   Triggering Conditions List

According to the ISO21448 [5] the triggering conditions are the specific conditions of a scenario that serve as an initiator for a subsequent system reaction leading to hazardous behaviour. To identify the possible conditions that can bring up the function to unknown hazards, parameters of the defined ODD will be modified. An own database with the potential triggering conditions based on the taxonomy described in Annex C of the ISO21448 [5] and the BSI standard [27] was developed for this purpose. This database includes categories and different levels of subcategories, which adds granularity to each subcategory. For example, the main category is at the top (e.g. environmental conditions, road conditions,...) and the more granular conditions are at the bottom (e.g. heavy snow). The main category, environmental conditions in this example, follows other subcategories such as the *weather conditions* or *illumination* and, then, these subcategories are split again into other subcategories. In the case of *weather conditions*, this subcategory is split into rain, snow, fog and other climate conditions to continue with more fined granularity, which includes different intensities as light, medium and heavy.. The main purpose of using this approach is to provide granularity to cover the maximum variety of situations, which should help to discover more shortcomings of function during the analysis.

2.4   Relevant Scenarios

In our use case, a scenario is defined as the combination of the previously defined ODD combined with potential triggering conditions. Based on this definition, the relevant scenarios are the compilation of scenarios that includes the selected triggering conditions in which the output of the function will be analysed to know whether the selected triggering condition could lead to a hazardous behaviour. In this step, only the triggering conditions that makes senses for the defined ODD will be taken into account. For simplicity, in a first iteration only a single triggering condition is added to the ODD to better identify the cause and origin of the hazard.

2.5   Hazard Analysis and Risk Assessment

HARA methodology is always performed in Functional Safety processes in which associated hazards to the system are analysed and classified according to the level of danger and caused injuries. This classification used the Automotive Safety Integrity Level (ASIL) which uses the parameters, Exposure (E), which is the possibility of occurrence of the hazard within the operation situation; Severity (S), which is the estimation of the harm that the hazard might cause; and Controllability (C) that is ability to avoid the harm (see ISO262626 [3] part 3). But unlike the process implemented in fuctional safety standard, the ASIL level is not used in the SOTIF analysis process and only the identification of the hazards are used.

As a part of the HARA analysis and the given scenario, the following identified hazards can be extracted: *"a collision due to the inability to completely brake before reaching an obstacle"* and *"activation of the emergency brake due to a false object detection"*

2.6   Qualitative Analysis

In this step, the impact of the defined scenarios on the function has to be analysed to know if they could lead to a performance limitation which could further effect a hazard. To do this, first, the function is split into the three main categories: perception, decision, and actuation. The perception part is also divided into perception sense and perception algo, a shorter reference to perception algorithms. This differentiation is done to separate the part in which perception only provides data from the perceived reality through sensor input and perception algo in which information is extracted based on that perceived data to get any environmental information, e.g. objects, driving road. In this use case, the perception sense includes the sensor drivers, data fusion, and some data post-processes like filtering ground from the point clouds. The block perception algo includes the costmap generator, which generates an occupancy grid from the filtered point cloud to determine the objects that surround the SPIDER. Decision part includes the node, called collision detector, that goes through the generated occupancy grid and detects the closest object and its distance to the robot. The output of the node is the trigger of the emergency brake in case the object violates the calculated allowed minimum distance or the object distance if an object is detected but the emergency brake is not yet necessary. Finally, the actuation part is done by the commands to steering, braking and propulsion. In the given use case it includes the emergency brake from the SPIDER. The main reason for this categorization is to identify the components and their location in the system architecture in which the performance limitations could occur. For this reason, collaboration with domain experts and developers is crucial to better identify the origin of the hazards. A discussion has to be done for each selected scenario to identify how it could affect the function output. For example, for the scenario that includes medium or high snow level, these specific conditions may affect the perception sense part of the function, since it can include ghost points in the perceived data, and the severity of the effect of the limitation is further rated by NO/Low/Medium/High (S0-S3). Therefore, this triggering condition could lead to the previously identified hazard *"activation of the emergency brake due to false object detection"*. Another specific scenario is the one in which the surface is slippery due to heavy rain. This kind of surface reduces the friction of the wheels (actuation part) and increases the distance necessary to completely stop the robot. This triggering condition has an impact on the surface friction of the ODD and could lead to the hazard *"a collision due to the inability to completely brake before reaching an obstacle"*. Similar discussions have to be done through the whole list of selected scenarios to identify the potential hazardous scenarios. An excerpt of this analysis can be shown in Fig. 4. In this use case, it was assumed the controllability (C) of the function is always C3 since it is a level 4 function and no backup operator is implemented.

Triggering Conditions	Cause	Impact / Consequences on vehicle level	Risk Assessment Severity (S0 - S3)	Risk Assessment Exposure (E1-E4)	Intended reaction (System) (Behaviour that can be realized)	Deviating Behavior (Y/N) (Does the Intended Reaction not correspond to the Common Reaction? If yes, then a SOTIF measure is necessary.)	SOTIF Measure (Additional security measure to minimize the risk. The aim is to minimize exposure.)
F01_IC_PER_SEN_01							
[F01_L01] Limitation F01-01_Maximum_perception_range							
Heavy Snow (visibility (PR20) < 0.5 km AND precipitation rate (PR18) > 5.0 mm/hr)	The visibility of the lidar sensos might be drastically reduce to make that D_perception < D_object	a collision due to the inability to completely brake before reaching an obstacle	S2	E1	The robot should detect the object and brake before a collision with the object	Y	- Regarding the current HW setup, this is a limitation due to the selected sensor technology. Redundance with radars could increase the realibity of the function in this scenario
[F01_L02] Limitation F01-02_Reduction_detection_accuracy							
Heavy Fog (visibility (PR20) < 0,2 km)	The fog particles could be detected as objects, which generate false positives	activation of the emergency brake due to a false object detection	S1	E2	The function should be able to differenciate between object and environmental noise to avoid the creating of false positives	Y	- Improving the algorithms for a more precise object detection. - Include sensor redundance to make the fuction stronger to this effect
F02_IC_ACT_01							
[F02_L01] Limitation F02-01_Reduction_actuation_eficiency							
Heavy Rain (precipitation rate (PR18) > 7,6 mm/hr)	The rain wets the asphalt and could increase the necessary distance to completely stopped the robot (D_brake > D_rss)	a collision due to the inability to completely brake before reaching an obstacle	S2	E1	The Drss guarantees the robot completely stops before reaching the object, avoiding the collision	Y	- Improving the algorithms to detect rainy scenarios and adapt the D_rss parameters to the current situation (e.g. decrease the a_min,brake)

Fig. 4. Triggering conditions analysis sheet excerpt

2.7   Testing and Evaluation

The first step in this process is the definition of the Key Performance Indicators (KPIs), which captures the behaviour in a nominal scenario and set the considered acceptable criteria to release the function. This nominal scenario, sometimes also called functional scenario, is the one used in optimal conditions without the inclusion of any of the triggering conditions. An example of a KPI could be Time To Collision (TTC) [28], which represents the time that the ego vehicle needs until it reaches the target vehicle or an obstacle according to the current ego and target velocities and its distance between the two vehicles. This metric can be defined by the formula (2.2). Similar to RSS formula (2.1), it is assumed that $v_{target} = 0$ since there is a static object instead of a target vehicle defined in the ODD.

$$TTC = d/(v_{ego} - v_{target}). \qquad (2.2)$$

Afterwards, the results obtained in the different levels of the verification and validation procedures have to be compared with the nominal conditions and ensure they are within the defined acceptable limits.

2.8   SOTIF Modifications

The main goal of applying SOTIF measures is to improve the output of the function and minimise the risk level that applied triggering conditions might lead to. Following the goal of the principle of ALARP (As Low As Reasonably Practicable) [29], which assumes that the efforts to achieve zero risk could be not feasible and it has to be taken into account the necessary efforts needed to reduce the risk as much as reasonable. For example, there are some cases in which it is not possible to further risk reduction or the associated efforts to reduce it are not worth it. Returning to the proposed use case, in that case where a weather conditions is included as potential triggering conditions in the scenario as heavy snow, the visibility is drastically reduced. There is a chance that the snow could limit the perception range of the sensors and it can lead to the previously defined hazard: *"a collision due to the inability to completely brake before reaching an obstacle"* in which the relationship $D_{perception} < D_{brake}$ could apply to lead to the specified hazard. According to the situation, modifications have to be applied to improve the output on the specified scenario. For example, diversity of sensor technologies, which are stronger against the described issue or an external hardware to measure the specific triggering condition (fog level on the environment) could be applied to mitigate the occurrence of the hazard. In cases in which the effectiveness of the SOTIF measures are not enough to pass the defined acceptance criteria level, these scenarios have to be considered and evaluated within the *"Residual Risk Evaluation"* block.

2.9   Residual Risk Quantification

In case the maximum efforts to minimize the risks are reached and there is not other possible way or feasible way to further improve the function, the evaluation of the existing residual risk has to be calculated. The risk could be expressed in a function as follows:

$$R = f(S, O)$$

According to the given formula, the risk (R) can be defined by the severity (S) and probability of occurrence (O). In this function, the severity is the specified in the analysis for the associated hazard. On the other hand, finding the right occurrence probabilities of each triggering condition presents a more complex problem since there are a wide variety of situations from weather to road conditions. Moreover, finding or calculating these probabilities could change between countries, where the availability of some of them may not be publicly accessible, which makes the problem even harder. At the end of this block, a quantitative evaluation of each identified risk ($R_0...R_N$) should be provided. For example, the number of kilometres or the number of hours until the function could lead to a hazard.

2.10 SOTIF Argumentation

Finally, the output of the previous blocks, which includes the carried out measures covered by functional modification and verification measures, such as simulations and testing, as well as the remained evaluated risks for each triggering condition, are included as inputs for the results of the SOTIF argumentation where both, reports (e.g. identified triggering conditions, relevant scenarios...) and metrics (e.g. number of hours until hazards behavior appears, KPIs,...), should be included.

3 Outlook

In this publication, a methodology to extract and evaluate the triggering conditions of an ADAS/ADS function is described. Since driven kilometres or simulations may not be enough in some situations, by using the introduced approach, a profound understanding of the system as well as the discovery of unknown hazardous scenarios could be provided. The addition of the triggering conditions analysis in theuse case helps the engineers to discover the ones that might lead to a hazard, and also provide more parameters in order to evaluate the risks of the function. For this purpose, the paper goes through all blocks of the proposed approach in which a description and a goal for each one is given as well as the relationship between them. The use case is illustrated by using the collision avoidance function implementation in our mobile robot HiL platform.

In future research works, the residual risk evaluation will be investigated in more detail to be able to provide a quantitative argument at the end of the process, which can provide specific metrics (e.g. validated number of kilometres) that will be used to characterize the safety of a function to achieve the demanded acceptance criteria. Moreover, in the following research, we want to extend this methodology in different approaches of the collision avoidance function to see how different sensor setups (e.g., RADAR+LIDAR, RADAR+LIDAR+CAMERA) can affect the function validation by combination of simulation and real-world testing.

Acknowledgments. Research leading to these results has been performed in the project FRACTAL A Cognitive Fractal and Secure EDGE based on an unique Open-Safe-Reliable-Low Power Hardware Platform Node, under grant agreement No. 877056. The project is co funded by grants from Germany, Austria, Finland, France, Norway, Latvia, Belgium, Italy, Switzerland, and Czech Republic and -Electronic Component Systems for European Leadership Joint Undertaking (ECSEL JU). The publication was written at Virtual Vehicle Research GmbH in Graz and partially funded within the COMET K2 Competence Centers for Excellent Technologies from the Austrian Federal Ministry for Climate Action (BMK), the Austrian Federal Ministry for Digital and Economic Affairs (BMDW), the Province of Styria (Dept. 12) and the Styrian Business Promotion Agency (SFG).

References

1. National Transportation Safety Board (NTSB). Collision between a sport utility vehicle operating with partial driving automation and a crash attenuator, Mountain View, California, 23 March 2018 (2020). www.ntsb.gov/investigations/AccidentReports/Reports/HAR2001.pdf
2. Bonnefon, J.-F.: 18 the Uber accident, pp. 93–98 (2021)
3. ISO26262: Road vehicles - Functional safety, International Organization for Standardization, Geneva, CH, Standard (2018)
4. ISO/SAE 21434:2021 Road vehicles - Cybersecurity engineering, International Organization for Standardization, Standard (2021)
5. ISO 21448: Road vehicles - Safety of the intended functionality, International Organization for Standardization, Geneva, CH, Standard (2021)
6. Khatun, M., Glaß, M., Jung, R.: Scenario-based extended hara incorporating functional safety and sotif for autonomous driving. In ESREL-30th European Safety and Reliability Conference, November 2020
7. Kinalzyk, D.: SOTIF process and methods in combination with functional safety. In: Yilmaz, M., Clarke, P., Messnarz, R., Reiner, M. (eds.) EuroSPI 2021. CCIS, vol. 1442, pp. 612–623. Springer, Cham (2021). https://doi.org/10.1007/978-3-030-85521-5_41
8. Martin, H., Winkler, B., Grubmüller, S., Watzenig, D.: Identification of performance limitations of sensing technologies for automated driving. In: 2019 IEEE International Conference on Connected Vehicles and Expo (ICCVE), pp. 1–6 (2019)
9. Ul4600 standard for safety: Evaluation of autonomous products, International Organization for Standardization, Standard (2021)
10. Kalra, N., Paddock, S.M.: Driving to safety: how many miles of driving would it take to demonstrate autonomous vehicle reliability? Transp. Res. Part A Policy Pract. **94**, 182–193 (2016). www.sciencedirect.com/science/article/pii/S0965856416302129
11. Dosovitskiy, A., Ros, G., Codevilla, F., Lopez, A., Koltun, V.: CARLA: an open urban driving simulator. In: Proceedings of the 1st Annual Conference on Robot Learning, pp. 1–16 (2017)
12. Rong, G., et al.: Lgsvl simulator: a high fidelity simulator for autonomous driving, arXiv preprint arXiv:2005.03778 (2020)
13. Schlager, B., et al: State-of-the-art sensor models for virtual testing of advanced driver assistance systems/autonomous driving functions. SAE Int. J. Connected Autom. Veh. **3**(3), 233–261 (2020). https://doi.org/10.4271/12-03-03-0018
14. Pilz, C., Steinbauer, G., Schratter, M., Watzenig, D.: Development of a scenario simulation platform to support autonomous driving verification. In: 2019 IEEE International Conference on Connected Vehicles and Expo (ICCVE), pp. 1–7 (2019)
15. Abdulazim, A., Elbahaey, M., Mohamed, A.: Putting safety of intended functionality sotif into practice. In: SAE WCX Digital Summit. SAE International, April 2021. https://doi.org/10.4271/2021-01-0196
16. Vaicenavicius, J., Wiklund, T., Grigaite, A., Kalkauskas, A., Vysniauskas, I., Keen, S.D.: Self-driving car safety quantification via omponent-level analysis. SAE Int. J. Connected Autom. Veh. **4**(1), 35–45 (2021). https://doi.org/10.4271/12-04-01-0004

17. Scholtes, M., et al.: 6-layer model for a structured description and categorization of urban traffic and environment. IEEE Access **9**, 59131–59147 (2021)
18. Jama and Sakura. Automated driving safety evaluation framework ver. 1.0 guidelines for safety evaluation of automated driving technology (2021). www.jama-english.jp/publications/Automated_Driving_Safety_Evaluation_Framework_Ver1.0.pdf
19. ASAM e. V. ASAM OpenODD (2021). www.asam.net/project-detail/asam-openodd/
20. Ito, M.: Odd description methods for automated driving vehicle and verifiability for safety. JUCS J. Univ. Comput. Sci. **27**(8), 796–810 (2021). https://doi.org/10.3897/jucs.72333
21. Mekki-Mokhtar, A., Blanquart, J.-P., Guiochet, J., Powell, D., Roy, M.: Safety trigger conditions for critical autonomous systems. In: 2012 IEEE 18th Pacific Rim International Symposium on Dependable Computing, pp. 61–69 (2012)
22. Expósito Jiménez, V.J., Schwarzl, C., Martin, H.: Evaluation of an indoor localization system for a mobile robot. In: 2019 IEEE International Conference on Connected Vehicles and Expo (ICCVE), pp. 1–5 (2019)
23. Virtual Vehicle Research GmbH. SPIDER: mobile platform for the development and testing of autnomous driving functions (2021). www.v2c2.at/spider/
24. Taxonomy and definitions for terms related to driving automation systems for on-road motor vehicles, SAE International, Standard (2021)
25. Shalev-Shwartz, S., Shammah, S., Shashua, A.: On a formal model of safe and scalable self-driving cars (2018)
26. Gassmann, B., et al.: Towards standardization of AV safety: C++ library for responsibility sensitive safety. In: 2019 IEEE Intelligent Vehicles Symposium (IV), pp. 2265–2271 (2019)
27. BSI PAS 1883:2020-operational design domain (ODD) taxonomy for an automated driving system (ADS). Specification, The British Standards Institution, Standard (2020)
28. Balas, V.E., Balas, M.M.: Driver assisting by inverse time to collision. In: 2006 World Automation Congress, pp. 1–6 (2006)
29. Malekzadeh, M., Bate, I.: Making an ALARP decision of sufficient testing. In: 2014 IEEE 15th International Symposium on High-Assurance Systems Engineering, pp. 57–64 (2014)

A Statistical View on Automated Driving System Safety Architectures

Rainer Faller[1]($\boxtimes$) and Krystian Radlak[2]

[1] exida.com GmbH, Munich, Germany
`rainer.faller@exida.com`
[2] Warsaw University of Technology, Warsaw, Poland
`Krystian.Radlak@pw.edu.pl`
`http://www.exida.eu`

Abstract. This paper discusses the challenges involved in meeting tolerable risk targets for automated driving (AD) functions of SAE L3 and above with current sense-plan-act safety architectures, including sensors. The evaluation is performed for classes of safety-related driving scenarios. Illustration by fault-trees is used to facilitate understanding by Functional Safety practitioners. It is intended to contribute to the discussion on how much diverse redundancy of sensors and algorithms is necessary, since diverse redundancy is costly and may increase complexity depending on the fusion strategy. Based on the evaluation of exemplary low and high frequency safety-critical traffic scenarios, this paper provides evidence that a diverse redundant system consisting of two channels will most likely not meet the tolerable risk target. It shows two consequences. First, the correlation or common cause failures between sensor measurements needs to be better understood and quantified. Second, extension of the AD architecture by a warning subsystem, as practiced in other industries, may decrease the risk of injury. The quantitative advantage and safety objectives are elaborated.

Keywords: Automated driving · Tolerable risk · Quantitative SOTIF analysis for diverse redundant safety architectures

1 Functional Safety and Safety of the Intended Functionality

As known by Functional Safety practitioners, the statistical evidence for a high degree of correctness of the functional safety specification and its implementation may be more difficult to achieve than the evidence for a sufficiently low probability of random Hardware failures. Consequently, the automotive standardization committees distinguish *Functional Safety* from *Safety of the intended functionality* (SOTIF). This allows for a more clear distinction between failures of the electrical and electronic system (E/E-system) and the functional insufficiency of the specified intended functionality. **Automated driving system (ADS) vendors must demonstrate that both safety objectives meet the tolerable risk target.**

M. Trapp et al. (Eds.): SAFECOMP 2022 Workshops, LNCS 13415, pp. 23–34, 2022.
https://doi.org/10.1007/978-3-031-14862-0_2

1.1 Terms

This paper uses the following terms and definitions.

Term	Definition
AD, ADS	Automated driving (system)
E/E system	Electrical and/or Electronic system
Functional safety	The distinction introduced by the automotive standardization committee of Functional Safety and SOTIF resulted in different definitions
[ISO 26262-1 [2]]	Absence of unreasonable risk due to hazards caused by malfunctioning behaviour of E/E systems
[IEC 61508-4 [1]]	Part of the overall safety relating to the *Equipment under Control* (EUC) and the *EUC control system* that depends on the correct functioning of the E/E/PE Safety-related systems and other risk reduction measures
SOTIF	Safety of the intended functionality - absence of unreasonable risk due to hazards resulting from functional insufficiencies of the Intended functionality or its implementation. [3]
Tolerable risk	Risk which is accepted in a given context based on the Current values of society. [ISO/IEC Guide 51:1999; [1]]
Positive Risk Balance (PRB)	The licensing of automated systems is not justifiable unless it promises to produce at least a diminution of harm Compared with human driving. [5]
PMHF	Probabilistic Metric for random Hardware Failures [2]
ODD	Operational Design Domain - specific conditions under which a Given driving automation system is designed to function. [3]
V2V	Vehicle-to-Vehicle communication
Golden reference or oracle	Trusted executable (simulation) model used to check that the function(s) with respect to the requirements Specification have been correctly implemented

2 Tolerable Risk

The specification of the tolerable risk is beyond this paper. The paper uses the acceptance criterion mentioned in ISO/FDIS 21448:2022 [3] Annex C.2.1 of 1e–8 death/h. Automotive OEMs may have different, yet unpublished requirements.

The RAND Corporation demonstrates in the excellent paper [6], that an OEM cannot statistically prove the PRB targets by extensive driving tests before delivery to customers. This paper advocates for the use of extensive simulations, which can, however, only partially remedy this problem.

Furthermore, statistical evidence obtained by recording incident-free driving kilometers may be of limited value for safety justification. This is because it is unclear whether the critical driving scenarios and different operating profiles experienced during the recorded driving tests reflect the ones in a new environment. Therefore, this paper focuses on statistical evidence based on evaluation of large sets of different driving scenarios foreseeable for the Operational Design Domains. Before road permission is granted for new ODDs, one must confirm that no untested driving scenarios are to be expected.

3   Current Sense-Plan-Act Architectures

Initially, sense-plan-act architectures were designed as a safety-related control system using diverse redundant perception sensors, including various cameras and RADAR. Safety-conscious designers extended such control systems by including a protection subsystem and additional inputs, including LIDAR, high-definition map, and high-precision inertial and global navigation satellite systems. Moreover, the designers attempted to reduce perception sensor sharing. The protection subsystem monitors the safety-related behavior of the control system. Their simplest form, such subsystems are designed to immediately shut down the application upon detection of an unsafe state, immediately achieving a safe state. ADS for SAE L3 and above cannot assume an immediately achievable safe state, and therefore require an additional subsystem to ensure fault-tolerance or fail-degraded operation. Literature search, including the available reports linked on NHTSA's VSSA index [7] did not reveal substantial enhancements of safety architectures for SAE L3[1] and above.

Quoted from [16], **Tesla** uses two fully independent *Full Self-Driving* (FSD) chips along with their own power subsystem, DRAM, and flash memory. The two independently derived plans from both chips are then consequently sent to the safety system which compares them to ensure an agreement was reached. It is not published, whether the two FSD chips execute the same software or use some form of (algorithmic) diversity. Other companies coming from the AD algorithmic side such as **Mobileye**, use diverse redundancy architectures serving a similar purpose with the *True Redundancy*[tm] monitoring [15] of the safety-related behavior of the control system. Mobileye calls the whole monitoring philosophy *Responsibility-Sensitive Safety* (RSS).

4   Challenge of Control and Protection System Architecture

This section evaluates various classes of safety-related scenarios to identify conditions under which control and protection system architectures are sufficient to meet the tolerable risk target:

- E/E systematic (Software) failures, ch. [4.2];
- Critical driving scenarios with low demand frequency, ch. [4.3];
- Critical driving scenarios with high demand frequency, ch. [4.4].

For simplicity, this paper models a control and protection system architecture and does not extend the model by the channel required for fault-tolerance or fail-degraded operation. Moreover, the SOTIF and systematic failure calculations use mean values from Bernoulli trials (success/fail). Fault-trees are used to provide visualization for functional safety practitioners. Only undetected failures are modeled.

---

[1] SAE J3016 [4] defines six levels of driving automation, from Level 0 (no driving automation) to Level 5 (full driving automation).

4.1   Probabilistic Target to Demonstrate

In this paper, it is assumed that the control and protection subsystem shall meet the probabilistic tolerable risk target with a single-sided confidence limit of $CL \geq 95\%^2$. This is shown in Fig. 1 using a normal distribution.

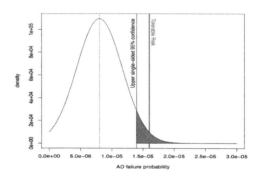

Fig. 1. AD failure probability vs tolerable risk

Safety objective:

$Q(\text{C+P}) :=$ Probability of the control and protection system
　　　　　　of violating the safety goal(s)

$\omega(\text{C+P}) :=$ Frequency of the control and protection system
　　　　　　of violating the safety goal(s)

$\omega(\text{C+P}) < \lambda(\text{tolerable risk}) = \text{1e-8/h}$

The control and protection subsystems are assumed to fail independently or due to common cause failure on the same demand scenario. This is represented by the following formula, which is a simplification of that given by IEC 61508-6:2010 Annex B.3.2.2.2

$$Q(\text{C+P}) = Q(\text{C}) \cdot Q(\text{P}) + CC(\text{C,P})$$

where $CC(\text{C,P})$ denotes the common cause failure of the control and protection subsystem, and using the β-factor common cause model [9,10] gives

$$CC(\text{C,P}) = \beta(\text{CC}) \cdot \min(Q(\text{C}), Q(\text{P}))$$
$$Q(\text{C+P}) = Q(\text{C})(1 - \beta) \cdot Q(\text{P})(1 - \beta) + \beta \cdot \min(Q(\text{C}), Q(\text{P}))$$

Note that the use of min() is explained by the stress/strength model. Both subsystems fail at the same stress if the stronger of the two fails, that is, the subsystem with the lower failure rate.

---

[2] ISO 26262-8 §14.4.5.2.4/.5 requires only 70% for statistical proven-in-use argumentation from field observation.

4.2   Functional Safety Related to Systematic E/E-failures

ISO 21448 [3] broadly defines SOTIF as the absence of unreasonable risk due to hazards resulting from functional insufficiency of the intended functionality or its implementation. This will include systematic failures during Software development. Hence they are not individually modelled but as part of the SOTIF evaluation in the following two chapters. The contribution of random Hardware failures has already been subtracted when determining the tolerable risk target for SOTIF and systematic failures.

4.3   SOTIF - Low Demand Frequency Events

This section evaluates critical driving scenarios with low demand frequency. The scenario parameters are assigned reasonable, assumed values. A rear-end collision due to the sudden occurrence of a traffic jam is an example of a low frequency scenario. Low frequency is assumed to comprise 2 incidents per year[3], with impact severity leading to irreversible injury or death. This gives a demand frequency of:

$$T_{operation} = 400 \, \text{h (operating time of a vehicle per year)}$$
$$AD_{operation} = 50\% \text{ (portion of } T_{operation} \text{ in automated driving)}$$
$$\omega(\text{low demand}) = 2/T_{operation}(\text{AD, year})$$
$$\omega(\text{low demand}) = 2/(400\text{h} \cdot 0.5) = 0.01/\text{h}$$

Extensive testing against a perfect oracle is used to expose SOTIF and systematic failures and quantify their probability with respect to external scenarios and internal state changes. Such testing corresponds to the use of Bernoulli trials with two possible outcomes, success or failure. This results in a binomial distribution. Many methods have been published to estimate the minimum number of successful test cases (zero failure) required to show that the assumed SOTIF and systematic failure rates are not surpassed [11,12]. Among the many methods, this paper uses a direct derivation of the binomial distribution formula [11]. This approach tends to be conservative than other methods.

In the following exemplary calculations we use very optimistic assumptions to show that even then the tolerable risk target will not be met. For the low demand frequency scenario we assume that the on-demand Protective subsystem passes 60,000 independent tests successfully. The more complex algorithms of the control subsystem, e.g., using machine learning (ML), are assumed to show a realistic false-negative rate of FN $\leq$1%. One could argue that the control and protection subsystem are subject to the same test set and number of tests. But the more complex algorithms of the control subsystem would most likely show more non-compliance/failures. Hence a higher failure probability is used for the

---

[3] Applicable field data not yet available.

control subsystem than for the protection subsystem throughout this paper.

$$Q(C) = 1.0\text{e-}2 \text{ (assumed False Negative (FN)} = 1\%)$$
$$Q(P) = 5.0\text{e-}5$$
$$\text{CL} = 95\%$$
$$n(P) = \frac{ln(1 - \text{CL})}{ln(1 - Q(P))} \text{ (binomial distr., zero failure [12])}$$
$$n(P) \approx 60{,}000 \text{ successful independent tests and simulations}$$
$$\beta = 1\% \text{ (smallest } \beta \text{ per IEC 61508-6)}$$
$$Q(\text{C+P}) = ((1\text{-}\beta) \cdot Q(C)) \cdot ((1\text{-}\beta) \cdot Q(P)) + \beta \cdot \min(Q(C), Q(P))$$
$$Q(\text{C+P}) = ((1\text{-}0.01) \cdot 1.0\text{e-}2) \cdot ((1\text{-}0.01) \cdot 5.0\text{e-}5) + (0.01 \cdot 5.0\text{e-}5)$$
$$Q(\text{C+P}) = 4.9\text{e-}7 + 5.0\text{e-}7 = 9.9\text{e-}7$$
$$\omega(\text{C+P, low demand}) = Q(\text{C+P}) \cdot \omega(\text{low demand})$$
$$\omega(\text{C+P, low demand}) = 9.9\text{e-}7 \cdot 0.01/\text{h} = 9.9\text{e-}9/\text{h}$$
$$\omega(\text{C+P, low demand}) < \lambda(\text{tolerable risk})$$

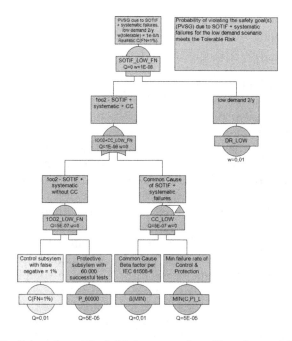

Fig. 2. Fault-tree for critical driving scenarios of low demand frequency

If the simulation results referenced in ch. [5.1] don't confirm the common cause factor model, then following [13] the worst-case estimate for Q(C+P) would be given by the sum of n(Q)+n(P), where n(P) ≫ n(Q). This effectively means the diverse redundant architecture is modelled as one black-box.

$$\omega(\text{C+P, low demand}) \approx 5.0\text{e-}5 \cdot 0.01/\text{h} = 5.0\text{e-}7/\text{h}$$
$$\omega(\text{C+P, low demand}) > \lambda(\text{tolerable risk})$$

Result: The tolerable risk target may be met if the common cause model shows to be comparable to simulation results presented in [8]. Else, following [13], the tolerable risk target will be missed by a factor of 50.[4]

4.4 SOTIF - High Demand Frequency Events

This section evaluates a critical driving scenario with high demand frequency. Cut-in maneuvers are an example. Fleet data evaluation for collision scenarios indicate a high demand frequency comprising 3 incidents per h. Excluding construction sites, reduced speed limit and focusing on impact potentially leading to irreversible injury or death, reduces the demand frequency to DR = 0.09/h. Intuitively these scenarios are well tested and controlled; otherwise, incidents would be frequent. However, the statistical evidence is very difficult to procure. As such the following assumption is made: evidence regarding control and protection subsystems gathered from testing and field experience is more valuable for high frequency scenarios than for low frequency scenarios.

$$Q(C) = 1.0\text{e-}2 \ (\text{assumed FN} = 1\%)$$
$$n(P) = 1,000,000 \text{ successful independent tests}$$
$$Q(P) = 3.0\text{e-}6 \ (\text{at CL} = 95\%)$$
$$Q(\text{C+P}) = ((1\text{-}0.01) \cdot 1.0\text{e-}2) \cdot ((1\text{-}0.01) \cdot 3.0\text{e-}6) + (0.01 \cdot 3.0\text{e-}6)$$
$$Q(\text{C+P}) = 2.94\text{e-}8 + 3.0\text{e-}8 = 5.94\text{e-}8$$

$$\omega(\text{high demand}) = 3/\text{h}$$
$$\omega(\text{C+P, high demand}) = Q(\text{C+P}) \cdot \omega(\text{high demand})$$
$$\omega(\text{C+P, high demand}) = 5.94\text{e-}8 \cdot 3/\text{h} = 1.78\text{e-}7/\text{h}$$
$$\omega(\text{C+P, high demand}) > \lambda(\text{tolerable risk})$$

The statistical evidence using the worst-case estimate of [13] will be worst, even when using a much lower demand frequency resulting from the above men-

---

[4] Note: The fault-tree, Figs. 2, doesn't consider the common cause factor in the independent failure branch [1oo2_LOW_FN, 1oo2_HIGH_FN]. This may be avoided by using the common cause feature of the fault-tree tool *Isograph Reliability Workbench*[tm]. However, doing so would obscure the principle of common cause modeling. Nonetheless, adequate results are produced for small β and Q.

tioned ODD restrictions.

$$n(C) + n(P) = 1,000,000 \text{ successful independent tests}$$

$$Q(C + P) = -\frac{ln(1 - \text{CL})}{(n(C) + n(P))} \text{ (IEC 61508-7 Annex D for large n)}$$

$$Q(C + P) = 3.0\text{e-6 (at CL} = 95\%)$$

$$\omega(\text{high demand, reduced ODD}) = 0.09/\text{h}$$

$$\omega(\text{C+P, high demand}) = Q(\text{C+P}) \cdot \omega(\text{high demand})$$

$$\omega(\text{C+P, high demand}) = 3.0\text{e-6} \cdot 0.09/\text{h} = 2.7\text{e-7}/\text{h}$$

$$\omega(\text{C+P, high demand}) > \lambda(\text{tolerable risk})$$

Result: The tolerable risk target is missed even when ODD restrictions are applied.

5   Consequences

5.1   Common Cause β Factor

The results of statistical system modeling for (diverse) redundant architectures are largely determined by the common cause factor or by correlation between the diverse redundant signal paths. Therefore, understanding of the common cause factor and the correlation between control and protection subsystems must be improved **and quantified**. Note, that ISO 26262-9 ch. 7 contains a list of classes of common cause initiators, but avoids quantification.

A novel SOTIF *Dependent Performance Analysis* (DPA) can be used to produce such quantification [8]. The DPA is based on the use of Bayesian networks. The conditional probabilities of the Bayesian networks are used in conjunction with Monte-Carlo simulations of the overall system (control, protection and warning subsystems) to evaluate the common cause failures triggered by dominant input variables. The Bayesian networks are systematically developed by the ADS design engineers using all inputs of each processing step of the sense-plan-act data flow. The conditional probabilities of the dominant input variables are quantified by field data evaluation and focused testing.

5.2   Architectural Consequence

The authors propose to extend the safety architecture by a warning subsystem. Human drivers hold a substantial advantage over current ADSs due to their ability to look further ahead and intuit critical situations. Shown in Fig. 3[5], the proposed warning subsystem is designed to enhance the current ADSs by looking further ahead for changes without taking autonomous action, and thus avoiding false positive (FP) system reactions. Evaluation of AD simulation results using input from critical real life scenarios has shown that earlier reaction by way

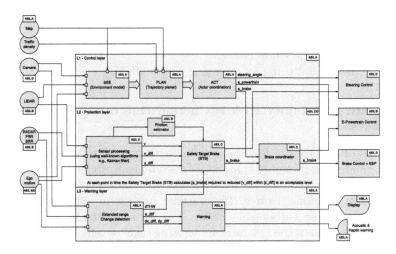

Fig. 3. Example of a control, protection and warning architecture

of increased warning range is more important than a corresponding increase in braking deceleration.

The warning subsystem should operate as follows.

(1) Upon sensing one of the following, alert and call-back the driver, but do not take autonomous action
   – Upcoming high demand frequency scenario.
     Ex: RADAR in predicting and avoiding accidents by looking at least two vehicles ahead.
   – Situation known by the DPA to be associated with an increased Common Cause factor of the sensors and algorithms.
     Ex: Sudden low friction and ghosting on wet road surface.
   – Situations which are new, or have not undergone sufficient analysis and testing during development.
     Ex: Aggressive driver cut-ins which may not be handled by AD functions developed using the *Notional Crash-Relevant Zone* concept. Evaluation of RADAR data may see these cut-ins happening occurring further ahead.
   – Situations likely to over-stress the control and protection subsystem algorithms and their execution, such as an excessively high number of objects, or a high likelihood of hidden objects suddenly appearing.
   – Near miss scenarios previously experienced by the fleet.
(2) Subject to deployment of the technology, warn nearby vehicles using **vehicle-to-vehicle communication** (V2V). Note that the authors explicitly recommend V2V communication and not vehicle-to-backend-to-vehicle communication as the warning chain should have minimum latency, which vehicle-to-backend-to-vehicle communication may not be capable of providing.

---

5 The justification of the ASIL allocation in the figure is beyond this paper.

(3) Acquire distributed measurements from nearby vehicles by V2V communication. These measurements are spacial- and temporal-diverse and hence, reduce the common cause factor.
(4) Support field monitoring by reporting to the OEM.

5.3   Quantitative Injury Risk Reduction Due to the Warning Subsystem

SAE L2+ is often used to describe systems with capabilities that lead drivers to expect greater functionality than SAE L2 systems. Systems of SAE L2+ and above are subject to conflicting requirements for the lowest possible FN and FP (ex. phantom braking) rates. The warning subsystem will not increase the FP rate as it takes no autonomous action. Furthermore, the future use of V2V communication reduces the FN rates by alerting nearby vehicles, and providing the control and protection subsystems with additional information concerning nearby vehicles.

[14] provides a mathematical relation between speed reduction and reduction of collision risk of death. They present that risk r (either road death risk or injury risk) relates to speed v according to $r = C \cdot e^{\beta v}$ (where C, β are constants) and speed is changed from $v1$ to $v2$, then the proportion of risk change will be

$$\frac{(r2 - r1)}{r1} = e^{\beta(v2 - v1)} - 1.$$

Given that the warning subsystem cannot cause FPs, the measurement range of the long range sensors could be extended, providing the driver with an earlier warning and pre-loading the control and protection subsystems. The impact of an earlier warning is now considered for two different scenarios, (a) a car driving at high speed along a highway, (b) a car driving at low speed in dense traffic.

Assuming that drivers of novel SAE L3 AD vehicles initially display a similar level of attention and responsibility as drivers of conventional vehicles, the calculations using [14] with the proposed $\beta = 0.08$ show that the warning subsystem can **reduce the risk of death for the highway and dense traffic example even without V2V communication (see table below).** The calculation of the risk reduction takes into account only the reaction of the driver enabled by the earlier warning, no automatic action. Also the evaluation of AD simulation results confirms that earlier response through increased warning range is more important than a corresponding increase in braking deceleration.

5.4   Further Benefits of the Warning Subsystem

The proposed control, protection and warning architecture provides further safety advantages. The protection and warning subsystems monitor the functional safety and SOTIF control subsystem failure rate. This monitoring allows designers to use their engineering judgement to postulate reasonable SOTIF control subsystem failure rate claims upfront, without requiring statistical proof.

Initial speed	Extended warning range	First driver reaction	Second reaction till warning distance consumed	Reduction of risk of death
130 km/h	+75 m	@0.8 s for 0.7 s, 1.5 m/s^2	@1.5 s for 0.62 s, 3.5 m/s^2	**60.6%**
60 km/h	+25 m	@0.8 s for 0.4 s, 1.5 m/s^2	@1.2 s for 0.33 s, 4 m/s^2	**42.6%**

Such postulation is necessary, as statistical proof via extensive driving tests prior to product delivery is impossible [6]. However, such an approach has a disadvantage: if the postulated claims are incorrect, that is, the failure rates are much higher than claimed, then the system will violate the tolerable risk target until the incorrect case is detected by field monitoring, and once detected, functionality must be limited by over-the-air update or recall.

In addition, the OEM's development and maintenance team would be informed upon activation of the warning or protection subsystems indicating that the AD subsystem was subject to scenarios or failure modes not experienced during development. The OEM can then decide whether to avoid similar situations by implementing (over-the-air) deactivation of AD functions for certain driving scenarios, or in extreme cases, a full product recall.

6 Conclusion

This paper provided evidence to support concerns that contemporary sense-plan-act safety architectures are insufficient to meet tolerable risk targets for systems of SAE L3 and greater. A review of the literature, including reports provided by the *National Highway Safety Traffic Association's voluntary safety self-assessment index* [7], provided no evidence of substantially enhanced architectures. Safety concerns are increased by attempts to further reduce sensor diversity, such as *Tesla Vision*. To counteract these concerns, this paper proposes a warning subsystem safety architecture, which can substantially reduce collision risk of death without the immediate need for V2V communication. The authors of this paper hope this will prompt an open discussion on alternative safety reasoning that incorporates statistical argumentation for the testing and validation of ADS.

The authors consider V2V communication with nearby vehicles as a necessary safety enhancement to fully handle high-demand scenarios. Note that the authors explicitly recommend V2V communication and not vehicle-to-backend-to-vehicle communication as the warning chain should have minimum latency, which vehicle-to-backend-to-vehicle communication may not be capable of providing. The driver of a vehicle directly affected by a critical scenario may react too slowly to a warning and hands-on request. However, the control subsystems and the drivers of nearby vehicles will be provided with a sufficiently advanced warning to allow them to react appropriately. In addition, the communication of measurement data will provide the control subsystems of nearby vehicles with an advanced view of the situation, and reduce the common cause factor. This would justify the use of mean probability for the complete set of vehicles that could potentially be confronted with the critical scenario. The analysis of an architecture that uses V2V communication will be the subject of a future paper.

Acknowledgements. We thank the reviewers of an earlier version of this paper for their careful readings and insightful comments. The work of K. Radlak was supported by the National Centre for Research and Development under the project LIDER/51/0221/L-11/19/NCBR/2020.

References

1. IEC 61508, Functional safety of electrical/electronic/programmable electronic safety-related systems (2010)
2. ISO 26262, Road vehicles - Functional safety (2018)
3. ISO/FDIS 21448, Safety of the intended functionality (SOTIF) (2022)
4. SAE J3016, Taxonomy and Definitions for Terms Related to Driving Automation Systems for On-Road Motor Vehicles (2018)
5. German Federal Minister of Transport and Digital Infrastructure, Ethics Commission, Automated and Connected Driving (2017)
6. Kalra, N., Paddock, S.M.: (RAND Corporation): how many miles of driving would It take to demonstrate autonomous vehicle reliability? (2016). https://www.rand.org/content/dam/rand/pubs/research_reports/RR1400/RR1478/RAND_RR1478.pdf
7. National highway traffic safety administration, automated driving systems voluntary safety self-assessment (VSSA) disclosure index (2022). https://www.nhtsa.gov/automated-driving-systems/voluntary-safety-self-assessment
8. Werling, M., (BMW), Faller, R., (exida), Betz, W., Straub, D. (TUM): Prospective Safety Integrity Analysis for L3+ Systems (2022)
9. Rausand, M., Barros, A., Hoyland, A.: System reliability theory: models, statistical methods, and applications, 3rd ed, ISBN-13: 978–1119373520 (2021)
10. Guey, C.N.: (Energy Laboratory, MIT): a method for estimating common cause failure probability and model parameters: the inverse stress-strength interference (ISSI) technique, MIT-EL 84–010 (1984)
11. Darby, J.L.: (Sandia National Laboratories): sample sizes for confidence limits for reliability, SAND2010-0550 (2010)
12. Bailey, R.T.: Estimation of zero-failure data. Risk Anal. **17**(3), 375–380 (1997)
13. Bishop, P., Povyakalo, A.: A conservative confidence bound for the probability of failure on demand of a software-based system based on failure-free tests of its components. Reliab. Eng. Syst. Saf. **203**, 107060 (2020)
14. Stipdonk, H.: The mathematical relation between collision risk and speed; a summary of findings based on scientific literature (2019). https://etsc.eu/wp-content/uploads/The-mathematical-relation-between-collision-risk-and-speed.pdf
15. Mobileye, true redundancy[tm] - the realistic path to deploying AVs at scale. https://www.mobileye.com/true-redundancy/
16. Full self-driving computer (FSD Computer) and FSD chip - tesla. https://en.wikichip.org/wiki/tesla_(car_company)/fsd_chip#Operation

Building a Test Bed for the Periodical Technical Inspection of Sensors Perceiving the Environment in Autonomous Vehicles

Felix Müller[1]([✉]) [iD], Philipp Nenninger[1], and Eric Sax[2]

[1] Institute of Energy Efficient Mobility (IEEM),
Karlsruhe University of Applied Sciences (HKA), 76133 Karlsruhe, Germany
{felix.mueller,philipp.nenninger}@h-ka.de
[2] Institute for Information Processing Technologies (ITIV),
Karlsruhe Institute of Technology (KIT), 76131 Karlsruhe, Germany
eric.sax@kit.edu

Abstract. With the introduction of the first available autonomous vehicles, the safety and reliability of these systems becomes even more relevant than it was in regard to driver assistance systems, as the driver is not necessarily available to immediately take over in controlling the vehicle. Especially the environmental perception of the individual vehicle plays a key part in its ability to navigate the public roads. At the same time, the sensors used for the perception are very likely to differ between individual vehicles over their lifespan due to maintenance and environmental differences as well as different incidents, that might impact their functionality. The periodical technical inspection of road vehicles is an established tool to ensure the technical capabilities of vehicles that are using public roads. In this paper, we present a more detailed overview of some of our suggestions to advance the periodical technical inspection for passenger cars with regard to advancing driver assistance systems and autonomous driving vehicles as these systems are having a wider impact on the technical state of the vehicle. The focus in this paper is put specifically onto the sensors for the environmental perception of the surroundings of the vehicle. We therefore present herein a test bed with artificial targets for the periodical technical inspection to evaluate the sensor systems and facilitate the vehicles roadworthiness classification based on the promising results of our preliminary tests.

Keywords: Autonomous driving · Periodic Technical Inspection · Roadworthiness · Environmental perception

1 Introduction

Over the last years, the main reason for traffic accidents with the involvement of vehicles was driver error [1]. To reduce the number of accidents and their consequences, the European commission has set the goal to reduce fatalities on the road to near zero by 2050 [2]. To accomplish this vision, certain driver assistance systems are set to become mandatory for new cars [3], while the automotive industry is working on the development

© The Author(s), under exclusive license to Springer Nature Switzerland AG 2022
M. Trapp et al. (Eds.): SAFECOMP 2022 Workshops, LNCS 13415, pp. 59–70, 2022.
https://doi.org/10.1007/978-3-031-14862-0_3

of autonomous driving functions, to remove the factor of human error. In addition to passive safety systems, the continuous advancement of technical capabilities is one of the factors, that contributes to the reduction of fatalities while the number of vehicles has risen over the years [4]. In order to achieve the set goal, it is necessary that the measures taken are working correctly. One of these measures to provide exactly that, is the periodical technical inspection of road vehicles to ensure the technical fitness of the vehicles in operation on public roads. It was introduced in 1906 in Baden, Germany and has been around in one form or another since then with updated procedures and scope [5]. The current basis for the roadworthiness inspections performed in the European Economic Area is laid out in [6] and differs slightly in the individual countries. In order to accommodate the introduction of autonomous vehicles on public roads [7], an update to the guidelines of the periodical technical inspection is necessary. First steps in this direction have been published in [8] and [9].

2   Periodic Technical Inspection in Germany

As the regulation can differ in the individual countries, and for different vehicle classes, this brief summary for the periodical technical inspection focuses on the situation in Germany, and here in particular on passenger class vehicles, which are commonly referred to as M1 in the legal documents. While we aim to provide suggestions that can be applied to all different kinds of vehicles, the explanation will focus on passenger cars to increase clarity.

The periodical technical inspection of road vehicles is specifically designed with different approaches: a visual inspection, by taking performance measurements and by observing the behavior of the vehicle or its systems in reaction to an action performed by the inspector. This is done in order to accommodate the various approaches that can be used by the vehicles manufacturer to implement the intended functions [10]. The current focus is mostly on the mechanical state of the vehicle, as can be seen when looking at the list of the included characteristics stated in [11, Anlage VIIIa, 6].

For the inspection of parts of the electric installation as well as for the identification of the vehicle, an electronic inspection has been introduced which reads information from the vehicle network [12]. The whole inspection of the vehicle has to be performed non-destructively, without the disassembly of equipment or parts from the vehicle and without modifying, altering or impairing the electronic systems of the vehicle, including for example, the creation of new error codes [11, Anlage VIIIa, 5].

2.1   Driver Assistance Systems in the Periodic Technical Inspection

Vehicles with driver assistance systems are already on the road today in large numbers. Some are equipped with sensors to detect the surrounding of the vehicle and their percentage can be expected to grow. As the driver is supposed to be in control at all times while the vehicle is operated, the driver can intervene in the case of a system malfunction. This is mirrored in the periodical technical inspection, as these systems are only rudimentarily included. For example, by checking the presence and the state of the front facing camera solely visually, as has been shown in [8, section V]. Starting with Level 3 of the classification defined in SAE J3016, the driver is considered to be the fallback and has to be ready to take control, but does not have to monitor the vehicle at all times [13, p. 25–26]. Therefore we argue, that the inspection has to include the autonomous driving systems in greater detail as is the case now for the driver assistance systems as in specific situations, like slow highway driving or automated parking garages, the driver can, for example, focus on writing emails or watch videos during the systems engagement and does so not necessarily detect a malfunction of the system in time.

3   Sensor Verification in the Field

Testing sensors in the field commonly differs from the tests that are performed with the sensors during development or production. Especially as part of the production of the sensor and the vehicle that is equipped with the sensor, a calibration of the sensor and the system is performed. In the field, the sensors for vehicles are not tested or verified on a regular basis, except for the internal self-tests of the units. Further work is only performed, if the self-tests report errors that might then be investigated in a workshop. In the event that a calibration of the sensors is necessary, different vehicle manufacturers employ different strategies to calibrate the sensors. The strategies used might differ between different sensors as well. Specifically, the extrinsic parameters, meaning position and orientation of the sensor in relation to the vehicle, are of interest and are commonly adapted in these scenarios [14]. This calibration can happen online while the vehicle is moving, or in the workshop using specifically designed calibration equipment. An example for a multi- manufacturer compatible aftermarket unit can be seen in [15], but similar systems are offered by different manufacturers.

4   Advancing the Periodical Technical Inspection

For the purpose of the following discussion, we assume the driver assistance systems or autonomous driving systems in the vehicle under test have passed their respective type approval processes that are or will be put in place or have been approved by the competent authorities in a similar way and the use of these systems is legal on the road. These stages include the verification, that these systems perform as described and intended in at least the associated tests that are needed to acquire the aforementioned approval. An example for the required tests can be found in [16] regarding the first Level 3 driving function, the Automated Lane Keeping System, although local laws can require more and different tests for granting the type approval.

In order to keep with the basic idea of the periodical technical inspection, the principles set forth in [11, Anlage VIIIa, 4.] are applied as a basis for the design of the tests. This means, that the advanced driver assistance systems and the automated driving systems shall be examined by their composition, condition, function and effectiveness. With the introduction of the test of electronic components during the periodical technical inspection into German law, it was laid out that the inspection should ensure that original parts or approved spare parts are used, no illegal technical changes have taken place and that function and effectiveness of the systems is part of the check, while the time and money spend on the inspection have to be in a reasonable relation to the objectives

[17, p. 63]. The source concludes, that complex function and effectiveness tests, for example to assess driving dynamic control systems, cannot be incorporated under these constraints at that point. As we agree with this assessment, and deem it valid today as well, an alternative approach to inspect the driving systems is required. As stated in [9], the inspection should therefore cover at least:

– the sensors detecting the surroundings,
– the actuators performing the driving function,
– the control units running the associated software and
– the software to perform the driving function itself.

4.1 Sensors for the Environmental Perception

As cars are moving towards more advanced assistance systems and first autonomous driving capabilities, the number of sensors fitted to the vehicles will increase. Projections estimate up to six radar sensors, seven cameras, eight ultrasonic sensors and four lidar sensors for a level 5 autonomous vehicle to track the surroundings of these cars [18]. In addition to these sensors, a number of other sensors will be integrated in the cars, to detect other specific conditions like wet roads or the sirens of emergency vehicles [19]. Therefore, standardized tests have to be implemented to test these sensors beyond their simple presence in the vehicle as is the case now during the periodical technical inspection [8, Section V].

For this work, we assume a vehicle is equipped with different set of sensors for different tasks. As such, we assume the following sensors to be present for the detection of the surroundings of the vehicle for this work:

– front facing sensors for the main driving task: cameras, radars, lidar sensors
– sensors to capture the near surroundings and cover the space behind the vehicle: cameras, radars, lidar sensors, ultrasonic sensors
– additional sensors, that can be mounted as necessary: moisture sensors to monitor road conditions, microphones to detect emergency services

This list should not be considered final for all automated driving vehicles, as advancement in technology and regulations might introduce more or different sensors in the future. Additionally, different sensors are present in the vehicle to detect different states and measure different signals. These include, for example, the driver attention sensor in Level 3 cars or the steering angle sensor.

For the purpose of this paper, we want to focus on the sensors detecting the environment and surroundings of the vehicle, because the sensors and their calibration are likely to be impacted by the daily use of the vehicles as they are subject to vastly different conditions as well as being mounted in positions, that cause them to be affected by accidents and various repairs as well as neglect by the vehicle owners. In regards to repairs for example, in most vehicles, the front facing camera is affected when the windscreen is replaced, while often the calibration for the front facing radar is invalid, as soon as the vehicles front is dismantled. This is even the case in unrelated repairs, for example while exchanging the coolant radiator.

4.2   Test Bed for the Sensor Systems in the Periodical Technical Inspection

In Germany, different places can be visited to have the periodical technical inspection performed. These include special testing centers of varying sizes, as well as regular repair shops for vehicles, that are visited by the engineers performing the inspection. The goal was to find a solution, that can be integrated in as many testing facilities as possible, in order to keep the access to these inspections as easy and available as possible. Therefore, we argued in [8], that a test bed would be the best approach, to enable the inspection of the autonomous driving systems in the already available testing centers. This test bed could thereby be integrated in the already available test beds for checking the headlight alignment and would hereby only use minimal additional space and benefit from the high standards, that these headlight test beds are already build to. An example for this would be the permissible limits for flatness deviations that only allow a deviation of up to 11mm over a length of 8m for the test bed [20]. The concept for our suggested test bed is shown in Fig. 1. Shown are, for illustration purposes, a possible target for a camera sensor at position $(x_0|y_0|z_0)$ as well as two lidar targets at $(x_1|y_1|z_1)$ and $(x_2|y_2|z_2)$ and a corner reflector for a radar sensor at $(x_3|y_3|z_3)$.

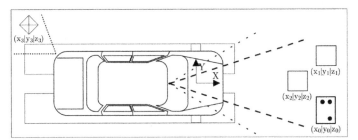

Fig. 1. Concept of the proposed test bed for sensors detecting the surroundings of the vehicle in automated driving vehicles. Extended version of the work laid out in [8]. The wide spaced dashed lanes represent the cameras field of view, the narrow spaced dashed lane is used for the radar sensors accordingly and the bold dashed line visualizes the lidars field of view.

4.3   Positioning of the Vehicle on the Test Bed

To use the suggested test bed to verify that the sensors are locating the targets in the correct position, it is of integral importance, that the vehicle is located in a known position within the test bed. This can be achieved in different ways and for different levels of ease as well as different costs. For a lower cost solution, we suggest to use the baseline of the suggested coordinate system, to position the vehicle along the x-axis in a reliable way. This could be easily and reliably done, by having an indent to position the center of the front wheels in the correct position in regard to the x-axis as shown in Fig. 1. This leaves the position along the y-axis as well as the rotation around the z-axis. To identify the position of the vehicle in this regard, using laser distance sensors could be an option and is the path we are currently using as a basis.

4.4 Inspection of the Sensor Systems

For the sensors detecting the environment, two main goals are present in the inspection. While one of them is the general detection of objects in the surroundings of the car and therefore the question of is the sensor working at all, the second one is, if the objects are located correctly in relation to the vehicle. The first question covers if there are blind spots in the designed detection area and if a defined object can be detected at all, while the second question is supposed to cover correct mechanical and electronic calibration. Of course, this requires that all the sensors used in the detection of the surroundings are subject to the inspection. We deem it necessary, that this inspection is carried out for every sensor individually, and not after sensor fusion has been performed on the measurements. This is to ensure, that a possible defect in the detection system would not be compensated by the detection capabilities of another sensor system, especially in the rather good conditions these tests will be performed in, for example in non-blinding, bright conditions, during the day, in a workshop and in dry conditions. In addition to that, it would reduce the chance of an already not optimal working system to pass the inspection.

As a key differentiation to calibration solutions on the market today and distributed by OEMs and aftermarket suppliers, the goal for this solution is not to provide calibration capabilities, but instead allow the verification of the current calibrations of the vehicle, while offering a single solution that can be used on all different vehicles regardless of the manufacturer. This would allow to keep the footprint of the inspection equipment low and in addition would help to keep the complexity of the solution to a minimum to in turn keep the cost of the individual inspection low.

As the sensors cannot be disassembled according to the regulation for the periodical technical inspection in Germany, in addition, doing so would invalidate the calibration and is therefore not an option regardless of the regulation, the sensors are to be tested inside of the vehicle.

4.5 Positioning of Targets

As a result of different possible mounting positions on the various vehicles for the different sensors, the targets have to be movable in order to accommodate the different makes and models of vehicles, therefore, Fig. 1 shows one exemplary setup. While the front facing cameras are mostly mounted behind the rear-view mirror, especially the radar sensors can be mounted in vastly different locations. Common positions include the air inlet in the front of the vehicle, but various vehicles have their radar sensors mounted near the bottom of the vehicle front, for example, where fog lights would be commonly mounted [21]. Another approach that has been adopted, is to mount the radar sensors with the front facing camera behind the rear-view mirror. Including not only the sensors for the main driving task, but also the sensors for the near surroundings and the space behind the vehicle, a lot more sensors and their respective targets become relevant for the inspection. Therefore, it is necessary to have the targets mounted in a way, that they can be repositioned in order to accommodate the different viewing areas for the individual sensors on the individual vehicles. A condition for the repositioning of the targets is hereby, that they are to be precisely locatable in the workshop to verify the measurements of the vehicle.

4.6 Sensor Targets for the Inspection

Using simulation devices as are used in different tests especially during development of the systems, such as radar target simulators, in order to inject virtual targets into the sensors, would be a way to gain very flexible test conditions, although they might have to be configured differently for the different systems under test. This would add additional possible points of failure during the inspection. In addition, a passive target is a more cost-effective solution and appears to be better suited for the harsher conditions in this setting, as they are comparable to a workshop. Thus, we consider this to be the way to focus the question of the target on.

We argue, that the test with a special artificial target is sufficient to answer the two questions proposed in Sect. 4.4 and allows to keep the development costs of the vehicles low and the additional software in the vehicle at a minimum while minimizing the potential attack surface for security threats. Using targets that resemble a human or other real objects could cause the detection algorithm, that probably incorporates artificial intelligence in the near future and which would work in the vehicle on the road, to be fitted too much to the artificial target and therefore would not recognize, for example, a real human or car. With an abstract artificial target, this risk can be minimized.

In regard to the specific design of the targets itself, different targets are to be designed in order to test the different sensors and their operating principles. In general, the goal for the design of the targets is not to test the edge cases in which the sensors fail, as this is part of the development process and the assessment of the system performance before these systems are introduced into public roads. It is more a verification of the correct calibration of the sensor system and therefore we deem the focus in the development for the targets should be on reliable detection in order to assess the systems locating performance.

1. **Cameras**: In order to verify the correct function of cameras, our suggestion is to design a target that consists of a board, which has specific dimensions, that can be used to estimate the distance between the target and the camera [22]. Given the camera system is supposed to be in a calibrated state, the system can pinpoint the location of the target in relation to the vehicles camera and therefore in relation to the whole vehicle. Using an artificial target that consists of simple shapes like circles and rectangles reduces the needed complexity in the detection and allows for an easier estimation of the position, as sharp contrasts can be used to allow for a better detection. An example for such a target can be seen in Fig. 1 marked with $(x_0|y_0|z_0)$, although a different target might yield better results and therefore the shown target is not necessarily our final suggestion and should be seen as for illustration purposes.
2. **Lidar Sensors**: While lidar sensors are also operating on the basis of light, a similar approach can be used as a target for the test, specifically we deem the target consisting of a board as sufficient for the test of the detection. It would have to be not as elaborate designed, as the lidar sensor can measure the distance and position of the target in relation to the sensor and therefore to the vehicle directly. Adding a reflective pattern to the target can improve the detection reliability, as the intensity can be measured by the lidar sensor and can be used in a similar way as the contrast in the detection

reliability of the camera target. First tests using just a rectangular target showed promising results as outlined in Sect. 4.7 [23].

3. **Radar Sensors**: While a board looks like a suitable and space efficient solution for camera and lidar sensors we used a different approach while looking for suitable targets for radar sensors, especially as boards would have to be aligned very accurately. As a potential target for radar systems, we experimented with spheres and corner reflectors so far. Beneficial for a sphere would be the indifference of the used frequency [24], as long as the sphere has a certain minimal radius to be suitable for the used wavelengths. Unfortunately, given that the radar cross section of a sphere differs in relation to the diameter of the sphere and that the sphere would have to be quite small (we used a sphere with a diameter of 15 cm) in order to be fitted to a test bed, this resulted in difficulties detecting the spheres low radar reflections in our test setup due to radar reflections that were produced by random other objects in a workshop that would be present in a similar manner in a real inspection test bed. Using a common corner reflector (we used an edge length of 14 cm) gave a larger radar cross section and therefore better results. The corner reflector was therefore more reliable to detect, than the spheres in the noise of the measurements [25].

4.7 Exemplary Test Performed in Regard to the Lidar System

To verify the approach of using planar targets for the test of the lidar system we used a lidar of the type OS-1 128 (Rev. C, Firmware version 2.1.2) made by Ouster, Inc. The targets consisted of a PVC board with a dimension of 220 mm × 220 mm and an attached piece of reflective pattern of 200 mm × 200 mm, that can be found on various road signs. The version we used was classified as RA 2 according to [26] and used microprisms to reflect the incoming light. The targets were mounted to aluminum extrusions, to reach the desired height adjustment and allow positioning. Two targets were placed in the field of view of the Lidar scanner, positioned as shown in Fig. 1, marked with $(x_1|y_1|z_1)$ and $(x_2|y_2|z_2)$, and their center positioned in $(2, 5m|0m|1m)$ and $(3, 0m|0, 5m|1, 5m)$ in regard to the shown coordinate system. Measurements for a campaign are shown in Fig. 2, with the sensors resolution set to 1024 × 128 with 10Hz for measurement 1, 1024 × 128 with 20 Hz for measurement 2 and 2048 × 128 with 10 Hz for measurement 3. While slight errors in the overall positioning of the targets are a result of the manual positioning in relation to the vehicle and the other target by using a tape measure, the results are still usable as the targets have not been moved between the different measurements and therefor the individual datapoints and their distribution is a result of the measurements and our algorithm calculating the center of the targets. The individual measurements of each campaign show, that our approach looks promising in allowing to pinpoint the location of a target reliably within Millimeters in consecutive measurements and within the tolerances of the sensor [27]. Even though the Range Accuracy is lower for retroreflectors than for Lambertian targets, our measurements showed, that the setup manages to come close to the stated ± 1 cm precision that is outlined in the datasheet for lambertian targets in the evaluated distance.

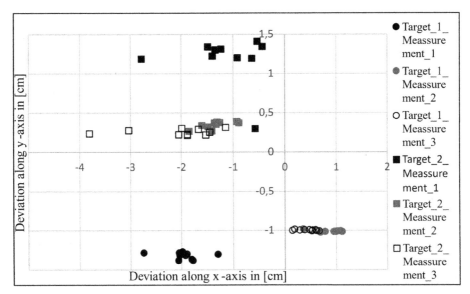

Fig. 2. Deviation of the position of the targets from their intended position. Each measurement campaign consisted of ten measurements taken. Target 1 is shown in round markers, while measurements for Target 2 are shown with square markers.

4.8 Required Information About the Vehicle Under Test

In order to perform the suggested tests on the vehicle, certain information has to be known about the vehicle. Specifically, information about the sensors in regard to their type, number, placement and characteristics. In addition to the information regarding the sensors, some information about the vehicle as a whole has to be known. Specifically, the dimensions of the vehicle and the location of the origin of the coordinate system is of relevance to perform the tests. A certain amount of this information is already known for the vehicle under test and stored in a database for use during the periodical technical inspection, for example if it is fitted with cameras, radars etc. and a description of where the sensors in question is mounted [12].[1] This is already part of the inspection today, as the sensors are visually inspected for obvious damage.

To advance the periodical technical inspection as we suggest in our work, the information already available today would no longer be sufficient to correctly place the targets for the sensor tests around the vehicle. As presented in Sect. 4.5, placing the targets correctly requires knowing where the sensor is located exactly and what field of view is covered by it.

---

[1] [12] notes, that the so-called system data that is collected for the vehicles contains "information on the actual installation of the vehicle systems and the corresponding examination procedures" and can contain "for example, physical quantities, fault codes, algorithms, identification features or tamper-proof displays".

Given the fact that some of this information is already known for each vehicle, the database and workflow to gather this information and to make it available for the periodical technical inspection is already established and can be amended without developing further or new systems.

In addition, the measurements that are collected by the vehicle have to be communicated to the test equipment, for the comparison with the known truth. Therefore, the appropriate messages have to be known or defined to access the gathered information.

4.9 Related Work and Differentiation

Meanwhile, another project aims to incorporate automated driving functions in to the periodical technical inspection. The "ervast" project proposes the use of a target vehicle and a proving ground to assess the performance of the driving systems [28]. In contrast, our approach allows for the integration of the test procedures into the testing centers, that are already in use today and would therefore allow for an easier and broader adoption while maintaining a controlled environment for comparable testing conditions between different inspection facilities and between different test dates.

5 Conclusion and Future Work

In this paper, we present an option for the advancement of the periodical technical inspection of passenger cars. Specifically, we focus on the integration of a test bed into the periodical technical inspection to evaluate the performance of the sensor systems for the environmental perception of the individual vehicle under test. We outline our suggestion for the test bed, its inclusion into existing procedures and facilities as well as first results of our tests in this regard and further considerations on the necessary prerequisites.

The first tests, like the one presented in this paper, give us the confidence, that our approach is promising and is capable of aiding the quest for safer roads. The presented work focuses on the test of sensor systems while our goal is to design a complete test approach, that would also allow to assess the other aspects of the autonomous driving systems in order to be able to give a sound evaluation of the vehicles road worthiness.

Our future work will therefore combine our approaches for the different sensor systems and incorporate the outlined constituents of the driving system, including the vehicles software, the control modules and other hardware in regard of the function to give a sound evaluation of the individual vehicles capabilities to reliably perform the driving task. In addition to this, we are planning on investigating different targets, to optimize the measurements and the repeatability of the performed test, for example by using a combination of lambertian and retro reflectivity to optimize detection and measurement accuracy for Lidar targets.

Acknowledgments. This work has been funded by GTÜ Gesellschaft für Technische Überwachung mbH, Stuttgart, Germany. The authors wish to thank Peter Neugebauer and Mario Schnäbele for their contributions to this research project.

References

1. Statistisches Landesamt Baden-Württemberg: Straßenverkehrsunfälle seit 1977 nach Ursache, Lage und Typen [road traffic accidents since 1977 by cause, location and types], https://www.statistik-bw.de/Verkehr/Unfaelle/10025137.tab?R=LA. Accessed 09 Jun 2022
2. European commission: Europe on the move - safe mobility: a Europe that protects (2018). https://ec.europa.eu/transport/road_safety/system/files/2021-07/20180517_mobility_safety_final.pdf. Accessed 09 Jul 2022
3. European commission: Europe on the move - new safety features in your car (2019). https://ec.europa.eu/docsroom/documents/34588/attachments/1/translations/en/renditions/native. Accessed 09 Jun 2022
4. Statistisches Landesamt Baden-Württemberg: Heilig's Blechle - 125 Jahre Automobil [Heilig's Blechle - 125 years of automobiles] (2021). https://www.statistik-bw.de/Service/Veroeff/Querschnittsver!F6ffentlichungen/806911001.pdf. Accessed 09 June 2022
5. Mayer, H.: Und dann macht es bumm: Geschichte des TÜV [And then it goes boom: History of the TÜV] 15 January 2016. https://www.faz.net/aktuell/technik-motor/technik/die-technischen-ueberwachungsvereine-im-wandel-der-zeit-14007191.html. Accessed 09 Jul 2022
6. Directive 2014/45/EU of the European Parliament and of the Council of 3 April 2014 on periodic roadworthiness tests for motor vehicles and their trailers and repealing Directive 2009/40/EC including Corrigendum OJ L 219, p. 25, 22 Aug 2019, (2014/45/EU)
7. A. Donath, A.: S-Klasse mit Level 3: Mercedes darf hochautomatisiert fahren [S-Class with Level 3: Mercedes may drive with conditional automation], 09 December 2021. https://www.golem.de/news/s-klasse-mit-level-3-mercedes-darf-hochautomatisiert-fahren-2112-161688.html. Accessed 09 Jul 2022
8. Müller, F., Nenninger P., Sax, E.: Analysis of requirements for autonomous driving systems. In: 2020 11th IEEE Annual Information Technology, Electronics and Mobile Communication Conference (IEMCON), pp. 87–93 (2020). https://doi.org/10.1109/IEMCON51383.2020.9284853
9. Gierl, M., Müller, F., Kriesten, R., Nenninger, P., Sax, E.: Challenges for periodical technical inspections of intelligent cars. In: Reports on Energy Efficient Mobility, vol. 1, pp. 9–14 (2021). https://doi.org/10.5281/zenodo.4569409
10. Braun, H., Bönninger, J., Missbach, S., Süssbier,R.: Erkennen und Bewerten von Mängeln an elektronischen Systemen und Bauteilen im Kraftfahrzeug [Detection and evaluation of defects in electronic systems and components in motor vehicles], Kirschbaum, Bonn (2015). ISBN 978-3-7812-1920-5
11. Straßenverkehrs-Zulassungs-Ordnung [2nd road traffic licensing regulations], Version including revisions until 18 May 2017
12. Bundesministerium für Verkehr, Bau und Stadtentwicklung: Einundvierzigste Verordnung zur Änderung straßenverkehrsrechtlicher Vorschriften [Forty-first Ordinance on the Amendment of Road Traffic Regulations]", Teil 1 Nr. 11, pp. 470–501 (2006). http://www.bgbl.de/xaver/bgbl/start.xav?startbk=Bundesanzeiger_BGBl&jumpTo=bgbl106s0470.pdf. Accessed 09 June 2022
13. SAE J3016: Taxonomy and Definitions for Terms Related to Driving Automation Systems for On-Road Motor Vehicles, revised version of April 2021
14. Winner, H., Hakuli, S., Lotz, F., Singer, C.: (ed.): Handbuch Fahrerassistenzsysteme: Grundlagen, Komponenten und Systeme für aktive Sicherheit und Komfort [Handbook of Driver Assistance Systems: Fundamentals, Components and Systems for Active Safety and Comfort], 3rd revised and supplemented revision, Wiesbaden, Springer Vieweg (2015)

15. Bosch aftermarket: DAS 3000 Die neue computergesteuerte Mehrmarken- Justagevorrichtung für Fahrerassistenzsysteme [DAS 3000 The new computer-controlled multi-brand adjustment device for driver assistance systems]. https://www.boschaftermarket.com/xrm/media/images/country_specific/de/equipment_5/adas_driver_assistance_system_2/xx_pdfs_40/facelift_das_3000.pdf. Accessed 09 Jun 2022

16. United Nations: Addendum 156 – UN Regulation No. 157 Uniform provisions concerning the approval of vehicles with regard to Automated Lane Keeping Systems (2021)

17. Bundesrat: 41. Verordnung zur Änderung straßenverkehrsrechtlicher Vorschriften [41st Ordinance on the Amendment of Road Traffic Regulations], 925/05, 23 December 2005. https://dserver.bundestag.de/brd/2005/0925-05.pdf, Accessed 09 Jul 2022

18. Malaquin, C.: Towards ADAS to Imaging radar for automotive market and technology trends. In: Microwave & RF Conference (2019)

19. Walz, E.: Mercedes-Benz cleared to offer its DRIVE PILOT 'eyes off the road' level-3 autonomous driving system on vehicles in Germany. https://m.futurecar.com/5054/Mercedes-Benz-Cleared-to-Offer-its-DRIVE-PILOT-Eyes-Off-the-Road-Level-3-Autonomous-Driving-System-on-Vehicles-in-Germany. Accessed 09 Jul 2022

20. Bundesministerium für Verkehr und digitale Infrastruktur: Richtlinie für die Überprüfung der Einstellung der Scheinwerfer von Kraftfahrzeugen bei der Hauptuntersuchung nach § 29 Straßenverkehrs- Zulassungs-Ordnung (StVZO) (HU-Scheinwerfer-Prüfrichtlinie) [Guideline for checking the setting of motor vehicle headlights during the periodic technical inspection in accordance with § 29 of the German Road Traffic Licensing Regulations (StVZO) (HU Headlight Inspection Guideline)], 12. November 2018, https://www.amz.de/sites/default/files/2019-09/amz_Verkehrsblatt_2018_174-web.pdf. Accessed 09 Jul 2022

21. Koch, K.: Challenges of radar sensor integration into modern vehicles, smart energy and systems (2019)

22. Geugis, W.: Inbetriebnahme von Fahrerassistenzkameras und Implementierung einer Objektdetektion unter ROS und OpenCV [Commissioning of driver assistance cameras and implementation of object detection using ROS and OpenCV], B.Eng. Thesis, IEEM, Hochschule Karlsruhe, Germany (2021)

23. Merz, P.: Ansätze zum Test der Verkehrssicherheit von Laserscannern in hochautomatisierten Fahrsystemen [Methods to test the roadworthiness of Lidar sensors in highly automated driving systems], B.Eng. Thesis, IEEM, Hochschule Karlsruhe, Germany (2021)

24. Mihat, A.: Approaches to Testing Highly Automated Driving Systems in Production and Field Radar System, M.Sc. Thesis, University DeOviedo, Spain, and IEEM, Hochschule Karlsruhe, Germany (2019)

25. Ilgen, B.: Implementierung eines Testansatzes für Radarsysteme in Kraftfahrzeugen [Implementation of a test approach for radar systems in motor vehicles], B.Eng. Thesis, Esslingen University of Applied Sciences and IEEM, Hochschule Karlsruhe, Germany (2021)

26. DIN 67520:2013-10 — Retro-reflecting materials for traffic safety - Photometric minimum requirements for retro-reflective sheetings

27. Ouster, Inc.: OS1 mid-range high-resolution imaging Lidar, datasheet rev. 7 January 2021. https://data.ouster.io/downloads/datasheets/datasheet-revc-v2p1-os1.pdf. Accessed 09 Jun 2022

28. Projekt ervast: Einsatz dynamischer Verkehrselemente für die Prüfung automatisierter Fahrfunktionen [Use of dynamic traffic elements for the testing of automated driving functions]. https://www.ervast-projekt.de/. Accessed 09 Jun 2022

Testing and Verification of the Deep Neural Networks Against Sparse Pixel Defects

Michal Szczepankiewicz[1], Krystian Radlak[2,3(✉)], Karolina Szczepankiewicz[4], Adam Popowicz[4], and Pawel Zawistowski[2]

[1] NVIDIA, Warsaw, Poland
msz@nvidia.com
[2] Warsaw University of Technology, Warsaw, Poland
{krystian.radlak,pawel.zawistowski}@pw.edu.pl
[3] Vay Technology, Berlin, Germany
[4] Silesian University of Technology, Gliwice, Poland
{karolina.szczepankiewicz,adam.popowicz}@polsl.pl

Abstract. Deep neural networks can produce outstanding results when applied to image recognition tasks but are susceptible to image defects and modifications. Substantial degradation of the image can be detected by automatic or interactive prevention techniques. However, sparse pixel defects may have a significant impact on the dependability of safety-critical systems, especially autonomous driving vehicles. Such perturbations can limit the perception capabilities of the system while remaining undetected by human observer. The effective generation of such cases facilitates the simulation of real-life challenges caused by sparse pixel defects, like occluded or stained objects. This work introduces a novel sparse adversarial attack generation method based on differential evolution strategy. Additionally, we introduce a novel framework for sparse adversarial attack generation, which can be integrated into the safety-critical systems development process. An empirical evaluation demonstrates that the proposed method outperforms and complements state-of-the-art techniques allowing for complete evaluation of an image recognition system.

Keywords: Dependability · Adversarial attacks · Deep learning · Evolution algorithms · Differential evolution

1 Introduction

Deep neural networks (DNNs) are a prominent group of machine learning algorithms used in applications such as computer vision, speech recognition, natural language processing, and bioinformatics [23]. The popularity of these methods continues to grow as they typically outperform classical algorithms [1]. However, DNNs are highly sensitive to minor intensity variations of individual pixels within the input image, potentially leading to the incorrect classification of an observed object [10].

Root causes of such sparse pixel defects vary, but they can ultimately provoke an incorrect decision from a classifier. The impact of corrupted pixels within an image can

M. Trapp et al. (Eds.): SAFECOMP 2022 Workshops, LNCS 13415, pp. 71–82, 2022.
https://doi.org/10.1007/978-3-031-14862-0_4

be diminished via various mitigation methods, depending on the source of the corrupted pixels in the image. Perturbations that are introduced intentionally are known as adversarial attacks. These attacks can be generated by attaching foil or stickers either to the target objects [9], or directly to the lens of the imaging system [17]. Such attacks present significant risk to safety critical systems such as nuclear systems, aircraft flight control systems, autonomous vehicles, unmanned aerial vehicles, smart grids, or healthcare devices. Sparse pixel defects can also occur unintentionally, due to random sensor faults caused by electric signal instabilities, malfunctioning or aging complementary metal-oxide-semiconductor (CMOS) or charge-coupled device (CCD) sensors [22]. Such distortions can be enhanced by miniaturization of high-resolution, low-cost image sensors and poor lighting conditions.

Ensuring that algorithms with DNN components can operate safely when encountering sparse pixel defects is a crucial step in their deployment within safety critical applications. System verification and validation include different testing activities to address: the capability of the sensor processing algorithms to function correctly within their environment, the ability of the decision making algorithms to handle both known and unknown scenarios, and the robustness of the overall system or specific functions. The dependability of DNNs against sparse pixel defects can be verified by injecting system inputs that trigger potentially hazardous behavior that may modify the ultimate decision of the given DNN. However, the generation of all test cases which may cause failure of the system is infeasible due to the combinatorial explosion of all possible corrupted pixel patterns within the image. Hence, verification of the diagnostic coverage of safety mechanisms requires a dedicated approach to discover appropriate input triggers. Existing adversarial attack generation methods present a potential solution to generate test cases to verify the dependability of DNNs against sparse pixel defects.

The main contributions of this paper are as follows. First, we introduce novel method for sparse pixel defects generation using a differential evolution strategy (DES). Additionally, we provide a novel framework for evaluation sparse pixel defects. Second, we address how the existing adversarial attacks generation methods can be used in verification activities for autonomous driving systems. Third, we highlight why sparse adversarial attacks should be considered during development of safety related applications based on DNNs algorithms. Our approach can be considered as an extension of one pixel attack, presented by Su et al. [29], which uses differential evolution (DE) to generate sparse adversarial perturbations. Our work is additionally inspired by the use of an efficient method for generating optimal solutions for very complex optimization problems without requiring costly matrix algebra operations [2]. We empirically evaluate the ability of the DES to generate sparse pixel defects and compare it to state-of-the-art methods for adversarial attack generation. The results show that the proposed DES-based method outperforms the one pixel attack strategy and enables the generation of additional unique sparse pixel detection combinations. We also show that exhaustive testing and verification of the impact of the sparse pixel defects in a traffic sign recognition system requires the use of multiple adversarial attack generation methods.

2 Related Work

In the context of DNNs, sparse pixel defects are typically considered to be malicious attacks intentionally introduced into the input image. The literature proposes a plethora of adversarial attack models. The models are typically classified into two groups, in the same manner as threat models, depending on the attacker's knowledge of the DNN's architecture. During a white-box attack the attacker has access to model parameters such as gradients, structures, and even training data of the target network [10]. During a black-box attack, the attacker has access only to the output class decision made by the classifier or the resulting confidence scores [18]. For both groups, various approaches have been presented for the generation of sparse adversarial attacks. A common approach for white-box attacks is the use of gradient based methods which integrate the l0-constraint [3]. Black-box attacks commonly use local search [8,21] or other heuristic algorithms [29].

The majority of attacks substantially modify the content of the original image, limiting their practical applicability and rendering them unlikely candidates for real-life scenarios [8]. However, adversarial attacks can introduce realistic and unacceptably high levels of risk due to the hazards caused by hardware malfunction or deliberate attack scenarios [15]. High risk can be generated by specific input data perturbations that modify the minimum number of pixels in order to adjust the classifier's decision. Such noisy patterns may occur in many scenarios. Raindrops reflecting sunlight onto a traffic sign could mislead an automated vehicle, or sparse, colorful flowers within a field of crops could cause an unmanned aerial vehicle to incorrectly localize a mission target [19]. Revealing and understanding the source of DNN vulnerabilities can further improve the robustness of classification methods, and adversarial examples can be used to train DNN classifiers [25].

Sparse pixel defects can also occur unintentionally, due to random sensor faults caused by electric signal instabilities or malfunctioning CMOS or CCD sensors [22]. Such malfunctions can be caused by age or poor lighting conditions, and can introduce defective pixels which continually report maximum or minimum intensity or measure brightness with a positive offset. The total deterioration of a pixel is caused by damage to the readout system within the output transistors. A brightness offset results from dark current generated by carriers thermal activity within the photosensor of a pixel. Pixel faults can be introduced during sensor production [4]. Such faults can be corrected by dark frame subtraction, implemented immediately post-production. The majority of remaining defects result from the occasional impact of high-energy particles onto the sensor surface, causing the formation of permanent atomic defects, often characterized by additional temporary instabilities [12].

The natural aging of a sensor can be characterized by an increase in the number of defects during each year of operation. Chapman et al. [5] present experimental calculations of this rate as a function of camera pixel size. The authors reveal that a reduction in pixel size corresponds with an increase in the number of new defects in the matrix, which is disadvantageous for the majority of applications requiring camera miniaturization (e.g., automotive solutions). They showed experimentally that for matrices with 2 μm pixels, new defects occurred at a rate of 0.1 defect/year/mm^2. For small sensors with a typical size of 20–40 mm^2, this corresponds with the appearance of 2–4 new defects and uncorrected pixels per year, which may have undesired impact on perception system and introduce unreasonable risks. Therefore, adversarial attack generation methods can be used in fault injection testing to verify the robustness and dependability of DNN algorithms used in autonomous driving systems.

3   Proposed DES-based Approach

Adversarial attack generation can be defined as an optimization problem that can be solved using evolutionary strategies. Let $f : \mathbb{R}^{U \times V} \longrightarrow [0, 1]^n$ be a classifier that supports multiple classes, where $U \times V$ denotes the resolution of the original input image X and n is the number of classes.

Let $\mathbf{x}_i = (r_i, g_i, b_i)$ denote the i-th pixel within the image, located at spatial coordinates (u_i, v_i). With X as an input, the probability that the model's output belongs to the class y_i is $f_{y_i}(X)$. The objective of a sparse adversarial attack is to modify the smallest number of pixels in the original input image X that causes $f_{y^*}(\hat{X}) \xrightarrow{\hat{X}} 0$, where $\hat{X}$ denotes the modified image and y^* is the true class of the image. Therefore, the generation of an adversarial perturbation can be formulated as an optimization problem, in which the objective is to discover a specific subset of pixels that, when modified, will change the original decision of the classifier. Such a problem can be solved using evolutionary algorithms, but requires an appropriate definition of the individuals and fitness function.

Let K be the number of pixels that are perturbed by the sparse adversarial attack. A single individual $\mathbf{w}_i$ in a population W represents a single adversarial attack, and can be expressed as a vector of the coordinates and resultant RBG values of K modified pixels: $\mathbf{w}_i = \big((u_1, v_1, r_1, g_1, b_1), \ldots, (u_K, v_K, r_K, g_K, b_K)\big)$, where (u_k, v_k) denotes the coordinates of the k-th modified pixel within image X and (r_k, g_k, b_k) represents the resultant RGB values of the k-th modified pixel. Thus, the size of an individual corresponding to a K-pixel attack is $5 \times K$, for example, an individual representing a five pixel attack consists of 25 vector elements: five pixels $\times$ ([two coordinates] + [three intensity values]).

3.1   Use of the DE

Su et al. [29] proposed a basic version of the DE algorithm for the generation of a single-pixel attack. The original DE approach introduced in [28] is a population-based optimization method belonging to the family of evolutionary strategies.

Let us assume the following notation: λ is the number of individuals in the population, t is the generation counter, $W^{(t)}$ is the population of the t-th generation, $\mathbf{w}_i^{(t)}$ is the i-th individual in the t-th generation, $\mathbf{w}_{i,j}^{(t)}$ is the j-th vector element of the i-th individual in the t-th generation.

Algorithm 1 outlines the basic DE algorithm, with the operations defined as follows:

– During *initialization*(), the coordinates of all λ individuals in the initial population are sampled from a uniform distribution (i.e., the initial population is randomly generated).

```
t ← 1
W^(t) ← initialization()
while !stop do
    for i ∈ 1..λ do
        m_i^(t) ← dm(i, W^(t))
        o_i^(t) ← crossover(m_i^(t), w_i^(t))
        w_i^(t+1) ← es(o_i^(t), w_i^(t))
    end for
    t ← t + 1
end while
```

Algorithm 1: Original version of DE algorithm.

– The differential mutation step, $dm(i, W^{(t)})$, randomly selects three indices $r1$, $r2$, and $r3$ (where $r1 \neq r2 \neq r3$, $r1 \neq i$) from the range $\{1, 2, .., \lambda\}$. The mutant individual $\mathbf{m}_i^{(t)}$ is then created by summing the individual $\mathbf{w}_{r1}^{(t)}$ and the product of a difference vector of individuals $\mathbf{w}_{r2}^{(t)}$ and $\mathbf{w}_{r3}^{(t)}$ and a scaling factor F, which defines the range of mutation:

$$\mathbf{m}_i^{(t)} = \mathbf{w}_{r1}^{(t)} + F \cdot (\mathbf{w}_{r2}^{(t)} - \mathbf{w}_{r3}^{(t)}). \tag{1}$$

– The binomial crossover process, $crossover(\mathbf{m}_i^{(t)}, \mathbf{w}_i^{(t)})$, handles the cross exchange of vector elements between the mutated offspring $\mathbf{o}_i^t$ and the individual $\mathbf{w}_i^{(t)}$:

$$\mathbf{o}_i^{(t)} = \begin{cases} \mathbf{m}_{i,j}^{(t)}, & \text{with probability } p_1 \\ \mathbf{w}_{i,j}^{(t)}, & \text{with probability } 1 - p_1, \end{cases} \tag{2}$$

for $j \in \{1, 2, ..., (5 \times K)\}$.

– During the elite succession step, $es(\mathbf{o}_i^{(t)}, \mathbf{w}_i^{(t)})$, the fitness of an individual $\mathbf{w}_i^{(t)}$ is tested against its offspring $\mathbf{o}_i^{(t)}$, and the fittest of the two is selected:

$$\mathbf{w}_i^{(t+1)} = \begin{cases} \mathbf{o}_i^{(t)}, & \text{if } f(\mathbf{o}_i^{(t)}) < f(\mathbf{w}_i^{(t)}) \\ \mathbf{w}_i^{(t)}, & \text{otherwise.} \end{cases} \tag{3}$$

3.2   Use of the DES

The DES [2] is a crossover between DE and the covariance matrix adaptation evolution strategy (CMA-ES) [11]. Experimental results [2] indicate that the DES outperforms the CMA-ES in higher dimensionalities and multimodal settings, which is an important attribute in the context of generating adversarial attacks.

The variant of DES utilized in this work is presented in Algorithm 2. Optimization begins with the generation of the initial population $W^{(1)}$ of λ individuals sampled from a uniform distribution. The t-th iteration of the main loop proceeds as follows. The current population is evaluated using the quality function Q. The midpoint $\mathbf{m}^{(t+1)}$ is then calculated using the best μ individuals from the population. The difference between

```
1: t ← 1
2: initialize
3: (W^(1) = {w^(1)_{1,...,λ} : w^(1)_i ∼ U(0, 1)})
4: while !stop do
5:     evaluate(W^(t); Q)
6:     m^(t+1) = (1/μ) Σ_{i=1}^{μ} w^(1)_i
7:     Δ^(t) ← m^(t+1) − m^(t)
8:     if t = 1 then
9:         p^(t) ← Δ^(t)
10:    else
11:        p^(t) ← (1 − c_c)p^(t−1) + √(μc_c(2 − c_c))Δ^(t)
12:    end if
13:    for i = 1, ..., λ do
14:        pick at random τ_1, τ_2, τ_3 ∈ {1, ..., H}
15:        j, k ∼ U(1, ..., μ)
16:        d^(t)_i ← √(c_d/2)(w^(t−τ_1)_j − w^(t−τ_1)_k)
17:                  + √(c_d)Δ^(t−τ_2) · N(0, 1)
18:                  + √(1 − c_d)p^(t−τ_3) · N(0, 1)
19:        w^(t+1)_i ← m^(t+1) + d^(t)_i
20:    end for
21:    t ← t + 1
22: end while
23: return w_{best}
```

Algorithm 2: DES variant used in the experiments.

consecutive midpoints $\Delta^{(t)}$ is accumulated via $\mathbf{p}^{(t)}$. Following this, the new population is created in an iterative fashion. Each individual $\mathbf{w}_i^{(t+1)}$, for $i \in \{1, 2, ..., \lambda\}$, is created independently by translating the population's midpoint $\mathbf{m}^{(t+1)}$ using a generated mutation vector $\mathbf{d}_i^{(t)}$. This is independently repeated λ times to construct the entire population.

The parameters that control this process are λ, the population size; μ, the number of individuals which are able to reproduce; H, the history size; and c_c and c_d, the mutation weighting parameters. Further details on the algorithm can be found in the original work [2]. Note that the algorithm presented here does not incorporate the optional noise term used to calculate the difference vectors in the original work.

4   Integration into Safety-Critical Systems Development

The presented framework provides methods for generation of sparse adversarial attacks and included methods are capable of delivering unique and effective sparse attack samples. The framework could be easily integrated into the scope of safety-critical development lifecycle. ISO 26262 [13] requires or recommends fault injection testing as a method for various purposes, i.e. including system development (hardware-software integration and testing, system integration test and vehicle integration testing), hardware development (hardware integration test), and software development (unit verification, integration testing, embedded software testing). As a result, this testing approach can bring safety argumentation for various aspects of the safety concept, i.e. correctness of safety requirements implementation at the hardware-software/system/vehicle level, effectiveness of safety mechanisms and correctness of functional performance, hardware design verification and completeness/correctness of the hardware safety requirements implementation, software verification at the unit, integration and embedded software levels. The potential verification of DNN's performance against adversarial attacks might be organised in a way as presented at the Fig. 1, which corresponds to simulating random hardware faults for camera sensor or systematic software faults in the image acquisition and pre-processing stage.

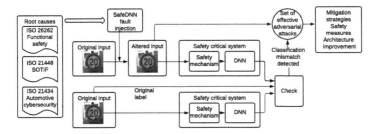

Fig. 1. Verification concept of the traffic sign recognition system.

The algorithms available in the framework are used for the purpose of generation of multiple and unique adversarial attacks for input images. Both altered and original images are passed through the safety mechanism block, which contains image pre-processing supposed to remove unwanted image perturbations which cause image misclassification. Classification outputs for the original and altered images are later on compared within the checker. In case of the misclassification, such altered images are collected for further investigation. Gathered effective sparse attacks samples can be used to verify newly developed improvements or refinements of existing measures, all of which can be introduced in the DNN architecture or development process, e.g. model architecture update by introducing randomization-based defenses [16], introduction of adversarial training [14], improvements of the safety mechanism for image pre-processing (like denoising [24]) or introduction of additional mechanisms (like consistency-based defenses [31], KNN-based defenses [30], provable defenses [26]).

The approach is utilized offline for the test set and can be repetitively executed after any refinement is introduced into the process or architecture (including extension of the test set). It is also fully independent from the applied validation strategy and, for example, is suitable for bootstrapping and every cross-validation strategy (i.e. exhaustive, non-exhaustive, nested). The approach could be also extended to cover redundant models that are executed on separate channels (by means of decomposition) and provide results and argumentation for technical independence.

5 Results

This section evaluates the effectiveness of the proposed framework in the context of dependability verification of traffic sign recognition system presented in the Fig. 1. Each experiment used a simple convolutional neural network, SimpleCNN [6], which consists of two convolutional and three fully connected layers. The first and second building blocks of a SimpleCNN are convolutional layers with batch normalization (reducing internal covariate shift), pooling, and rectified linear activation. These layers constitute the feature extraction section of the network. The classification section of a SimpleCNN consists of a flattening layer, two fully connected layers with rectified linear activation, and one fully connected layer with no activation function applied. Additionally, two popular DNN architectures were used in the experiments: VGG16 and Resnet50. All networks were trained on the German Traffic Sign Recognition Benchmark (GTSRB) [27]. The SimpleCNN model reached 96.4% accuracy across the entire GTSRB test set, whereas VGG16 and Resnet50 achieved 97.1% and 97.3% respectively. The sparse adversarial attacks were generated using only correctly classified images from the test set.

The proposed DES-based method was compared with the one pixel attack method [29], which uses attacks generated by DE. Additionally, we compared the DES-based approach to state-of-the-art methods for the generation of sparse adversarial attacks: SparseFool (SF) [20], CornerSearch (CS) [8], Projected Gradient Descent (PGD) [8], and SparseRS (RS) [7]. The effectiveness of each attack method was evaluated, using the GTRSB data set, by measuring the fraction of attacks that were successful and assuming that an equal number of pixels were modified in each image. A *successful* (or *effective*) adversarial attack causes incorrect recognition of a traffic sign (and is detected by the Check step in Fig. 1); an *unsuccessful* attack causes no change in the classifier's decision. In the context of DES and DE, which operate on a population of individuals, an attack is assumed to be successful if at least one individual from the maintained population modifies the original decision of the analyzed DNN.

As the DES is derived from DE, both algorithms were initialized with the same number of individuals and generations. The initial population, of size $\lambda = 1000$, was generated via random sampling of a uniform distribution. The stop criterion was defined as a maximum generation limit of $I_{max} = 5000$. A "bounce back" repair strategy was implemented: if a generated individual had color values that were outside the RGB intensity range or pixel coordinates that were outside the image, then the problematic values were mirrored back into the search space at the boundary that they exceeded. The state-of-the-art methods tested alongside the DES were evaluated using default parameter settings within implementations created by the authors. During the execution of each algorithm we recorded both the total number of attacks and the ratio of successful attacks.

The results of the numerical experiments using the GTSRB data set are presented in Table 1. The best results are highlighted in red. The proposed DES-based method outperforms the state-of-the-art techniques when one pixel is modified. Attacks of this type are particularly useful for DNN evaluation, as they occur more frequently in real-world applications and industrial deployment (e.g., due to hot pixels in CMOS matrices). The difficulty of generating successful adversarial attacks using only one faulty pixel is demonstrated as expected; each algorithm showed greatest improvement between one and three pixels, with the introduction of further pixels bringing minimal benefit. For each method, a larger number of faulty pixels corresponds with a higher chance of perturbing regions of the input image which contain features crucial for the DNN classifier to reach a correct decision. The proposed DES always outperforms the original DE algorithm in the generation of successful sparse adversarial attacks. These results also prove the superiority of DES over DE in the generation of adversarial attacks activity.

Table 1. Summary of the attack success rate for the new method and competitive techniques on GTSRB dataset while using different numbers of pixels (K).

	SimpleCNN						VGG16						Resnet50					
	Effective attacks [%]																	
K	DES	DE	SF	CS	PGD	RS	DES	DE	SF	CS	PGD	RS	DES	DE	SF	CS	PGD	RS
1	49.8	46.0	45.1	44.7	32.5	47.3	43.2	39.3	40.3	40.1	28.2	42.7	43.9	39.5	39.9	39.7	30.5	41.9
3	67.1	64.9	85.8	86.3	71.4	83.2	59.3	55.9	80.4	80.2	62.9	78.4	58.8	56.5	82.6	80.0	65.3	79.2
5	81.5	79.5	92.2	92.5	79.8	94.7	74.2	70.8	84.3	85.1	71.8	86.1	73.3	71.0	85.7	84.3	70.3	85.5
7	83.2	81.4	95.5	95.9	82.4	96.4	76.1	73.1	85.5	88.1	73.1	87.4	74.7	72.0	87.1	88.6	71.7	88.9
9	86.0	84.1	97.1	96.9	83.5	97.3	80.2	76.1	87.1	90.9	74.8	89.8	79.2	77.2	89.9	91.1	73.9	89.5

Table 2. Summary of the uniqueness rate for the new method and competitive techniques on GTSRB dataset for 1-pixel attacks on SimpleCNN model.

SimpleCNN, 1-pixel attacks					
Unique attacks [%]					
DES	DE	SF	CS	PGD	RS
5.2	0.6	4.5	4.2	0	4.7

An identical trend is present in the results for the more complex DNN models that were tested: the DES-based algorithm generates the most successful adversarial attacks when a single pixel of the input image is modified. However, the rate of successful adversarial attacks is lower for the more complex models than for the simpler model, although the accuracy results are similar. This could be due to the complex models generating their output decision as a function of more features of the input image and more complex relationships between those features, compared to the simpler model. Hence, the generation of the correct combination of pixel coordinates and colors required to produce a successful attack is a more demanding task, particularly when modifying only a small number of pixels.

We further investigated the collected set of effective adversarial attacks and evaluated the uniqueness rate of each method for one pixel attacks against the SimpleCNN model. The uniqueness rate was defined as the percentage of images for which only a single method was able to generate a successful adversarial attack. The results, presented in Table 2, show that the proposed DES-based method has the highest uniqueness rate for sparse adversarial attacks. The DE method generated few unique successful adversarial attacks, the majority of which were discovered by the DES-based approach. Moreover, the PGD method has zero effectiveness, as all the successful attacks it generated were also discovered by the CS method. Although the presented results show that a high percentage of the data set can be effectively attacked by individual methods, the combined use of different methods is required to generate the highest possible coverage of successful adversarial attacks, which proves high usability of the proposed framework for the purpose DNN models verification against sparse adversarial attacks. For larger numbers of modified pixels the uniqueness rates are lower, as multiple methods can achieve high effectiveness.

A selection of the adversarial attacks generated for an exemplary "General caution" traffic sign from the GTSRB data set are shown in Fig. 2. The successful adversarial attacks caused the model to misclassify the image, bringing the confidence score of the classifier to zero for the correct class. For the cases shown in Fig. 2b, Fig. 2c, Fig. 2d, and Fig. 2f, the sign was incorrectly classified as "right-of-way at the next intersection". For the case shown in Fig. 2e, the sign was incorrectly classified as "pedestrians". Interestingly, successful attacks can be generated by modifying pixels outside the region of the sign itself, as shown in Fig. 2e. This suggests that the classification processes use sections of the image outside of the object of interest, and indicates unexpected weaknesses of the training methods which should be addressed by the safety engineers and developers of DNNs.

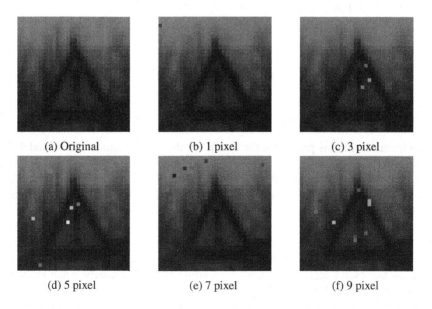

(a) Original   (b) 1 pixel   (c) 3 pixel

(d) 5 pixel   (e) 7 pixel   (f) 9 pixel

Fig. 2. Exemplary successful n-pixel attacks obtained for "General caution" traffic sign.

6   Conclusions

This paper introduced a framework that contains state-of-the-art methods for the generation of sparse adversarial attacks against DNNs, together with a novel DES-based attack method. The newly introduced method was compared with both similar and state-of-the-art algorithms dedicated to the generation of sparse adversarial attacks. Experiments conducted on the GTRSB data set show that the proposed method outperforms the original DE-based algorithm in every tested scenario. Importantly, the proposed method causes DNNs to produce a substantially larger number of misclassifications when modifying only one pixel of the input image. Attacks of this type are more likely to occur in real-world scenarios, and the identification of them greatly facilitates the design of safety measures and mechanisms for systems that utilize DNNs. Our framework proved its usefulness in supporting testing activities required to reach conformance to ISO 26262 and successful deployment of DNNs algorithm in safety critical systems.

Acknowledgements. This work was supported by the National Centre for Research and Development under the project LIDER/51/0221/L-11/19/NCBR/2020 and by SZiR-2 project granted by Warsaw University of Technology under the program Excellence Initiative: Research University (ID-UB)

References

1. Alom, M.Z., et al.: A state-of-the-art survey on deep learning theory and architectures. Electronics **8**(3), 292 (2019)
2. Arabas, J., Jagodziński, D.: Toward a matrix-free covariance matrix adaptation evolution strategy. IEEE Trans. Evol. Comput. **24**(1), 84–98 (2020)
3. Carlini, N., Wagner, D.: Towards evaluating the robustness of neural networks (2017)
4. Carrère, J.P., Place, S., Oddou, J.P., Benoit, D., Roy, F.: CMOS image sensor: process impact on dark current. In: 2014 IEEE International Reliability Physics Symposium, pp. 3C.1.1-3C.1.6 (2014)
5. Chapman, G.H., Leung, J., Namburete, A., Koren, I., Koren, Z.: Predicting pixel defect rates based on image sensor parameters. In: 2011 IEEE International Symposium on Defect and Fault Tolerance in VLSI and Nanotechnology Systems, pp. 408–416 (2011)
6. Cheng, C., Huang, C., Nührenberg, G.: NN-dependability-kit: Engineering neural networks for safety-critical autonomous driving systems. In: IEEE/ACM International Conference on Computer-Aided Design (ICCAD), pp. 1–6 (2019)
7. Croce, F., Andriushchenko, M., Singh, N., Flammarion, N., Hein, M.: Sparse-rs: a versatile framework for query-efficient sparse black-box adversarial attacks. CoRR **abs/2006.12834**, https://arxiv.org/abs/2006.12834 (2020)
8. Croce, F., Hein, M.: Sparse and imperceivable adversarial attacks. In: Proceedings of the IEEE/CVF International Conference on Computer Vision, pp. 4724–4732 (2019)
9. Eykholt, K., et al.: Robust physical-world attacks on deep learning visual classification. In: 2018 IEEE/CVF Conference on Computer Vision and Pattern Recognition, pp. 1625–1634 (2018)
10. Goodfellow, I.J., Shlens, J., Szegedy, C.: Explaining and harnessing adversarial examples (2015)

11. Hansen, N.: The CMA evolution strategy: a comparing review. In: Towards a New Evolutionary Computation: Advances on Estimation of Distribution Algorithms, pp. 75–102 (2006)
12. Hopkinson, G.R., Goiffon, V., Mohammadzadeh, A.: Random telegraph signals in proton irradiated CCDs and aps. In: 2007 9th European Conference on Radiation and Its Effects on Components and Systems, pp. 1–8 (2007). https://doi.org/10.1109/RADECS.2007.5205515
13. ISO: ISO 26262 (Part 1–12) - Road Vehicles - Functional Safety, 2nd edn, December 2018. www.iso.org
14. Kurakin, A., Goodfellow, I., Bengio, S.: Adversarial machine learning at scale. arXiv preprint arXiv:1611.01236 (2016)
15. Kurakin, A., Goodfellow, I., Bengio, S.: Adversarial examples in the physical world (2017)
16. Lecuyer, M., Atlidakis, V., Geambasu, R., Hsu, D., Jana, S.: Certified robustness to adversarial examples with differential privacy. In: 2019 IEEE Symposium on Security and Privacy (SP), pp. 656–672. IEEE (2019)
17. Li, J., Schmidt, F., Kolter, Z.: Adversarial camera stickers: a physical camera-based attack on deep learning systems. In: Proceedings of the 36th International Conference on Machine Learning, vol. 97, pp. 3896–3904 (2019)
18. Li, Y., Li, L., Wang, L., Zhang, T., Gong, B.: Nattack: Learning the distributions of adversarial examples for an improved black-box attack on deep neural networks (2019)
19. Modas, A., Moosavi-Dezfooli, S., Frossard, P.: Sparsefool: a few pixels make a big difference. In: 2019 IEEE/CVF Conference on Computer Vision and Pattern Recognition (CVPR), pp. 9079–9088 (2019)
20. Modas, A., Moosavi-Dezfooli, S.M., Frossard, P.: Sparsefool: a few pixels make a big difference. In: Proceedings of the IEEE/CVF Conference on Computer Vision and Pattern Recognition, pp. 9087–9096 (2019)
21. Narodytska, N., Kasiviswanathan, S.P.: Simple black-box adversarial perturbations for deep networks. arXiv preprint arXiv:1612.06299 (2016)
22. Plataniotis, K., Venetsanopoulos, A.: Color Image Processing and Applications. Springer, Berlin (2000). https://doi.org/10.1007/978-3-662-04186-4
23. Pouyanfar, S., et al.: A survey on deep learning: algorithms, techniques, and applications. ACM Comput. Surv. **51**(5), 1–36 (2018)
24. Radlak, K., Szczepankiewicz, M., Smolka, B.: Defending against sparse adversarial attacks using impulsive noise reduction filters. In: Real-Time Image Processing and Deep Learning 2021, vol. 11736, p. 117360O. International Society for Optics and Photonics (2021)
25. Shafahi, A., et al.: Adversarial training for free! In: Advances in Neural Information Processing Systems, vol. 32 (2019)
26. Sinha, A., Namkoong, H., Volpi, R., Duchi, J.: Certifying some distributional robustness with principled adversarial training. arXiv preprint arXiv:1710.10571 (2017)
27. Stallkamp, J., Schlipsing, M., Salmen, J., Igel, C.: Man vs. computer: Benchmarking machine learning algorithms for traffic sign recognition. Neural Netw. **32**, 323–332 (2012)
28. Storn, R., Price, K.: Differential evolution - a simple and efficient heuristic for global optimization over continuous spaces. J. Global Optim. **11**, 341–359 (1997)
29. Su, J., Vargas, D., Sakurai, K.: One pixel attack for fooling deep neural networks. IEEE Trans. Evol. Comput. **23**(5), 828–841 (2019)
30. Wang, Y., Jha, S., Chaudhuri, K.: Analyzing the robustness of nearest neighbors to adversarial examples. In: International Conference on Machine Learning on Machine Learning, pp. 5133–5142. PMLR (2018)
31. Xiao, C., Deng, R., Li, B., Yu, F., Liu, M., Song, D.: Characterizing adversarial examples based on spatial consistency information for semantic segmentation. In: Proceedings of the European Conference on Computer Vision (ECCV), pp. 217–234 (2018)

Observing the Impact of Multicore Execution Platform for TSP Systems Under Schedulability, Security and Safety Constraints

Ill-ham Atchadam, Laurent Lemarchand, Frank Singhoff$^{(\boxtimes)}$, and Hai Nam Tran

Univ. Brest, Lab-STICC, CNRS, UMR 6285, 29200 Brest, France
{ill-ham.atchadam,laurent.lemarchand,
frank.singhoff,hainam.tran}@univ-brest.fr

Abstract. Avionic systems are integrating more and more functions to cope with the increasing number of features on modern aircrafts. These systems are subject to many requirements that have to be considered during their design. Time and Space Partitioning (TSP), which consists of isolating applications within partitions, is a well-known means to assign avionic applications to computing units according to security, schedulability, and safety constraints. Multicore execution platforms are becoming popular in avionic systems. In this paper, we propose to investigate the partitioning of avionic applications over such execution platforms while considering schedulability, security, and safety constraints. We propose a design space exploration approach using a multi-objective meta-heuristic, that provides trade-offs between schedulability and security while considering safety and multicore platforms with different numbers of cores. We illustrate how this meta-heuristic can investigate key parameters such as hardware shared resource overhead.

Keywords: Time and space partitioning · Scheduling · Safety · Security · Architecture exploration · Multi-objective optimization · Multicore

1 Introduction

SWaP (size, weight, and power) are great challenges in the avionic domain. Avionics systems were designed based on a federated approach [10] where each function had its own dedicated computing system [2]. To cope with the increasing number of functions embedded in an aircraft, the integrated avionic modular (IMA) [9] approach has been proposed to provide a pool of shared computing, communications, and I/O resources that is partitioned for use by multiple avionics functions [25]. IMA considers time and space partitioning (TSP) which guarantees time and space isolation between functions on the shared hardware

ⓒ The Author(s), under exclusive license to Springer Nature Switzerland AG 2022
M. Trapp et al. (Eds.): SAFECOMP 2022 Workshops, LNCS 13415, pp. 83–96, 2022.
https://doi.org/10.1007/978-3-031-14862-0_5

resources. Space isolation is obtained by memory protection between partitions while time isolation is enforced by offline partitioned scheduling.

Avionic functions implemented as real-time tasks in TSP systems have stringent constraints on safety, security, and schedulability. Safety is enforced by both the isolation through partitioning to prevent fault propagation and by the active redundancy, i.e. replications of tasks and partitions. Security requires that malicious entities cannot compromise the confidentiality of data exchanged between tasks. This can be achieved through encryption mechanisms. Implementation of safety and security measures must not affect system's schedulability as timing constraints must be respected to ensure the correct functionality of the system.

Problem Statement. A safe and secure TSP system implies additional tasks, partitions, and communications for safety, and additional overheads for encryption. This leads to a non-negligible increase in computation need, which may lead some tasks to miss their deadlines. Therefore it is important to propose approaches that can overcome the overheads due to security and safety requirements. This can be achieved by increasing the computing capacity of the system with multicore execution platforms. In this paper, we investigate how the use of multicore platforms may help in improving the safety and security of TSP systems while not jeopardizing their schedulability.

Contributions. In this paper, we propose a Design Space Exploration (DSE) approach based on the Pareto Archived Evolutionary Strategy (PAES) meta-heuristic that provides trade-offs for multi-objective optimization problems (MOOP) between safety, security, and schedulability for TSP systems on multicore platforms. We explore the tasks to partitions assignment in TSP systems when communications are secured and tasks are replicated. We show that our approach allows designers to explore the gain in terms of schedulability while considering security and safety. To validate the approach, we conduct two experiments. We analyze the search space by varying the number of cores. A first experiment provides consistent results showing schedulability improvements when the number of cores is increased, which assesses the relevance of our DSE. A second experiment illustrates the interest of our DSE, the experiments investigate the impact of multicore hardware shared resources on schedulability.

The rest of this paper is structured as follows. Section 2 presents the background together with the system model and assumptions taken in our work. Section 3 describes our DSE approach. Section 4 shows the experiments conducted to evaluate the DSE approach. Section 5 discusses related work and positions our contribution. Finally, Sect. 6 concludes the paper.

2   Background and Assumptions

In this section, we present system model and assumptions taken in our work. Then, we also present the context of security and safety that we consider.

2.1   System Model and Assumptions

In this paper, we consider a multicore TSP systems of m applications $(A_1, ..., A_m)$ where each application is a set of tasks. Systems considered are composed of a set n periodic tasks $(\tau_1, ..., \tau_n)$. We assume a multi-core architecture of d identical cores $(CO_1, ..., CO_d)$.

Each task τ_i is defined by a set of parameters $(C_i, T_i, D_i, CI_i, CL_i, A_i, P_i, CO_i)$. C_i, called the capacity of the task τ_i, represents its worst-case execution time. A task is released every T_i unit of time and has a deadline at D_i. We assume that the initial request of all the tasks is at time 0. A task is characterized by a tolerance level CI_i (hard or soft) to meet its deadline. A task is classified based on a confidentiality level CL_i (Top-secret, Secret, Unclassified). A_i represents the application to which the task τ_i belongs. P_i characterizes the partition to which the task τ_i is assigned. A partition is characterized by an execution time duration. We assume that all the partitions have the same properties and are executed based on an offline cyclic scheduling with a fixed interval called *major time frame* (MAF). Finally, a task is assigned to a core CO_i and core migration is not allowed at runtime.

We assumed that tasks communicate with each other through intra-partitions, or inter-partition communications depending on their assigned partitions. Intra-partition communications are communications between tasks in the same partition while inter-partition communications are about tasks assigned to different partitions. These communication services are provided by an application programming interface (API) such as the one proposed by the ARINC653 standard [5]. Both intra and inter-communications introduce overheads on the tasks concerned by the communications (i.e. sending and receiving tasks). As shown in [17], these overheads depend on the size of the exchanged data.

An offline cyclic scheduling is fixed for the partitions. Partitions are executed cyclically on an interval time called major time frame (MAF). Tasks inside partitions are executed concurrently based on a given scheduling policy (i.e. fixed-priority scheduling).

Figure 1 shows an example of scheduling of a multicore system with four tasks, assigned to two partitions and two cores. We note that τ_1, τ_3 and τ_2 are respectively assigned to core CO_1 and CO_2. For tasks to partitions assignment, τ_1, τ_2, τ_3, τ_4 are respectively assigned to partitions P_1, and P_2. The same MAF is assumed for all cores. Then when a partition is activated, only its tasks are executed concurrently on the cores depending on the tasks to cores assignment. Cores that have no task in the activated partition are in idle mode. They are not used till the activation of a partition with tasks assigned to them. In this example, we assumed that there is a communication from τ_1 to τ_2 and another from τ_1 to τ_3. Then τ_2 has to wait for τ_1 completion time before being starting its execution. This explains why even if τ_1 and τ_2 are on different cores, and τ_2 is the only task on CO_2, τ_2 could not start at time 0. It has to wait for the completion of τ_1.

Finally, we also consider overheads introduced by the hardware shared resources (level-2 cache, bus, memory, etc.) when multiple cores execute simul-

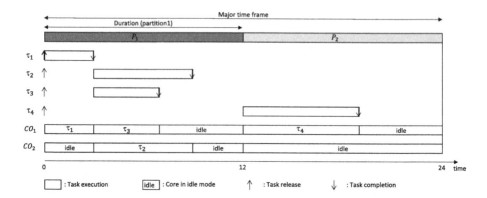

Fig. 1. Example of a multicore TSP system scheduling

taneously [3]. In [14], it has been proven that they are non-negligible and have
to be considered when performing the schedulability analysis of a multicore real-
time system. This issue is part of the key point addressed by the CAST-32A.
CAST-32A is a guidance for Avionics Multi-Core Processing that highlights some
parameters that may impact safety, security and performance. It considers that
contention for shared resources has an impact on the execution time of tasks.

2.2   Security and Safety

Security. We assumed that attacks can be operated on intra-partition and
inter-partition communications through attacks such as eavesdropping [26] and
code injection [19] (e.g. a code injected by a malicious employee). They violate
the confidentiality of a system, which normally restricts the access of data only
to authorized entities.

A communication is said to be vulnerable if it violates security rules defined
by a security model. In this work, we assume the Bell-La Padulla (BLP) [1]
security model with regard to confidentiality vulnerabilities. It is based on the
No read-up/no write-down principle. A communication from task τ_i to τ_j is
considered as a confidentiality violation if $CL_i > CL_j$. In this communication,
τ_i performs a write down and τ_j performs a read up, which violates the rules.

When a communication from task τ_i to τ_j is vulnerable, functions of a library
implementing encryption and decryption are called. Then an encryption (resp.
decryption) call is added to task τ_i (resp. τ_j) source code. Assuming the worst-
case situation where the encryption key is set up at each release of a task, we
also added a key set up function to both source code tasks. This process changes
the capacities of tasks τ_i and τ_j as follows where C_i' and C_j' represent their new
capacities. $C_{encryption\_function}$, $C_{decryption\_function}$, and $C_{encryption\_key\_function}$
represent respectively the execution times of the encryption, decryption, and
key set up functions.

$$C'_i \leftarrow C_i + C_{encryption\_function} + C_{encryption\_key\_function}$$
$$C'_j \leftarrow C_j + C_{decryption\_function} + C_{encryption\_key\_function}$$

$$(a)$$

Safety. We consider safety problems induced by arbitrary failures [15]. It includes the detection that some messages are not sent or received, the detection of incorrect messages sent with errors, and the detection of extra sent messages. We assume the worst-case situation where the replication is applied to all the software components (tasks and partitions). Then with such safety constraints, each task and partition is implemented by three instances. We impose that two instances of the same task are not allowed to be placed on the same partition. This paper is not an answer to multicore plaforms with hardware single point failure; e.g. when cores are interconnected by a bus, the bus is a single point of failure, while it is not the case if cores are interconnected with a crossbar.

2.3 Multi-objective Optimization

Multi-objective optimization problems (MOOP) [4] are characterized by multiple conflicting objectives to optimize: the optimization of one objective can deteriorate other objectives. Then it becomes difficult or sometimes impossible to build solutions that optimize simultaneously all the objectives. Thus, design space exploration is an alternative that helps to explore the space of solutions and propose a set of trade-offs between the objectives. The designer can then choose, between the trade-offs, the most appropriate solution to the specifications needed for his system.

The simplest approach is to investigate all the possible solutions in order to find the best trade-offs. However, for a large-scale problem, we can face a combinatorial explosion of the design space and the exhaustive search can become very time-consuming. Thus a multi-objective evolutionary algorithm (MOEA) [4] such as PAES [13] is an alternative to compute in fewer time solutions close to the best trade-offs. During the exploration, solutions are compared to each other using the Pareto dominance principle [13]. A solution $s1$ dominates a solution $s2$, if for all the objectives $s1$ is not worse than $s2$ and $s1$ is better than $s2$ for one objective at least. $s2$ is not a good trade-off and is discarded. Non dominated solutions found during the exploration constitute the Pareto set of solutions.

3 Design Space Exploration (DSE) Approach for Multicore TSP Systems

In this section, we present a DSE approach that computes trade-offs between security and schedulability while considering safety constraints and resources constraints such as the number of cores and partitions. Since security, schedulability, and safety are conflicting requirements that lead to a multi-objective optimization problem, we adopt the PAES algorithm in our approach.

PAES is a meta heuristic framework. It starts with random solution(s) and transforms them using exploration operators, keeping the most interesting ones generation after generation. In order to customize PAES framework for isolving efficiently our problem, we need to identify (1) specific initial solutions, (2) constraints to perform the feasibility tests, (3) objective functions to optimize, (4) mutation operators to generate new solutions. These components are detailed in the next section.

The entry point of the PAES being the initial solution, we proposed an initial solution adapted to our problem. During the design space exploration, new solutions are generated through mutation operations that consider tasks to partitions and cores assignments and communications security. Feasibility tests are performed according to the respect of security, schedulability, and safety constraints. Feasible solutions are evaluated according to objective functions based on schedulability and security analysis.

Initial Solution. We design the initial solution by resolving all confidentiality vulnerabilities in the system (as described in Sect. 2.2), placing all the initial tasks in the same partition running on a single core. Then we triplicate the tasks, the communications between tasks, and the partitions to ensure safety. We proceed with a schedulability analysis of this solution. If it is schedulable, there is no need to continue with the exploration: we consider this solution as an optimal solution since it is fully secured, schedulable and safe with the minimal number of cores. Otherwise, we add this initial solution to the archive.

Instead of starting the exploration with an archive containing one solution as specified in the original PAES algorithm, we fill the archive with several solutions. We made this choice to improve solution diversity and exploration of the design space. We fill the archive with solutions modeling various tasks to cores assignment and communications security. Then we added solutions with all tasks assigned to a single core and with all tasks of a partition assigned per core. For these solutions, we decided to resolve all or no security vulnerabilities.

Objective Functions and Constraints. In the PAES meta-heuristic, the constraints are conditions that should always be respected. Otherwise, the concerned solutions are considered not valid. Objective functions are defined to tolerate some violations and should be optimized in order to propose the best trade-offs between conflicting objectives. We defined the constraints and the objective functions based on schedulability, safety, and security issues. In our model, tasks can be either hard deadline tasks or soft deadline tasks. As a constraint, a solution is considered invalid and is rejected if a hard deadline task misses its deadline. Missed deadlines are tolerated for soft deadline tasks.

– C1: No missed_deadlines for hard deadline tasks

Our first objective function is defined by the number of soft deadline tasks that missed their deadlines. This number is computed through a scheduling simulation of the solution. The function is noted below:

– F1: Minimize (number of missed soft deadlines)

Since we decide to investigate tasks to core assignment to evaluate their impact on the considered systems, our second objective function represents the number of cores used in a given solution:

– F2: Minimize (number of cores)

The problem depicted in this paper addresses the confidentiality of communications between tasks. We defined the constraints below for security vulnerabilities based on BLP rules for communicating tasks:

– C2: No data received by Unclassified task from Secret or Top-secret task

Each model that compromises one of these constraints is rejected. Otherwise, any communication violating the other BLP rules is tolerated. This allows the definition of the security objective function:

– F3: Minimize (number of tolerated confidentiality violations)

The equation F3 represents the number of tolerated communications that violate BLP rules.

Since we address safety issues by applying active redundancy, each task of our model is triplicated. By definition, this redundancy imposes that two instances of the same task should never be placed on the same partition. Then we assumed as safety constraints that every solution with two instances of a task placed on the same partition should be automatically rejected.

– C4: Two instances of the same task cannot be placed in the same partition

In order to find trade-offs for our MOOP, all the defined objective functions have to be minimized. Constraints and objective functions are computed with the Cheddar tool in which our DSE heuristic has been implemented [24].

Mutation Operator. Since PAES works with a neighborhood-based search, the design space is explored by mutating a solution to another nearby. We are interested in tasks to partitions assignment, tasks to cores assignment, and the security of communications between tasks.

The first mutation operator changes the tasks to partitions assignment of a solution. It is defined with two different options. The first option consists of moving all tasks of a randomly chosen application to a randomly chosen partition. The second option consists of moving a randomly chosen task to a randomly chosen partition.

The second operator is similar to the first one but changes tasks to cores assignment. Thus, the first option consists of moving all the tasks of a randomly chosen application to be executed on a randomly chosen core. The second option is operated by moving a randomly chosen task to be executed on a randomly chosen core.

Notice that the change of tasks to partitions or tasks to cores assignment has an impact on the schedulability of the solution.

The third operator concerns communications of the solution. It is realized by a random choice of a communication. If the communication presents security vulnerabilities, then we secure it by adding security functions. Otherwise, we remove the security functions and the communication becomes unsecure.

After each mutation operation, we conduct feasibility tests to check the respect of schedulability and security constraints. If the new solution generated by the mutation does not respect one of the constraints, it is rejected and another mutation operation is performed. Otherwise, if the solution respects all the constraints, then schedulability and security analysis are performed to evaluate the objective functions of the solution.

In the next section, we propose to validate and illustrate our DSE approach through experiments.

4   Test Cases and Evaluation

In these experiments, we evaluate our DSE approach with a case study with the objective of proposing a set of solutions representing good trade-offs between security and schedulability while considering safety and multicore executing platforms with different numbers of cores.

We highlight that our choices of tasks model, considered faults, and encryption algorithms are classic and from known benchmarks, but can be adapted.

Case Study. We use a case study composed of a set of two applications: a flight controller application ROSACE (Research Open-Source Avionics and Control Engineering) [20] and a digital signal processing application CFAR (Constant False Alarm Rate detection) [22]. ROSACE is a real-time benchmark composed of fifteen dependent and periodic tasks with the WCETs of tasks and their period taken from [20]. CFAR is a target detection application composed of four dependent tasks with the WCETs taken from the StreamIT benchmark profiled in [22]. We assume for ROSACE and CFAR, an average data size of 8 bytes.

We assumed that cores are identical and have the same predefined MAF. The partitions are identical with a duration of 1250 us. We also supposed that the tasks are periodic and their deadlines (soft or hard) and security levels are fixed independently by the designer as inputs.

Results of the Experiment. Considering the two applications, the initial system model is made of 19 tasks. With our safety assumptions, we triplicated partitions, tasks, and communications. This implies 57 tasks with at least 3 partitions for the DSE. By considering one of the additional initial solutions defined in 3 that runs each application per partition, we assume a DSE with a maximal number of 6 partitions. Then, we explore multiple solutions with 3, 4, 5, and 6 partitions since the safety imposes a minimum of 3 partitions.

We assumed that intra-partition (resp. inter-partition) communications are performed through blackboards (sampling ports). For their cost, we consider the execution times of the APEX calls SFPBench Benchmark proposed in [16]. Considering the data size of our case study, for blackboards (resp. sampling ports), it gives a cost of 0.76 us/0.32 us (resp. 4.24 us/5.04 us) for read/write.

For confidentiality vulnerabilities securing, we used the blowfish encryption algorithm [23]. With a frequency of 1.2 GHz, we computed the time execution of security functions based on values provided by the crypto++ benchmark [8] and the data size of our applications. Then for both applications, the execution times of encryption, and encryption key refreshment are respectively 0.166 us, and 88.83 us. We consider the decryption execution time equal to the encryption execution time.

About the shared hardware resource overheads, we only consider the interconnection overhead. We conduct the DSE first by considering the best case with negligible interconnection overhead. Second, we conduct another DSE by assuming the overhead percentage provided in [14]. It depends on the number of cores of the considered system. Then for a system with only one core, there is no interconnection overhead. For a system netween 2 and 4 cores (resp. between 5 and 8), the interconnection overhead on each task corresponds to 10% (resp. 13%) of its capacity. For systems with more than 8 cores, we assume a 26% overhead. Each DSE was performed for 20000 iterations which takes 12 h.

The solution with minimum cores corresponds to the solution with all tasks assigned to a single core. It has a high number of missed deadlines (45 over 57 tasks). By increasing the number of cores to 57 cores (i.e. number of tasks), more tasks are able to meet their deadlines (e.g. from 45 to 0 missed deadlines when inter-core communication is considered negligible). This confirms the impact of multicore platforms on safe and secure TSP systems. This is explained by the fact that using more cores increases the computation capacity of the system.

Since these solutions are extreme, we propose to investigate the design search space, in order to find interesting trade-offs. The DSE proposes a set of 52 (resp. 40) different trade-offs with no interconnection overhead (with interconnection overhead). Figure 2 shows the set of non-dominated solutions.

For the system model with negligible interconnection overhead, our DSE tool was able to decrease from 45 to 11 the number of cores required for a fully secured, safe, and no missed deadlines solution (Fig 2(a)). Our DSE is able to detect a minimal number of cores that corresponds to a fully secured, safe, and no missed deadlines solution. This solution considers a better grouping of tasks on the cores in order to propose a reduced number of cores while not allowing any task to miss its deadline. The tasks to cores assignment of this solution is so irregular that it will be very time-consuming and almost impossible to get manually such an assignment considering 57 tasks to assign to 11 cores. This shows the effectiveness of our DSE in proposing good trade-offs while considering schedulability, security, safety, and different numbers of cores.

The DSE with non-negligible interconnection overhead also proposes a solution that reduces to 11 the number of cores for a fully secured, safe, and no

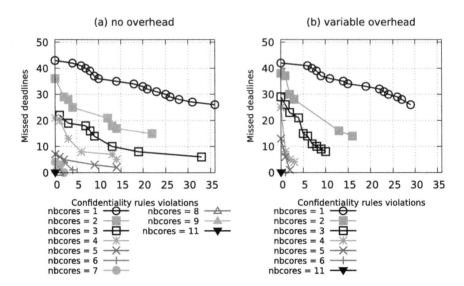

Fig. 2. Schedulability vs. confidentiality with inter-core communication variation

missed deadlines solution (Fig 2(b)). Contrary to the above-mentioned solution, it has a different tasks to cores assignment and used 4 partitions instead of 3 partitions. This can be explained by the fact that the above-mentioned solution updated with interconnection overhead was not able to keep no missed deadline. Then the DSE was able to explore different tasks to partitions and tasks to cores assignments to avoid missed deadlines without using more cores. Those solutions are not intuitive and motivate the use of our DSE approach.

As expected, we observe in the figures that the more the number of cores increases, the easier it becomes to ensure the security of safe TSP systems while minimizing the number of missed deadlines. This confirms the relevance of the proposed DSE.

The speedup relates to the number of cores can be compromised by a high shared hardware resource overhead. As shown on the graphs, trade-offs with no security vulnerabilities proposed by the DSE with non-negligible interconnection overhead have a number of missed deadlines greater than or equal to the equivalent in the DSE with negligible interconnection overhead. Let us consider the fully secure solutions with 5 cores. With no interconnection overhead, there are 7 missed deadlines (Fig 2(a)) while there are 13 missed deadlines when considering interconnection overhead (Fig 2(b)). This can also explain that with interconnection overhead, solutions with 6, 7, 8, and 9 cores are dominated by the other solutions and then rejected by the PAES. This illustrates that overhead related to shared hardware resources is a key parameter in the design of safe and secure multicore TSP systems.

No optimal result is known, since the search space size is in the order of 10^{146}. Thus an exhaustive search should be no tractable. Comparison could be made with other heuristic approaches only, without a guarantee on optimality.

5 Related Work

In this section, we position our work by presenting different approaches that addressed the design of multicore platforms for TSP systems with schedulability, safety, and/or security constraints/objectives.

Many researchers have investigated TSP systems on multicore platforms. In [21], the authors depicted that multicore platforms can intervene in ensuring high-performance requirements. For this purpose, they identified some conditions such as privileging the intra-partition parallelism, which assumes the possibility of running parallel tasks of the same partition on different cores. In [7], the authors proposed the evolution of a TSP unicore system to a TSP multicore system while considering inter and intra-partition parallelism mechanisms. The former consists of activating simultaneously many partitions on different cores. The work in [12] proposed a similar idea towards the design and analysis of TSP multicore systems. The authors specifically focused on symmetric multiprocessing (SMP) architectures where each core has access to a common shared memory and I/O resources with a single operating system for all the cores. They defined patterns for SMP/TSP multicore systems with which they extended the Ocarina code generation tool.

Since safety and security are important requirements for TSP systems, several researchers showed interest in these domains. In [6], the authors proposed a survey for validation and certification of TSP multicore systems deployed on the Xtratum hypervisor [18]. For example, it highlights fault tolerance for safety and data protection for security. The authors of [11] addressed multicore platforms not specifically for TSP systems, but for real-time systems in general. They also addressed the systems' security vulnerabilities. Then the authors added security mechanisms such as a hash algorithm to their systems and then proposed a DSE to optimize their schedulability while exploring the security tasks to cores assignment possibilities.

The potential schedulability benefits of deploying TSP systems on multicore platforms have led to multiple researches on the design and analysis of such systems. Some have addressed their security and safety vulnerabilities. Few have studied the assignment of tasks to cores through a DSE for real-time systems in general. We propose a DSE approach for multicore TSP systems that investigates not only tasks to cores assignment but also tasks to partitions assignment and securing communications alternatives in order to find trade-offs. We also integrate safety constraints into our proposal. As far as we know, no work has proposed such a set of combinations.

6 Conclusion

In this paper, we investigate the impact of multicore platforms on safe and secure TSP systems by proposing an approach to explore their design space. Our DSE approach covers the different possibilities of tasks to partitions assignment, tasks to cores assignment, and securing communications, which is a combinatorial problem. Our approach is based on a meta-heuristic which proposes trade-offs between schedulability and security for a safe TSP system while considering different numbers of cores.

As expected, our approach shows that for a safe and secure TSP system with some missed deadlines, increasing the number of cores effectively helps to optimize the system schedulability. Better solutions can also be obtained by moving some tasks from one partition to another or from a core to another. This first result confirms the relevance of our DSE.

To illustrate the interest of our approach, we test the DSE by considering shared hardware resources overhead existing in multicore platform. This overhead results from tasks on different cores accessing simultaneously the same hardware resources. It may increase considerably the required number of cores to keep a certain level of schedulability. Our experiments show that the shared hardware resources overhead, the number of cores, the number of partitions, tasks to partitions and cores assignments are key parameters in the design of multicore safe and secure TSP systems.

In this paper, the multicore hardware resource overheads introduced in the DSE was limited while it exists various sources and types of such overhead in multicore platforms (from the cache, interconnection or memory systems). In the future, we want to integrate in the DSE some of these overheads. We also intend to consider other security vulnerabilities such as those related to integrity or/and availability since we only consider confidentiality vulnerabilities.

Artefact All experiment data presented in this paper are available at http://beru.univ-brest.fr/svn/CHEDDAR/trunk/artefacts/DECSOS22/.
Programs and scripts written to produce these experimental data are available at http://beru.univ-brest.fr/svn/CHEDDAR/trunk/src/framework_examples/architecture_exploration_tools/.

References

1. Bell, D.E., La Padula, L.J.: Secure computer system: Unified exposition and multics interpretation. Tech. rep, MITRE CORP BEDFORD MA (1976)
2. Bieber, P., Boniol, F., Boyer, M., Noulard, E., Pagetti, C.: New challenges for future avionic architectures. AerospaceLab (4), 1 (2012)
3. Chai, L., Gao, Q., Panda, D.K.: Understanding the impact of multi-core architecture in cluster computing: a case study with intel dual-core system. In: Seventh IEEE international symposium on cluster computing and the grid (CCGrid 2007), pp. 471–478. IEEE (2007)

4. Coello, C.A.C., Lamont, G.B., Van Veldhuizen, D.A., et al.: Evolutionary Algorithms for Solving Multi-objective Problems, vol. 5. Springer, New York (2007). https://doi.org/10.1007/978-1-4757-5184-0
5. Committee, A.E.E.: Arinc 653: avionics application software standard interface, supplement 1 (2003)
6. Coronel, J., Tsagkaropoulos, M., Mylonas, D., Balbastre, P., Kollias, V., Crespo, A.: Validation of securely partitioned systems over multicore architectures based on xtratum. In: Proceedings on Data systems in aerospace (DASIA) (2013)
7. Craveiro, J., Rufino, J., Singhoff, F.: Architecture, mechanisms and scheduling analysis tool for multicore time-and space-partitioned systems. ACM SIGBED Rev. **8**(3), 23–27 (2011)
8. Dai, W.: Crypto++ 5.6. 0 benchmarks. http://www.cryptopp.com/benchmarks.html (2009)
9. (Firme), R.: Integrated Modular Avionics (IMA) Development Guidance and Certification Considerations. RTCA (2005)
10. Garside, R., Pighetti, F.J.: Integrating modular avionics: a new role emerges. IEEE Aerosp. Electron. Syst. Mag. **24**(3), 31–34 (2009)
11. Hasan, M., Mohan, S., Pellizzoni, R., Bobba, R.B.: A design-space exploration for allocating security tasks in multicore real-time systems. In: 2018 Design, Automation & Test in Europe Conference (DATE), pp. 225–230. IEEE (2018)
12. Hugues, J., Honvault, C., Pagetti, C.: Model-based design, analysis and synthesis for multi-core and tsp avionics targets (2018)
13. Knowles, J., Corne, D.: The pareto archived evolution strategy: a new baseline algorithm for pareto multiobjective optimisation. In: Proceedings of the 1999 Congress on Evolutionary Computation-CEC99 (Cat. No. 99TH8406), vol. 1, pp. 98–105. IEEE (1999)
14. Kumar, R., Zyuban, V., Tullsen, D.M.: Interconnections in multi-core architectures: understanding mechanisms, overheads and scaling. In: 32nd International Symposium on Computer Architecture (ISCA 2005), pp. 408–419. IEEE (2005)
15. Lala, J.H., Harper, R.E.: Architectural principles for safety-critical real-time applications. Proc. IEEE **82**(1), 25–40 (1994)
16. Gohring de Magalhaes, F., Torres Aurora Dugo, A., Lefoul, J.B., Nicolescu, G.: On the benchmarking of partitioned real-time systems. arXiv e-prints, pp. arXiv-2007 (2020)
17. de Magalhaes, F.G., Dugo, A.T.A., Lefoul, J.B., Nicolescu, G.: On the benchmarking of partitioned real-time systems. arXiv preprint arXiv:2007.10794 (2020)
18. Masmano, M., Ripoll, I., Crespo, A., Metge, J.: Xtratum: a hypervisor for safety critical embedded systems. In: 11th Real-Time Linux Workshop, pp. 263–272. Citeseer (2009)
19. Mo, Y., Garone, E., Casavola, A., Sinopoli, B.: False data injection attacks against state estimation in wireless sensor networks. In: 49th IEEE Conference on Decision and Control (CDC), pp. 5967–5972. IEEE (2010)
20. Pagetti, C., Saussié, D., Gratia, R., Noulard, E., Siron, P.: The rosace case study: from simulink specification to multi/many-core execution. In: 2014 IEEE 19th Real-Time and Embedded Technology and Applications Symposium (RTAS), pp. 309–318. IEEE (2014)
21. Patte, M., Lefftz, V., Zulianello, M., Crespo, A., Masmano, M., Coronel, J.: System impact of distributed multi core systems. Technical Report ESTEC Contract 4200023100 (2011)

22. Rouxel, B., Puaut, I.: StR2RTS: Refactored streamit benchmarks into statically analyzable parallel benchmarks for WCET estimation & real-time scheduling. In: 17th International Workshop on Worst-Case Execution Time Analysis (WCET 2017), Schloss Dagstuhl-Leibniz-Zentrum fuer Informatik (2017)

23. Schneier, B.: Description of a new variable-length key, 64-bit block cipher (Blowfish). In: Anderson, R. (ed.) FSE 1993. LNCS, vol. 809, pp. 191–204. Springer, Heidelberg (1994). https://doi.org/10.1007/3-540-58108-1_24

24. Singhoff, F., Legrand, J., Nana, L., Marcé, L.: Cheddar: a flexible real time scheduling framework. In: ACM SIGAda Ada Letters, vol. 24, pp. 1–8. ACM (2004)

25. Watkins, C.B., Walter, R.: Transitioning from federated avionics architectures to integrated modular avionics. In: 2007 IEEE/AIAA 26th Digital Avionics Systems Conference, pp. 2-A. IEEE (2007)

26. Zou, Y., Wang, G.: Intercept behavior analysis of industrial wireless sensor networks in the presence of eavesdropping attack. IEEE Trans. Ind. Inf. **12**(2), 780–787 (2015)

Security Assessment Prospects as Part of Vehicle Regulations

Mona Gierl[1]([⊠]) [iD], Reiner Kriesten[1], and Eric Sax[2]

[1] Institute of Energy Efficient Mobility, University of Applied Sciences, International University
Campus 5, 76646 Bruchsal, Germany
{mona.gierl,reiner.kriesten}@h-ka.de
[2] Institute for Information Processing Technologies, Karlsruhe Institute of Technology,
Engesserstr. 5, 76131 Karlsruhe, Germany
eric.sax@kit.edu

Abstract. Vehicle regulations provide uniform provisions to improve road safety and environmental protection. The World Forum for the harmonization of vehicle regulations works continuously on keeping the regulations up to date considering current technological innovations and scientific progress. With the advances in automotive connectivity, cybersecurity engineering is becoming mandatory for connected cars. Thus, present roadworthiness assessments have to be extended with adequate security assessment methods. Within this paper, the current state of the type approval and periodic technical inspection regulations for passenger cars are presented. Further, the UN R155 Cybersecurity Regulation [1] and the ISO/SAE 21434 [2] are analyzed to provide the state of the art about ongoing cybersecurity standardization and regulation efforts in the automotive domain. In addition, cybersecurity assessment challenges are derived and the need for corresponding assessments through accredited institutions is discussed.

Keywords: Automotive cybersecurity assessment · Vehicle regulations · Type approval · Periodic technical inspection

1 Introduction

Over the last few years, researchers have demonstrated attacks on vehicles to have an impact on road safety [3–5]. Independent of the vehicle type, the road safety and environmental performance are essential factors concerning all traffic participants and therefore are supplementarily controlled by regulations. At present, vehicles have to meet specified technical requirements before road admission and pass regular inspections while in operation to be approved for road usage. These vehicle regulations are formulated by regulatory bodies with the intent to improve road safety and decrease environmental pollution. Depending on the country and national approval schemes, different requirements are mandated, yet, harmonization efforts are presented by e.g., the United Nations (UN) Working Group WP.29. Within the UN regulatory framework, three agreements are presented:

1. 1958 Agreement concerning the adoption of harmonized technical UN regulations for wheeled vehicles, equipment and parts [6]
2. 1997 Agreement covering periodic technical inspections [7]
3. 1998 Agreement known as UN Global Technical Regulations (GTRs) [8]

The UN regulations of the 1958 Agreement prescribe technical requirements and administrative procedures for the approval of newly developed vehicles, while the UN Rules of the 1997 Agreement refer to regular inspections taking place periodically throughout the lifetime of the vehicle. Finally, the UN GTRs of the 1998 Agreement were established in parallel to the 1958 Agreement and provide "globally harmonized performance-related requirements and test procedures" [8] without defining administrative procedures for type approval, to also allow countries with other certification schemes (e.g., self-certification in the US, Canada, etc.) to participate in the harmonization efforts.

As technology evolves, the technical requirements and test or inspection methods within the regulations have to adapt to keep up with recent vehicle safety considerations. In this context, two essential guidelines for the development of vehicles exist: ISO 26262 Road vehicles - Functional safety (since 2011) and ISO/SAE 21434 Cybersecurity Engineering (since 2021) which serve as a reference for the manufacturer. Thus, with the recent ISO/SAE 21434 Cybersecurity Standard [2], security can be seen as a key aspect which needs to be considered over the whole vehicle lifespan.

Problem Statement. The assessment of roadworthiness is a sovereign task assigned to competent authorities and inspectors. In case of not fulfilling the requirements or showing defects, the vehicles are withdrawn from road admission to reduce the risk of fatal injuries. Depending on each vehicle's technology, the examination criteria vary. Due to digitization and advances in connectivity, the risk of malicious attacks adds to the current spectrum of possible sources of faults potentially impacting road safety. However, it is challenging to detect the effects of an attack on the vehicle and it generally requires full system knowledge and suitable security testing methods. For this reason, the question arises to what extent security assessments by accredited organizations can contribute to improved road safety.

Contribution. Within the paper, we want to show that accredited organizations should conduct security assessment and are able to provide valuable security assessment results for road users. To do so, the scope and the process of vehicle regulations within the framework of type approval and periodic technical inspections are presented. Subsequently, the link to cybersecurity is drawn by addressing the respective UN R155 regulation as well as by listing the relevant work products of the ISO/SAE 21434 standard. In summary, the paper provides the recent status of legal security assessments and derives future challenges and requirements for assessments from them.

Note. In this paper, the term security refers to the short form of cybersecurity.

In Sect. 2, background information on the type approval and the periodic technical inspection is given. In terms of content, the legal situation and the general processes are addressed. Section 3 establishes the link to security and addresses the respective challenges in assessing security. Afterwards, Sect. 4 provides insight into related work in the product development and post development phase. Section 5 elaborates on two important automotive security initiatives, namely the ISO/SAE 21434 and the UN R155. And finally, Sect. 6 identifies and discusses open research areas.

2 Regulatory Background

To obtain and to maintain road admission, the condition of the vehicle has to adhere to regulatory requirements. A distinction can be made between the type approval which the manufacturer has to apply for previous to production and the periodic technical inspection which occurs regularly over the years of operation. A summary of the scope of type approval and periodic technical inspection is given in Table 1

2.1 Type Approval

For the sake of vehicle safety and environmental protection, vehicles have to meet type approval regulations addressing uniform technical requirements "for wheeled vehicles, equipment and parts which can be fitted to and/or be used on wheeled vehicles" [6]. Thus, vehicle manufacturers have to adhere to country specific type approval regulations to obtain a certificate of compliance, and to be allowed to produce their approved vehicle or respective system or component. Efforts have been made to harmonize existing regulations with the target to reduce barriers to international trade [6]. Namely, the Regulation 2018/858/EU [9] is applicable all over Europe and refers to the UN 1958 Agreement which formulates the above mentioned uniform technical requirements for contracting parties and is currently signed by 64 states including the European Union (EU) [10]. Thus, once the vehicle or its components approved according to the UN regulations, the approval is mutually recognized by all contracting parties and no further tests or approvals are necessary for international trade.

The procedure of a type approval involves three parties: the manufacturer, an accredited technical service and the approval authority. The manufacturer is responsible to provide justification of met requirements and competent approval authorities are the auditors. After conformance evaluation of the technical service, the application is forwarded to the approval authority which issues the certificate. In addition to administrative efforts, the selection of test methods and the performance of the conformance tests by the technical service is of particular interest. Important qualities are a uniform procedure, which is consistent, objective, and repeatable. Furthermore, the prescribed regulatory requirements and testing procedures shall always comply with current roadworthiness standards. An excerpt from the 2018/858/EU illustrates this:

"In order to ensure a high level of vehicle functional safety, to ensure the protection of vehicle's occupants and other road users, and to ensure the protection of the environment and health, the technical requirements and environmental standards that apply to vehicles, systems, components and separate technical units should continue to be harmonised and adapted to reflect the technical and scientific progress." [9].

2.2 Periodic Technical Inspections (PTI)

In 2021, the german federal motor transport authority ("Kraftfahrt-Bundesamt", kba) found that a majority of operating passenger cars - namely 12.5 million (25.9%) – were first registered between 5 to 9 years ago (see Fig. 1.) [11]. Over the years in use, all vehicles are subject to wear and tear which may cause technical errors or other deficiencies. As in 2020, 27.2% of the defects in passenger cars were found in the lighting equipment and other parts of the electronic system while 18% of the defects were found in the brake system [12]. Hence, chances are that a malfunctioning technical system impacts the road safety and poses a hazard to all road users.

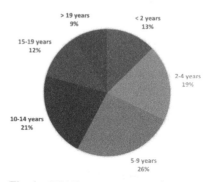

Fig. 1. 2021 Passenger car rate in Germany by registration age [12]

Periodic roadworthiness inspections aim to ensure the safe and environmentally acceptable condition of vehicles in use [13]. With the 1997 Agreement, the UN has adopted harmonized rules for the periodic technical inspection for wheeled vehicles which are also applied by the EU within the 2014/45/EU [13]. Still, the EU directive prescribes minimum requirements and is often supplemented by stricter requirements at national level. A summary of current roadworthiness test procedures of different countries is provided in [14]. In order to get a better understanding of the PTI, the subsequent section describes the procedure in Germany.

The frequency of the inspection varies depending on the vehicle class and country (e.g., passenger cars in Germany are inspected every 2–3 years). According to [13], an inspection includes the identification of the vehicle, braking equipment, steering, visibility, lighting equipment and the according parts of the electrical system, axles, wheels, tires, suspension, chassis and its attachments, other equipment, nuisance, and supplementary tests for passenger-carrying vehicles. The examination is based on visual and performance tests, whereas no disassembly may be carried out. The inspection assesses the vehicle's equipment, condition, function, and performance. For evaluation, individual functions such as the lights, windshield wipers, or other buttons or levers are operated manually and the vehicle is visually inspected from all sides. Furthermore, for the assessment of safety relevant electronic systems, a vehicle diagnostic communication standard, namely the ISO 20730 Road vehicles - Vehicle interface for electronic Periodic Technical Inspection (ePTI), was published in 2021 [15]. Within the ISO 20730-3, an ePTI system list is included, which summarizes the ePTI-relevant systems. Electronic systems in Germany are checked using a PTI-Adapter, which is connected via the On-Board Diagnostics (OBD) interface. In addition, the PTI-Adapter can be used for the brake performance measurement on the brake test bench. Other important components are the exhaust emission test and the headlamp aiming system. Overall, the fundamental basis for all periodic technical inspections is built upon the comparison between the examined vehicle behavior and the desired system response.

The 2014/45/EU provides a catalog on inspection items with their respective test methods, reasons for failure, and a classification of the severity of the resulting deficiencies. The deficiencies are divided into three categories: minor, major, and dangerous. German law extends these deficiencies categories with a fourth, which can be translated as "unroadworthy". Road admission is withdrawn in case of major or worse deficiencies.

Table 1. Content and scope of type approval and periodic technical inspections

	Type approval	Periodic technical inspection
Objective	Conformance, roadworthiness and environmental impact checks	Uncover vehicle deficiencies or manipulation, roadworthiness and environmental impact checks
Point in time	Application prior to production	Periodically during years of operation
Scope	vehicle type, system or component	systems and components of manufactured, whole vehicle
Methods	Document review, sampling, test lane, simulation, hardware in the loop, etc	Visual inspection, electronic interface (OBD), brake tester, headlamp aiming device, exhaust gas analyzer, test drive
Data access	Manufacturer provides documentation package, upon request further data has to be provided, intellectual property of manufacturer is handled confidential (white box testing)	Fault memory and diagnostic information dependent on vehicle capabilities and electronic interface support (black box testing)
Peculiarity	–	Inspection without disassembly

3   Cybersecurity Challenges over the Years of Vehicle Operation

Attacks on the vehicle take place during their usage time and may affect driving safety if the attack is successful, one of the most famous examples being the white hat attacks on an Jeep Cherokee [3]. Simultaneously, whenever a vehicle shows major or worse defects, the vehicle is withdrawn from road admission to reduce the risk of fatal injuries. This raises the research question:

Research Question RQ1. To what extent are attacks able to trigger defects and should security evaluations be part of roadworthiness assessments by accredited organizations?

For a security evaluation to be part of vehicle regulations, the following challenges have to be considered:

– Challenge I: The threat landscape is dynamic and changes with advances in technology. This influences the selection of appropriate countermeasures. Hence, existing lists of threats have to be extended regularly.

- Challenge II: Security countermeasures can "age" due to new attacker techniques which may be able to bypass implemented countermeasure making them meaningless and increasing the risk of new attacks.
- Challenge III: Security measures are "not visible" during normal operation since they are generally preventive. Compared to known driving functions, e.g., the emergency braking system, security measures do not control actuators.
- Challenge IV: Identifying the impact of an attack on the vehicle requires expert knowledge in the security domain. Thus, the inspector should have the required experience and qualifications to perform consistent security roadworthiness assessments.

The challenges show that the assessment of security differs fundamentally from the assessment of other systems or components of the vehicle. While driving functions can usually be validated through test drives by specifying worst-case scenarios for the respective system in the regulations (e.g., braking force or reaction times to be observed), security measures do not control actuators and do not show system reactions to the driver during normal operation. The conflict lies much more in the fact that if the vehicle would be deliberately penetrated during a "security inspection", the affected driving function may be automatically deactivated to prevent compromise, while this step would be irreversible until the vehicle is brought to a contract workshop of the manufacturer, which would be associated with undesirable costs.

4 Related Work

Adapting regulations to the state of technology is a continuous challenge and requires an understanding of prevailing standards and about the measures taken by the manufacturer. An extensive listing of all standards and measures of the manufacturer would go beyond the scope of this paper, instead a brief overview of relevant scientific publications shall be given. In terms of automotive security, the according ISO/SAE 21434 and the UN R155 are presented in Sect. 5. For the measures taken by the manufacturer, a distinction must be made between the security assessment efforts in the product development phase and the post development phase. The assessment during development is for verification and validation and should take place as early as possible. In the post development phase, the focus is on maintaining the security through monitoring and incident response, so that the vehicle remains roadworthy over the years of operation despite the previously mentioned dynamic threat landscape.

Product Development Phase. During automotive security engineering, a risk-based approach is chosen to select appropriate countermeasures based on threat and risk analyses in the concept phase. On the basis of identified risks, security goals and requirements are derived and summarized within the security concept which is implemented and tested during the product development phase. The artifacts from development and especially the test results from the product development phase can be used to check conformance to vehicle regulations (see Sect. 5). In the context of type approval, Brennich et al. [16] regard security testing as an indispensable means for compliance. They appeal to a holistic security testing concept under selection of suitable security testing techniques.

A survey on automotive security testing methods was conducted by Pekaric et al. [17]. Within the survey, they applied five security testing techniques (model-based security testing, code-based testing and static analyses, penetration testing and dynamic analyses, and security regression testing) according to [18] and assigned these to the different phases of the automotive life cycle. The literature review has shown a clear emphasis on verification efforts during product development, whereby it identifies a gap in the testing of changes in the post development phase by pointing out a lack of automotive security regression tests.

Post Development Phase. In the post development phase, besides the application of access control mechanisms and firewalls to restrict the access on resources, Intrusion Detection Systems (IDS) are used for the detection of attacks. A survey of current IDS for intra vehicle networks is given in [19]. The paper points out that most features neglect the context of in-vehicle data and mainly focus on cyber feature analysis. The potential of context-aware security is investigated by Grimm et al. [20], who aim to pave the way for intelligent security measures which are enriched with context aware attack data. In addition, the post development phase is characterized by software updates over the air, which enable the remote download of bug fixes or even new features during the years in operation. However, a particular challenge is posed by the variety of software variants which makes verification approaches necessary to guarantee a secure update process. The ICARUS method [21], for example, represents a contract-based approach that tracks and models changes in the system throughout the whole product line.

5 State of the Art – Security Standard and Regulations

In total, we want to highlight two formal automotive initiatives. First, the ISO/SAE 21434 - Cybersecurity Engineering since August 2021, which is addressed to manufacturers and suppliers and covers the state of the art in development. This standard can be used to derive what engineering results can be expected for type approval. Secondly, the UN R155 regulation on cybersecurity which was published in January 2021. It represents the minimum requirements for the security of modern vehicles and will come into force in the EU for new vehicle types from 2022 [22].

5.1 ISO/SAE 21434 – Cybersecurity Engineering

The ISO/SAE 21434 is designed to serves as a guidance document for the development of new vehicles. The implementation of the standard is not mandatory, but development artifacts can be used as compliance arguments for the regulations. Understanding the security engineering process helps to understand what is to be expected for future type approvals.

The security process within the ISO/SAE 21434 was established according to the safety processes of ISO 26262 [23] and also addresses the different phases of the V-Model (concept, product development and post development phases). Besides the three V-Model phases, management of cybersecurity, continual cybersecurity activities, and risk assessment are further elaborated by the standard.

– Cybersecurity management: Cybersecurity also involves considerations on an organizational level to ensure cross-institutional governance. The cybersecurity management is responsible to establish and maintain security policies including, e.g., the definition of processes and according rules.
– Continual cybersecurity activities including monitoring, security event assessment, vulnerability analysis, and vulnerability management.
– Risk assessment methods describing the procedure to identify threats and classify the resulting risk corresponding to their impact.

Detailed insights into the standard are already provided by literature [24, 25]. Whereas, [26] describes the interrelationships with adjacent standards (e.g., ISO 27000, ISO 9001, etc.). In terms of type approval, the manufacturers are responsible to disclose relevant engineering documentation to the technical service which generates the required evidence to show compliance with the security regulation (see Sect. 2.1). To do so, the presentation of available work products from the application of the ISO/SAE 21434 is preferred. A summary of security activities and work products is given in Annex A of the standard.

In summary, the ISO/SAE 21434 serves as a security engineering framework. The framework is requirements based and does not elaborate on specific technologies. Instead, it comprises of security requirements, recommendations and assigns each requirement a working package. The working packages can be seen as engineering artifacts which can be used to evidence type approval conformance. Besides the engineering phase, the implemented countermeasures and continual security activities are of interest in the operational phase.

5.2 UN R155 Cybersecurity Regulation

The UN R155 is the first cybersecurity regulation addressing type approval and was published in January 2021. It comprises uniform provisions concerning the approval of vehicles with regards to cybersecurity and cybersecurity management system (CSMS). According to the UN R155, a CSMS is a "systematic risk-based approach defining organisational processes, responsibilities and governance to treat risk associated with cyber threats to vehicles and protect them from cyber-attacks" [1]. In detail, it requires the management of security risks by setting up organizational structures and processes to ensure security over the entire vehicle life cycle. According to [22], the necessary processes include:

– Risk identification and management in vehicle design
– Verification of risk management, e.g., through testing
– Ensure risk assessments to be appropriate and up-to-date
– Monitor attacks and incident response
– Enable analysis of occurred security attacks
– Continuous assessment of cyber security measures also considering new threats and vulnerabilities

To attain type approval, manufacturers have to provide the responsible authorities with sufficient argumentation in form of documentation and test reports. Evaluation for acceptance includes analysis of documentation, organizational audits, review of test reports, and verification by sampling or respective testing [1]. The regulations not only pose challenges for the manufacturer, but also for the approval authorities that have to meet the necessary competence for evaluation. Of special interest are the threats and mitigations annexed to the regulation, since they have to be explicitly addressed during development by the manufacturer. The list is composed of seven threat domains: Back-end servers, their communication channels, their update procedure, unintended human actions facilitating a cyber-attack, their external connectivity and connections, vehicle data/code, and potential vulnerabilities that could be exploited if not sufficiently protected or hardened.

Compared to the ISO/SAE 21434, the UN R155 is less extensive and not all engineering artifacts are of relevance. This is due to the regulation's objective to maintain road safety and not to repeat the verification and validation process of the manufacturer. Rather, the focus of the UN R155 is on the implementation of a CSMS and concentrates on the appropriateness of risk analysis and selected mitigation strategies, so that vehicles are protected against attacks throughout the entire operating time. In order to maintain the security over the years of operation, the manufacturer is - according to paragraph 7.4.1. of UN R155 - obliged to report his monitoring results to the technical service at least once a year and thus confirms that the implemented measures are still effective.

6 Discussion and Future Assessment Prospects

The importance of security engineering throughout the whole vehicle lifecycle is underlined by the ISO/SAE 21434 and is used here as a basis for further considerations. From the standard, it is evident that security engineering does not just consist of individual measures that are added on top of the developed product, but rather of security management processes and technical countermeasures.

The state of the art in Sect. 5 indicates that a regulatory framework which references the ISO/SAE 21434 already exists to assess vehicle security prior to market entry. Nevertheless, type approval previous to UN R155 was a one-time evaluation. Once approved and without system changes, the system was allowed to be produced in series allowing the system to be integrated in different vehicle models. However, the effectiveness of security measures is dynamic as new attack methods might bypass mitigation strategies. The UN R155 has responded to these challenges by requiring the manufacturer to have a CSMS. This means that the manufacturer is obliged to present his monitoring results to the technical service at least once a year. Still, at the same time, there are no comparable regulations considering security in the periodic technical inspection. The PTI is an important assessment of the vehicle safety over the years in use, and with the introduction of the CSMS, the PTI should also determine whether the measures taken by the implemented CSMS affect the vehicle as expected. One example is the control of software versions in the vehicle, which are currently only used as inspection criteria in the PTI in the event of recalls. With the help of or in combination with the unique software identification number of the UN R156 on software updates [27], a uniform procedure in the PTI is conceivable, but has not yet been implemented, since the development of this unique software identifier is currently still being discussed for type approval. In this regard, it is necessary to establish relevant inspection criteria and corresponding methods.To do so, the main focus is to address the security challenges listed in Sect. 3 and to consider the available knowledge in science and research. As a first step towards a PTI for intelligent vehicles, we identified in [28] the framework conditions and initial starting points to determine which information can be used to assess the equipment, condition, function, and performance of the vehicle security. Whereas the type approval examines vehicle types, e.g., models of a vehicle, systems or components, within the periodic technical inspections each vehicle is inspected individually. Depending on the year of manufacture and equipment, a diversity of vehicles occurs, but which are all to be judged consistently, within the given time constraints and by the same deficiencies catalog. Hence, for future security assessments, the question of classification of security defects arises while tuning should also be considered as attack motivation.

Overall, it is important that an evaluation of the security measures should follow a holistic approach and consider the approaches from Sect. 4 but should also consider the possibilities within the framework of type approvals and periodic technical inspections. Furthermore, the objectives of the 2018/858/EU and 2014/45/EU regulations are precisely formulated, they demand the requirements and test methods to always correspond to the technical and scientific progress. Accordingly, international initiatives exist in the area of vehicle compliance for road safety. For instance, the WP.29 is continuously developing new specifications for type approval and periodic technical inspection. This is also how the UN R155 security regulation was developed, as well as other type approval regulations relating to driver assistance systems (e.g., UN R157 Automated Lane Keeping Systems). In total, the advantage is that all activities and meetings regarding the approval of automated, autonomous and connected vehicles are bundled within the Working Party on Automated/Autonomous and Connected Vehicles (GRVA), whereas the full documentation is publicly available online [29].

In addition to the efforts of the UN, the EU Commission is responsible for initiatives and the improvements of vehicle safety in the EU. As a consequence, the EU published the roadworthiness package consisting of three parts: 2014/45/EU on periodic technical inspections, 2014/47/EU on technical roadside inspections, and 2014/46/EU on vehicle registration documents [30]. CITA, the International Motor Vehicle Inspection Committee, is also committed to road safety and is an "international association of public and private sector organizations actively involved in mandatory road vehicle compliance" [31]. In addition to regular studies concerning roadworthiness testing, they also publish position papers discussing the EU legal framework including the roadworthiness package. Thus, in [32] CITA identifies the need for ADAS sensor testing and requires the detection of software and hardware tampering. They especially demand for data access and increased software testing [32].

All these initiatives reflect the trend toward security assessment as part of vehicle regulation and therefore show that accredited organizations should also assess the security to evaluate the roadworthiness. However, for the concrete implementation, the upcoming challenges and the potentials of the assessment have to be identified. As a consequence, this gives rise to the following open research question:

Remaining Research Question RQ2. How can security be assessed by accredited organizations within roadworthiness assessments?

This question should provide the impulse and motivation for future work. Yet if one thing should have become clear, it is that the ISO/SAE 21434 and the UN R155 are setting the foundation for prospect security assessment efforts and further initiatives for improved vehicle road safety can be expected in the future.

7 Conclusion

The assessment of roadworthiness is a sovereign task and has to be in accordance with current road safety standards. With the availability of connected vehicles, cybersecurity has established itself to being an additional evaluation criterion. Legally two mandatory occasions exist to attain road admission, namely type approval (see Sect. 2.1) and periodic technical inspection (see Sect. 2.2).

The cybersecurity challenges over the years of operation have been listed and it became apparent that the inspection of driving functions differs from the evaluation of security features. As a successful attack might lead to defects in the car, we discussed the question of whether security assessment should be part of mandatory roadworthiness tests by accredited organizations. We further concluded that existing approaches are restricted to the requirements given in the ISO/SAE 21434 and the UN R155. As a result, the implementation of the regulations, e.g., the security conformance checks conducted by approval authorities and especially security assessment during periodic technical inspections, must be further emphasized in the future.

For future reference, it is planned to answer the remaining research question and investigate, among other things, which attacks affect the vehicle and what system reactions can be recorded in the process, as well as what information is relevant for the evaluation by the inspection engineer. Therefore, it is planned to examine current and prospect automotive security solutions.

Acknowledgment. The presented work has been funded by GTÜ Gesellschaft für technische Überwachung mbH in Stuttgart, Germany.

References

1. UN Regulation No. 155 - Uniform provisions concerning the approval of vehicles with regards to cyber security and cyber security management system (2021)
2. ISO/SAE International: 21434:2021 Road vehicles - Cybersecurity engineering (2021)
3. Charlie Miller, Chris Valasek: Remote Exploitation of an Unaltered Passenger Vehicle (2015)
4. Sommer, F., Dürrwang, J., Kriesten, R.: Survey and classification of automotive security attacks. Information **10**, 148 (2019). https://doi.org/10.3390/info10040148
5. Pekaric, I., Sauerwein, C., Haselwanter, S., Felderer, M.: A taxonomy of attack mechanisms in the automotive domain. Comput. Stand. Interfaces **78**, 103539 (2021). https://doi.org/10.1016/j.csi.2021.103539
6. UN/ECE: Text of the 1958 Agreement. ECE/TRANS/WP.29/2016/2 (2015)
7. Text of the 1997 Agreement. ECE/TRANS/WP.29/2020/38 (2020)

8. UN/ECE: Text of the 1998 Agreement. ECE/Trans/132
9. Regulation (EU) 2018/858 of the European Parliament and of the Council of 30 May 2018 on the approval and market surveillance of motor vehicles and their trailers, and of systems, components and separate technical units intended for such vehicles, amending Regulations (EC) No 715/2007 and (EC) No 595/2009 and repealing Directive 2007/46/EC (2018)
10. UN/ECE: Status of the Agreement. ECE/TRANS/WP.29/343/Rev.29 (2021)
11. Kraftfahrt-Bundesamt: Bestand an Kraftfahrzeugen und Kraftfahrzeuganhängern nach Fahrzeugalter (Number of motor vehicles and trailers by vehicle age). FZ 15 (2021)
12. Kraftfahrt-Bundesamt: Jeder dritte Personenkraftwagen wies Mängel auf (Every third passenger car had defects) (2020)
13. Directive 2014/45/EU of the European Parliament and of the Council of 3 April 2014 on periodic roadworthiness tests for motor vehicles and their trailers and repealing Directive 2009/40/EC (2014)
14. European commission: roadworthiness certificate and the proof of test. https://ec.europa.eu/tra nsport/road_safety/road-safety-member-states/roadworthiness-certificate-and-proof-test_en
15. ISO: 20730 Road vehicles - Vehicle interface for electronic Periodic Technical Inspection (ePTI) (2021)
16. Brennich, T., Moser, M.: Putting automotive security to the test. ATZ Electron. Worldw. **15**, 46–51 (2020). https://doi.org/10.1007/s38314-019-0155-9
17. Pekaric, I., Sauerwein, C., Felderer, M.: Applying security testing techniques to automotive engineering. In: ARES 2019, pp. 1–10. https://doi.org/10.1145/3339252.3340329
18. Felderer, M., Büchler, M., Johns, M., Brucker, A.D., Breu, R., Pretschner, A.: Security testing: a survey. In: Advances in Computers, vol. 101, pp. 1–51. Elsevier (2016)
19. Al-Jarrah, O.Y., Maple, C., Dianati, M., Oxtoby, D., Mouzakitis, A.: Intrusion detection systems for intra-vehicle networks: a review. IEEE Access **7**, 21266–21289 (2019). https://doi.org/10.1109/ACCESS.2019.2894183
20. Grimm, D., Stang, M., Sax, E.: Context-aware security for vehicles and fleets: a survey. IEEE Access **9**, 101809–101846 (2021). https://doi.org/10.1109/ACCESS.2021.3097146
21. Guissouma, H., Schindewolf, M., Sax, E.: ICARUS - incremental design and verification of software updates in safety-critical product lines. In: Proceedings of 47th Euromicro Conference on Software Engineering and Adanced Applications, pp. 371–378. https://doi.org/10.1109/SEAA53835.2021.00055
22. UN/ECE: UN Regulations on Cybersecurity and Software Updates to pave the way for mass roll out of connected vehicles (2020)
23. ISO: 26262:2011 Road vehicles - functional safety, vol. (2011)
24. Macher, G., Schmittner, C., Veledar, O., Brenner, E.: ISO/SAE DIS 21434 automotive cybersecurity standard - in a nutshell. In: Casimiro, A., Ortmeier, F., Schoitsch, E., Bitsch, F., Ferreira, P. (eds.) SAFECOMP 2020. LNCS, vol. 12235, pp. 123–135. Springer, Cham (2020). https://doi.org/10.1007/978-3-030-55583-2_9
25. Schmittner, C., Macher, G.: Automotive cybersecurity standards - relation and overview. In: Romanovsky, A., Troubitsyna, E., Gashi, I., Schoitsch, E., Bitsch, F. (eds.) SAFECOMP 2019. LNCS, vol. 11699, pp. 153–165. Springer, Cham (2019). https://doi.org/10.1007/978-3-030-26250-1_12
26. Costantino, G., de Vincenzi, M., Matteucci, I.: In-depth exploration of ISO/SAE 21434 and its correlations with existing standards. IEEE Comm. Stand. Mag. **6**, 84–92 (2022). https://doi.org/10.1109/MCOMSTD.0001.2100080
27. UN Regulation No. 156 - Proposal for a new UN Regulation on uniform provisions concerning the approval of vehicles with regards to software update and software updates management system (2021)

28. Gierl, M., Müller, F., Kriesten, R., Nenninger, P., Sax, E.: Challenges for periodic technical inspections of intelligent Cars VEHICULAR 2022: the eleventh international conference on advances in vehicular systems, technologies and applications, pp. 41–46
29. UN/ECE: Vehicle Regulations Wiki, https://wiki.unece.org/display/trans/Home+Vehicle+ Regulations
30. European commission: tougher vehicle testing rules to save live. https://ec.europa.eu/transp ort/road_safety/eu-road-safety-policy/priorities/safe-vehicles/vehicle-inspection/tougher-vehicle-testing-rules-save-live_en
31. CITA: international motor vehicle inspection committee. https://citainsp.org/about-us/
32. CITA: future EU legal framework for access to in-vehicle data. Position Paper (2022)

UNECE Threat List Case Study: Prediction of Cyber Risks in the Automotive Domain Using Regression Analysis

Abdelkader Magdy Shaaban[✉], Sebastian Chlup, and Christoph Schmittner

AIT Austrian Institute of Technology, Vienna, Austria
{abdelkader.shaaban,sebastian.chlup,christoph.schmittner}@ait.ac.at
https://www.ait.ac.at/

Abstract. Cybersecurity has become a significant factor in the automotive industry. It is responsible for protecting data and critical components of the vehicle against cyberattacks. Automobile manufacturers should ensure their vehicle's cybersecurity, considering the UNECE regulation for road vehicle approval. Estimating risk severity is critical in this domain for specifying appropriate security mechanisms to address existing cyber risks. To have an accurate risk evaluation, we need to consider multiple factors of likelihood and impact, which indicate the probability of risk occurrence and its severity. However, establishing a relationship amongst multiple factors of impact and likelihood remains a challenging problem that needs to be addressed. In this work, we propose applying machine learning regression analysis to create correlations between various independent factors of likelihood and impact for predicting dependent variables that indicate the assessment of cyber risk severities. We use the UNECE threat list as a case study to show how machine learning regression approaches may help predict realistic cyber risk estimations in the automotive domain. Finally, we evaluate outcomes to demonstrate the effectiveness of regression analysis for evaluating cyber risks in the automotive sector.

Keywords: Cybersecurity · Threats · Risk evaluation · Regression analysis

1 Introduction

Cybersecurity is essential in the automotive industry. It protects critical units as well as software that controls functional safety in cars from different types of cyber threats. Any malicious code injected into the automotive network causes damage or failure of a specific unit or the entire vehicular system [1]. Replacing mechanical units with embedded technology raises safety concerns in the automotive domain [2]. In addition, incorporating internet connectivity to modern

M. Trapp et al. (Eds.): SAFECOMP 2022 Workshops, LNCS 13415, pp. 110–122, 2022.
https://doi.org/10.1007/978-3-031-14862-0_7

vehicles for advanced features like autonomous driving, connecting with other cars or external terminals, and software updates create new cybersecurity challenges. Any internet-enabled device can be hacked, which is valid for today's automobiles [3]. A vulnerable point in a vehicle may cause the entire vehicle to become out of control. An attack could occur if malicious code is inserted into communication buses of a vehicle, causing the vehicle's standard functionality to be interrupted and potentially leading to disastrous results. It is essential to identify and address the exact security vulnerabilities in the early stages of the vehicle engineering process. Beyond that, it becomes costly and challenging to implement security countermeasures [4].

Estimating cyber risks is essential for implementing the appropriate risk mitigation measures. The difficulties are determining the likelihood and impact of potential threats and obtaining more accurate results where multiple factors should be considered appropriately. Additionally, increasing estimating factors will make building relationships among these factors more challenging, which will require significant time and effort.

The risk assessment process uses several methods for evaluating the vehicular risk level based likelihood and impact parameters. The following formula shows one of the most common risk assessment methods:

$$Risk = Likelihood * Impact \qquad (1)$$

Equation 1 is feasible if we only have one value for likelihood and impact, where the likelihood represents the probability of a particular cyber incident to happen, and the impact describes the level of impact in case a cyber attack takes place. Estimating the risk represents the severity level of a cyber attack against any part within the vehicular network. For example, if the impact level is 3 and likelihood is 4, the overall risk estimation yields a 12 which indicates risk assessment based on numerical values. However, in the automotive sector multiple factors shall be considered for more accurate risk estimation. Therefore, regression analysis could be the most appropriate solution for dealing with these issues. It allows for the understanding and development of correlations between several independent variables to estimate or predict one value indicating cyber risk. A set of factors for estimating likelihood and risk in the automotive industry, is presented and discussed in [5].

Furthermore, in this work, we use these factors and estimate the likelihood and impact of multiple cyber threats in the automotive domain based on the United Nations Economic Commission for Europe (UNECE) threat list [6]. We build a novel dataset on our knowledge, which includes a collection of independent variables (defined in terms of the proposed factors) and a single dependent variable, representing the final cyber risk value. There are multiple regression analysis techniques are used in this work such as multiple linear - backward elimination, polynomial, decision tree, random forest, and support vector regression. We use the Python language [7] for applying these regression techniques. In the following step, we examine the effectiveness of each technique in the context of the testing dataset to determine whether these techniques give more accurate results for predicting cyber risks and fulfilling the overall research objective for estimating one single value (i.e., risk) concerning multiple factors of likelihoods and impacts.

2   UNECE Automotive Potential Threats

According to the "UN regulation on uniform provisions concerning the approval of vehicles about cybersecurity and their cybersecurity management systems" [8] the approval authority or the technical service should verify that the vehicle manufacturer has a cybersecurity management system and that it is in compliance with the regulation before the vehicle can be certified. The approval authority or technical service should ensure that vehicle manufacturers apply their cybersecurity management system throughout the vehicle lifecycle, including development, production, and post-production. The vehicle manufacturer shall also demonstrate that their cybersecurity management system is adequality considered, including risks and mitigations presented in Annex 5 in [8]. The Annex consists of three main sections; Section A contains a list of threats, vulnerabilities, and attack methods. Section B discusses a set of security mitigation (i.e., set of measures for reducing a risk) for threats within a vehicle, whereas Section C, includes security mitigations relevant to threats outside the vehicles. The spreadsheet version of that list holds more details about threats, as described in [6].

Some other details are defined in the spreadsheet version, representing the vehicle architecture components where the attack may be initiated. This information is classified into four main categories (i.e., Internal architecture, Physical, Wireless, and External). We used these details to estimate relevant factors that represent the likelihood of each threat. In addition, seven categories proposed in the spreadsheet represent anticipated outcomes when any of these threats are triggered within the vehicular network. These proposed parameters are studied to estimate initial factors representing impact parameters [9].

The proposed factors and their estimation processes for representing the likelihood and the impact in the UNECE threat list are discussed in detail in [9]; where Sect. 2.1 and Sect. 2.2 discuss the estimation process of these factors and how these support creating a newly introduced dataset for estimating cyber risks in the automotive domain.

2.1   Estimation of the Likelihood Factors

The UNECE threats list [6] provides an explanation of the various vehicle units that could serve as the starting point for an attack. We make use of these descriptions and enhance them in order to build a set of likelihood values that are concentrated on an attack on a particular vehicle unit from where an attack could be initiated [9]. Multiple factors for evaluating the likelihood of potential threats for the estimation of cyber risks in the automotive domain are defined, as described in [5]. Table 1 represents these factors as a set of multiple dimensions

Table 1. Proposed factors of the likelihood parameter values

Factors	Rates			
	[1% - 25%]	]25% - 50%]	]50% - 75%]	]75% - 100%]
Capabilities	Amateur	Mechanic, Repair shop, etc.	Hacker, Automotive expert, etc.	Expert
Availability	Public	Information for maintenance availability	Information for OEM, system integrator, etc. availability	Information for ECUs' company availability
Reachability	Untrusted network	Private network	Part time accessible	Physical access
Equipment needed	Standard devices	Specialize devices	Tailor-made device	Multiple Tailor-made devices

of the likelihood for each threat that could happen [9]. Because of this, we would be describing these factors using percentage values. These percentages describe a probabilistic rate for each of the factors that determine the overall possibility of occurrence of a specific cyber threat.

As described in the table, we proposed four factors for estimating the likelihood of each threat, as follows [9]:

- **Capabilities**: This factor is a numerical representation of an attacker's capability to attack a system or a system unit. For example, if the attacker is an Amateur, we suggest that the capability factor could be up to 25%. If the attacker is an expert at automotive hacking, this factor could reach the maximum expected rate (i.e., 100%).
- **Availability**: This factor represents the availability of target data/unit. For example, if data is available through the car maintenance process, the availability could reach 50%. According to the Original Equipment Manufacturer (OEM), system integrator, or other sources, the availability rate could be as high as 75%. This will happen if the data is available through them.
- **Reachability**: This factor reflects how easily data may be accessed. Physical access to the data may have the highest success rate; however, private network access may only have a 50% success rate.
- **Equipment needed**: This factor provides a numerical estimate of the possibility of a threat if customized equipment is required. Therefore, a high success rate (100%) is possible if multiple tailored devices are used to attack one or more specific targets in the automobile environment.

According to the previously discussed parameter values described in the UNECE spreadsheet, we utilised and updated them to estimate our proposed factors. The outcomes are described as four factors (i.e., Capabilities, Availability, Reachability, and Equipment needed) for each threat in order to define multiple dimensions of the probability of a threat occurring rather than a single value. Equation 2

$$Likelihood = \left\lceil \left(\frac{(Capability + Availability + Reachability + Equipment)}{N} \right) * S_f \right\rceil \quad (2)$$

where:

- S_f: Scaling factor for estimating the likelihood value is within the range of 1 to 4, where 1 is low, and 4 is high representation value of a particular cyber incident that could happen.
- N: is the sum of all likelihood proposed factors.

2.2 Estimation of the Impact Factors

The process of impact assessment is an activity that endeavours to evaluate risk whenever prospective threats and security vulnerabilities are defined. Many factors need to be considered regarding automotive security to ensure that various types of impacts do not damage the vehicle or cause other cyber incidents [9]. It should be avoided that a cybersecurity attack [10]:

- causes immediate damage to the environment or human lives (**safety**),
- causes loss of control over personal information (**privacy**),
- causes financial damage (**finance**),
- negatively impacts the operation and traffic flow (**operation**).

The proposed numerical numbers for these four factors of impact are presented in Table 2. These factors include safety, financial, operational, and privacy. The hazard level is represented in what is known as the Automotive Safety Integrity Level (ASIL) [11] for the safety category in the automotive sector. ASIL was developed to help discover appropriate risk mitigation methods so that unacceptably high risks can be avoided. ASIL values can be any of the following four classes: A, B, C, or D, with D being the highest possible level of safety and A representing the lowest possible level [12]. In this study, we use numerical representations 1, 2, 3, and 4 to describe ASIL A, ASIL B, ASIL C, and ASIL D, respectively. In the same way that we used numerical values for the other categories of the impact (i.e., financial, operational, and privacy) to represent the varying degrees of these categories, with "1" being the lowest level and "4" representing the highest level [9]. As a result, we suggested using these four aspects (i.e., safety, financial, operational, and privacy) to ascertain the severity of the impact in the event that a cyber-attack was conducted against the vehicle network.

Table 2. Impact levels [9]

Factors	Impact Levels			
Safety	ASIL A (1)	ASIL B (2)	ASIL C (3)	ASIL D (4)
Financial	1	2	3	4
Operational	1	2	3	4
Privacy	1	2	3	4

The UNECE threat list identify seven categories of potential impact are outlined in the spreadsheet of potential threats, which describes the potential impact of each threat as follows [6]:

- Safe operations of vehicle affected,
- Vehicle functions stopped working,
- Software modified, performance altered,
- Software altered but no operations effects,
- Data integrity breach,
- Data confidentiality breach, and
- Other, including criminality.

These seven categories are updated and represented in numerical values in the range between 1 "low impact" to 4 "high impact" to evaluate the severity of each threat listed on the spreadsheet separately. In the course of our research, we investigated these categories for each threat based on personal diligence to estimate a fundamental impact level [9]. Then we estimate the impact according to the previously proposed factors (i.e., safety, financial, operational, and privacy).

Equation 3 is defined in order to evaluate a single preliminary estimation of the impact value of each threat based on the previously discussed and estimated factors.

$$Impact = \left\lceil \left(\frac{(Safety + Financial + Operational + Privacy)}{M} \right) * S_f \right\rceil \quad (3)$$

where:

- S_f: Scaling factor for estimating the impact value is within the range of 1 to 4, where 1 is low, and 4 is high representation value of the impact when a particular cyber incident happen.
- M: is the sum of all impact proposed factors.

2.3   Building the Dataset

One of the most important cornerstones of our research study is the creation of a new dataset that includes our factors that define numerous likelihood and impact dimensions for each threat identified in the UENCE threat list. In order to provide a rough estimate of the proposed factors for each threat, Table 3 depicts a heat map of some selected threats in our dataset.

The table describes the preliminary estimation of the likelihood and impact factors. Furthermore, we identify approximate numerical values of risk assessment values based on the previously discussed factors in Sect. 2.1 and Sect. 2.2. The risk value is defined as a dependent value estimated according to previously discussed likelihood and impact factors (i.e., independent variables). Based on expert knowledge and initiatives with consultations with vehicle domain specialists, we determine a preliminary estimation of the likelihood and impact of each threat in the UNECE list. Afterwards, we estimate cyber risk for each identified threat according to Eq. 1.

Table 3. The estimation of the likelihood and impact for some selected UNECE threats

	Threat Title	Likelihood				Impact				
	Example of attack methodologies	Reachability	Capability	Availability	Equipment	Safety	Financial	Operational	Privacy	Risk
1	Abuse of privileges by staff	28%	46%	38%	30%	2	3	1	4	6
2	Unauthorised internet access to the server	59%	64%	46%	60%	3	3	3	4	12
3	Unauthorised physical access to the server	15%	39%	38%	17%	1	3	1	4	6
4	Attack on server stops it functioning	9%	18%	15%	11%	1	4	1	4	3
5	Loss of information in the cloud	7%	7%	15%	9%	3	3	3	4	4
6	Unauthorised physical access to the server	45%	80%	67%	15%	3	3	3	4	12
7	Information leakage or sharing	9%	11%	31%	11%	1	3	1	4	3
8	Unauthorised manipulation of software	50%	71%	100%	49%	1	1	2	1	6

2.4 Regression Analysis

Regression analysis is a method for examining the correlation among more than one independent factor and a single dependent factor [13]. Those factors are referred to as variables. The primary objectives of regression analysis are to understand the relationship between the independent variables to predict a single dependent variable [14]. As described in Eq. 4 represents the most common multiple linear regression function.

$$Y = a_0 + a_1X_1 + a_2X_2 + \ldots + a_nX_n \tag{4}$$

The symbol "Y" indicates the dependent variable or the predicted value that needs to be estimated, and the symbols "X1," "X2," and "Xn" represent the dependent variables. The regression coefficients are a0, a1, and an. Therefore, the "Y" represents the cyber risk that needs to be calculated using numerous likelihood and impact factors (i.e., Xs). In this study, the regression analysis is utilized to establish correlations between all independent variables of the likelihood and impacts and predict a value representing the risk associated with cyber-attacks.

3 Case Study: UNECE Automotive Threats List

The threat list by the UNECE for the automotive sector is studied as part of this research work to estimate preliminary values of the likelihood and impact to build a dataset for our research work and demonstrate how regression analysis could support predicting risks. The UNECE threats list describes how different vehicle units might be the way to trigger an attack. We use these descriptions and update them to define a set of likelihood and impact values of an attack based on a specific vehicle unit, where an attack could be initiated from.

3.1 Regression Approaches

This section applies multiple regression approaches to predict cyber risk. Then we compare the outcomes to show how regression analysis can interconnect multiple impact and likelihood factors to predict values representing cyber risks. The dataset is split into training and testing data; we used the 80:20 ratio for the splitting strategy. Figure 1 illustrates the outcomes our the regression methods used in this work in comparison with the testing data in our dataset.

Approach (a) - Multiple Linear Regression - Backward Elimination Technique: The backward elimination is utilized to estimate cyber risks in the automotive sector. This strategy aims to eliminate the factors that are not significant and then improve the model with the help of adjustment factors in order to get the predicted values [15]. The *p-value* plays a significant role in assessing whether or not part of the input data should be discarded throughout the cyber risk evaluation procedure. According to the estimation of the Significance Level (SL), we define it as *0.05*, which indicates that regression results with the *P-values* above the SL that should be discarded. In our model, we repeated this elimination process until the backward technique eliminated two factors from the likelihood and impact (i.e., *p-value* higher than SL). The process for describing the relationships between independent and dependent variables is based on four variables (i.e., Reachability, Capability, Safety, and Operational). Figure 1a illustrates the outcomes of predictions using the multiple linear - backward elimination.

It depicts the curve fitting of the predicted values to demonstrate how well they match up with our testing data. Some predicted values closely match the fitting curve, while others do not. For example, the regression predicts 4.57834, whereas it was given within the testing data is 4.34568. In addition, it estimates a 9.08642 risk value, but it was given a 7.07953.

Approach (b) - Random Forest (RF) Regression: A Random Forest (RF) is a regression and classification technique that uses several decision trees and a method called Bootstrap and Aggregation; most generally referred to as bagging. The primary concept of this technique is to incorporate multiple decision trees to estimate the final result instead of depending only on a single decision tree to decide on the final result [16]. This technique is proposed to be integrated into this work to show how the RF regression can predict cyber risks in the automotive domain. Figure 1b illustrates the outcomes of the RF regression algorithm.

As described in Fig. 1b, some of the predicted values are fit the testing data, whereas others are not. For example, one of the given risks as input is estimated as 4.34568, when the RF predicts that threat's risk as 4.28321. However, some other risks are not fitting to the testing data. For instance, another threat's risk was evaluated as 3.33333, where the RF predicted the risk as 5.27296.

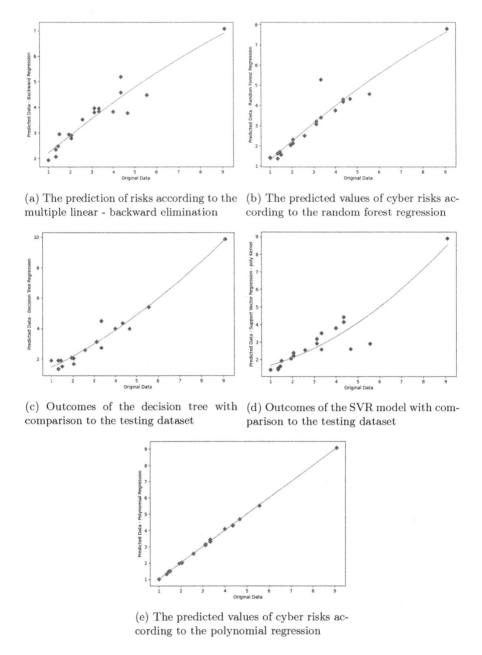

(a) The prediction of risks according to the multiple linear - backward elimination

(b) The predicted values of cyber risks according to the random forest regression

(c) Outcomes of the decision tree with comparison to the testing dataset

(d) Outcomes of the SVR model with comparison to the testing dataset

(e) The predicted values of cyber risks according to the polynomial regression

Fig. 1. Prediction of cyber risks using regression approaches

Approach (c) - Decision Tree (DT) Regression: Decision tree regression is a recursive partitioning algorithm that divides data into divisions. It splits the data into two branches so that the sum of the squared deviations from the mean in the two branches is as small as possible. In this work, we use the Mean Squared Error (MSE) to measure the quality of a split. Each of the new branches is then split in half again. The procedure continues until each node exceeds a minimum node size and is designated a terminal node [17]. In our work, we use the DT regression for predicting cyber risks and comparing outcomes with the testing data, as shown in Fig. 1c.

It shows that the DT regression prediction data are more fit to the fitting curve. For example, a threat's risk is previously estimated as 9.08642, while the DT predicts 9.87654.

Approach (d) - Support Vector Regression (SVR): The regression problem is a generalization of the classification problem for a model that produces a continuous-valued output rather than a finite-valued output. Using a regression model, we can determine the value of a continuous-valued multivariate function. SVR aims to reduce the prediction error representing the difference between the expected and desired outputs in a given situation [18]. The work of the SVR is the same as Support Vector Machine (SVM), which aims to find the best fit line in predicting values. Hyperplanes are utilized in SVR to predict the continuous output. Support Vectors are defined as the data points on either side of the hyperplane that is closest to the hyperplane. Mathematical functions, referred to as the kernel, must be defined to take data as input and convert it to the correct format to determine the hyperplane suitable to a particular model [19]. Therefore, the kernel helps find a suitable hyperplane without affecting the computational cost [20].

As part of this research endeavor, we find that the Radial Basis Function (RBF) kernel is suitable for our model to predict values compared to the testing data set. Figure 1d illustrates outcomes of the SV model and describes the fitting curve according to the testing data.

According to the figure (i.e., Fig. 1d), we can observe that multiple predicted values are represented close to the curve. Consider the following example: the estimated cyber risk for a threat was 2.03704; however, the SVR predicted 1.9706, which was better than the multiple linear and decision tree approaches (i.e., it was estimated as 2.78924 multiple linear and 1.66667 decision tree). In addition, SVR estimates some other data that is not quietly fitting the curve. The SVR estimated 6.25232 for one of the threat risk values, which was given in the testing data by 9.08642.

Approach (e) - Polynomial Regression: Polynomial regression is a subset of multiple regression in which successive power terms are included. Polynomial models are a flexible curve fitting technique [21]. This type of regression analysis represents the relationship between the independent and dependent variables as a polynomial of n degrees [22]. In this work, we utilize this regression technique to estimate risks in the automobile industry. Outcomes of this technique is depicted in Fig. 1e.

In Fig. 1e, we can see that all of the predicted values are fitting with the limits of the curve, demonstrating the effectiveness of the polynomial regression technique in predicting values that are relatively near to the test data.

3.2   Results Evaluation

As presented in Sect. 3.1, we show results of different regression algorithms utilized in this work to predict automotive cyber risks. This section evaluates the effectiveness of each regression technique employed in this study. Therefore, we evaluate the r-squared value to determine how close the predicted values are to the testing data. Table 4 represents the r-squared values of each regression technique.

Table 4. The estimation of r-squared values for each regression technique

Regression Techniques	R-Squared Value
Polynomial	0.99962616
Support Vector	0.98801774
Decision Tree	0.9595138
Random Forest	0.91307856
Multiple Linear	0.90658347

As shown in the table, polynomial regression is the most effective technique. The r-square rate is at 99.9%, representing the predicted values close to the testing data. However, the multiple linear - backward technique rate is approximately 90% close to the testing data. Random forest is less accurate than other techniques, such as support vector and decision tree. In this case, we may conclude that the polynomial is considered the most powerful technique for anticipating cyber risks in the automotive sector.

4   Summary, Conclusion, and Future Work

This study shows how regression analysis can predict cyber risks in the automotive industry. Different types of regression techniques used in this study include multiple linear - backward elimination, support vector, decision tree, polynomial, and random forest. We conducted the UNECE threat list in this work as a case study and calculated the likelihood and impact of each threat. Then, we built a novel dataset for regression analysis using a preliminary calculation of cyber risks. A training data set is defined for training our regression models, and a testing dataset is used to evaluate outcomes. Results of applied regression techniques are compared and evaluated using the r-squared function to determine whether predicted values are closely related to the previously calculated risks (i.e., testing data). According to our findings and taking into account the characteristics of out data set, the polynomial regression is more powerful in predicting risks than other regression analysis techniques.

Currently we have created a novel dataset with about 90 threats from the automotive domain. The next step in our research is to integrate more cyber attacks into our dataset to improve the resolution for predicting more specific cyber risks in the automotive sector and to investigate the effects on the results of the different regression techniques.

Acknowledgement. The ECQA Certified Cybersecurity Engineer and Manager - Automotive Sector is co-funded by the Erasmus+ Call 2020 Round 1 KA203 Programme of the European Union under the agreement 2020-1-CZ01- KA203-078494. This work is partially supported by Grant of SGS No. SP2021/87, VSB - Technical University of Ostrava, Czech Republic.

References

1. Shaaban, A.M., Schmittner, C., Gruber, T., Mohamed, A.B., Quirchmayr, G., Schikuta, E.: Ontology-based model for automotive security verification and validation. In: Proceedings of the 21st International Conference on Information Integration and Web-Based Applications & Services, iiWAS2019, pp. 73–82, NY. Association for Computing Machinery (2019)
2. Macher, G., Armengaud, E., Brenner, E., Kreiner, C.: Threat and risk assessment methodologies in the automotive domain. Procedia Comput. Sci. **83**, 1288–1294 (2016)
3. McAfee: Automotive security best practices. Technical report, McAfee (2016)
4. Kastebo, M., Nordh, V.: Model-based security testing in automotive industry. Master's thesis, Department of Computer Science and Engineering, University of Gothenburg, Gothenburg, Sweden (2017)
5. Shaaban, A.M., Schmittner, C., Bonitz, A.: The design of a divide-and-conquer security framework for autonomous vehicles. In: The Eighth International Conference on Advances in Vehicular Systems, Technologies and Applications, pp. 94–102 (2019)
6. United Nations Economic Commission for Europe UNECE. CSOTA ad hoc "threats 2" (2017). https://wiki.unece.org/download/attachments/45383725/ TFCS-ahT2-06%20%28Chair%29%20Table%20on%20CS%20threats%20- %20changes%20agreed%20by%20ahT2%20-%20non-cleaned%20up.xlsx?api=v2. Accessed 26 April 2022
7. Python: Python language (2022). https://www.python.org. Accessed 07 June 2022
8. The Task Force on and Cyber Security and Over-the-Air issues. Proposal for amendments to ECE/TRANS/WP.29/GRVA/2020/3 - draft new UN regulation on uniform provisions concerning the approval of vehicles with regard to cyber security and of their cybersecurity management systems (2020)
9. Shaaban, A.: An ontology-based cybersecurity framework for the automotive domain - design, implementation, and evaluation. PhD thesis, Faculty of Computer Science, University of Vienna, Austria (2021). https://utheses.univie.ac.at/ detail/59948

10. Schmittner, C., Latzenhofer, M., Magdy, S.A., Hofer, M.: A proposal for a comprehensive automotive cybersecurity reference architecture. In: The 7th International Conference on Advances in Vehicular Systems, Technologies and Applications (2018)
11. ISO/FDIS: ISO/FDIS 26262-9 Road vehicles - Functional safety - Part 9: Automotive safety integrity level (ASIL)-oriented and safety-oriented analyses. Technical report, International Standard (2018)
12. Ali, A.A.: ISO 26262 functional safety standard and the impact in software lifecycle. J. Univ. Appl. Sci. (2017). http://rgdoi.net/10.13140/RG.2.2.12486.16963
13. Rong, S., Bao-Wen, Z.: The research of regression model in machine learning field. In: MATEC Web of Conferences, vol. 176, p. 01033 (2018). EDP Sciences
14. Gallo, A.: A refresher on regression analysis (2015). https://hbr.org/2015/11/a-refresher-on-regression-analysis. Accessed 10 Feb 2022
15. Vu, D.H., Muttaqi, K.M., Agalgaonkar, A.P.: A variance inflation factor and backward elimination based robust regression model for forecasting monthly electricity demand using climatic variables. Appl. Energy **140**, 385–394 (2015)
16. Dutta, A.: Random forest regression in Python (2022). https://www.geeksforgeeks.org/random-forest-regression-in-python/. Accessed 04 May 2022
17. Xu, M., Watanachaturaporn, P., Varshney, P.K., Arora, M.K.: Decision tree regression for soft classification of remote sensing data. Remote Sens. Environ. **97**(3), 322–336 (2005)
18. Awad, M., Khanna, R.: Support vector regression. In: Efficient Learning Machines, pp. 67–80. Apress, Berkeley, CA (2015). https://doi.org/10.1007/978-1-4302-5990-9_4
19. Raj, A.: Unlocking the true power of support vector regression (2020)
20. Sethi, A.: Support vector regression tutorial for machine learning (2020). https://www.analyticsvidhya.com/blog/2020/03/support-vector-regression-tutorial-for-machine-learning/. Accessed 28 Apr 2022
21. Ostertagová, E.: Modelling using polynomial regression. Procedia Eng. **48**, 500–506 (2012)
22. Abhigyan: Understanding polynomial regression!!! (2020). https://medium.com/analytics-vidhya/understanding-polynomial-regression-5ac25b970e18. Accessed 26 Apr 2022

Watch: A Validation Framework and Language for Tool Qualification

Luiz Cordeiro, Christian Becker, Markus Pielmeier, and Julian Amann[(✉)]

BMW Group, Petuelring 130, 80809 Munich, Germany
{luiz.cordeiro,christian.ck.becker,markus.mp.pielmeier,
julian.amann}@bmw.de

Abstract. ISO 26262:2018 is one of the most important standards for functional safety within the automotive domain. One crucial aspect of the standard is software tool qualification. The goal of software tool qualification is to ensure that none of the used software tools (compilers, code generators, etc.) is introducing a safety-related malfunctional behavior. Therefore, for each tool a so-called tool confidence level (TCL) is determined, and based on this appropriate tool qualification methods are chosen such as the validation of a software tool. As an input for the TCL determination all relevant use cases of a tool must be considered.

In the context of the development of advanced driver-assistance systems (ADAS) such as automated driving, the TCL determination can be already a very complex task. Our internal ADAS software stack consists of more than 23 million source lines of code, with close to 2000 developers working on this stack in parallel triggering more than 20000 CI (continuous integration) builds per day. Since we are following an agile development methodology our toolchain can change every day.

To be able to withstand these continuous changes we developed *Watch*. *Watch* is a software validation framework and domain-specific language to support tool qualification for automotive functional safety. *Watch* helps to identify all used tools within our toolchain, ensures that the correct version of a tool has been used, and allows us to define in a formal way how a tool can be used within our environment. Furthermore, it offers the possibility to formulate qualification toolkits.

Keywords: Functional safety · ISO 26262 · Tool qualification

1 Introduction and Motivation

ISO 26262 [1] is a crucial standard for functional safety (FuSa) for road vehicles. Toolchains used within that context of software development are getting more and more complex and safety-relevant, due to increasing requirements such as automated driving. A part of the ISO 26262 standard is dedicated to tool qualification. This activity includes finding all relevant tools, identifying their impact, coming up with mitigations if necessary, and as an ultimate goal building trust in the used tools. For instance, the computation of software quality metrics, such as code coverage, requires the use of specific tools. It must be ensured that the correct and expected tools are used exactly in the

© The Author(s), under exclusive license to Springer Nature Switzerland AG 2022
M. Trapp et al. (Eds.): SAFECOMP 2022 Workshops, LNCS 13415, pp. 127–139, 2022.
https://doi.org/10.1007/978-3-031-14862-0_8

way, they were intended for. For instance, one requirement could be that a certain tool is only allowed to be used in the combination with specific command-line options. Since different tools are used to make FuSa relevant statements there is a high need to identify all involved tools and to make sure that those tools work and are used properly. To get reproducible FuSa statements, it makes sense to automate the process of generating them (e.g. automatic generation of software quality metrics such as code coverage) and to embed them in a Continuous Integration/Continuous Delivery (CI/CD) environment. In a rapidly developing and agile environment, this can become a very labor-intensive task, since there can be frequent changes and adaptations to the existing environment (e.g. regular version updates of tools or new use cases for tool usage), which then always triggers a new FuSa evaluation. This paper introduces Watch, a validation framework, and language for supporting automotive functional safety within CI/CD environments. The framework can be used to support tool qualification, by automating the following activities:

- Detect all involved tools within a toolchain
- Ensure that only predefined tools in a specific version are used
- Ensure that tools are only used in a specific way using a domain-specific language called Watch
- Ensure that specific output artifacts are generated
- General End-to-End testing of FuSa related toolchains and tools

2   Related Work

The ISO 26262 (Road vehicles - Functional safety) [1] consists of 12 parts. Tool qualification is discussed in part 8 (supporting processes) clause 11. Besides this, some overall foundations, common vocabulary, as well as overall management of functional safety, are discussed in parts 1, 2, and 3. The standard defines the term tool classification level (TCL). Furthermore, it describes how a TCL can be determined by the analysis of all relevant use cases of a tool, by evaluating if a tool has a safety impact (Tool Impact = TI), and by considering the probability that a safety-relevant error made by a tool can be detected (tool error detection = TD). Given all the use cases for a specific tool, the TI and the TD probability a TCL can be derived. Besides this for every safety-relevant item such as an automated driving system an ASIL (automotive safety integrity level) is determined. Given the TCL and the corresponding ASIL, the standard suggests different tool qualification methods. Depending on the ASIL some of the tool qualification methods are highly recommended by the standard. For instance, given a tool that is functional safety relevant that was not developed by a safety standard and should now be used in the context of an ASIL D software component, the standard suggests performing a validation of the software tool. For more details, we refer to the standard.

Besides the ISO 26262, there is also a large body of supporting literature (such as [2, 3] or [4]) about functional safety, the ISO 26262 standard itself, and in particular about tool qualification according to ISO 26262. [5] gives also a very good and brief introduction to the topic tool qualification according to ISO 26262 and describes a practical process of how tools can be manually assessed. The process described in [5] is very close to what we have done in our software stack before we had our Watch based approach.

Within the automotive domain there exist several domain-specific languages (DSL) for different purposes. [6] describes a DSL called Franca IDL for software architecture models for safety-relevant automotive software systems. The language can be seen mainly as an interface definition language, that enables developers to treat architecture like code. The paper describes how an agile development methodology and ever shorter development cycles force companies to switch from manual processes to automated and scalable solutions such as DSLs.

Another very interesting and elaborate standard for tool qualification that originates from the aerospace domain is DO-330/ED-215 [7]. It shares similar goals for tool qualification as ISO 26262 part 8 clause 11, but the main focus is airborne and ground-based software systems. Nevertheless, the ideas are transferable to automative safety assessment processes.

The Tool Integration Language (TIL) described in [8] is a domain-specific modeling language that allows expressing toolchains in a formalized way. For instance, it provides different modeling elements to describe tools, interactions between tools (e.g. service calls or data exchanges), trace links, users, and repositories. The formal approach of TIL helps to identify potential risks related to tool integration when combining different tools in a toolchain. Furthermore, [9] describes ideas to generate real toolchains from TIL models. [8] shows also some ideas in the direction of an automated tool qualification based on TIL. Nevertheless, the tool qualification problem based on TIL is not solved and requires an upfront TIL model of the toolchain.

3 The Watch Framework and Language

3.1 End-To-End Testing of FuSa Relevant Toolchains

A Qualification Toolkit. The validation of a software tool can be realized by implementing a software qualification toolkit. A software qualification toolkit consists of an extensive test suite for the specific tool under consideration. The test suite must cover functional and non-functional aspects of the software tool. Since we usually do not have the source code of the software tool we want to investigate, we must treat the tool as a black box. Black-box testing means that our tests consist of end-to-end tests (also known as acceptance tests). We give the tool some predefined input, where the expected output is known. Then we run our tool with the given data and wait for the result. Finally, we check if the generated results of the tool match our expectations. If all tests succeed, and our test cases cover all our use cases and edge cases our tool is qualified to be used within our safety-relevant toolchain. To not risk any open gaps in the test cases we highly recommend an external review and assessment of the test suite for a specific tool. Our personal experience is that it takes a few review rounds until all relevant use and edge cases are covered.

Example: Generating Software Quality Metrics. To make this more concrete let's consider an example. Imagine a hypothetical implementation of a toolchain that is used to provide software quality metrics (details of software quality metrics can be found for example in [10]). In this specific case, we will consider how statement coverage is computed within this toolchain. Later it will be shown how the Watch framework can be applied to this toolchain. The given toolchain is a much-simplified pipeline compared to that what we use in our production environment. Figure 1 gives an overview of the hypothetical statement coverage toolchain.

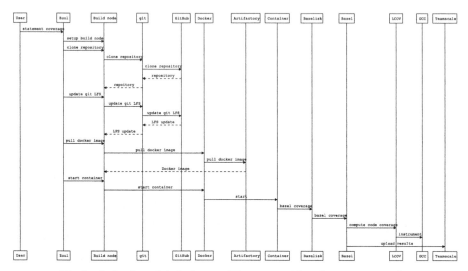

Fig. 1. A simple toolchain for providing users with code coverage metrics

The code coverage metric toolchain (Fig. 1) is triggered by a user. Usually, this happens when a code change is performed. Zuul [11], an open-source continuous integration environment, is then requested to compute the current code coverage for the existing source code and given change. The task performed by Zuul, such as code coverage metric computation, is defined as a so-called build job. Before Zuul can start a build job it needs to set up a build node. A build node is the place where a build job (e.g. code coverage computation build job) is performed. This involves different steps, such as copying credentials, certificates and setting up a clean and hermetic environment. Afterwards, the source code for which the code coverage needs to be computed is fetched. This is done in this example using Git [12], a version control system. Git communicates here with GitHub, a well-known hosting platform for Git-based software repositories. As a next step, a feature called Git LFS (Large File System) is used to download large build artifacts. Following this, a docker image pull is performed. Docker is a solution for managing virtual containers [13]. The pulled image contains an environment (Ubuntu 20.04 LTS) that has all tools in place that are needed to perform the current task of determining the code coverage. This includes tools such as Bazel [14], a build system, LCOV, a tool for instrumentation of the source code under investigation, and GCC a compiler. After the instrumentation, compilation, and test runs are performed the resulting code coverage information is stored in a system called Teamscale. Teamscale gives the developer a visual presentation of the determined code coverage information, i.e. raw numbers of different coverage types, and shows besides a lot of other metrics which lines were executed and which ones were skipped by the implemented tests.

A toolchain for code coverage can be very complex. In our production environment it consists of services and build servers that are hosted in different networks, machines, physical places, and cloud environments. On every instance of a machine different tools and even different environments are used. Additionally to this within a highly agile environment frequently changes are performed to our infrastructure and our build setup (version updates, introduction of new tools, removal of old ones, etc.). Overall, this makes tool qualification for FuSa very challenging. With the Watch framework we address this problem at different levels. The Watch framework provides functionalities for black-box and white-box testing of toolchains (see Fig. 2).

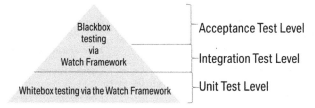

Fig. 2. The Watch framework covers black-box and white-box testing of toolchains

Black-Box Testing via the Watch Framework. Instead of considering each individual tool on its own within the code coverage toolchain, we can abstract the collection of tools to one single tool, and therefore, we could tread the whole toolchain as one single black box. To get the black box toolchain qualified we need to implement a qualification toolkit for it. This works by covering all relevant test cases of the toolchain. For instance, we can set up a test for which the test coverage is known. Afterwards, we let the code coverage toolchain run and wait for the final result. If the expected code coverage meets the determined code coverage, then the black-box test was successful. A sufficient extensive test suite could cover all relevant use cases and could serve as a qualification toolkit. Also, later changes to the toolchain would not affect the qualification toolkit, since it does not know and care about the implementation details at all. The Watch framework provides the functionalities to formulate such a qualification toolkit.

See Fig. 3 for an example of how the Watch framework can be applied to a toolchain for code coverage. The Watch framework offers the possibility to define in a declarative manner end-to-end tests using YAML. End-to-end tests can interact with tools. There are numbers of predefined tools and actions that can be triggered by Watch. The Watch framework can also act on events of tools. In the given example (see Fig. 3) it waits for Zuul CI (our continuous integration system) to finish a build job. There are also some time constraints on this activity. Once Zuul CI finishes validation can take place. The validation in the example includes checking the log file of the used coverage tool to make sure that we get the expected code coverage and also includes an HTTP request to the tool Teamscale to ensure that the proper information is given. In a real-world scenario the test suite is much more extensive. The defined YAML file can be read and executed by Watch. Watch was implemented in-house with the help of Python. It supports currently several tools of our toolchain and was custom-tailored to our toolchain and use cases.

Nevertheless, the basic concept of a generic test framework for end-to-end testing and the formulation of declarative tests can also be applied in other areas.

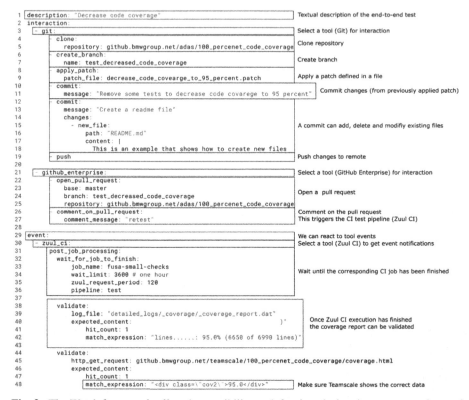

Fig. 3. The Watch framework offers the possibility to define in a declarative manner end-to-end tests using YAML. End-to-end tests can interact with tools. There is a number of predefined tools and actions that can be triggered by these tools. The Watch framework can also act on events of tools such as the finalization of a build job in a CI Tool such as Zuul CI.

The end-to-end testing framework can also be applied to subparts of bigger toolchains or individual tools. For instance, in our production environment, we used it to set up a qualification toolkit for *strace* (more details on this tool will follow in Sect. 3.2). We formulated using the Watch framework 57 individual tests that can be grouped in 11 logical test suites. Since Watch formulates tests (see Fig. 3) in a high-level declarative manner, it was also easy for our external safety assessment (performed by an external company) to review our tests (qualification toolkit). During the analysis, some gaps and issues were found that could be addressed by extending the test suite. Similarly, we developed for GitHub Enterprise (our version control system) 15 end-to-end tests that mainly focus on the code review feature of GitHub Enterprise Server, since for other potential errors of GitHub Enterprise Server we have other mitigations in place. We execute our test suites in regular nightly and weekly runs in our CI/CD environment to make sure our used tools work as expected. This allows us also to do for instance frequent version updates of GitHub Enterprise Server (that are necessary for different reasons, such as security patches) since we can guarantee that for our use cases the updated tool works as expected. We applied the framework also to other tools of our toolchain.

3.2   White-Box Testing: Low-Level Testing of CI Jobs

Low-Level Testing Aspects. After the coverage of high-level testing using the Watch framework in the previous sections, the upcoming sections will focus on low-level testing aspects. Since we try to generate our FuSa statements in an automated way, the corresponding processes and toolchains for this endeavor are usually embedded into our CI system. Therefore, we also speak quite often about CI jobs which can be considered as the environment where our toolchain is executed. Low-level testing in this scope means whether the right tool version with the correct parameters was used during the whole process of a CI job. Especially for the tool management [ISO-26262-8: 7.4] it is important to make sure that the right tool versions were used with the corresponding parameters within the CI system. If this was not the case, it could happen that a tool (version) is invoked in a way that was not qualified according to ISO 26262. How to mitigate this problem with the Watch framework will be explained in the next sections.
The Problem: How to Identify All Tools in a Continuous and Fast-Changing Environment? Before tools can be monitored and later may be qualified, it is necessary to gather all used tools in a certain CI job (toolchain). Most of the time CI jobs do already exist (because of research activities or pre-series prototypes) and should then be investigated regarding functional safety aspects. It might be that there is no knowledge or too little knowledge about which tools are used in a CI job at all. To build up the tool landscape (overview of used tools), there are different approaches, e.g.:

- Interview experts: Each CI job should have an expert (that person that set up the job). Interviewing that person can help to understand the purpose of the CI job and to find out which tools are supposed to be used.
- Reengineering from source code: Another approach is to analyze source/configuration code and check which tools are configured to run before, during, and after the main task of the CI job.
- Using process monitoring (e.g. *strace*): *Strace* is a tool that monitors all system calls for a certain command or process identifier (PID) on Linux. Similar tools exist also for other operating systems such as Windows or macOS. If you start the main process of a CI job with *strace*, it is possible to see all system calls (tools with arguments and environment variables) that were running. Also, the process tree can be generated by analyzing log files generated by *strace*. This helps to indicate which tool has been invoked by which other tool.

Experience has shown that the first two approaches are recommended to be used when a CI job/toolchain gets investigated for the first time. Although it can be very hard to interview the corresponding experts, it helps to understand the intention of the CI job. However, this can be very helpful for further investigations like the reengineering part for instance. As already mentioned in the *Introduction & Motivation*, in a rapid and agile development it can be a very labor-intensive task to do the manual steps like interviewing or reengineering. Therefore, the third approach should be used to automate the creation of the current tool landscape. Automatic detection of tools and their use proved to be quite helpful in our environment with nearly 2000 developers since it can happen quite easily that a tool version is updated or somewhere in a bash script the way how a command-line tool is invoked is changed, without considering all aspects of tool qualification.

Maintaining Tool Versions. As already stated, it is mandatory to keep track of the used tools including tool versions. Therefore, it makes sense to automate the check whether a certain tool was used with a specific version. The Watch framework is capable of doing that: It reads from a configuration the expected properties of a tool. This configuration file contains the tool name, maintainer, tool path, hash of binary and/or a version, and how the version can be obtained by the command line for example by using `--version`. This tool is then executed after or before the main run of a CI job. If a version was updated and does not match the configuration anymore, the job maintainer (toolchain maintainer) will be notified or the change request (pull request) will be rejected. An example configuration could look like the following:

```
{
    "tool_name": "gcov",
    "responsible_person": "any_person@company.de",
    "comment": "",
     "tool_configs": [
       {
         "version": "9.3.0",
         "version_config": {
           "checksum": "0211f049f5b1121fbd03…9ead1",
           "version_command": "--version",
           "version_string": "gcc (Ubuntu 9.3.0) 9.3.0",
           "valid_until": "",
           "paths": [
             "/usr/bin/gcc"
           ]
}}]
},
```

The format of the shown configuration file is JSON (JavaScript Object Notation). Every tool should have at least one responsible person who exactly knows why and how this tool is intended to be used. Furthermore, a tool can have configurations that describe how to obtain the tool version, e.g. by using the "`version_command`" compared to the "`version_string`" and/or comparing the checksum with the configured and the actual one.

Ensure that Artifacts are Generated. There is also the possibility to ensure that some specific artifacts are generated. The following code is a snippet from an artifact definition file (artifacts.json):

```
{
    "artifact": "internal_release_mt_InternalRelease.tar.bz2",
    "base_dir": "bazel-out/x64_windows-fastbuild/bin/ib_vip/var",
    "format": "tar.bz2",
    "comment": ""
}
```

The Watch framework ensures that all artifacts defined in this file do exist. This is done by triggering the Watch checker at the right time (after the artifact is generated, usually done at the end of a build job run). It then checks if the artifact can be found at the defined location. It is also possible to define the expected output format and there is also the option to define a regular expression to check the file for particular content in the case the file is a text file.

Maintaining Tool Invocations. It might be necessary to make sure that certain tools are only executed with pre-defined parameters. However, it might be difficult to make sure that tools were really executed only with defined arguments within a CI job. The Watch framework is able to do that by using *strace*.

The generated *strace* log information contains also the PID (Process ID), binary path and arguments passed to the tool. With this information, the Watch framework can be configured to read in the *strace* log and additionally a directory where all tool configurations are stored. The tool configurations are written in the Watch language and can for example contain the following Watch code:

```
MustContain("--input", "/home/user/input.json") AND
MayContain("--job_name", "test-.*") AND
NoRemainingParams
```

This configuration means, that the command-line parameter of a certain tool invocation needs to have the "`--input /home/user/input.json`" argument and can also have the "`--job_name test-job`" argument for instance (but not necessarily).

The argument *MustContain* is mandatory, whereas the *MayContain* implies optional. Also, regular expressions can be used to avoid configuration duplication for different input arguments. With the *NoRemainingParams* set, Watch will throw an error if there are any other command-line parameters passed to the tool. The configured order of arguments does not matter, this makes the comparison more flexible. Watch will also log any binary that is not configured but was executed. With this approach not only tools can be validated but it can also be assured that certain binaries were actually executed. This allows to validate if certain test binaries or unknown (untracked) binaries were executed. This check is an automation of observing each tool invocation of a toolchain. Figure 4 gives an overview of the described implementation.

The Watch Language. In this section, we want to give a brief overview of the Watch language. Figure 5 shows the grammar of the Watch language. The main intent of the language is to formulate constraints for command-line arguments.

For tools that have a safety manual, it's important to make sure that every invocation of it follows the manual. To do so, the Watch framework provides a mini domain-specific

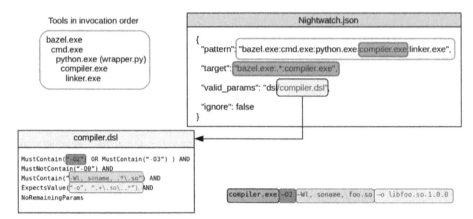

Fig. 4. The tool invocation order is monitored by *strace*. This serves as an input to the Watch framework. In so-called Watch files (e.g. Nightwatch.json) we define the expected tool invocation order (e.g. Bazel gets called before Python, the compiler gets called before the linker) and reference a Watch file (e.g. dsl/compiler.dsl). The Watch file makes use of the Watch language, a language specifically designed for checking tool invocations.

```
Expression:                                                   MustContain:
    (head=Statement | head=Group) (op=Operator tail=Expression)?      "MustContain" "(" values=Values ")"
;                                                             ;

Statement:                                                    MustNotContain:
    MayContain | MustContain | MustNotContain | ExpectsValue | NoRemainingParams    "MustNotContain" "(" values=Values ")"
;                                                             ;

Group:                                                        ExpectsValue:
    "(" exp=Expression ")"                                        "ExpectsValue" "(" key=STRING "," values=Values ")"
;                                                             ;

Operator:                                                     NoRemainingParams:
    AndOperator | OrOperator | XorOperator                        values="NoRemainingParams"
;                                                             ;

AndOperator: /(?i)and/ ;                                      Values:
OrOperator: /(?i)or/ ;                                            arguments += STRING[',']
XorOperator: /(?i)xor/ ;                                      ;

MayContain:                                                   Comment:
    "MayContain" "(" values=Values ")"                            /\s*#.*$/
;                                                             ;
```

Fig. 5. Formal grammar definition of the Watch language

language (called *Watch*) for the tool responsible to configure how their tool should be used. The language contains the following assertions:

- *MustContain*: Indicates obligatory parameters. An invocation without any of the parameters informed would be considered a violation.
- *MustNotContain*: Parameters that ought not to be used. Their presence constitutes a violation.
- *ExpectsValue*: For parameters that receive values (for example "-o output.o"), this construct allows the tool responsible to indicate what constitutes valid parameters.
- *MayContain*: Parameters that are allowed but not obligatory. It's relevant to indicate these parameters when the tool responsible decides to use also the *NoRemaining-Params* construct.

- *NoRemainingParams*: This means that the set of previously declared rules should match all parameters that can be used with the tool. If the tool is called with any parameter not covered by one of these rules, it's a violation.

The power of the Watch language approach is that the tool responsible can really fine-tune how precise their configurations should be, and differentiate critical tool usages from non-critical.

Drawbacks of the Approach. However, there are also downsides of using this approach:

- Performance: Strace is very resource-consuming and can lead to a much higher running time (up to 3 or 4 times) of the whole CI job. Therefore, it is necessary to take care that the build job that should be monitored is not running too long or should not be executed in short cycles. Additionally, the more tools are invoked, the bigger the strace logs. Watch needs to be programmed in a way that it can handle those log files. Nerverthless, we are using Watch in our frequently triggered check pipeline (on every change request/pull request) to perform some partial checks on our software stack. For longer runs e.g. code coverage measurement our current approach is to use a nightly run of the Watch framework.
- Configuration Effort: In a frequently changing environment it can be a lot of effort to adapt and to change the configuration of the tools. It is a maintenance of configurations that is mandatory to make sure that the toolchain is executed as intended. Nevertheless, the reconfiguration can also be seen as a kind of to-do list for tool qualification. It shows version updates, changes in tool invocation, etc.

As described system monitoring via *strace* is costly and results in long CI build runs. Therefore, we decided to run full FuSa checks via *strace* and the Watch framework only nightly and before important releases (e.g. deliveries to ECUs), because they are not needed for each change (20000 CI runs per day). This gives us the best tradeoff between performance and reaction time to safety-related toolchain issues. For discovering toolchain issues even earlier we introduced some lightweight checks in our per regular build jobs to detect toolchain issues. For instance, we check the version number of known/expected tools by invoking them with the appropriate commands (e.g. `gcc -version`) and validate the checksum of tools. This can be done also without running *strace*. Nevertheless, the lightweight checks have some gaps that are covered by your nightly runs using system monitoring.

Practical Use-Cases and Evaluation. Figure 6, represents a CI job that runs different tools like Bazel as a build tool, a code generator based on Python, a compiler, a linker, and many other tools (visualized by Tool1).

It might be only a guess that the correct tool versions were used, but no proof. Furthermore, every tool can expect and handle a lot of parameters. The Watch framework can ensure that tools like GCC, Bazel, or any other executed tool were invoked with the expected parameters. Last but least, the Watch framework can also be configured to check intermediate or final artifacts if they were produced, and it can compare the artifacts with a configured hash.

Manual inspection of the toolchain is error-prone and takes some effort. Alone the task of tool identification took us about 1 to 2 weeks within our software stack. Given

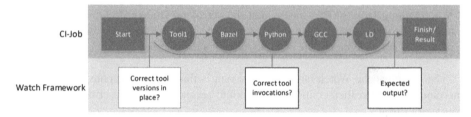

Fig. 6. Practical use-case of the watch framework

biweekly release cycles, the Watch framework helps us to reduce the effort to a few hours.

4   Conclusion and Outlook

Agile development, shorter development cycles, and safety-relevant systems in the domain of advanced driver-assistance systems force us to automate our repetitive work [15]. The Watch framework helps us to automate tedious tasks, such as ensuring that we are using the correct versions of every tool in our toolchain, discovering newly introduced tools, or ensuring tools can be only used in a restricted way. Furthermore, it helps us to implement tool qualification toolkits for complex toolchains (acceptance test) or parts of it (integration and component tests). Nevertheless, there is still some room for improvements. As we pointed out our solution comes with performance drawbacks because system monitoring via *strace* results in some not to be neglected overhead. There are some promising alternatives to *strace* that could be considered that may have a lower impact on the performance. Also, the Watch language could be further improved. The version of the Watch language described in this paper is actually our internal version 2.0 of the language. There is also quite some room for improvements such as introducing new keywords to formulate better constraints. Overall, the current solution is already used in our production environment and resulted in positive feedback from users.

References

1. International Standardization Organization, ISO 262626 Road vehicles – Functional safety, no. ISO 26262. ISO, Geneva, Switzerland (2018)
2. Gebhardt, V., Rieger, G.M., Mottok, J., Gießelbach, C.: Funktionale Sicherheit nach ISO 26262: Ein Praxisleitfaden zur Umsetzung. dpunkt.verlag (2013). ISBN 978-3-89864-788-5
3. Slotosch, O., Wildmoser, M., Philipps, J., Jeschull, R., Zalman, R.: ISO 26262 - Tool chain analysis reduces tool qualification costs. Automot. Saf. Secur. 2012, 27–38 (2012)
4. Ross, H.L.: Funktionale Sicherheit Im Automobil. Carl Hanser GmbH (2014). ISBN 978-3-446-43632-9
5. Hillebrand, J., Reichenpfader, P., Mandic, I., Siegl, H., Peer, C.: Establishing confidence in the usage of software tools in context of ISO 26262. In: Flammini, F., Bologna, S., Vittorini, V. (eds.) SAFECOMP 2011. LNCS, vol. 6894, pp. 257–269. Springer, Heidelberg (2011). https://doi.org/10.1007/978-3-642-24270-0_19

6. Schlichthärle, S., Becker, K., Sperber, S.: A domain-specific language based architecture modeling approach for safety critical automotive software systems (2020)
7. R. T. C. for aeronautics. RTCA, DO-330 software tool qualification and considerations. RTCA (2011)
8. Asplund, F., Biehl, M., Loiret, F.: Towards the automated qualification of tool chain design. In: Ortmeier, F., Daniel, P. (eds.) SAFECOMP 2012. LNCS, vol. 7613, pp. 392–399. Springer, Heidelberg (2012). https://doi.org/10.1007/978-3-642-33675-1_36
9. Biehl, M.: A modeling language for the description and development of tool chains for embedded systems, PhD Thesis, KTH, Embedded Systems (2013)
10. Myers, G.J., Sandler, C., Badgett, T.: The Art of Software Testing, 3rd ed. Wiley Publishing, Hoboken (2011)
11. The Zuul contributors, Zuul - a project gating system. 2022. Accessed 16 Jan 2022. https://zuul-ci.org/docs/zuul/
12. Chacon, S., Straub, B.: Pro Git, 2nd ed. Apress, USA (2014)
13. Turnbull, J.: The Docker Book: Containerization is the new virtualization (2014)
14. Google, L.: Bazel (2022). Accessed 16 Jan 2022. https://bazel.build/
15. Beyer, B., Jones, C., Petoff, J., Murphy, N.R.: Site Reliability Engineering: How Google Runs Production Systems, 1st ed. O'Reilly Media, Inc., Sebastopol (2016)

Criteria for the Analysis of Gaps and Limitations of V&V Methods for Safety- and Security-Critical Systems

Enrico Ferrari[1] , Rupert Schlick[2] , Jose Luis de la Vara[3(✉)] , Peter Folkesson[4] , and Behrooz Sangchoolie[4]

[1] Rulex Innovation Labs, Genoa, Italy
enrico.ferrari@rulex.ai
[2] Austrian Institute of Technology, Vienna, Austria
rupert.schlick@ait.ac.at
[3] Universidad de Castilla-La Mancha, Albacete, Spain
joseluis.delavara@uclm.es
[4] RISE Research Institutes of Sweden, Gothenburg, Sweden
{peter.folkesson,behrooz.sangchoolie}@ri.se

Abstract. As society increasingly relies on safety- and security- critical systems, the need for confirming their dependability becomes essential. Adequate V&V (verification and validation) methods must be employed, e.g., for system testing. When selecting and using the methods, it is important to analyze their possible gaps and limitations, such as scalability issues. However, and as we have experienced, common, explicitly defined criteria are seldom used for such analyses. This results in analyses that consider different aspects and to a different extent, hindering their comparison and thus the comparison of the V&V methods. As a solution, we present a set of criteria for the analysis of gaps and limitations of V&V methods for safety- and security-critical systems. The criteria have been identified in the scope of the VALU3S project. Sixty-two people from 33 organizations agreed upon the use of nine criteria: functionality, accuracy, scalability, deployment, learning curve, automation, reference environment, cost, and standards. Their use led to more homogeneous and more detailed analyses when compared to similar previous efforts. We argue that the proposed criteria can be helpful to others when having to deal with similar activities.

Keywords: Verification & Validation · V&V method · Gaps · Limitations · Analysis criteria · Safety-critical systems · Security-critical systems

1 Introduction

Safety- and security-critical systems such as industrial robots and connected vehicles with advanced driving support play a major role in society. They support many daily-life activities and we strongly rely on them. On the other hand, as the use and complexity of these systems are increasing, system manufacturers and component suppliers

© The Author(s), under exclusive license to Springer Nature Switzerland AG 2022
M. Trapp et al. (Eds.): SAFECOMP 2022 Workshops, LNCS 13415, pp. 35–46, 2022.
https://doi.org/10.1007/978-3-031-14862-0_9

require methods that help them to confirm that safety, cybersecurity, and privacy (SCP) requirements are satisfied [8], i.e., V&V (verification and validation) methods.

V&V can be defined as the process of determining whether the requirements for a system or component are complete and correct, the products of each development phase fulfill the requirements or conditions imposed by the previous phase, and the final system or component complies with specified requirements [15]. This is necessary so that a safety- and security-critical system can be deemed dependable. From a general perspective, a method corresponds to a particular procedure for accomplishing or approaching something, especially a systematic or established one [24]. In this paper, we focus on methods for V&V of safety- and security-critical systems. Examples of these methods are fault injection [21] and model-based testing [17].

The new as well as automated features of safety- and security-critical systems, such as AI-based recognition, require that dedicated V&V methods are applied to them [8]. The methods must consider how to cope with the scale and complexity of the systems as well as their high level of inter-connection.

In addition, it is important to analyze if the methods present some gaps or limitations, such as scalability issues or high cost. However, the analysis and later selection and use of the methods are not always as systematic and thorough as they could. As we have experienced in various collaborative projects, e.g. [4, 14, 22], analysis criteria are usually not explicitly agreed upon, defined, and thus applied. This results in analyses that vary in scope and depth, ultimately hindering result comparison and comparison of V&V methods.

As a solution, we present a set of criteria for the analysis of gaps and limitations of V&V methods for safety- and security-critical systems. By gap we refer to an unexplored idea, i.e., some feature that nobody has ever implemented or studied in a V&V method. For example, nobody might have ever determined the extent to which a new method is applicable for compliance with a safety standard. On the other hand, by limitation we refer to a constraint that reduces the applicability of a method in certain situations. For example, formal verification methods often suffer from scalability issues. We consider both gaps and limitations in the scope of the V&V methods.

The criteria for the analysis of gaps and limitations have been identified in the context of VALU3S (Verification and Validation of Automated Systems' Safety and Security) [1], a large-scale industry-academia project that aims to evaluate and improve state-of-the-art V&V methods and tools. Thirty-three organizations agreed upon the use of nine criteria: functionality, accuracy, scalability, deployment, learning curve, automation, reference environment, cost, and standards. Sixty-two people used the criteria to analyze 53 V&V methods, resulting in a more homogeneous and more detailed analyses when compared to similar previous efforts.

The result of this analysis is a comprehensive and sound classification of gaps and limitations that can help researchers in the field to better identify weak points in V&V methods and therefore to improve the techniques in a more precise way. This can support also large projects such as VALU3S in a uniform evaluation of reference, existing results, as well as of the obtained ones.

The rest of the paper is organized as follows. Section 2 presents the background of the paper. Section 3 describes the criteria for the analysis of gaps and limitations of

V&V methods for safety- and security-critical systems, whereas Sect. 4 describes the application of the criteria. Section 5 presents our main conclusions and future work.

2 Background

2.1 The VALU3S Project

Manufacturers of automated safety- and security-critical systems and of their components have been allocating an enormous amount of time and effort developing and conducting research on these systems. They need to make sure that the systems function in the intended way and according to specifications, which is not a trivial task. For example, system and thus V&V complexity rises dramatically the more integrated and interconnected these systems become with the addition of automated functionality and features to them. This also translates into an overhead on the V&V process, making it time-consuming and costly.

Within this context, the VALU3S project [1] aims to evaluate state-of-the-art V&V methods and tools, improve them, and design a multi-domain framework that provides a clear structure around the components and elements needed for V&V [2]. The main expected benefit is to reduce the time and cost needed for V&V of safety- and security-critical systems with respect to SCP requirements. This is done through identification, classification, and development of evaluation methods, tools, environments, and concepts for system V&V with respect to the mentioned requirements.

The consortium of VALU3S consists of partners from 10 different European countries, including 25 industrial partners, six research institutes, and 10 universities. Thirteen use cases with SCP requirements are studied in detail from six domains: aerospace, agriculture, automotive, healthcare, industrial robotics/automation, and railway.

One of the first tasks of the project dealt with the review of state-of-the-art and state-of-the-practice V&V methods [29]. The methods were planned to be applied in the project use cases with the intention to improve how SCP requirements were addressed, ensured, and confirmed. Fifty-three methods were reviewed and classified according to the categories shown in Fig. 1. A line between two categories indicates that some relationship was identified between V&V methods of the corresponding categories. The methods were then studied in more detail to identify their main gaps and limitations [30]. This paper presents the criteria selected for such an analysis of gaps and limitations, as well as its outcome. Next, effort was spent on addressing the gaps and limitations, thus on improving the methods [31].

2.2 Related Work

The criteria for the analysis of gaps and limitations of V&V methods for safety- and security-critical systems were referred to in a prior publication on workflow modelling by VALU3S partners [7]. However, the definition of the criteria, information about how they were applied, and application examples were not provided.

The selection and use of criteria to validate and evaluate V&V methods has been widely addressed. For example, new methods must show that they fulfil certain characteristics so that they can be regarded as effective and efficient V&V means. Examples of

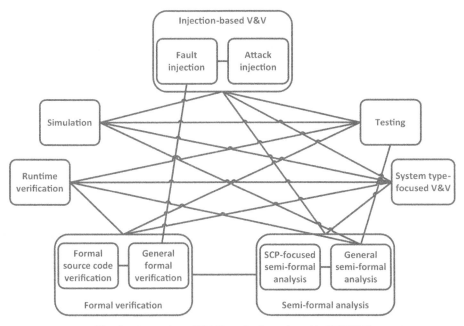

Fig. 1. Categories of V&V methods analyzed in VALU3S

such criteria include accuracy [20], cost [25], and scalability [18], among others. It is easy to find publications that have used our criteria for the analysis of gaps and limitations, or similar criteria, when studying and discussing V&V methods. What distinguishes this paper from this kind of prior publications is that: (1) we present a set with nine different criteria, not only one or a few; (2) we explicitly focus on the analysis of gaps and limitations as a way to identify improvements; and (3) we present criteria selected and used for analyses of tens of V&V methods in the scope of a large collaborative effort between industry and academia. The latest requires an agreed, clear definition of the criteria so that they are homogeneously applied. In addition, publications that have paid attention to a reduced set of criteria have resulted in narrower analyses.

Other publications have proposed criteria and metrics for characterization and evaluation of engineering products and processes, e.g., software ones [10, 16], as well as of V&V methods, e.g., [19, 23, 27]. On the one hand, the depth of these pieces of work is different, as we do not deal with definition of detailed metrics and measurement procedures for the different criteria presented. The analyses in VALU3S have mostly been qualitative. Quantitative information was based on prior studies. On the other hand, the breadth of our set of criteria is larger, as we consider further criteria.

Regarding prior research projects on V&V, it is common that they reviewed V&V methods, typically at the beginning of the projects, e.g., [3, 6]. It is also common that the projects evaluated the methods developed at later stages, e.g., [5, 9]. For the first effort, we are not aware of any other large-scale industry-academia project that has explicitly defined and agreed on a set of criteria so that all the partners use them. For the latter, the differences with this paper are the same as those publications referred in the previous paragraph: different depth and different breadth.

In summary, prior work has proposed and used criteria for evaluation of V&V methods. However, its scope and breadth do not match the needs identified in VALU3S for analysis of gaps and limitations, thus the needs of similar efforts.

3 Criteria for the Analysis of Gaps and Limitations of V&V Methods

To better identify gaps and limitations of V&V methods, we propose a set of criteria that aims to cover the main aspects to consider, ranging from more functional issues to more operational ones. The criteria are proposed to guide further development in V&V methods. There could be overlaps between criteria, but we decided to leave a loose boundary between them in order to make them applicable to different methods.

The nine criteria proposed for analysis of gaps and limitations are defined below. The examples provided have been extracted from the deliverable of the VALU3S project that reports the analysis of gaps and limitations conducted [30].

1. **Functionality**, in relation to the capabilities and features of a V&V method, and to its practicality in general, as well as to the range of V&V activities that it supports. It could be determined that a method could better address some V&V need. Note that, this evaluation is done considering what is in the scope of the method: a functionality unrelated to the method should not be considered a gap.

   Example: *Test Oracle Observation at Runtime* only performs analyses on an individual behaviour and it is not exhaustive.
2. **Accuracy**, regarding whether the outcome from using a V&V method conforms to an expected correct value or a quality level, corresponding to a qualitative assessment of correctness or freedom from error. It is important that a method is reliable enough, especially when employed for some critical application. Notice that this includes both the accuracy of a single instance (i.e., could we trust that if a method says that a situation is safe, it is actually safe) and the statistical accuracy (i.e., how far estimates of V&V are from the actual values).

   Example: *Behaviour-Driven Formal Model Development* requires input from both formal methods and domain experts, so its accuracy depends on the quality of the communication and understanding between them.
3. **Scalability**, to analyse if a V&V method requires too many computational resources (time or memory) and therefore can be applied only to limited or simplified scenarios. This narrows the applicability of a method.

   Example: High accuracy of *CPU Verification* demands high computation power and limits the testing capacity for software.
4. **Deployment**, for consideration of possible problems of a V&V method when put into operation in real-world contexts. For instance, issues in integrating a method with others and a lack of proper tool support can negatively impact deployment.

   Example: *Human Interaction Safety Analysis* currently lacks tool support for efficient use.

5. **Learning curve**, to evaluate the expected progress by a person in gaining experience or new skills to successfully use a V&V method. For cost-effective use, a method might require high-level technical knowledge or skills.

    Example: *Fault Injection in FPGAs* requires comprehensive knowledge in FPGAs.

6. **Automation**, regarding the degree of automatic operation of a V&V method. For instance, if a method is not fully automated and requires large intervention, such as tuning by human users, the corresponding V&V process could become long and error prone. When dealing with large-scale complex systems, automatability of the whole V&V process could become a key feature.

    Example: For *Model-Based Mutation Testing*, building test models is not easily automatable.

7. **Reference environment**, to assess whether a V&V method works only for some settings and conditions, e.g., in a simulated environment. As a consequence, there might be no warranties that findings are still valid for other environments, e.g., for operation in the real world.

    Example: *Vulnerability and Attack Injection* requires a prototype or a real system.

8. **Cost**, considering if using a V&V method requires significant investments in terms of, e.g., hardware, software, time, or human resources. In general, the lower the costs, the better.

    Example: *Simulation-Based Robot Verification* may require a large amount of hardware resources depending on the number of tests to be performed.

9. **Standards**, which indicate the extent to which aspects related to regulations and standards, and the compliance with them, are taken into consideration by a V&V method. This is especially important for critical domains such as avionics and railway, in which compliance with standards and certification are required so that a system is allowed to operate. It can also be determined that a method is against some recommendation in a standard. For example, Fault correction with artificial intelligence is not recommended for railway (EN 50128 standard).

    Example: No explicit and direct link with compliance has been established between *Knowledge-Centric System Artefact Quality Analysis* and most assurance/engineering standards.

4   Application of the Criteria for the Analysis of Gaps and Limitations of V&V Methods

The criteria defined in Sect. 3 have been applied for identifying the gaps and limitations in the set of methods introduced in [8]. This contributes to the validation of the criteria. The activity was performed within the VALU3S project by 62 people, who analyzed 53 V&V methods adopting the criteria. In this section, two different analyses are reported. In Subsect. 4.1, two methods are analyzed in detail in order to better show the criteria and how they could be applied. In Sect. 4.2, the main results obtained applying the criteria to all the methods are synthetically reported.

4.1 Application of the Criteria to Two Methods

The results of the application of the criteria to two methods are reported in detail in this section. The two methods have been selected to ensure that various types of methods are covered and that a wide range of criteria is used. The first method (Model-implemented Fault Injection) is an experimental one, i.e., it is based on the observation of the behaviour of the system under certain circumstances. On the other hand, the second method (Knowledge-Centric System Artefact Quality Analysis) is an analytical one, since it is based on the analysis of defined metrics that does not require system execution.

In **Model-implemented Fault Injection**, separate blocks modelling faults are injected into a model of the System Under Test (SUT) [28]. MATLAB and LabVIEW are examples of tools used to build such system models. This method is used to verify and validate the system's capability to handle faults. The fault handling includes attributes such as fault detection, correction, or fallback with or without the fault handling mechanisms implemented. This type of fault injection method is used for a system's evaluation at early design stages [11].

- *Functionality.* (i) The method can be improved by adding techniques such as pre-injection analysis and post-injection analysis [12] to reduce the number of the tests and still get the same or improved results in terms of time, cost, and effort. Pre-injection analysis is done before any fault injection experiments are performed while post-injection uses the results of previous fault injection experiments. (ii) Adding more fault models will increase the functionality of the method.
- *Accuracy.* The accuracy of the method depends on the accuracy of the modelled faults and systems. Since the model of the system might not accurately represent the real system in a real environment, supplemental V&V activities (e.g., acceptance tests) are recommended to be performed at later development stages.
- *Scalability.* Exhaustive fault injection or full system monitoring may require a lot of computational resources depending on the complexity of the target system and its environment.
- *Deployment.* (i) The model-implemented fault injection method is not feasible for final implementations of systems. (ii) The method must be adapted to the simulation tool environment used, e.g., MATLAB toolboxes and MATLAB versions used.
- *Learning curve.* The method requires knowledge and skills regarding the simulation tool environment, e.g., MATLAB/SIMULINK skills.
- *Automation.* The configuration of fault injection campaigns and result analysis are done manually.
- *Reference environment.* This method is only applicable for the simulation environment.
- *Costs.* (i) Software such as MATLAB/SIMULINK is not open source and needs investments. (ii) There is also some cost involved in terms of time when conducting model implemented fault injection. For example, exhaustive fault injection or full system monitoring increases V&V cost.
- *Standards.* No relevant gap or limitation has been identified. Examples of standards including requirements which this method may fulfil are ISO 26262, IEC 62061, ISO 13849, and IEC 61508.

Knowledge-Centric System Artefact Quality Analysis is a method to assess the quality of systems artefacts, such as textual requirements specifications and system models, by exploiting knowledge bases, e.g., an ontology [26]. The assessment is quantitative according to different artefact characteristics (correctness, consistency, and completeness) and to different metrics (e.g., based on the number of elements with a given property in an artefact, such as the number of vague words in a requirement).

- *Functionality*. The amount of model-specific quality analysis means is currently limited. Most of the available support focuses on textual requirements.
- *Accuracy*. A detailed study of quality analysis accuracy has not been conducted.
- *Scalability*. Issues can arise with large and complex system artefacts. Tool solutions have nonetheless been developed to mitigate it.
- *Deployment*. Connectors with the system artefact sources are required, i.e., means to connect with tools (for requirements management, system modelling, etc.) or files to get system artefact data.
- *Learning curve*. There is a barrier in the need for knowing how to create and properly manage ontologies.
- *Automation*. Creation and management of ontologies, as well as of connectors to system artefact sources, would benefit from automation support.
- *Costs*. Creation and management of ontologies is mostly a manual effort that can require significant time.
- *Standards*. No explicit and direct link with compliance has been established for most assurance/engineering standards. Nonetheless, the method (i) has been applied for many systems under regulatory requirements, and (ii) supports INCOSE rules for writing requirements [13], among other reference documents.

4.2 Application Results

The analysis of 53 V&V methods led to identification of 400 gaps and limitations, which corresponds to about 7.5 gaps or limitations for each method. The methods were selected according to the needs and challenges of VALU3S industrial use cases.

Table 1 shows the number of gaps for each criterion, which ranges from 16 to 69. The criterion with more gaps or limitations is Functionality; this is understandable since many functionalities could be added to each method. For the other criteria, on average, about one gap or limitation has been defined for each method, except Standards and Reference Environment, which have less than 0.5 gaps/limitations for each method. This limited number is probably due to the fact that Reference Environment and Standards are as relevant for some methods as for others. For example, some methods could be applied in contexts where no clear standard is defined or they could be natively defined in a reference environment, so no issue regarding this is envisaged.

Regarding the number of gaps for each method, the ones with the highest number of gaps/limitations are Model-based Testing and Penetration Testing, with 15 gaps/limitations each.

Referring to the categories of methods illustrated in Fig. 1, the average number of gaps/limitations per method is reported in Table 2. The category with the highest number of gaps/limitations is Attack Injection, with about 11.3 for each method. On the other side, only 5.8 gaps/limitations were found on average for Testing methods.

Figure 2 shows the average number of gaps/limitations for each criterion and method category. A detailed analysis of this plot can help to qualitatively understand which types of gaps are more frequent in each category. For example, for the Testing methods, a higher number of gaps or limitations connected to Accuracy have been identified, while fewer limitations were pointed out as regards to Functionality. Understanding if some methods share the same type of gaps and limitations and which type of gaps/limitations are more frequent could clarify the direction where the improvements should be carried out.

Table 1. Number of gaps and limitations for each criterion.

Gap/limitation criterion	# of gaps & limitations
Functionality	69
Accuracy	56
Scalability	49
Deployment	47
Learning curve	45
Reference environment	25
Costs	50
Automation	43
Standards	16
Total	400

Table 2. Average number of gaps and limitations for each category of V&V methods.

Gap/limitation criterion	Average # of gaps & limitations
Attack injection	11.3
Fault injection	8.1
Simulation	7.8
Testing	5.8
Runtime verification	8.3
Formal source code verification	9.0
General formal verification	6.4
SCP-focused semi-formal analysis	6.9
General semi-formal analysis	7.0
System-type-focused V&V	10.0

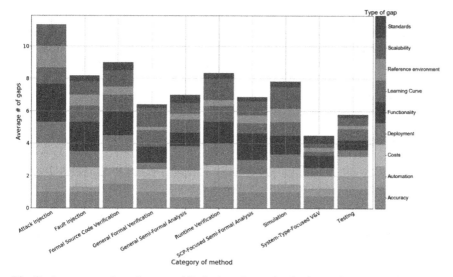

Fig. 2. Average number of gaps and limitations for each criterion and category of methods.

4.3 Discussion

This section complements the insights provided in the previous section by discussing some relevant general aspects of the criteria for analysis of gaps and limitations of V&V methods and of their application.

First of all, the criteria were agreed upon and selected in the scope of a given project, VALU3S, with a specific purpose and specific needs. The criteria fit these purpose and needs, such as the identification of improvement opportunities in V&V methods for safety- and security-critical systems, focusing SCP requirements, to later realize the corresponding improvements. Although other efforts and projects might differ in scope and purpose, we are still confident that the criteria presented are general enough to apply to many similar situations. The overall characteristics to assess of a V&V method are the same regardless their application context, although characteristics some might be more relevant than others. For example, standards can be regarded as a more important criterion for safety-critical systems than for other system types.

Regarding the completeness of the criteria, we acknowledge that other researchers might decide that different criteria need to be considered or that the set of criteria proposed needs to be refined. For instance, and considering again the example of safety-critical systems, it could be valuable to explicitly consider tool qualification aspects when analyzing the automation and standards, or as a complement to them. It is important to ensure that, e.g., tools work as expected, identify errors effectively, and do not introduce errors according to the requirements of safety standards. Our main argument is that the set of criteria has been suitable for VALU3S, thus we consider that it could also be for others. Indeed, we plan to propose the use of the criteria in similar future efforts, such as new large-scale industry-academia projects that plan to review V&V methods.

As indicated above, one of the main benefits that we have found in the definition of an explicit and agreed set of criteria for analysis of gaps and limitations is that it has resulted in a more homogeneous assessment of V&V methods. In other projects, we have experienced that different people considered different aspects when reviewing V&V methods and to a different extent, leading to a more difficult comparison and more limited identification of improvement opportunities. A simple broad, but still precise, comparison such as the one shown in Fig. 2 could not be provided for the prior projects in which we have been involved.

5 Conclusion

As we increasingly rely on safety- and security-critical systems, it is essential that their dependability is confirmed by using adequate V&V methods. To this end, the possible gaps and limitations of the methods must be analyzed. Explicitly defined criteria can aid in making these analyses more precise, homogeneous, and comparable.

In this paper, nine criteria for classifying gaps and limitations have been proposed: functionality, accuracy, scalability, deployment, learning curve, automation, reference environment, cost, and standards. The criteria have been applied in the VALU3S project on a set of 53 V&V methods belonging to different categories and application fields. The outcome helps in addressing the efforts in improving available V&V methods. We also consider that the use of the criteria aids in obtaining more homogeneous analyses of gaps and limitation of V&V methods, also contributing to a more accurate comparison of V&V methods and method types.

As future work, the criteria will guide the development of new V&V methods to overcome existing gaps and limitations, as well as the improvement of existing methods. Moreover, the impact of the use of criteria for addressing current gaps and limitations is planned to be evaluated.

Acknowledgments. The research leading to this paper has received funding from the VALU3S (H2020-ECSEL grant agreement no 876852; MCIN/AEI ref. PCI2020-112001; NextGen.EU/ PRTR), iRel4.0 (H2020-ECSEL grant agreement no 876659; MCIN/AEI ref. PCI2020-112240; NextGen.EU/PRTR), ETHEREAL (MICINN/AEI ref. PID2020-115220RB-C21; ERDF), and Treasure (JCCM SBPLY/19/180501/ 000270; ERDF) projects, and from the Ramon y Cajal Program (MICINN RYC-2017-22836; ESF). We are also grateful to all the VALU3S partners that have provided input and feedback for the selection of the criteria and that applied them.

References

1. Agirre, J., et al.: The VALU3S ECSEL project: verification and validation of automated systems safety and security. Microprocess. Microsyst. **87**, 104349 (2021)
2. Aguirre, J., et al.: Multidimensional framework for characterizing verification and validation of automated systems. In: EDCC (2022)
3. Amalthea4public project: D3.1 - Analysis of state of the art V&V techniques (2015)
4. AMASS project: https://cordis.europa.eu/project/id/692474
5. AMASS project: D1.7 - AMASS solution benchmarking (2019)
6. AMASS project: D3.1 - Baseline and requirements for architecture-driven assurance (2018)

7. Bauer, T., et al.: Cross-domain modelling of verification and validation workflows in the large scale European research project VALU3S. In: Orailoglu, A., Jung, M., Reichenbach, M. (eds) Embedded Computer Systems: Architectures, Modeling, and Simulation. SAMOS 2021. LNCS, vol. 13227. Springer, Cham (2022). https://doi.org/10.1007/978-3-031-04580-6_25

8. de la Vara, J.L., et al.: A proposal for the classification of methods for verification and validation of safety, cybersecurity, and privacy of automated systems. In: QUATIC (2021)

9. ElasTest project: D7.3 - Public demonstrator artifacts (2019)

10. Fenton, N.E., Pfleeger, S.L.: Software Metrics - A Rigorous and Practical Approach, 3rd edn. CRC Press, Boca Raton (2015)

11. Folkesson, P., Ayatolahi, F., Sangchoolie, B., Vinter, J., Islam, M., Karlsson, J.: Back-to-back fault injection testing in model-based development. In: Koornneef, F., van Gulijk, C. (eds.) SAFECOMP 2015. LNCS, vol. 9337, pp. 135–148. Springer, Cham (2015). https://doi.org/10.1007/978-3-319-24255-2_11

12. Grinschgl, J., et al.: Efficient fault emulation using automatic pre-injection memory access analysis. In: 2012 IEEE International SOC Conference, pp. 277–282. Niagara Falls, NY (2012)

13. INCOSE: Guide for Writing Requirements (2019)

14. iRel40 project: https://cordis.europa.eu/project/id/876659

15. ISO: ISO/IEC/IEEE 24765: Systems and software engineering - Vocabulary (2017)

16. Kan, S.: Metrics and Models in Software Quality Engineering, 2nd edn. Addison Wesley, Boston (2002)

17. Kramer, A., Legeard, B.: Model-Based Testing Essentials-Guide to the ISTQB Certified Model-Based Tester: Foundation Level. Wiley, Hoboken (2016)

18. Ma, T., Ali, S., Yue, T.: Testing self-healing cyber-physical systems under uncertainty with reinforcement learning: an empirical study. Empir. Softw. Eng. **26**(3), 1–54 (2021). https://doi.org/10.1007/s10664-021-09941-z

19. Miller, L., et al.: Guidelines for the verification and validation of expert system software and conventional software. US Nuclear Regulatory Commission (1995)

20. Moreno, V., Génova, G., Parra, E., Fraga, A.: Application of machine learning techniques to the flexible assessment and improvement of requirements quality. Softw. Qual. J. **28**(4), 1645–1674 (2020). https://doi.org/10.1007/s11219-020-09511-4

21. Natella, R., et al.: Assessing dependability with software fault injection: a survey. ACM Comput. Surv. **48**(3), 44 (2016)

22. OPENCOSS project: https://cordis.europa.eu/project/id/289011

23. OPENCOSS project: D1.3 - Evaluation framework and quality metrics (2013)

24. Oxford UK Dictionary: Method. https://www.lexico.com/definition/method (2021)

25. Panesar-Walawege, R.K., et al.: Supporting the verification of compliance to safety standards via model-driven engineering: approach, tool-support and empirical validation. Inf. Softw. Technol. **55**(3), 836–864 (2013)

26. Parra, E., et al.: Advances in artefact quality analysis for safety-critical systems. In: 30th International Symposium on Software Reliability Engineering (ISSRE) (2019)

27. Roza, M.: Verification, validation and uncertainty quantification methods and techniques. NATO (2014)

28. Svenningsson, R., Vinter, J., Eriksson, H., Törngren, M.: MODIFI: a MODel-implemented fault injection tool. In: Schoitsch, E. (ed.) SAFECOMP 2010. LNCS, vol. 6351, pp. 210–222. Springer, Heidelberg (2010). https://doi.org/10.1007/978-3-642-15651-9_16

29. VALU3S project: D3.1 - V&V methods for SCP evaluation of automated systems (2020)

30. VALU3S project: D3.3 - Identified gaps and limitations of the V&V methods listed in D3.1 (2021)

31. VALU3S project: D3.6 - Final description of methods designed to improve the V&V process (2022)

3rd International Workshop on Dependable Development-Operation Continuum Methods for Dependable Cyber-Physical System (DepDevOps 2022)

3rd International Workshop on Dependable Development-Operation Continuum Methods for Dependable Cyber-Physical Systems (DepDevOps 2022)

Miren Illarramendi[1], Aitor Arrieta[1], and Irune Agirre[2]

[1] Software and Systems Enginering, Mondragon Unibertsitatea,
Mondragon-Arrasate, Spain
{millarramendi,aarrieta}@mondragon.edu
[2] Dependable Embedded Systems, Ikerlan Research Centre,
Mondragon-Arrasate, Spain
iagirre@ikerlan.es

1 Introduction

In recent years it has become evident that the use of software to perform critical functions is on the rise. As a result, dependable embedded systems are getting more intelligent and automated. For instance, the automotive industry is a clear witness of this trend, where more and more Advanced Driver-Assistance Services (ADAS) are already embedded in cars. This results in a dramatic increase of software complexity, which also requires hardware platforms with higher computing power. All these trends hinder the safety certification, as it is increasingly difficult to guarantee at design time that system errors are prevented or controlled in such a way that there will be no unreasonable risk associated to the electrical/electronic system component at operation time. These challenges are leading to the need for new development practices that reduce the overall system development time and costs without compromising safety and certification.

The rise of new connection technologies (e.g., 5G) bring new opportunities in terms of the download of frequent software updates of new (improved) releases and sending back operation-time information for fixing bugs and enhance the design. Advances done in new development practices like DevOps have shown effectiveness in software development while reducing overall development costs. The DevOps paradigm aims at having seamless methods for the Design-Operation Continuum of software systems. This paradigm has shown promising results in different domains, including web and mobile engineering. Its practices can bring several advantages to dependable CPSs, including bug fixing based on operational data, inclusion of new functionalities, etc.

However, in the context of dependable CPSs, several challenges arise, requiring DevOps paradigms to have adaptions from several perspectives: the environment in which the CPS operates needs to be considered when updating the software, dependability of software needs to be ensured to a certain level, software fault might lead to severe damages, etc. Furthermore, the safety-critical industry has well established safety-lifecycles dictated by safety standards and adopting the DevOps paradigm has several open research challenges.

The International Workshop on Dependable Development-Operation Continuum Methods for Dependable Cyber-Physical Systems (DepDevOps) is dedicated to explore new ideas on dependability challenges brought by over-the-air-software updates to the critical domain, with special focus on safety, security, availability, and platform complexity of emerging dependable autonomous systems. This is a fundamental step for the adoption of DevOps approaches in dependable embedded systems. Over the air updates can bring several benefits to dependable Cyber-Physical Systems, like solving security vulnerabilities, adding new functionalities or bug fixing and they are a key enabler for improving the design based on operation time data. In addition to this, the workshop aims to identify novel tools and architectures that enable the developers implement a streamlined and automatic workflow that makes methods and tools to be seamlessly used during design phases as well as in operation.

The third edition of DepDevOps was held as part of the 41th International Conference on Computer Safety, Reliability, & Security (SAFECOMP 2022).

2   H2020 Projects: Dependable DevOps

The DepDevOps project has been organized by researchers from two H2020 projects that are in-line with the workshop:

- Adeptness: Design-Operation Continuum Methods for Testing and Deployment under Unforeseen Conditions for Cyber-Physical Systems of Systems (https://adeptness.eu/).
- UP2DATE: New software paradigm for SAfe and SEcure (SASE) Over-the-Air software updates for Mixed-Criticality Cyber-Physical Systems (MCCPS) (https://h2020up2date.eu/).

which means that the topics of the workshop are in line with the research objectives of these projects and as both projects are in their second year, the papers presented during the workshop will be considered as inputs and inspiration for the next stages.

3   Acknowledgments

As chairpersons of the workshop, we want to thank all authors and contributors who submitted their work, Friedemann Bitsch, the SAFECOMP Publication Chair, and the members of the International Program Committee who enabled a fair evaluation through reviews and considerable improvements in many cases. We want to express our thanks to the SAFECOMP organizers, who provided us the opportunity to organize the workshop at SAFECOMP 2022. Particularly we want to thank the EC and national public funding authorities who made the work in the research projects possible. We hope that all participants will benefit from the workshop, enjoy the conference and accompanying programs and will join us again in the future!

4 International Program Committee

Erwin Schoitsch	AIT Austrian Institute of Technology
Friedemann Bitsch	Thales Deutschland GmbH
Jon Perez	Ikerlan
Leonidas Kosmidis	Barcelona Supercomputing Center (BSC)
Shaukat Ali	Simula Research Laboratory
Mikel Azkarate-Askasua	Ikerlan
Blanca Kremer	Ikerlan
Urtzi Markiegi	Mondragon Goi Eskola Politeknikoa (MGEP)
Aitor Agirre	Ikerlan
Wasif Afzal	Mälardalen University
Kim Gruettner	OFFIS
Paolo Arcaini	Barcelona Supercomputing Center (BSC)

A Guided Search for Races Based on Data Flow Patterns

Andreas Neubaum[(⊠)], Loui Al Sardy[(⊠)], Marc Spisländer[(⊠)], Francesca Saglietti[(⊠)], and Sara Kretschmer

Software Engineering (Informatik 11), Friedrich-Alexander-Universität Erlangen-Nürnberg, Martensstr. 3, 91058 Erlangen, Germany
{andreas.neubaum,loui.alsardy,marc.spislaender, francesca.saglietti,sara.kretschmer}@fau.de

Abstract. A strategy for searching for exploitable races is derived, implemented and evaluated. It aims at the detection of inconsistent behaviour due to irregularly interleaved instructions of concurrent threads. The search for internal races focuses on particular data flow patterns targeting the occurrence of internal races by enforcing different orders of reading and writing operations; it is guided by symbolic expressions of interleaved paths and constraint solving. The possibility of propagating internal races to system races is subsequently considered. An exemplifying application of the approach proposed illustrates its practicality.

Keywords: Software vulnerability · Thread · Interleaving · Scheduling · Race · Data flow pattern · Symbolic execution · Constraint solving

1 Introduction

The increasing impact of potential cyber-attacks on the behaviour of automated processes is evident. Such attacks are frequently based on existing software vulnerabilities which may be intentionally exploited via knowledge or trial [5, 8, 9]. This hazardous situation urgently asks for efficient verification techniques designed to explicitly address the detection of exploitable vulnerabilities of predefined type before allowing for operation. For this purpose, typical testing approaches rely on so-called fuzzing, i.e. on generating high numbers of test cases by mutation such as to increase the chances of triggering incorrect behaviour during testing. Unfortunately, the growing complexity of software lowers the probability of randomly activating weaknesses present in the code.

In order to overcome this deficiency, the project SMARTEST2 – following a strategy already started by the predecessor project SMARTEST – rather pursues the goal of developing intelligent techniques devoted to a more systematic identification of vulnerabilities of predefined type. These are based on the extraction (via static analysis) of logical constraints to be successively systematically solved (if possible), or (more often) heuristically satisfied [2]. Evidently, such an approach cannot claim completeness, as it is not intended to address any arbitrary weakness. On the other hand, for selected

M. Trapp et al. (Eds.): SAFECOMP 2022 Workshops, LNCS 13415, pp. 47–58, 2022.
https://doi.org/10.1007/978-3-031-14862-0_10

vulnerability classes it could be shown to provide superior detection strategies when compared to weakness-unspecific fuzzers.

The present article intends to elaborate on this topic by focusing on testing and analysis techniques aiming at the pre-operational exploitation of races caused by irregularly interleaved instructions belonging to two concurrent threads. Such races represent relevant software vulnerabilities [9]. The approach concentrates on the selection of interleavings instantiating specific data flow patterns which, although not guaranteeing an exhaustive search, are considered as particularly race-prone.

2   Related Work

An overview of tools targeting vulnerabilities was presented in [11]; such tools range from generic fuzzers (e.g. AFL [20], Radamsa [13]) relying on random input variation to provoke runtime errors to more sophisticated analysis techniques targeting specific anomalies. While generic fuzzers allow to address an unlimited spectrum of anomalies, when confronted with particular vulnerability classes their power reveals as limited [1].

More refined approaches (like KLEE [4] or QSYM [19]) systematically support code coverage by extracting path predicates via symbolic execution; these can be successively analysed by constraint solvers (like STP [7] or Z3 [6]) to generate test cases. Even when achieving high coverage, however, test cases may not necessarily be tailored to uncover specific weaknesses.

On the other hand, there are dedicated techniques targeting the occurrence of races. Some of them (like CHESS [10] and KISS [15]) select a subset of interleaved executions and check their correctness via assertions. Both the sample incompleteness and the assertion inaccuracy, however, may restrict the chances of identifying exploitable races.

Further approaches focus on the identification of interleavings characterized by a selection of data flow patterns considered as hazardous.

Among them, Ctrigger [14], RaceFuzzer [16] and Penelope [17] aim at executing interleavings meeting predefined patterns by varying the underlying scheduling (not the input data), successively evaluating the correctness of the resulting execution.

Also MAPLE [18] considers given data flow patterns and test data in order to identify interleaved executions covering the target set of patterns by means of a more refined pattern classification. A limitation of such approaches lies in their dependence on given test data not subject to further variation.

Finally, MEMICS [12] aims at instantiating patterns as well, overcoming the aforementioned limitation by selecting appropriate input data via constraint solving. On the other hand, it takes the execution of pattern-based interleavings as sufficient evidence for their inappropriateness without evaluating their actual behaviour.

The approach taken in the following is based on similar reading/writing patterns extended, however, to include branching effects due to predicates on variable values. In addition, it essentially differs from the approaches mentioned above by requiring concrete evidence about behavioural inconsistencies due to interleaving effects. To do so, it targets the generation of data-specific scenarios based on different interleavings before explicitly comparing the results (resp. the corresponding internal states). This helps avoid relying on unsharp assertions or on acceptance criteria based on generalized reading/writing effects rather than on observable behaviour.

3 Race-Prone Data Flow Patterns

3.1 Terminology and Assumptions

In the following, the term *interleaving* is used to denote any sequence of interleaved instructions belonging to two programs. In general, such a sequence cannot be guaranteed to be executable by concurrent program runs. A *scheduling* determines in which sequence to interleave the thread instructions. A (*system*) *race* is an event occurring whenever two executions of the same input result in different interleavings producing different outputs. Similarly, an *internal race* denotes an event occurring whenever two partial executions of the same input (until predefined thread-specific checkpoints) result in different interleaving prefixes ending in different internal states.

Assumptions. The following conditions are assumed to hold:

1. Number and codes of concurrent threads as well as upper bounds on the number of loop iterations can be determined in advance.
2. Deadlocks can be excluded.
   Assumptions 1 and 2 are considered as acceptable in the context of technical processes automatically controlled by software, as typically addressed in this article; hereby, threads are assumed to be based on asynchronous sensor messages and not to require synchronous communication or exclusive access to shared resources.
3. While executing basic instructions (i.e. assignments or predicate evaluations) no interruption is enabled; if required, the validity of this constraint may be enforced by appropriate locking mechanisms.
4. No side effects occur during the evaluation of branching predicates; if required, the validity of this constraint may be enforced by maintaining the original semantics while separating the side effect constructs from the mere evaluation of the predicates.

Data Flow Annotations. For any variable v, the following notation will be used to annotate data flow properties:

- def(v) denotes a definition of v, i.e. a writing access to v,
- def-clear(v) characterizes a control flow (sub)path involving no definitions of v,
- c-use(v) denotes a computational use of v, i.e. a reading access to the value of v for the purpose of assigning a value to any variable or parameter,
- p-use(v) denotes a predicative use of v, i.e. a reading access to the value of v for the purpose of evaluating a branching condition.

Graphical Elements. For arbitrary variables v and z the following notation will be used to characterize nodes of the control flow graph CFG_T of a thread T:

- $[def_T(v)]$ denotes a node including an instruction overwriting v;

- [c-use$_T$(v), def$_T$(z)] denotes a node including an instruction overwriting z by making use of the value of v;
- [p-use$_T$(v)] denotes a branching node involving the evaluation of a predicate on v.

Execution Modes. The following abbreviations will be used to represent consecutive or interleaved execution modes concerning control flow paths $X_1,\ldots,X_n$, where $n \in \mathbb{N}$:

- $<X_1,\ldots,X_n>$ denotes the successive executions of $X_1, X_2,\ldots$ and X_n (in this order);
- $<X_1 \| X_2>$ denotes the interleaved execution mode of X_1 and X_2;
- $S(<X_1\|X_2>)$ denotes the interleaving of X_1 and X_2 defined by scheduling S.

3.2 Pattern 1

The first race-prone pattern considered addresses the concurrent execution of two instructions, each involving a definition of the same variable v. Evidently, the final value of v is determined by the one instruction executed last. Assuming these instructions to assign different values to v implies that the internal state of each thread depends on the order of their execution.

Given two arbitrary threads T_i ($i \in \{1,2\}$) with control flow graphs CFG$_{Ti}$ consider the following thread-specific path prefixes

$$P_i:<A_i, [def_{Ti}(v)], B_i>,$$

where A_i denotes a subpath of CFG$_{Ti}$ from its entry to a predecessor node of [def$_{Ti}$(v)] and B_i denotes a def-clear(v) subpath of CFG$_{Ti}$ starting at a successor node of [def$_{Ti}$(v)]. In general, subpath B_i is not required to reach the exit node; in particular, there may be further definitions of v occurring after B_i. Consider interleaving any given pair of such subpaths by applying first a scheduling S_0 to $<A_1\|A_2>$ such as to induce a partition of each A_i into $<A_i', A_i''>$ where S_0 operates on A_i', but not on A_i''; this initial scheduling is successively extended in two alternative ways, namely by applying a scheduling S_1 to $<B_1\|A_2''>$ resp. S_2 to $<A_1''\|B_2>$; in particular, the resulting interleavings

$$I_1:<A_0, A_1'', [def_{T1}(v)], S_1(<B_1\|A_2''>), [def_{T2}(v)]> \text{ and}$$
$$I_2:<A_0, A_2'', [def_{T2}(v)], S_2(<A_1''\|B_2>), [def_{T1}(v)]>$$

share a common prefix $A_0 = S_0(<A_1'\|A_2'>)$ and reach an internal race at their conclusion if the following constraint C_1 is fulfilled:

$$C_1 = exec_1 \wedge exec_2 \wedge \left[expr_1(v) \neq expr_2(v)\right],$$

where for each $j \in \{1,2\}$ exec$_j$ denotes the predicate expressing the executability of I_j and expr$_j$(v) denotes the symbolic expression of the value of v after executing I_j.

3.3 Pattern 2

The second race-prone pattern addresses the concurrent execution of two defining instructions concerning two variables v and z, where the definition of z makes use of the current value of v. Evidently, the value of v actually used to overwrite z depends on the order of execution. Therefore, pattern 2 addresses pairs of interleavings differing in the order of execution of two such defining instructions.

Consider the following thread-specific path prefixes

$$P_1:<A_1, [\text{def}_{T1}(v)], B_1> \text{ and } P_2:<A_2, [\text{c-use}_{T2}(v), \text{def}_{T2}(z)], B_2>,$$

where for $i \in \{1,2\}$

- A_i denotes a subpath of CFG_{Ti} from its entry to a predecessor node of $[\text{def}_{T1}(v)]$ (in case $i = 1$) resp. to a predecessor node of $[\text{c-use}_{T2}(v), \text{def}_{T2}(z)]$ (in case $i = 2$),
- B_i denotes a def-clear(v) and def-clear(z) subpath of CFG_{Ti} starting at a successor node of $[\text{def}_{T1}(v)]$ (in case $i = 1$) resp. at a successor node of $[\text{c-use}_{T2}(v), \text{def}_{T2}(z)]$ (in case of $i = 2$).

Any given pair of such subpaths may be interleaved in two different ways, namely by applying first a scheduling S_0 to $<A_1 \| A_2>$ (inducing a partition $A_i = < A_i', A_i''>$) and then a scheduling S_1 to $<B_1 \| A_2''>$ resp. S_2 to $<A_1'' \| B_2>$ such that the resulting interleavings

$$I_1:<A_0, A_1'', [\text{def}_{T1}(v)], S_1(< B_1 \| A_2''>), [\text{c-use}_{T2}(v), \text{def}_{T2}(z)]> \text{ and}$$
$$I_2:<A_0, A_2'', [\text{c-use}_{T2}(v), \text{def}_{T2}(z)], S_2(<A_1'' \| B_2>), [\text{def}_{T1}(v)]>$$

share a common prefix $A_0 = S_0(<A_1' \| A_2'>)$ and reach an internal race at their conclusion if the following constraint C_2 is fulfilled:

$$C_2 = \text{exec}_1 \wedge \text{exec}_2 \wedge [\text{expr}_1(v) \neq \text{expr}_2(v) \vee \text{expr}_1(z) \neq \text{expr}_2(z)],$$

where for each $j \in \{1,2\}$ exec_j denotes the predicate expressing the executability of I_j and $\text{expr}_j(\text{var})$ denotes the symbolic expression for any variable var after executing I_j.

3.4 Pattern 3

The third race-prone pattern addresses two different orders concerning the concurrent execution of a defining instruction of a variable v and a branching construct (i.e. an if-then-else or a loop construct), where the branching predicate depends on the value of v. Evidently, the code portion to be executed after the evaluation of the branching predicate (i.e. the THEN part or the ELSE part resp. the loop body or the loop exit) may depend on the order of execution. In order to increase the chances of a race, pattern 3 enforces the traversal of subpaths diverging after evaluating the branching predicate.

Assuming CFG_{T2} to contain a branching node $[\text{p-use}_{T2}(v)]$ with two exits pointing to the starts of two subgraphs G_1 and G_2 sharing only an empty exit node, consider the path prefixes

$$P_1:<A_1, [\text{def}_{T1}(v)], B_1>,$$
$$P_{2I}:< A_2, [\text{p-use}_{T2}(v)], P(G_1), B_2>,$$
$$P_{2II}:<A_2, [\text{p-use}_{T2}(v)], P(G_2), B_2>,$$

where for $i, k \in \{1,2\}$

- A_i denotes a subpath of CFG_{Ti} from its entry to a predecessor node of $[def_{T1}(v)]$ (in case of $i = 1$) resp. to a predecessor node of $[p\text{-}use_{T2}(v)]$ (in case of $i = 2$),
- $P(G_k)$ denotes a path of G_k such that $V_1 \cup V_2 \neq \emptyset$ for sets V_k consisting of the variables defined on $P(G_k)$,
- B_i denotes a def-clear(var) subpath of CFG_{Ti} starting at a successor node of $[def_{T1}(v)]$ resp. at a successor node of the common exit of G_1 and G_2, where var $\in V_1 \cup V_2$.

Consider interleaving the pair (P_1, P_{2I}) by applying first a scheduling S_0 to $<A_1 \| A_2>$ (hereby inducing a partition on A_i) and then a scheduling S_1 to $<B_1 \| A_2''>$. Similarly, consider interleaving the pair (P_1, P_{2II}) by applying first the same scheduling S_0 to $<A_1 \| A_2>$ and then a scheduling S_2 to $<A_1'' \| <P(G_2), B_2>>$. The resulting interleavings

$$I_1: < A_0, A_1'', [def_{T1}(v)], S_1(< B_1 \| A_2''>), [p\text{-}use_{T2}(v)], P(G_1) > \text{ and}$$
$$I_2: <A_0, A_2'', [p\text{-}use_{T2}(v)], S_2(<A_1'' \| <P(G_2), B_2>>), [def_{T1}(v)]>$$

share a common prefix $A_0 = S_0(<A_1' \| A_2'>)$; an internal race can be provoked if executing different branches results in different values assigned to at least one variable, i.e. if the following constraint C_3 is fulfilled:

$$C_3 = exec_1 \wedge exec_2 \wedge [\vee_{var \in V}(expr_1(var) \neq expr_2(var))],$$

where for $j \in \{1,2\}$ $exec_j$ denotes the predicate expressing the executability of I_j and $expr_j(var)$ denotes the symbolic expression for any variable var $\in V = V_1 \cup V_2 \cup \{v\}$ after execution.

4   Pattern-Based Race Detection

Based on the theoretical background underlying the three data flow patterns introduced and described in Sect. 3, the present section is intended to propose an approach targeting the detection of races. This approach can be structured in two phases:

- Phase 1 (detection of internal races): guided by the race-prone patterns presented above, the search proceeds by iteration, repeatedly identifying concrete interleavings for which to solve the corresponding race constraints (C_1, C_2 resp. C_3) derived in Sect. 3. To do so, the underlying expressions are evaluated via tool-supported symbolic execution [3]. The resulting pattern-specific constraint is successively submitted to a constraint solver [6]. As soon as one of the constraints reveals as satisfiable, any of its solutions provides input capable of provoking an internal race.
- Phase 2 (extension to system races): internal races identified in phase 1 are analysed for extendibility towards the triggering of a race at system level.

The two phases are described in more detail in the following subsections.

4.1 Phase 1: Pattern-Based Identification of Internal Races

The search proceeds via the following four steps, each addressing the coverage of a particular design parameter (data flow pattern, pair of nodes, pair(s) of path prefixes and triple of schedulings); by appropriate iterations over these steps all possible combinations of the underlying parameters can be taken into account. The iterative process stops as soon as an internal race is found.

Step 1: Select Pattern. Select a data flow pattern among the three patterns introduced and illustrated in Sects. 3.2–3.4.

Step 2: Select Pair of Nodes. Select from CFG_{T1} node n_1 and from CFG_{T2} node n_2 such that both nodes can be taken to instantiate one of the patterns identified in step 1, i.e. pair (n_1, n_2) is of type

$$([def_{T1}(v)], [def_{T2}(v)]) \text{ in case of pattern 1,}$$
$$([def_{T1}(v)], [c\text{-}use_{T2}(v), def_{T2}(z)]) \text{ in case of pattern 2,}$$
$$([def_{T1}(v)], [p\text{-}use_{T2}(v)]) \text{ in case of pattern 3.}$$

Step 3: Select Pair(s) of Path Prefixes. Depending on the pattern considered, concrete pair(s) of path prefixes have to be determined: a pair (P_1, P_2) in case of patterns 1 and 2 resp. two pairs (P_1, P_{2I}) and (P_1, P_{2II}) in case of pattern 3. This is done by selecting for $i \in \{1,2\}$ concrete subpaths A_i, B_i and – as far as pattern 3 is concerned – $P(G_i)$, as introduced in Sect. 3. This selection process terminates, as upper bounds for the number of loop iterations are assumed to be known (Subsect. 3.1). If required in order to keep the number of candidate pairs within affordable boundaries, the maximum number of loop iterations allowed for A_i and B_i may be further reduced, at the cost, however, of decreased search accuracy.

Step 4: Select Schedulings and Analyse Resulting Interleavings. This step consists of the following tasks:

- **Select triple of schedulings.** As described in Sect. 3, interleavings I_1 and I_2 result by application of appropriate schedulings S_0, S_1 and S_2 to the pair(s) of path prefixes selected in step 3. As the chances of finding a common executable input of I_1 and I_2 increase with the length of the common prefix A_0, S_0 is initially defined such as to maximize its length (this is the case if A_1'' and A_2'' are sequences of length 0). As long as the search for races is not successful, future iterations consider further scheduling triples addressing sequences A_1'' and A_2'' of varying length.
- **Determine constraint.** The pattern-specific constraint (C_1, C_2 resp. C_3) derived in Sect. 3 depends on the path predicates $exec_j$ and on the variable-specific expressions $expr_j(var)$; these are determined via tool-supported symbolic execution (KLEE [4]) of both interleavings.
- **Analyse constraint for satisfiability.** The constraint determined is finally submitted to the constraint solving tool Z3 [6]. If it reveals as satisfiable, the tool provides an input triggering an internal race at the conclusion of the interleavings I_1 and I_2. Otherwise, the search continues – if possible – with a different tuple of design parameters.

4.2   Phase 2: Analysis of Extendibility from Internal Races to System Races

The detection of an internal race does not necessarily imply the presence of a software vulnerability capable of provoking a race at system level, but it can be considered as providing evidence about some internal inconsistency which may be further exploited to provoke a system race.

A simple attempt at exploiting an internal race consists of making use of the input x_{ir} triggering it (as determined in Step 4). A complete execution of x_{ir} requires to extend the interleavings I_1 and I_2 (so far limited to path prefixes) by scheduling suffixes allowing to reach the end of each thread.

A particularly simple extension allowing to interleave also the path suffixes P_{1suf} and P_{2suf} not yet consumed, is given by the sequential execution of the path suffixes; evidently, there are two different sequential schedulings S_{seq1} and S_{seq2} given by:

$$S_{seq1}\left(<P_{1suf}\|P_{2suf}>\right) = <P_{1suf}, P_{2suf}> \text{ and}$$
$$S_{seq2}\left(<P_{1suf}\|P_{2suf}>\right) = <P_{2suf}, P_{1suf}>$$

Extending the preliminary interleavings I_1 and I_2 via these sequential suffixes S_{seq1} and S_{seq2} yields two complete interleavings. In case the latter can execute input x_{ir} resulting in different outputs, the internal race is easily propagated to a system race.

On the other hand, if such a straightforward propagation from internal to system races is not feasible, a systematic search may be applied by

- analysing for each pair of interleaved path suffixes the satisfiability of the corresponding constraint required to expose a system race from the internal states reached after I_1 resp. I_2 and
- stopping as soon as any such constraint can be solved.

Evidently, the combinatorial effort required by such a search may be considerable, although inferior to the procedure introduced in [11] which did not allow to restrict it to path suffixes of limited length following the states exposing internal races.

5   Evaluation

5.1   Example

The following example considers the logic controlling two fictive machines sharing a common deposit and cooperating to the production of a bounded number W of work pieces out of a corresponding number of blanks: while the blank producer repeatedly creates a new blank from raw material and places it in the common deposit, the work piece producer repeatedly extracts a blank, processes it and deposits the resulting new work piece. Hereby, blanks require twice as much space as work pieces.

Both producers sense the number of blanks (# blanks in deposit) and of work pieces (# work pieces in deposit) actually stored and derive the amount of free space by

$$\text{free space} = C - 2 \cdot (\text{\# blanks in deposit}) - (\text{\# work pieces in deposit}),$$

where C denotes the deposit capacity in terms of the number of work pieces it can accommodate. As long as there are still work pieces to be produced and as soon as there is enough free space to deposit a blank resp. at least one blank ready to be processed, the corresponding producer starts its iteration which ends by depositing the artefact obtained. Trying to place a work piece in a full deposit causes it to fall down and break.

It is assumed that originally the production of one blank resp. of one work piece were designed as atomic (i.e. non-interruptible) regions, but that during maintenance efficiency arguments may have led to refine the atomic regions such as to reduce the overall production time; this refinement is shown in Fig. 1.

Blank Producer	**Work Piece Producer**
while # blanks produced < W	while # work pieces produced < W
if free space ≥ 2	if # blanks in deposit ≥ 1
start blank production;	extract blank;
wait until blank produced;	start work piece production;
place blank in deposit;	wait until work piece produced;
	place work piece in deposit;

Fig. 1. Control logic for cooperating producers (dotted frames denote atomic regions)

A producer may have to wait while the other processes its current piece; an upper bound for the maximum number of loop traversals during any such waiting phase is assumed to be known. In order to avoid the situation where both producers wait for each other, inputs C and W are constrained by the inequality $C \geq W + 1$.

5.2 Race Detection Capability and Effort

The application of the pattern-based guided search to the control logic shown above led to the detection of 3 internal races, the first 2 of which could not be propagated to a system race; this was actually due to problem-inherent reasons rather than to methodological weakness. The third internal race, however, which was detected after 1 h and 10 min, could be successfully extended to a system race after 6 further seconds. The search for further internal races continued until all pattern instances were checked and terminated after a total runtime of 5 h and 29 min without further detections.

The race scenario identified refers to the possibility that after having extracted a blank from a full deposit, the work piece producer may rely on the availability of at least one free slot; before depositing the work piece just produced, however, a new blank may be deposited by the concurrent blank producer, hereby causing the work piece to fall and break. Evidently, under the original atomic regions this would not have been possible.

5.3 Comparison with Random Search

In order to evaluate the benefits of using the patterns 1, 2 and 3 for the purpose of identifying races, the performance of the guided search proposed was compared – both in terms of detection capability and of effort required – with a purely random selection of inputs and schedulings.

The input data, namely the storage capacity C and the number W of work pieces to be produced, was generated according to a uniform random distribution under the following constraints:

$$C \geq W + 1 \quad \wedge \quad C, W \leq 10000$$

Each experiment consisted of successive steps. At each step an input was first randomly chosen and then repeatedly executed until the output differed from the output of its first execution (i.e. until a race occurred) or at the latest after the input had been executed 100 times. As long as no race was observed, a new step with a new random input followed. The steps were repeated as long as no race was observed and the total runtime of the experiment did not surpass 10 h. In case of successful race detection 5 independent experiments were carried out. On the other hand, due to its analytical rather than random nature, the corresponding pattern-based search for internal races was not replicated.

Different (work piece resp. blank) production times were experimentally simulated via sleep instructions; their impact on race detection was successively analysed. The results are summarized in Table 1; they show that, as long as no production times are considered, random detection revealed as superior in terms of searching speed when compared to the pattern-based approach. This is due to the relatively high number of random test runs carried out under this timing assumption which contributes to increase the chances of blind searching for races.

Already for small delays due to blank resp. work piece production, however, the experimental data shows that random search could not be relied upon to expose race vulnerabilities. In fact, with the production times slowly increasing, the number of random runs which can be evaluated within 10 h significantly drops, hereby heavily decreasing the chances of selecting race-exposing inputs and schedulings.

Table 1. Comparison of random search and pattern-based search for different production times

Production time		Random search		Pattern-based search	
Blank	Work piece	Success	Min - Max time	Success	Time
0 ms	0 ms	Yes	31 ms – 2362 ms (5 experiments)	Yes	70 min
1 ms	0 ms	No	10 h	Yes	70 min
1 ms	1 ms	No	10 h	Yes	70 min
2 ms	1 ms	No	10 h	Yes	70 min

On the other hand, the pattern-based search more seldom requires concrete code executions; therefore, an increase in production time(s) does not essentially impact on search time consumption, thus allowing for a higher number of searching runs to be carried out under comparable time constraints.

6 Conclusion

The increasing impact of exploitable software vulnerabilities on the behaviour of technical processes with high reliability demands requires novel verification approaches addressing the detection of individual weakness classes, among them irregular races caused by inappropriate interleaving of concurrent threads.

The present article proposed an approach which does not depend on the programming language and is based on three data flow patterns considered as promising in supporting the exposal of potential races occurring during the execution of two concurrent threads. The search space is reduced to candidate interleavings derived by instantiation of such patterns. The search can be successively guided by pattern-specific constraints derived from predicates and expressions gained via tool-supported symbolic execution. Whenever revealing satisfiable by constraint solving tools within acceptable time limits, this approach results in concrete data causing an internal race upon reaching a predefined operational state.

The benefits offered by this approach were confirmed in the light of experimental results. Its major limitation concerns the propagation of system races from the internal races identified, as this task may involve a heavier combinatorial effort. On the other hand, the detection of internal races already offers valuable support by providing concrete evidence capable of exposing the potential for semantic inconsistencies.

In view of the effort required, the approach focused on pairs of concurrent threads. An extension to include more threads may be addressed by future investigations.

Acknowledgment. The authors gratefully acknowledge that the work presented was supported by the German Federal Ministry for Economic Affairs and Energy (BMWi), project no. 1501600C (SMARTEST2).

References

1. Al Sardy, L., Neubaum, A., Saglietti, F., Rudrich, D.: Comparative evaluation of security fuzzing approaches. In: Romanovsky, A., Troubitsyna, E., Gashi, I., Schoitsch, E., Bitsch, F. (eds.) SAFECOMP 2019. LNCS, vol. 11699, pp. 49–61. Springer, Cham (2019). https://doi.org/10.1007/978-3-030-26250-1_4
2. Al Sardy, L., Saglietti, F., Tang, T., Sonnenberg, H.: Constraint-based testing for buffer overflows. In: Gallina, B., Skavhaug, A., Schoitsch, E., Bitsch, F. (eds.) SAFECOMP 2018. LNCS, vol. 11094, pp. 99–111. Springer, Cham (2018). https://doi.org/10.1007/978-3-319-99229-7_10
3. Baldoni, R., Coppa, E., D'Elia, D., Demetrescu, C., Finocchi, I.: A survey of symbolic execution techniques. ACM Comput. Surv. **51**(3), 1–39 (2018)
4. Cadar, C., Dunbar, D., Engler, D.: KLEE: unassisted and automatic generation of high-coverage tests for complex system programs. In: USENIX Symposium on Operating Systems Design and Implementation, pp. 209–224. USENIX Association (2008)

5. Cisco: Most common CWE vulnerabilities. Annual Cybersecurity Report (2018)
6. de Moura, L., Bjørner, N.: Z3: an efficient SMT solver. In: Ramakrishnan, C.R., Rehof, J. (eds.) TACAS 2008. LNCS, vol. 4963, pp. 337–340. Springer, Heidelberg (2008). https://doi.org/10.1007/978-3-540-78800-3_24
7. Ganesh, V., Dill, D.L.: A decision procedure for bit-vectors and arrays. In: Damm, W., Hermanns, H. (eds.) CAV 2007. LNCS, vol. 4590, pp. 519–531. Springer, Heidelberg (2007). https://doi.org/10.1007/978-3-540-73368-3_52
8. MITRE Corporation: Common Weakness Enumeration (CWE), Top 25 Most Dangerous Software Weaknesses (2020)
9. MITRE Corporation: Common Vulnerabilities and Exposures (CVE) including race reports CVE-2020-1839, CVE-2022-29582, CVE-2022-29527, CVE-2022-25165, CVE-2022-25090
10. Musuvathi, M.: Systematic concurrency testing using CHESS. In: Workshop on Parallel and Distributed Systems: Testing, Analysis, and Debugging. ACM (2008)
11. Neubaum, A., Al Sardy, L., Spisländer, M., Saglietti, F., Biener, Y.: Testing for IT security: a guided search pattern for exploitable vulnerability classes. In: Habli, I., Sujan, M., Gerasimou, S., Schoitsch, E., Bitsch, F. (eds.) SAFECOMP 2021. LNCS, vol. 12853, pp. 105–116. Springer, Cham (2021). https://doi.org/10.1007/978-3-030-83906-2_8
12. Nowotka, D., Traub, J.: MEMICS – Memory Interval Constraint Solving of (concurrent) Machine Code. Automotive – Safety & Security, LNI 210, pp. 69–83, Springer (2012)
13. Oulu University Secure Programming Group (OUSPG): Radamsa (2010)
14. Park, S., Lu, S., Zhou, Y.: CTrigger: exposing atomicity violation bugs from their hiding places. In: International Conference Architectural Support for Programming Languages and Operating Systems, vol. 37, pp. 25–36. ACM (2009)
15. Qadeer, S., Wu, D.: KISS: keep it simple and sequential. SIGPLAN Not. **39**, 14–24 (2004)
16. Sen, K.: Race directed random testing of concurrent programs. In: SIGPLAN Conference on Programming Language Design and Implementation, pp. 11–21. ACM (2008)
17. Sorrentino, F., Farzan, A., Parthasarathy, M.: PENELOPE: weaving threads to expose atomicity violations. In: International Symposium on Foundations of Software Engineering (FSE 2010), pp. 37–46. ACM (2010)
18. Yu, J., Narayanasamy, S., Pereira, C., Pokam, G.: Maple: a coverage-driven testing tool for multithreaded programs. In: International Conference on Object Oriented Programming Systems Languages and Applications, pp. 485–502. ACM (2012)
19. Yun, I., Lee, S., Xu, M., Jang, Y., Kim, T.: QSYM: a practical concolic execution engine tailored for hybrid fuzzing. In: USENIX Security Symposium, pp. 745–761. USENIX (2018)
20. Zalewski, M.: American Fuzzy Lop (AFL) (2017)

9th International Workshop on Next Generation of System Assurance Approaches for Critical Systems (SASSUR 2022)

9th International Workshop on Next Generation of System Assurance Approaches for Critical Systems (SASSUR 2022)

Jose Luis de la Vara[1], Alejandra Ruiz[2], and Antonio Kung[3]

[1] Department of Computing Systems, Universidad de Castilla-La Mancha, Albacete, Spain
joseluis.delavara@uclm.es
[2] TECNALIA Next - Quantum Technologies, TECNALIA R&I, Derio, Spain
alejandra.ruiz@tecnalia.com
[3] Trialog, Paris, France
antonio.kung@trialog.com

1 Introduction

System assurance and certification are amongst the most expensive and time-consuming tasks in the development of critical systems, e.g., safety-critical, security-critical, privacy-critical, mission-critical, and business-critical ones. Assurance and certification of critical systems require the execution of complex and labour-intensive activities, such as the management of compliance with hundreds or thousands of criteria defined in standards, the management of a large volume of assurance evidence artefacts, or the provision of convincing and valid justifications that a system is dependable. Therefore, the companies developing critical systems or components, as well as the companies assessing them, need approaches that facilitate these activities and ideally increase their efficiency. The challenges arising from system assurance and certification are further growing as a result of the technological advancements of critical systems, such as new connectivity, autonomy, and adaptation features.

Since 2012, the SASSUR workshop is intended to explore new ideas on assurance and certification of critical systems. It provides a forum for thematic presentations and in-depth discussions about specification, analysis, reuse, composition, and combination of assurance arguments, of assurance evidence, and of contextual information about critical products, in a way that makes assurance and certification more cost-effective, precise, and scalable. SASSUR aims at bringing together experts, researchers, and practitioners from diverse communities, such as safety, privacy, and security engineering, certification processes, model-based engineering, software and hardware design, and application communities (transport, healthcare, industrial automation, robotics, nuclear, defence, etc.).

2   This Year's Workshop

SASSUR is held again in 2022 after having been cancelled in 2020 and 2021 due to the covid pandemic. The program consists of four high-quality papers (in alphabetical order):

- An Approach for Deriving Reduced Collision Scenarios for Highly Automated Driving Systems, *by Marzana Khatun, Heinrich Litagin, Rolf Jung and Michael Glass*
- DevOps and Safety? SafeOps! Towards Ensuring Safety in Feature-Driven Development with Frequent Releases, *by Peter Munk and Markus Schweizer*
- Dynamic Checks of Evidence Models for Assurance Projects in Eclipse OpenCert, *by Jabier Martinez and Ángel Jesús Varela-Vaca*
- State of the Art Study of the Safety Argumentation Frameworks for Automated Driving System, *by Ilona Cieslik, Víctor J. Expósito Jiménez, Helmut Martin, Heiko Scharke, and Hannes Schneider*

We hope that all the authors and participants will benefit from the workshop, enjoy the workshop, and join us again in the future!

Acknowledgements. We are grateful to the SAFECOMP organization committee and collaborators for their support in arranging SASSUR, especially to Jérémie Guiochet and Erwin Schoitsch as Workshop Chairs, and to Friedemann Bitsch as Publication Chair. We also thank all the authors of the submitted papers for their interest in the workshop, and the program committee for its work. Finally, the workshop is supported by the CONNECT (HORIZON ref. 101069688) iRel4.0 (H2020-ECSEL ref. 876659; MCIN/AEI ref. PCI2020-112240; NextGen.EU/PRTR), VALU3S (H2020-ECSEL ref. 876852; MCIN/AEI ref. PCI2020-112001; NextGen.EU/ PRTR), ETHEREAL (MICINN/AEI ref. PID2020-115220RB-C21; ERDF), and Treasure (JCCM ref. SBPLY/19/ 180501/000270; ERDF) projects, and by the Ramon y Cajal Program (MCIN/AEI ref. RYC-2017-22836; ESF).

Workshop Committees

Organization Committee

Jose Luis de la Vara	Universidad de Castilla-La Mancha, Spain
Alejandra Ruiz	TECNALIA, Spain
Antonio Kung	Trialog, France

Programme Committee and Reviewers

Fabien Belmonte	Alstom, France
Markus Borg	RISE, Sweden
John Favaro	Intecs, Italy

Barbara Gallina	Mälardalen University, Sweden
Maritta Heisel	University of Duisburg-Essen, Germany
Garazi Juez	BMW, Germany
Sahar Kokaly	General Motors, Canada
Georg Macher	Graz University of Technology, Austria
Johnny Marques	ITA, Brazil
Jabier Martinez	Tecnalia, Spain
Thor Myklebust	SINTEF, Norway
Philippa Ryan Conmy	Adelard, UK
Christoph Schmittner	Austrian Institute of Technology, Austria
Irfan Sljivo	NASA, USA
Marc Zeller	Siemens, Germany

DevOps and Safety? SafeOps! Towards Ensuring Safety in Feature-Driven Development with Frequent Releases

Peter Munk and Markus Schweizer[(✉)]

Robert Bosch GmbH, 71272 Renningen, Germany
{peter.munk,markus.schweizer}@bosch.com

Abstract. The increasing importance of software and rising level of connectivity of safety-critical products such as vehicles enable continuously improving and adding the functionality. DevOps development principles support such kind of continuous deployment. However, safety-critical products shall fulfill safety standards. In addition, it is impossible to show that a new or updated functionality is safe without considering the entire system. We introduce the *SafeOps* approach that leverages the DevOps principles automation, feature-driven development, and monitoring during operations to fulfill the requirements of the ISO 26262 when iteratively extending and improving safety-critical products. We present concepts and existing approaches to increase the level of automation of safety engineering tasks like safety analysis and generation of safety artifacts and we show how the management of these artifacts can be supported. Furthermore, we outline future research questions and propose a first concept to obtain quick and systematic feedback of the quality of the safety concept from the deployed products, enabling to enter the DevOps cycle from a safety point of view.

Keywords: Dependability · Agile · CD · MBSE · MBSA · FTA · FMEA

1 Introduction

Software plays an increasingly important role in safety-critical industries. In the automotive domain, this trend is referred to as *software-defined vehicle (SDV)*, meaning the customer experience is mainly shaped by software. The trend includes continuously deploying new functionality and enhancing the product, enabled by the rising level of connectivity. As a result, SDVs motivate and propel the switch to service-oriented business models in the automotive industry, which start with a minimum viable product and extend the functionality, i.e., the set of features, available to customers over time.

Continuously improving and extending a service are the motivation of DevOps development principles in the information technology (IT) industry. The DevOps principles include iterative and feature-driven development (FDD), embracing automation wherever possible, which manifests in pipelines for continuous integration (CI) and continuous deployment (CD), and monitoring the operations of the service.

© The Author(s), under exclusive license to Springer Nature Switzerland AG 2022
M. Trapp et al. (Eds.): SAFECOMP 2022 Workshops, LNCS 13415, pp. 145–157, 2022.
https://doi.org/10.1007/978-3-031-14862-0_11

However, in safety-critical industries, safety standards like the ISO 26262 [7] in the automotive domain, demand a comprehensive safety case that usually refers to a set of documents with arguments and evidence showing the product's safety, i.e., the safety artifacts. All safety artifacts must be provided before deploying a new or updated feature. In our experience updating the safety case for a bug fix of a released product can take more than 2 weeks as of today.

For safety-critical services it is not sufficient to prove that a new or updated feature is safe, even if the features is implemented only in software, since safety is an emergent property of a system [12]. Instead, safety of the entire service including hardware and mechanical parts must be analyzed and shown each time a feature is released. This might be one of the reasons why, according to our impression, the safety community has not yet embraced the DevOps principles and specifically the automation possibilities to the extent that they are embraced by the software community or in the IT industry. This leads to a friction between product owners and software engineers on the one side and safety experts on the other side. The obligation to show the safety of an entire product or service for each release is only economically feasible if the level of automation in the management of safety artifacts and in tedious, repeating, and error-prone tasks in safety engineering, i.e., safety artifact generation, is increased. This allows to safety experts to focus on safety engineering tasks that require human creativity and cannot be automated. The need for more automation is enlarged by bug fixes and security patches, which also require an updated safety case before being released.

At the same time, the operations and field monitoring concept of today's automotive products is often based on component failures that require repairs in workshops, which are then reported to the Original Equipment Manufacturer (OEM) and successively along the supply chain [4]. Given the increasing connectivity of automotive products and services, a faster and more fine-grained way to monitor and analyze the quality of the safety concept over the complete product lifetime becomes feasible. Specifically in case of autonomous driving, the safety concept itself might require such continuous monitoring to deal with an evolving operational design domain, e.g., to identify previously unknown classes of vulnerable road users like eScooters.

As a result, we argue that the requirements of safety standards like the ISO 26262 must be aligned with DevOps development principles. In this paper, we present the *SafeOps* approach that leverages the DevOps principles automation, feature-driven development, and monitoring during operations to fulfill the requirements of the ISO 26262 when iteratively extending and improving an existing safety-critical product. Our contributions are as follows:

- We show how feature-driven development can be lifted from software to system level and aligned with the requirements of safety standards like the ISO 26262.
- We map important safety engineering tasks from the ISO 26262 to the DevOps cycle and list existing approaches and concepts to automate or support these tasks.
- We describe an automated approach to track and visualize the status of safety artifacts, i.e., the results of safety engineering tasks, in a dashboard.
- We introduce research questions and an initial concept to obtain quick and systematic feedback of the quality of the safety concept from the deployed products.

2   Foundations

According to a systematic mapping study from Jabbari et al. [8], DevOps is a development methodology aimed at bridging the gap between Development (Dev) and Operations (Ops), emphasizing communication and collaboration, continuous integration, quality assurance, and delivery with automated deployment utilizing a set of development practices. The DevOps methodology or various aspects that are commonly attributed to it become increasingly relevant in the automotive domain [2].

At the same time, most of the products and services in the automotive domain are built not only from software but include hardware and mechanical parts. A malfunction of such components can cause severe harm and thus, the product or service is considered safety critical. In this paper, we use the term safety for functional safety according to established standards such as the IEC 61508 and its derivations like the ISO 26262 for the automotive industry. These safety standards condense the state of practice for building safe electrical/electronic (E/E) products. Due to the authors background and expertise, we focus on the ISO 26262 in the following, but we assume that our approach is also applicable to the other safety standards in general.

In principle, a development compliant to ISO 26262 follows the V-Model as reference process model. The standard states that "development approaches or methods from agile software development can also be suitable for the development of safety-related software [...]. However, agile approaches and methods cannot be used to omit safety measures or ignore the fundamental documentation, process or safety integrity of product rigor required for the achievement of functional safety." [7, 5.2 Note 1] At the same time, the methods recommended by the ISO 26262 to achieve the required documentation, process or safety integrity rigor do not inherently support incremental updates and extensions of a product. While future versions of safety standards might better support such kind of development, safety remains an emergent property of the system that cannot be addressed sufficiently if only new or updated features are considered [12].

3   The SafeOps Approach

In the following, we present the SafeOps approach. We focus mainly on software-implemented features, since these can be added over the complete product life cycle. However, due to its holistic nature, the SafeOps approach can also be applied for features that include new or changed hardware or mechanical components.

3.1   Prerequisites

The SafeOps approach is based on the following main building blocks:

Model-Based System Engineering (MBSE). To support an efficient engineering of safety artifacts, which will be discussed in the next section, the development needs to follow MBSE practices. Specifically, different abstraction layers are modeled in a hierarchical manner in an appropriate modeling language, e.g. System Modeling Language[1] (SysML) from the Object Management Group (OMG), potentially with different

---

[1] https://omgsysml.org/.

viewpoints on each layer, e.g. a static and dynamic view, as proposed e.g. by [17]. Lower abstraction levels such as hardware, software, or mechanics typically require domain-specific modeling languages.

Due to the safety-critical nature of the product, the MBSE also includes safety aspects to synchronize development and safety engineering. Several extensions of appropriate modeling languages have been proposed to support this, e.g., the Risk Analysis and Assessment Modeling Language[2] (RAAML) extension to SysML, the Open Dependability Exchange (ODE) Metamodel[3], and EAST-ADL[4], an architecture description language for the automotive domain.

Several software tools exist to support the modeling and analysis of safety properties based on models, e.g., ANSYS Medini Analyze[5] or ENCO SOX[6] as industrial solutions and FASTEN [19], AutoFOCUS3[7], safeTbox[8], or HiP-HOPS[9] from academia.

Traceability Information Model (TIM). A model-centric development typically improves the traceability compared to document-based development approach. However, the SafeOps approach requires a TIM to link individual development and safety artifacts beyond the typical scope of a model. For example, the TIM supports links between documents or reports, components of an abstract system models, elements of domain-specific hardware models, and individual gates and events of a Fault Tree.

The TIM is machine-readable so traces and links can automatically be followed by tools or scripts i.e., this is beyond the often-used spread sheet based traceability matrix. The TIM works across tool borders because different engineering disciplines tend to stay with their preferred software environment and tooling. While Cleland-Huang et al. [3] describe this as one of the grand challenges for ubiquitous traceability, there exist commercial traceability solutions that promise to provide efficient traceability handling and analysis across a variety of development tools, e.g. Yakindu Traceability[10] or Eclipse CAPRA[11].

Version Control System (VCS) and Continuous Integration (CI) Pipeline. A VCS like git stores the development history of all artefacts under its control. Besides the source code, for which VCSs are very common, our approach requires that all development artifacts including system, hardware and software models, the requirements, the safety artifacts, and documents are managed by the VCS. The VCS also needs to support branching, i.e., a copy of all development artifacts is created and worked on, which can later be integrated back in the original trunk it was copied from. To support the branching

---

[2] https://www.omg.org/spec/RAAML/1.0/Beta1/About-RAAML.
[3] https://github.com/DEIS-Project-EU/ODEv2.
[4] https://www.east-adl.info.
[5] https://www.ansys.com/products/safety-analysis/ansys-medini-analyze.
[6] https://www.enco-software.com/software/.
[7] https://www.fortiss.org/ergebnisse/software/autofocus-3.
[8] https://www.safetbox.de/.
[9] https://hip-hops.co.uk/.
[10] https://www.itemis.com/en/yakindu/traceability/.
[11] https://projects.eclipse.org/projects/modeling.capra.

and merging back into the original trunk, the VCS provides an overview of changes in the individual artifacts, i.e., a diff view.

A CI pipeline allows to automatically run specific scripts or tools when a new version of artifacts is added to the VCS.

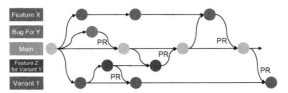

Fig. 1. A schematic overview of the different branches in a version control system (VCS). The central element is the main branch, from which feature and development branches are split. Filled circles denote updates of artifacts under version control. Once the development of a branch completes, a pull request (PR) is created to merge it back into the main branch. A variant of a product can be handled as separate branch with individual configuration and adaptions.

Feature-Driven Development (FDD). FDD means that individual functionalities are independently developed and incrementally added to a product [15]. We assume that a feature can also require changes to hardware of mechanical components, especially in early stages of the product life cycle. Furthermore, we assume that for the current version of the product, there already exists a valid and comprehensive safety case including all safety-relevant documents on the main branch of the VCS.

As shown in the schematic overview in Fig. 1, each feature is developed in an individual feature branch that originates from the main branch. Similar, bug fixes or security patches are developed in their own branches. Once the development of the feature is completed, a pull request (PR) is created to integrate the new feature into the main branch. One important aspect of the SafeOps approach is that this PR includes checking if the safety case provided by the new feature is again valid for the entire product and all relevant safety documents are available (see Sect. 3.3 for details). We recommend keeping the scope of features small and integrate them frequently back in the main branch, since in case another branch was integrated in the meanwhile, e.g., bug fix in Fig. 1, potential conflicts need to be resolved by another update from the main branch.

To support different variants of the same product, the VCS contains an additional branch for each variant, as shown in Fig. 1. New features might be developed specifically for a variant but merged into the main branch, too. The variant branch is updated from the main branch by keeping the variant-specific configuration or adaptions.

3.2 Safety Engineering Support

A schematic overview of the SafeOps approach is presented in Fig. 2. In the following, we present approaches to support or even automate the most relevant steps to fulfill the requirements of the ISO 26262 for each new feature.

Note that for each change request, the ISO 26262 requires an impact analysis describing the type of change, the affected work products, and the potential impact on functional safety. Since for each new feature, our approach considers all relevant steps in a delta mode, we argue that it includes this impact analysis.

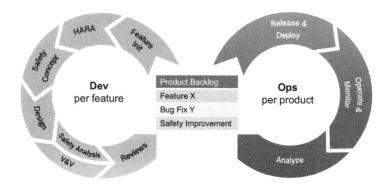

Fig. 2. A schematic overview of the SafeOps approach. The product backlog in the center lists the new features, bug fixes or safety improvements to be developed. The left *Dev* circle shows the steps to be performed during development of each feature in the given order. Safety analysis and V&V activities are performed in parallel. The right *Ops* circle shows the steps performed during product operation.

Hazard Analysis and Risk Assessment (HARA). Update the item definition and evaluate if the new feature has impact on the existing HARA. Note that both artifacts, the item definition and the HARA were copied from the main branch to the feature branch in the VCS. If the new feature introduces new hazards, at least one corresponding safety goal per hazard is defined. The new feature might also affect existing hazards. This can result in a modified Automotive Safety Integrity Level (ASIL) of existing safety goals.

Support or Automation. The analysis of the impact a new feature has on an existing HARA is an engineering task that requires human creativity and thus is very hard to automate. However, the manual analysis is supported by a knowledge database with documented experience, e.g., known hazards, situation catalogues, and safety goals, of former product versions.

Beckers et al. [1] present guide words inspired by Hazard and Operability (HAZOP) studies for the HARA. The authors propose a model-based approach using UML profiles to define the elements of the HARA and their relations. This allows to perform validation checks for the HARA, e.g., to check that every ASIL rated hazard is assigned to at least one safety goal. Zeller [23] proposes a simulation-based approach where the system and its context are simulated to identify new hazards.

Functional and Technical Safety Concept (FSC and TSC). As a prerequisite the safety goals from the HARA and requirements are known. Additionally, the new feature is represented in the functional and technical model. In case the set of safety goals or the rating of any safety goal was modified in the previous step, i.e., the HARA, update the FSC and TSC. The FSC and TSC are typically represented by safety-specific requirements at system and technical level. The FSC and TSC might also require modifications of the model, e.g., to represent an ASIL decomposition or include safety mechanisms.

Support and Automation. The derivation of a FSC and TSC is an engineering task that requires human creativity and expertise. In case new safety goals were identified, the FSC and TSC are carefully updated and the resulting additional or modified safety-specific requirements are added to the TIM. In case the rating of an existing safety goal was modified, we can leverage the TIM to automatically identify the affected safety-specific requirements. To derive and allocate safety requirements along the cause-effect chains, we recommend identifying the relevant outputs at the system level in the system model that potentially affect a safety goal. Following the cause-effect chain from these outputs in a backward direction allows to identify the relevant components and allocate safety requirements. This identification of the relevant components can be automated by scripts. Note again that the result of this automation might not be complete and human expertise is necessary to identify potential missing information in the model. Nevertheless, it ensures all obviously relevant components are included.

Verification and Validation (V&V). Depending on the ASIL of the requirement, the ISO 26262 recommends different V&V activities to be performed. We assume that these activities as well as their results are added to the VCS and part of the TIM and links to the tested requirement and the component under test in the model do exist.

Support and Automation. Some of the recommended V&V activities like requirements analysis, inspection, or error guessing based on experience are hard to automate. However, there exists many activities at different abstraction layers like fault injection, simulation, interface tests, or static code analysis that can be automated well or supported by models. The details are out of scope of this paper.

Safety Analysis. The goal of safety analysis is to show that the FSC and TSC as well as their implementation prevent faults from violating any of the safety goals. ISO 26262 recommends an inductive safety analysis, typically Failure Mode and Effects Analysis (FMEA), is performed independent of the ASIL rating and a deductive analysis (e.g. Fault Tree Analysis - FTA) for safety goals with ASIL C or D.

Support and Automation. Safety is a system property and should not be seen as composable [12]. This means that even if individual components are well-engineered and considered safe, the system assembled by these components might still violate safety goals due to unconsidered side-effects or interfaces not included in the models. At the same time, the VCS allows to generate a view that highlights the design changes compared to the previous version. This diff view supports the impact analysis to identify which safety analysis must be performed and to perform these safety analysis in *delta* mode, i.e., considering the entire system but focusing on the effects of the new feature.

Using MBSE for safety analysis this is known as Model-Based Safety Analysis (MBSA) [9] or Model-Based Dependability Analysis (MBDA) [20]. Typically, it requires that errors and their effects on the nominal behavior are incorporated in the model. Due to the updates of the model caused by the design and implementation of the new feature, MBSA and MBDA naturally support safety analysis in delta mode. Note that some of the following approaches are implemented in tools mentioned in Sect. 3.1.

Regarding FTA, Kaiser et al. [10, 11] present the concept of Component Fault Trees (CFTs), where components of the architecture model are annotated with their fault propagation behavior in an FTA-like manner. In the past we have shown that the concept of CFTs can be applied in the automotive domain as well [13]. When a new feature is added, the CFTs of the affected or additional components are checked and updated if necessary. Afterwards, the CI pipeline automatically builds the fault tree of each safety goal from the CFTs, computes the Minimal Cut Sets (MCSs), and stores the results in the VCS. This allows to generate a diff view of the MCSs with the new feature.

Regarding the FMEA we propose to use the static view of the MBSE models to generate the FMEA structure tree. Based on the dynamic view and the linked requirements, suggestions for the FMEA function network can be generated. Since the fault propagation is also contained in the model, e.g., in CFTs, suggestions for the FMEA failure network can be generated as well. However, to identify the complete set of errors the deductive nature of the FTA and the inductive nature of the FMEA must be considered. Hence, it is important that the generated failure network should be considered only as a suggestion. Finally, the CI pipeline automatically generates the FMEA spread sheet. The inputs to determine the risk priority number (RPN) and suitable safety measures must be manually provided by safety experts, as this is an engineering task. Papadopoulos et al. [16] extend Matlab Simulink models with safety-relevant information such as faults, failures, and hazards, to synthesize FMEA spreadsheets.

The goal of the DFA is to ensure a sufficiently high independence is achieved where required, e.g., between the nominal function and a checking function or between the corresponding components of all basic events in one cut set. In previous work, we proposed to leverage the models to suggest coupling factors, e.g., shared resource or components of identical type, and dependent failure initiators (DFIs) [14]. Since the models typically do not contain all relevant information for a complete DFA, the suggestions are checked and completed by safety experts. The manual input is then stored together with the model in such a way, that it is included in the suggestions the next time they are generated. This approach results in an DFA in delta mode and the diff view of the suggested DFA entries supports the safety experts to identify the effects the new feature has on the entire product.

Sari and Reuss [18] have shown how the DFA can be supported by EAST-ADL models. The authors propose various consistency checks at different levels of abstraction to analyze the correct ASIL decomposition. The focus lies on the analysis of the system architecture, based on the assumption that the hardware components are in fact sufficiently independent.

Confirmation Reviews. According to the ISO26262, all changes made to safety artifacts, including the HARA, FSC/TSC, V&V activities, safety analysis, and the safety case itself must be verified by appropriate confirmation reviews.

Support and Automation. The diff views generated by the CI pipeline allows reviewers to focus on changes and thus support an efficient confirmation process.

Release and Deployment. Once the feature is implemented and the safety artifacts are updated and reviewed, the feature branch is ready to be integrated into the main branch. Since all safety artifacts were updated in delta mode, they already consider the entire product. As a result, there always is a complete and consistent safety case of the entire product available on the main branch. Hence, the main branch is ready to be released and deployed, the details of which are outside the scope of this paper.

Artifact	Status	Review
HARA	done	done
FSC	done	in progress
TSC	done	in progress
FTA	in work	to do
FMEA	in work	to do
DFA	to do	to do
Test Specification	done	in progress
Test Results	95% pass	n.a.

Fig. 3. An exemplary overview of the SafeOps Dashboard indicating the status of the different safety artifacts and their reviews. The status of test results reflects the test outcome.

3.3 Safety Management Dashboard

To support an overview of the current state of the safety engineering artifacts during the development, we leverage the VCS and the CI pipeline. Every pull request triggers the following automated checks and presents the results in the *SafeOps Dashboard*. Optionally, the dashboard can be updated after every commit to provide the safety experts, feature owner, and engineers quick feedback on state of the safety-relevant development aspects. The SafeOps Dashboard lists all safety artifacts and presents their state in a color scheme: red means work on the artifact has not been started (to do), yellow means the work on the artifact is ongoing (in progress), and green means the work on the artifact is finished (done), as shown exemplary in Fig. 3. When all safety artifacts are in state green, the safety case is considered complete. We propose that only in case all safety artifacts are green, the pull request to the main branch is accepted. Note that the SafeOps Dashboard can present results of consistency checks on the TIM, e.g., that for each safety goal there exists at least one safety requirement or that all safety specific requirements are linked to at least one component in the model.

Initially, when a new branch is created, all safety artifacts are set to red state. When an artifact is modified, which is recognized by the VCS, its state is set to yellow. For most safety artifacts it is very hard to automatically determine if the work on them is finished. We leverage the fact that the ISO 26262 requires confirmation reviews for safety artifacts. Hence, whenever a review document is created for a safety-relevant artifact, the state of the artifact is set to green and the state of the review document itself is set to yellow. Note that the link between the artifact and the review is part of the TIM.

The SafeOps Dashboard also tracks V&V activities. Test specification is set to green only if all safety requirements are linked by at least one test specification and the specification was reviewed. Additionally, it reports test results and coverage metrics.

The ISO 26262 defines the safety plan as a document to manage and guide the execution of the safety activities including tasks and deliverables. Hence, our approach can be considered as an automated update of the safety plan, in other words safety management automation. Note that the SafeOps Dashboard can be applied outside the scope of the ISO 26262 as well, by tracking the state of the evidences used in the safety case.

3.4 Data-Driven Safety

The ISO 26262 requires that a "field monitoring process for potential safety-related incidents related to the item or its elements shall be implemented". We propose to leverage the connectivity of today's automotive products to perform this field monitoring in a fine grained, systematic, and fast way as compared to relying on workshops reporting failures in vehicle components to OEMs, which then forward these reports along the supply chain. When presented well, this feedback from products in the field supports safety experts to continuously improve the safety concept of the product and thus, enter the DevOps cycle from a safety point of view, as shown in Fig. 2.

The safety concept typically contains safety mechanisms that monitor or limit individual signals or parameters in the product. Whenever such a safety mechanism is triggered in the field, a set of relevant parameters is collected and sent to a backend. The set of the parameters is defined by safety experts during the design of the safety concept and should support the analysis of the situation in which the safety mechanism was triggered. The data is aggregated in the backend and visualized in an extension of the SafeOps Dashboard. For example, the number of times a safety mechanism was triggered is visualized by different colors of the respective components in the model.

The Data-Driven Safety Part requires further research, e.g., deriving concepts to monitor cases where errors were not detected but a safety goal was violated, identifying relevant parameters to be recorded, analyzing the correlation and causality in the collected data, especially with respect to metrics that focus on performance limitations or safety of the intended functionality (SOTIF) aspects like critical corner cases, and representing the gathered insights to the safety experts in ways to best support their work.

4 Related Work

Several authors have worked on the integration of safety specific aspects in agile or iterative development. However, only few have specifically considered combining safety with DevOps principles.

Siddique [21] presents the SafetyOps framework based on principles like interchangeable data between tools of the different disciplines and open application programmable interfaces (APIs). Vöst and Wagner [22] propose four main principles to keep continuous builds safe with main focus on safety test case generation from safety analysis artifacts. Zeller [23] presents an overview of model-based methods to enable CD considering all phases of the safety engineering life cycle. While the Dev part of the SafeOps approach is based on the previous works, our focus on the ISO 26262 allows us to provide more details with respect to the individual steps.

Fayollas et al. [4] present a concept called SafeOps, too, and focus lies on a field data monitoring for autonomous functions to either get more confidence during operation or to improve the assurance level. Gautham et al. [5] present a model-based approach to generate runtime monitors from design verification requirements of the IEC 61508. Heffernan et al. [6] present an approach to map safety requirements to logic formulae, which allows to generate runtime monitors operating in vehicles. This approach is well aligned with today's DevOps principles. While the authors conclude that "the challenge lies in the development of closed-loop reactive schemes for real-time fault protection", we argue that the derivation of fault protection schemes is an engineering task that requires human creativity, so systematic feedback on the quality of the safety case needs to be presented to the safety experts to improve the safety concept.

5 Conclusion and Future Work

We presented the SafeOps approach combining DevOps principles with safety, specifically the ISO 26262. Our approach is based on FDD and MBSE and requires a TIM, a VCS and a CI/CD pipeline. Safety is a system property that cannot be addressed sufficiently at component level. Thus, our approach keeps the safety case and all safety artifacts of the entire product on the main branch. New features are developed in separate branches and inherit a copy of all safety artifacts. We went through the most relevant steps of the ISO 26262 and presented concepts and existing approaches to increase the level of automation to support updating the safety artifacts to include the new feature, i.e., in delta mode. To support the management of the safety artifacts, we presented SafeOps Dashboards that automatically tracks the status of the safety artifacts. This way, engineers are better aware of safety tasks, which should help to reduce friction between the disciplines. In addition, the SafeOps approach ensures that the main branch is always ready to be released and there are no safety tasks blocking a frequent release cycle. Our first concept for data-driven safety demonstrates how field monitoring and connectivity can be used to obtain feedback on the quality of the safety concept. While the presented concept requires further research, it shows how to enter the DevOps cycle from a safety point of view and continuously improve the safety concept.

As future work, we will further research data-driven safety aspects mentioned in Sect. 3.4 and we plan to apply our SafeOps approach in a real product development, which might require tool qualification according to ISO 26262. Due to the rising level of connectivity, the scope of future safety-critical products might include parts that are executed in the cloud. The development of such systems requires expertise from the IT domain and the embedded domain, so we plan to investigate how development methods like SafeOps help to bring these domains together.

References

1. Beckers, K., Heisel, M., Frese, T., Hatebur, D.: A structured and model-based hazard analysis and risk assessment method for automotive systems–a disruptive study. In: Reliability Engineering & System Safety, vol. 158, pp. 185–195 (2017)
2. Belagatti, P.: The scene of DevOps in the automotive industry (2020). https://dzone.com/art icles/the-scene-of-devops-in-the-automotive-industry. Accessed 13 Apr 2022
3. Cleland-Huang, J., Gotel, O.C., Huffman Hayes, J., Mäder, P., Zisman, A.: Software traceability: trends and future directions. In: Proceedings of the Future of Software Engineering, pp. 55–69 (2014)
4. Fayollas, C., Bonnin, H., Flebus, O.: SafeOps: a concept of continuous safety. In: Proceedings of the EDCC (2020)
5. Gautham, S., Jayakumar, A., Rajagopala, A., Elks, C.: Realization of a model-based DevOps process for industrial safety critical cyber physical systems. In: Proceedings of the ICPS (2021)
6. Heffernan, D., MacNamee, C., Fogarty, P.: Runtime verification monitoring for automotive embedded systems using the ISO 26262 Functional Safety Standard as a guide for the definition of the monitored properties. IET Softw. **8**, 193–203 (2014)
7. International Organization for Standardization (ISO). ISO 26262: Road vehicles—functional safety (2018)
8. Jabbari, R., Ali, N., Petersen, K., Tanveer, B.: What is DevOps? A systematic mapping study on definitions and practices. In: Proceedings of the Workshop of XP (2016)
9. Joshi, A., Miller, S., Whalen, M., Heimdahl, M.: A proposal for model-based safety analysis. In: Proceedings of the DASC (2005)
10. Kaiser, B., Liggesmeyer, P., Mäckel, O.: A new component concept for fault trees. In: Lindsay, P., Cant, T. (eds.) Proceedings of the Workshop on Safety Critical Systems and Software (2003)
11. Kaiser, B., et al.: Advances in component fault trees. In: Proceedings of the ESREL (2018)
12. Leveson, N.: Engineering a Safer World - Systems Thinking Applied to Safety. MIT Press (2012)
13. Munk, P., Nordmann, A.: Model-based safety assessment with SysML and component fault trees: application and lessons learned. Softw. Syst. Model. **19**(4), 889–910 (2020). https://doi.org/10.1007/s10270-020-00782-w
14. Munk, P., Schweizer, M., Schneider, D., Adler, R., Velasco, S.: Model-based dependent failure analysis (2021). https://safetronic.fraunhofer.de/wp-content/uploads/2021/11/Safetronic21-ModelBased-DFA-Munk.pdf. Accessed 29 Apr 2022
15. Palmer, S., Felsing, J.: A Practical Guide to Feature-Driven Development. Prentice Hall (2002)
16. Papadopoulos, Y., McDermid, J., Sasse, R., Heiner, G.: Analysis and synthesis of the behaviour of complex programmable electronic systems in conditions of failure. Reliab. Eng. Syst. Saf. **71**, 229–247 (2001)
17. Pohl, K., Hönninger, H., Achatz, R., Broy, M.: Model-Based Engineering of Embedded Systems: The SPES 2020 Methodology. Springer, Heidelberg (2012). https://doi.org/10.1007/978-3-642-34614-9
18. Sari, B., Reuss, H.: A model-driven approach for dependent failure analysis in consideration of multicore processors using modified EAST-ADL. SAE Technical Paper (2017)
19. Ratiu, D., Nordmann, A., Munk, P., Carlan, C., Voelter, M.: FASTEN: an extensible platform to experiment with rigorous modeling of safety-critical systems. In: Bucchiarone, A., Cicchetti, A., Ciccozzi, F., Pierantonio, A. (eds) Domain-Specific Languages in Practice. Springer, Cham (2021). https://doi.org/10.1007/978-3-030-73758-0_5
20. Sharvia, S., Kabir, S., Walker, M., Papadopoulos, Y: Model-based dependability analysis: state-of-the-art, challenges, and future outlook. In: Mistrik, I., Soley, R., Ali, N., Grundy, J., Tekinerdogan, B. (eds.) Software Quality Assurance, Morgan Kaufmann (2016)

21. Siddique, U.: SafetyOps (2020). https://doi.org/10.48550/arXiv.2008.04461. Accessed 5 Feb 2022
22. Vöst, S., Wagner, S.: Keeping continuous deliveries safe. In: Proceedings of the ICSE-C (2017)
23. Zeller, M.: Towards continuous safety assessment in context of DevOps. In: Habli, I., Sujan, M., Gerasimou, S., Schoitsch, E., Bitsch, F. (eds.) SAFECOMP 2021. LNCS, vol. 12853, pp. 145–157. Springer, Cham (2021). https://doi.org/10.1007/978-3-030-83906-2_11

Dynamic Checks of Evidence Models for Assurance Projects in Eclipse OpenCert

Jabier Martinez[1]([✉]) and Ángel Jesús Varela-Vaca[2]

[1] Tecnalia, Basque Research and Technology Alliance (BRTA), Derio, Spain
jabier.martinez@tecnalia.com
[2] IDEA Research Group, University of Seville, Seville, Spain
ajvarela@us.es

Abstract. The modelling of regulatory frameworks and industry standards, including their argumentation and expected evidence, are used during assurance processes to demonstrate the compliance of systems. However, this is handled mainly in a static fashion, and using these models for dynamic evidence checking along the system life-cycle, including operation (checking the model at runtime), is not yet mainstream. This preliminary work shows a tool-supported modelling method for the automatic and dynamic evaluation of evidence. The solution is supported by an Eclipse OpenCert tool extension where the capabilities of evidence models are extended with automatic checks. The user monitoring the assurance project receives alerts when evidence are unsatisfied. It also exports a continuous log of these checks using the XES standard to enable traceability and historical creation of passing and failing checks for analysis and auditing purposes. While some evidence checks are generic, the diversity of checking processes required our solution to be extensible.

Keywords: Safety · Security · Reference frameworks · Dynamic check

1 Introduction

Reference frameworks for systems engineering, such as safety or security regulations, standards, industrial guidelines, or even in-house guidelines, represent a reasonable way to build trust in systems and have confidence in the process of their construction. To make explicit or to audit the compliance to a certain reference framework, assurance projects are conducted. An assurance case is a structured argument supported by a body of evidence, which provides a convincing and valid justification that a system meets its assurance requirements for a given application in a given operating environment [4]. Dynamic evidence checks can be useful for **processes** (e.g., organisational or engineering processes) with the need for continuous checking that the process is followed as established and the expected assets are produced and checked for validity. One specific type of

M. Trapp et al. (Eds.): SAFECOMP 2022 Workshops, LNCS 13415, pp. 158–165, 2022.
https://doi.org/10.1007/978-3-031-14862-0_12

process is **systems during operation** (e.g., self-adaptive systems) that need to demonstrate or validate correct functioning at runtime.

On the left side of Fig. 1, we illustrate an overview of assurance consisting of three layers. The reference frameworks provides guidance for assurance projects which, at the same time, provide guidance for the systems engineering itself, e.g., the creation of system assets and their characteristics, the verification and validation (V&V), or concrete activities to follow in the organization. The systems engineering project assets are intended to provide traceable evidences to fulfil the assurance needs, and consequently, the compliance to reference frameworks. On the right side of the figure we illustrate the modelling solution proposed in Eclipse OpenCert [6] as a tool for assurance management. Reference frameworks are modelled through the Common Assurance and Certification Metamodel (CACM) [11] with concepts such as requirements, activities, artefacts, roles, levels, and a large set of elements expressive enough to capture diverse reference frameworks. Then, for the assurance layer, two types of models are key, namely assurance case models, and evidence models. Assurance case models uses the Goal Structuring Notation (GSN) [7] and it is similar to the elements proposed in the Structured Assurance Case Metamodel (SACM) [10] such as claims, argumentation, evidences. The evidence models is another part of the CACM to capture the life-cycle of the evidences and more technical details about the evidences than in the assurance cases models. Finally, in the project assets, given the diverse nature and technological stack of each project, we have the actual assets of the systems engineering activities.

Traceability means are possible through the mapping models provided by the tool, and for the case of evidence models and the actual project assets, Uniform Resource Identifiers (URI) are used as attributes in the evidence model elements.

In the scope of this work, we focus on the part inside the square of Fig. 1. The concrete implementation in Eclipse OpenCert of this high-level picture is considered an iterative process where the assurance cases are built and the assurance is managed across the life-cycle. We make the following contributions:

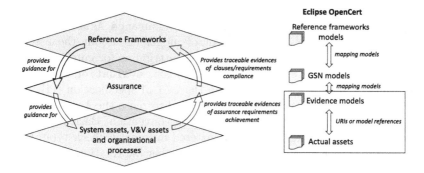

Fig. 1. Overview of reference frameworks, assurance, and project assets, with the corresponding models or expected project assets in Eclipse OpenCert.

– **Evidence checks:** The traceability information of evidence models to actual assets is enriched with an extensible method for their validation. That means that traces are not just pointers anymore, but also a way to automatically check that the pointed elements are valid. As basic example, an evidence can actually point to a file, but the file can be empty or incomplete with respect to the expected content.
– **Dynamic evidence checks:** The automation of evidence checks opens the door for a continuous validation of the evidence models. Our preliminary implementation allows to schedule validations, receive alerts for the user monitoring the assurance project, and exporting a continuous log.
– **Research results availability:** The tool extension is publicly available[1] to make this research reproducible and allow others to build on top of it.

The paper is organised as follows. The approach is detailed in Sect. 2, and the related work is presented in Sect. 3. Finally, a conclusion is drawn and perspectives are outlined in Sect. 4.

2   Approach

Section 2.1 provides technical details about how we integrated automatic evidence checks in the tool, how it is extensible, and it also presents some available generic checks that can be already used. Then, Sect. 2.2 presents how we included this functionality as part of a dynamic evidence checking loop, including the generation of logs.

2.1   Extensible Evidence Checks

Figure 2 shows an illustrative example of an evidence model. An `Artefact Model` contains `Artefact Definitions` with their corresponding `Artefacts` with its version, creation date etc. An `Artefact` can have several `Resources` where one of the attributes is the location. In this attribute, an URI is expected pointing to the actual resource. An `Artefact` can contain `Assurance Asset Evaluations` which semantics refer to any assessment of judgement about the asset. This way, each `Assurance Asset Evaluation` has attributes for entering free plain text named `criterion`, `criterion description`, `evaluation results`, and the `rationale`. Metamodel details are in the CACM specification [11].

Instead of modifying the CACM, we decided to reuse the `Assurance Asset Evaluation` concept defining a tool-supported convention. Basically, when the `criterion` match the identifier of a registered automatic check type, the tool will be able to launch an automatic check. If further information is needed (e.g., parameters), they will be obtained from the `criterion description`.

---

[1] Plugin org.cclipse.opencert.evidence.check at https://gitlab.eclipse.org/eclipse/opencert/opencert/-/tree/release/2.0.

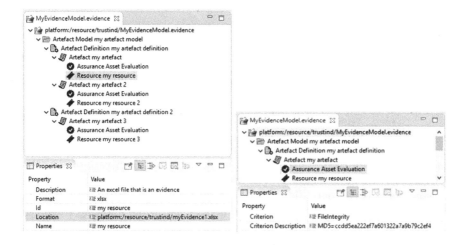

Fig. 2. Example of evidence model.

Eclipse OpenCert was enriched with an extension point to register automatic checks. The interface to be implemented is quite simple but allows complex operations. The method to implement just receive the `Assurance Asset Evaluation` element as input, and this allow to access the `Resource` and its URI, and the `criterion description` if needed. The user of the tool can, on demand, select and launch the evaluation or a set of evaluations.

Implemented checks: The checks can be extremely diverse. That is way extensibility was mandatory. However, a couple of predefined check are included by default: *FileExists*: Used to check that an asset that was considered finished actually exists. In a runtime context, it can be used to check that certain file did not disappear. The URI of the `Resource` is resolved (e.g., URIs using the protocols `file:/` or `platform:/resource/`) and it checks that the file exists. *FileIntegrity*: The monitoring of file integrity is a typical process in security

management where certain relevant files (e.g., access control information files, security or system configuration files) are checked against malicious or unintentional modifications. Different hashing algorithms can be used with the content of a file. Java includes MD5, SHA-1, SHA-256 and many others depending on the Java version. There are three ways to use this check type. 1) Using only the id without anything on the description will calculate the hash in the first check, and this hash will be used in all the subsequent checks. Default algorithm is SHA-256. 2) Specifying the hashing algorithm in the description (e.g., MD5, SHA-384). 3) Specifying both the hashing algorithm and the concrete expected hash (e.g., MD5=ccdd5ea222ef7a601322a7a9b79c2ef4). This is preferred to avoid that the integrity of the file was not respected in the first check.

Fig. 3. Artefact model with the toggle button (icon in the upper left corner) for dynamic evidence checking.

2.2 Dynamic Evidence Checks and Log Streaming

Figure 3 shows the toggle button available in the tool to activate or deactivate the dynamic evidence checks of the evidence model. Certain parameters are requested such as the periodicity of the checking and if a continuous log wants to be exported. The background process is launched while allowing to continue using the tool. However, the user is notified when any evidence check fails. Failing a check does not stop the process as the failing messages are included and accumulated in a status window.

The logs are exported in XES (1849-2016 IEEE Standard for eXtensible Event Stream)[2] using the OpenXES library. An example is shown in Listing 1.1. Each check is streamed as an `<event>` with information such as the id of the evaluation, whether it was satisfied, and the timestamp. Each complete validation of the evidence model is contained within a `<trace>`.

Listing 1.1. Example of XES from dynamic evidence checks

```xml
<?xml version="1.0" encoding="utf-8"?>
<log xes.version="1.0" xes.features="nested-attributes" openxes.version="1.0RC7">
        <extension name="Time" prefix="time" uri="http://www.xes-standard.org/time.xesext"/>
        <extension name="Concept" prefix="concept" uri="http://www.xes-standard.org/concept.xesext"/>
        <string key="concept:name" value="Evidence model ID: null Name: my artefact model"/>
        <trace>
                <string key="concept:name" value="instance_0"/>
                <event>
                        <string key="criterion" value="FileIntegrity"/>
                        <boolean key="check" value="true"/>
                        <string key="concept:name" value="Evaluation ID: integrity Name: integrity"/>
                        <date key="time:timestamp" value="2021-09-28T16:04:17.933+02:00"/>
                </event>
                <event>
                    ... more individual checks
                </event>
        </trace>
        <trace>
            ... more complete set of checks of the evidence model
        </trace>
</log>
```

3   Related Work

The system assurance is demonstrated as a crucial discipline for industrial sectors [13] specially in certification for safety-critical systems. Dynamic assurance cases [3,5] were described as one way to enable proactive assurance management. Dynamic safety assurance have been applied in multiple industrial contexts such

---

[2] https://xes-standard.org/ and https://www.xes-standard.org/openxes/start.

as autonomous systems [1,8], software-intensive systems [14], and embedded systems [9]. These approaches focused on theoretical or conceptual approaches by incorporating components to feed (back), improve or empower the assurance cases, e.g., machine learning components to analyse the operation of real systems. However, other approaches deal with dynamic assurance by continuous assessment, e.g., in software-intensive systems [14]. Most approaches contributed on the level of assurance and evidence models, i.e., GSN and evidence models (e.g., [1,3–5]), while our focus is on the validation of the evidence models against the actual evidence artefacts. Contrary to conceptual frameworks or industrial tools that might cover to some extent what we propose, we focused on the technical aspects to provide a publicly available tool focused on automatic and dynamic checks.

4   Conclusion and Perspectives

Eclipse OpenCert is a tool for assurance management. In this work, the tool has been extended to automate the validation of evidences, and to enable a dynamic validation at runtime. This preliminary study does not intend to demonstrate high conclusions but some goals and achievements in supporting some aspects. In this respect, the tool presented focused on demonstrating the integration of dynamic evidence checks on the Eclipse OpenCert tool following reference frameworks supporting the metamodels of CACM [11].

The future work and perspectives opened by this preliminary work include:

Correctness and validation: The preliminary implementation is functional and available but its design and implementation could be refined, i.e., through automatic tests simulating runtime processes beyond the manual testing we conducted so far, and a real system assurance case with configuration management problematic of many evidences coming from several components.

Further support for context-awareness: We mitigated the complexity in the diversity of systems engineering projects by making the approach extensible with regard to check types. However, the tool only allows to schedule the checks with a user-defined frequency. It can be envisioned that the tool should also be extensible for allowing another kind of context events (e.g., changes in specific assets) to automatically trigger the checks. Regarding the logs, the XES information can end up in large files after a large amount of time. For the moment, it is expected that other tools consume the XES and handle the stream.

Handling the implications of evidence checks: The tool support does not cover important aspects, such as how to respond to the failing checks (e.g., corrective actions) or which are the implications at higher levels. For instance, impact analysis could be performed to identify which argumentations at the assurance case level do not hold any more. Notably, our approach can help to identify rebutting defeaters (an evidence contradicting a claim), thus potentially contributing in the process of dialectic argumentation [2,12]. In this process, the objective will be to defeat the defeater through further argumentation so as to maintain the assurance case in a valid state. At even higher level, impact analysis can be performed at reference framework level, i.e., which parts of the reference framework is respected, and which are not because of the missing or incorrect evidence. In this sense, the approach can be extended to contribute to checkpointed safety cases for submission to regulators. Currently, the XES logs work directly at evidence model level, but not at higher levels.

Handling valid checks that are actually invalid: Our current approach does not consider evidences that might appear valid through the automatic check, but they are not. For instance, the environment might have changed causing the case to become invalid, or malicious actors can change an actual evidence artefact to promote false confidence that the system is safe when it actually is not. Dialectic argumentation to refine the assurance case (and the evidence model) seems to be a possible solution to alleviate these problems.

Acknowledgment. Jabier Martinez was supported by the TRUSTIND project (Creating Trust in the Industrial Digital Transformation), an Elkartek project funded by the Basque Government. The work of Angel J. Varela-Vaca has been funded by the projects COPERNICA (P20_01224), AETHER-US (PID2020-112540RB-C44/AEI/ 10. 13039 / 501100011033), and METAMORFOSIS (US 1381375). We would like to thank the anonymous reviewers for their valuable feedback.

References

1. Asaadi, E., Denney, E., Menzies, J., Pai, G.J., Petroff, D.: Dynamic assurance cases: a pathway to trusted autonomy. Computer **53**(12), 35–46 (2020)
2. Bloomfield, R., Rushby, J.: Assurance 2.0: a manifesto. In: Parsons, M., Nicholson, M. (eds.) Systems and Covid-19: Proceedings of the 29th Safety-Critical Systems Symposium (SSS 2021), pp. 85–108. Safety-Critical Systems Club, York, UK, final draft available as arXiv preprint arXiv:2004.10474 (2021)
3. Calinescu, R., Weyns, D., Gerasimou, S., Iftikhar, M.U., Habli, I., Kelly, T.: Engineering trustworthy self-adaptive software with dynamic assurance cases. IEEE Trans. Softw. Eng. **44**(11), 1039–1069 (2018)
4. Denney, E., Pai, G., Whiteside, I.: Hierarchical safety cases. In: Brat, G., Rungta, N., Venet, A. (eds.) NFM 2013. LNCS, vol. 7871, pp. 478–483. Springer, Heidelberg (2013). https://doi.org/10.1007/978-3-642-38088-4_37
5. Denney, E., Pai, G.J., Habli, I.: Dynamic safety cases for through-life safety assurance. In: ICSE 2015, pp. 587–590. IEEE Computer Society (2015)
6. Eclipse: Opencert platform (2022). https://www.eclipse.org/opencert
7. Goal Structuring Notation Standard Working Group: Goal Structuring Notation (2021). https://scsc.uk/gsn
8. McDermid, J.A., Jia, Y., Habli, I.: Towards a framework for safety assurance of autonomous systems. In: Artificial Intelligence Safety (2019)
9. Moncada, D.S.V., et al.: Dynamic safety certification for collaborative embedded systems at runtime. In: Model-Based Engineering of Collaborative Embedded Systems, pp. 171–196. Springer, Cham (2021). https://doi.org/10.1007/978-3-030-62136-0_8
10. OMG: Structured Assurance Case Metamodel (2017). https://www.omg.org/spec/SACM

11. Ruiz, A., et al.: AMASS platform validation, D2.9 (2019). https://www.amass-ecsel.eu/sites/amass.drupal.pulsartecnalia.com/files/D2.9_AMASS-platform-validation_AMASS_Final.pdf
12. The Assurance Case Working Group (ACWG): Assurance case guidance: challenges, common issues and good practice v1 (2021). https://scsc.uk/r159:1
13. Virvou, M., Matsuura, S.: Toward dynamic assurance cases. In: Knowledge-Based Software Engineering: Proceedings of the Tenth Joint Conference on Knowledge-Based Software Engineering, vol. 240 (2012)
14. Zeller, M.: Towards continuous safety assessment in context of DevOps. In: Habli, I., Sujan, M., Gerasimou, S., Schoitsch, E., Bitsch, F. (eds.) SAFECOMP 2021. LNCS, vol. 12853, pp. 145–157. Springer, Cham (2021). https://doi.org/10.1007/978-3-030-83906-2_11

An Approach for Deriving Reduced Collision Scenarios for Highly Automated Driving Systems

Marzana Khatun[1]([envelope])[ORCID], Heinrich Litagin[1], Rolf Jung[1], and Michael Glaß[2]

[1] University of Applied Sciences Kempten, Bahnhofstraße 61, 87435 Kempten, Germany
{marzana.khatun,heinrich.litagin,rolf.jung}@hs-kempten.de
[2] University of Ulm, Helmholtzstraße 16, 89081 Ulm, Germany
michael.glass@uni-ulm.de

Abstract. Scenario analysis is essential for the validation of highly automated driving (HAD) systems. The complexity of overall system safety is increasing in terms of Functional Safety (FuSa) and Safety of Intended Functionality (SOTIF). However, field testing of all possible safety-critical scenarios is hardly possible for automated vehicles. Therefore, scenario simulation is necessary for HAD to support the validation process and has gained acceptance in recent years. However, scenario-based analysis leads to an explosion of scenarios, so a scenario database is required at the beginning of the development phase. Hence, scenario reduction approaches need to be integrated in the conceptual phase to reduce the scenario modeling and testing effort. The contribution of this paper is to present simulation-based testing approaches for determining a reduced set of collision scenarios, taking into account the sensitivity of safety-critical parameters. Furthermore, a set of application scenarios is simulated to demonstrate the scenario reduction approaches by considering the detected collisions under a specific or restricted Operational Design Domain (ODD). In addition, this study supports the provision of a safety argument with evidence by introducing a variance-based sensitivity analysis and a scenario database that can be used as an input data set for an artificial intelligence system.

Keywords: HAD · FuSa · LC · Parameter variation · CarMaker

1 Introduction

Highly automated vehicles are expected to increase road safety and reduce the number of road accidents. The development of new techniques and methods for assistance systems with more capabilities and better performance is necessary to ensure the safety of automated vehicles. Nowadays, drivers must be able to take

Supported by organization IFM – Institut für Fahrerassistenz und vernetzte Mobilität.

control of driving tasks in various situations. According to the Society of Automotive Engineers (SAE) J3016, the level of automation is defined in six levels, ranging from level 0 (no automation of driving) to level 5 (full automation of driving) [1]. In the updated taxonomy, the levels are divided into two main areas [2] Level 0 - Level 2 are "driver support functions" where the driver is assumed to be active all the time while the vehicle is in operation, and Level 3 - Level 5 are "automated driving functions" where the driver is not heavily involved while the vehicle is in operation [2,3]. In this paper, Highly Automated Driving (HAD) systems are considered as partially and/or fully automated driving functions of a vehicle, such as a ego vehicle with automated lane change maneuver.

A study has shown that $ 594 billion lost in lives and injuries [4] and accident statistics are recorded as Road-Traffic Accident data German In-depth Accident Study (GIDAS), National Highway Traffic Safety Administration (NHTSA), the International Road Traffic and Accident Database (IRTAD) and others [5]. According to Thomas [5], *the GIDAS estimation for increased automation, accident can be reduced of 19 % by 2030, 23% by 2040, 50 % by 2050, 71 % by 2060 and almost total prevention by 2070.* However, the databases themselves are not freely accessible in detail for research purposes. Despite the challenges of accessing detailed accident databases, there are other challenges, such as the explosion of test scenarios that include vehicle parameters and environmental aspects, including SOTIF. The need for security becomes unavoidable in HAD systems due to the trustworthiness and/or performance of such systems, which can be measured by reliability analysis. Various methods such as statistics, Monte Carlo experiments, hazard analysis, and failure analysis are used for reliability estimation. For SAE Level 2 vehicles, safety methods and processes are specified in ISO 26262 (FuSa) [6] and SOTIF [7] to deal with unreasonable risks applicable in the automotive industry. The HAD systems applicable to SAE Level 3 or higher level of automation that indicate the modification, change or adaptation of the methods available and require new technologies such as artificial intelligence to make driving-related decisions. Consequently, unreasonable risks must be avoided when driving, whereby not only the human driver but also vehicle systems are responsible for reducing or preventing hazards. Therefore, HAD systems need to address the newly introduced systematic way to ensure the overall safety of automated vehicles.

Reducing the risk of collision is only possible if the vehicle performance is improved and the safety of the vehicle functions and features is ensured. For this reason, simulation-based tests using parameter variations are performed in the logical scenarios phase and shown in this study to determine the safety-critical vehicle parameters and/or combination of parameters. First, a series of pretest scenarios are simulated to determine the ranges of each safety-critical parameter with respect to collision detection. Second, a series of posttest scenarios with reduced parameter space on the safety-critical parameters including the sensitivity analysis. The variance-based sensitivity is investigated to determine the influences of the input parameters that have the potential to cause a collision.

For sensitivity analysis, a specific use case scenario as lane change maneuver on highway is investigated.

The remainder of this paper is presented as follows. Section 2 describes the currently available normative references and understanding of HAD automation level with scenario modeling and simulation. Later, in the Sect. 3, scenarios are described in a layer-based style and logical scenarios are simulated in tools such as CarMaker. Scenario reduction approaches including scenario description and modeling are presented in this section. Several application scenarios with parameter variation through collision detection are simulated to support the validation of the HAD systems. For further investigation, a set of parameters is examined for a variance-based sensitivity analysis. The sensitivity analysis result is based on collision detection for a specific application scenario with a constrained ODD. Finally, Sect. 4 summarizes the results and describes further work to strengthen the safety concept of HAD systems.

2   State-of-Art and Science

2.1   Standards and Regulations

Automated driving is expected to improve vehicle performance in most situations compared to conventional drivers. However, the complete avoidance of accidents or collisions remains a problem in the development of ADS safety. Avoiding unreasonable risks is an important measure for achieving an acceptable level of safety. Evidence is based on the use of proactive and reactive driving behaviors, avoidance of collisions to the extent practical while maintaining reasonable safety, and avoidance of discrimination based on road user-related characteristics. These assessments are typically made based on a combination of qualitative and quantitative evaluations (e.g. HARA, TARA, FMEA) as well as based on good engineering practices and existing standards such as SAE J3016 (Taxonomy and definitions) [1], ISO 26262 (FuSa) [6], ISO/PAS 21448 (SOTIF) [7], ISO/TR 4804 (Safety and cybersecurity for automated driving systems) [8]. It can be argued that the application of existing standards (applicable up to SAE L2) and engineering techniques and methods will lead to safer autonomous products. However, the currently available safety-related standards and research projects [9–11] are considered as the basis for safe automated driving.

2.2   Highly Automated Driving System

While the new techniques and methods for automated driving have been demonstrated in various research projects, there are complaints about the difficulties in achieving SAE Level 3 or higher automation safety. Currently, FuSa and SOTIF standards are applicable up to SAE automation level 2. However, to reduce the misunderstanding of automation levels, ADS is defined as *set of elements that provide a specific conditional or higher use case of automated driving in or for a specific vehicle* [8]. In addition, automated vehicle (AV) is expressed as *vehicle equipped with at least one conditional (SAE Level 3) or higher (SAE Level*

4/Level 5) automated driving system [8]. The introduction of the new assistance systems is about increasingly complex systems with different functions and scenarios to achieve SAE Level 3.

A holistic approach requires a range of different scenarios with accident probabilities based on road type, vehicle dynamics and environmental conditions. Thus, the accident data is the first measure for selecting the scenarios. Author Alexander [13] mentions, *in the vehicle development process, virtual validation and scenario-based testing will play an even greater role than before* [13]. In addition, the author of [14,15] presented scenario modeling using automated layer-based scenario (function) description and scenario (logic) reduction approaches [14,15]. However, logical scenario reduction with variance-based sensitivity analysis is the focus of this paper.

2.3   Variance-Based Sensitivity Analysis

Sensitivity analysis is a method to study the uncertainty of the result depending on the input factors and variance-based approach is vastly used in automotive engineering [17,18], in context of uncertainty and risk estimation. Quantitative sensitivity analysis is recommended for safety and is intended for highly automated driving systems. To ensure safety, the influences and interactions of the input parameters must be investigated. The variance-based sensitivity is used to assess the influences of the input parameters, and the function can be expressed as follows:

$$Y = f(\mathcal{S}) \tag{1}$$

where, S is a set of input parameters as described in Sect. 3. Functional decomposition has been considered using conditional expectations such as collision or no collision during lane change and difference in variance has been estimated from the simulation results. The detail expressions of variance-based approach is not described in this paper but the reduction approach with the variance approach is illustrated in detail. The variance-based approach is used to analyze the sensitivity and present the simulation results of the lane change function for HAD systems.

3   Scenario Reduction Approaches

Scenario-based analysis is not new and is used in various fields, e.g. rail transport, aviation and currently also in the automotive industry (see ENABLE-S3, Pegasus, VVM). This technique provides a rational method for determining accident or collision situations. Scenario-based analysis examines different combinations and ranges of parameters in a given driving situation and determines spectra of collision and non-collision scenarios. Scenario-based analysis typically consider a wide range of scenarios (base-case scenario, best-case scenario, and worst-case scenario [19]) and determining the effects of parameter variations. The focus of the scenario-based analysis is to explore the possible outcomes and understand the potential impact of variables in collision detection.

In the Pegasus project [10] scenarios are defined from different levels of abstraction, such as functional scenarios, logical scenarios and concrete scenarios [20]. According to author Menzel's proposal [12], *"functional scenarios include operational scenarios at a semantic level including linguistic scenario notation. The scenarios are consistent. The vocabulary used to describe functional scenarios is specific to the use case and domain and may have varying levels of detail* [12]. In addition, the authors of [12] describe the logical scenario as," *it includes operational scenarios at a state space level. Logical scenarios represent entities and the relationships of those entities using parameter ranges in the state space. The parameter ranges can optionally be specified with probability distributions.* In other words, the temporal sequence of scenes and parameter space, including the initial parameter set, is defined by the logical scenario. Furthermore, a concrete scenario describes the complete sequence of a single instance from a logical scenario [21]. It is assumed that the ODD can be defined not only at the functional scenario level, but also at the logical scenario level, taking into account aspects such as environment, sensor performance, or constraints for specific application scenarios.

3.1   Scenario Description

The basic scenario modeling is derived from the German accident type catalog [22]. For scenario modeling and simulation, lane change is considered as a feature of the HAD system. The identities of the highway, country, and city accident scenarios are 631 (vehicles traveling in the same direction), 661 (vehicles traveling in the opposite direction), and 211 (turning with oncoming traffic) from [22] are shown in Fig. 1.

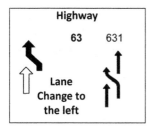
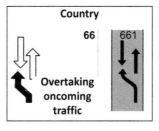
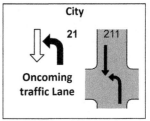

Fig. 1. Basic scenarios - accident types [22]

Lane Change (LC) scenarios are investigated for the scenario-based simulation using the basic scenarios (highway, country and city). The basic scenarios are modeled using tools like CarMaker. Modeled scenario indicate the accident types as mentioned in Fig. 1. The view of the modeled basic scenarios are shown in Fig. 2.

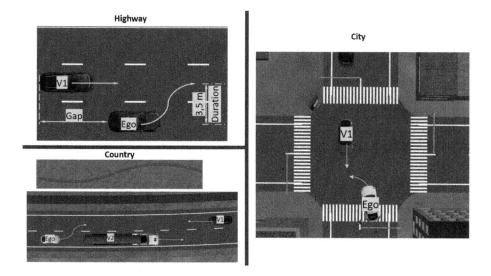

Fig. 2. Basic scenarios model in CarMaker

3.2   Logical Scenario Reduction

To describe the logical scenario, the type and behavior of the parameters in the situations are counted. The logical scenario can then be carried over into concrete scenarios where the specific parameters are defined and simulated to identify the hazardous scenario by means of the detected collisions. A set of assumed input parameters expressed as $S = \{P1, P2, P3.....Pf\}$ where, f is the number of input parameter's type that are varied to define the collision and hazardous situations while changing the lane by ego vehicle. For example, if f = 4, input parameter set $S = \{P1, P2, P3, P4\}$ and each of the parameter types from set S are assigned with set elements such as:

$$
\begin{aligned}
P1 &= \{a_i \mid P1 \in \mathcal{S}\}; a_i = \{a_1, a_2, \ldots, a_n\} \\
P2 &= \{b_j \mid P2 \in \mathcal{S}\}; b_j = \{b_1, b_2, \ldots, b_l\} \\
P3 &= \{c_k \mid P3 \in \mathcal{S}\}; c_k = \{c_1, c_2, \ldots, c_m\} \\
P4 &= \{d_q \mid P4 \in \mathcal{S}\}; d_i = \{d_1, d_2, \ldots, d_t\}
\end{aligned}
\tag{2}
$$

Here, n, l, m and t are the arrays of elements of P1, P2, P3 and P4, respectively, where four kinds of parameters are used in the input parameter set S. The sensitivity of the input variables is estimated based on the result of the collision detection. This allows the optimization of the critical input variables and their combination including their ranges for potential collisions. SAE automation level 3 requires efficient test scenarios and calibration of the parameter space to logical scenarios for validation. One favorable method to deal with the large number of scenarios is to cluster the scenarios from field data, which is labor intensive and costly. Another optimistic method is to use prior art knowledge to support scenario-based validation in the concept phase, which is the focus of this paper. Scenario clustering defines different situations with possible safety-related parameters, as shown in Fig. 2 for different sets logical scenarios. Therefore, several sets of logical scenarios (see Fig. 2) are simulated to determine the possible range of safety parameters. As an assumption, parameter sets for collision detection are considered. For each of the scenarios, a different set of input parameters is used, namely the speed of the ego vehicle, the distance between the vehicles, and other safety-related parameters. For example, four input parameters for LC on highways, seven input parameters for LC on rural roads, and three parameters for LC on city roads.

The proposed parameter variation with the reduction steps are as follows. Step 1: Consider a combination of the input parameter types (assume 4 parameter types). Step 2: Preparing the test sequence (*TS*) to vary the parameter types in an orderly manner. Step 3: Simulation of test sequence scenarios *F(TS)* and detection of collisions. Step 4: Reduction of the elements (P*reduced*) of the already varied parameter types (considering elements that yield only collision-free concrete scenarios). For each combination of the set *S*, steps 2 to 4 are repeated to determine the safety bounds of the parameters. Let us consider a combination (step 1) of the set *S* as (P1, P2, P3, P4) and P1 is varied in the first iteration stage.

The first iteration of possible test sequence scenarios is (step 2):

$$TS_1 = P1 \times P2(1) \times P3(1) \times P4(1) \tag{3}$$

The parameter set P1 is varied as the first iteration and other elements from the set *S* are considered as a singleton set containing the first element of the set and the test sequence scenario simulation function (step 3):

$$F(TS_1) = \begin{cases} 1 & \text{if elements from TS1 result a collision} \\ 0 & \text{if elements from TS1 result no collision} \end{cases} \tag{4}$$

The elements of P1 can be reduced (P*1reduced*) considering the results of collision detection and reused by considering only the elements where no collision occurs (step 4), which can be defined as $P'1$:

$$P_1 reduced = \{P_1' := P_1' \subset P1 \wedge \vdash F(TS_1 = 0)\} \tag{5}$$

For the second iteration, the set (P*1reduced*) is used as a singleton set, where P2 is varied in the test sequence of scenarios. The first element of P*1reduced* is the last element of P1 when no collision occurs as a simulation result. In other words, when the simulation results of the function *F(TS1)* changes the state from no collision to collision. The 2nd iteration steps of the possible test sequence scenarios, the test sequence scenario simulation function *F(TS2)* and the reduced parameter set of P2 are:

$$TS_2 = P_1'(1) \times P2 \times P3(1) \times P4(1) \tag{6}$$

$$F(TS_2) = \begin{cases} 1 & \text{if elements from TS2 result a collision} \\ 0 & \text{if elements from TS2 result no collision} \end{cases} \tag{7}$$

$$P_2 reduced = \{P_2' := P_2' \subset P2 \wedge \vdash F(TS_2 = 0)\} \tag{8}$$

The third iteration steps can be represented as:

$$TS_3 = P_1'(1) \times P_2'(1) \times P3 \times P4(1) \tag{9}$$

$$F(TS_3) = \begin{cases} 1 & \text{if elements from TS3 result a collision} \\ 0 & \text{if elements from TS3 result no collision} \end{cases} \tag{10}$$

$$P_3 reduced = \{P_3' := P_3' \subset P3 \wedge \vdash F(TS_3 = 0)\} \tag{11}$$

However, the study includes up to the fourth element, as mentioned in set S. Thus, the fourth iteration is the final phase, which can be expressed as follows:

$$TS_4 = P_1'(1) \times P_2'(1) \times P_3'(1)) \times P4 \tag{12}$$

$$F(TS_3) = \begin{cases} 1 & \text{if elements from TS3 result a collision} \\ 0 & \text{if elements from TS3 result no collision} \end{cases} \tag{13}$$

The reduced parameters from the previous simulation are used in the next iteration. The reduction of set P4 can be considered for another iteration if the length of parameter set S is increased. As a byproduct of scenario reduction approach, simulated scenario outputs including the input sets can be used in system like artificial systems as a type of machine learning to predict new output values. In other words, the simulated concrete scenarios can be used to create a scenario data set for training artificial systems such as machine learning.

3.3   Scenario Simulation and Sensitivity Analysis

The simulation for the logical scenarios is performed in CarMaker. The basic scenarios described in Sect. 3.2 consider different types of parameters and ODD. For the lane change maneuver, the parameter types and their limits are varied within the defined ODD. In order to reduce the simulation effort for the use case scenario and maintaining the systematic structure, different discretization steps are used while performing the scenario simulation in the different iteration stages as illustrated in Sect. 3.2 of this paper. Hazard scenarios are considered using accident data as described in [15,16], which correspond to the logical use case scenarios presented in Sect. 3.1. For each use case, multiple sets of input parameters with specific parameter space are used. For the highway scenario, there are more than three input parameters that strongly affect the results of the simulation by means of collision. For example, the collision probability is lower when the ego vehicle changes lanes without another vehicle on the road than when another vehicle is driving on the road. During the pre-test simulation, the limit range of the input parameters is realized with a wide parameter space as listed in Table 1 with upper and lower limit. The reduced range of input parameters is considered in the post-testing phase. The sequence of the input parameters is considered in the post-testing phase to detect the collision as a result of the variance-based sensitivity analysis.

Table 1. Input parameters ranges

Input parameters	Initial parameter	Lower to upper limit
Ego speed (Km/hr)	130	50 to 160
LC gap (Meter)	65	0 to 80
LC duration (s)	3	1 to 16
V1 speed (Km/hr)	140	80 to 160

To analyze the sensitivity of the input parameters the iteration steps mentioned in the previous Subsect. 3.2 has been considered. Defining the boundary range of the input parameters is the first step to identify the sensitivity of the parameters, the findings from the previously performed test scenarios are taken into account during the simulation process.

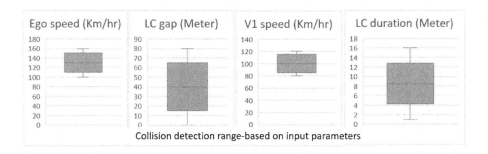

Fig. 3. Input parameters variation range

The variance-based method is used as a global sensitivity analysis because the results are interpreted directly based on the inputs. The output function simply depends on the set of model input parameters (S). For the LC highway scenario, four input parameters are varied sequentially. In other words, first the speed of the ego-vehicle was varied, then the LC distance and the LC duration or speed of the other vehicle (V1). The results of the first iteration were used as input parameters for the next iteration. The boundary of the critical range for the input parameters is represented in Fig. 3.

The results of the variance-based sensitivity analysis based on collision detection are summarized in Table 2. The variance of the output reflects the independent effect of the input parameters during the pretest phase and the posttest

Table 2. Variance-based sensitivity analysis

Input parameters	Pretest variance	Posttest variance	Delta variance
Ego speed	≈43%	≈45%	2.14%
LC gap	≈22%	≈43%	20.78%
LC duration	≈69%	≈24%	44.75%
V1 speed	≈40%	≈36%	4.00%

phase. It is noted that both test phases are considered for a restricted ODD, but with different discretization steps of the input parameters, in order to observe the influence of the input parameters with respect to the parameter space and the discretization process. The combination of input parameters is examined with reduced boundary range during the posttest phase and the variance of the results is monitored to identify the most critical input parameters. The discretization steps are higher in the pretesting phase and are reduced to half or less in the post testing phase of the sensitivity analysis. It was found that the discretization steps play an important role in the sensitivity analysis. For example, the discretization steps affect the results with the highest difference of 44.75%, while the ego speed is only 2.14%, as shown in Table 2. The simulation results show that the lane change gap and the duration of the lane change are the most safety-critical input parameters for the use case scenario.

4 Conclusion and Future Work

In the past, ADS safety approval was mostly performed by million-mile tests, which are difficult due to the complex system and new functionalities of the vehicle. Therefore, this study investigates a reduction of scenarios in terms of parameter variation. To support the deployment of safety systems, this paper proposes a demonstration process for scenario selection and testing using pretesting and post-testing to reduce scenarios. The collision probability was estimated at the logical scenario level using Monte carlo simulation. Based on the collision probability, another set of simulation was performed in CarMaker taking into account the reduced safety-critical parameter limits. As a byproduct of the simulation, a scenario database was created that can be used ADS features such as transverse guidance assist system.

Moreover, the sensitivity of input parameters is investigated and argued with test scenario iteration sets to validate the simulation results by using the standard sensor models, which can be replaced by real sensor models, and simulating the scenarios in a tool such as CarMaker. The reduced parameter space is evaluated by simulation and used for test scenario iteration to identify the safety limits of the parameters. However, when the complexity of the system increases with respect to a fully automated vehicle (SAE Level 5), emulator-based (e.g. Gaussian process emulator) sensitivity analysis can be used to reduce computational effort and cost. Future work will apply the proposed reduced approaches to other

ODDs with reduced parameter space and produce a set of safety specifications for SAE Level 3 automated vehicles. It is recognized that the parameter-based scenario data set only reflects the simulation but can be used for machine learning with optimization algorithms.

The key idea of the sensitivity analysis in this paper is to identify the most safety-critical input parameters during lane change through evidence such as simulation-based test results. Based on the variance-based approach, it was investigated that the duration of lane change is the most sensitive among the other input parameters in the implementation of lane change on the highway. As a result of the sensitivity analysis, it can also be shown that the discretization steps of the input parameters have significant effects on the output, which can be used in further scenario optimization techniques.

Furthermore, the scenario database is obtained by selected logical scenarios (highway, country and city) and several sets of concrete scenarios are simulated and can be used as an input for training an artificial intelligence, such as collision detection.

References

1. SAE J3016: Taxonomy and Definitions for Terms Related to Driving Automation Systems for On-Road Motor Vehicles, commonly referenced as the SAE Levels of Driving Automation (2019)
2. SAE blog: SAE levels of driving automation refined for clarity and international audience. https://www.sae.org/blog/sae-j3016-update. Posted 3 May 2021
3. Mobility Insider: What are the levels of automated driving? https://www.aptiv.com/en/insights/article/what-are-the-levels-of-automated-driving. Aptiv. Accessed 4 Jan 2020
4. NHTSA: Automated vehicles for safety: the evolution of automated safety technologies, United States department of transportation-benefits of automation (2019)
5. Winkle, T.: Safety benefits of automated vehicles: extended findings from accident research for development, validation and testing. In: Maurer, M., Gerdes, J.C., Lenz, B., Winner, H. (eds.) Autonomous Driving, pp. 335–364. Springer, Heidelberg (2016). https://doi.org/10.1007/978-3-662-48847-8_17
6. ISO 26262: Road vehicles - functional safety, standard, ed. 2, Part 1–12 (2018)
7. ISO/PAS 21448: Road vehicles - safety of the intended functionality, publicly available specification, ed. 1 (2019)
8. ISO/TR 4804: Road vehicles - safety and cybersecurity for automated driving systems - design, verification and validation, Technical report, ed. 1 (2020)
9. Leitner, A., Watzenig, D., Ibanez-Guzman, J. (eds.): Validation and Verification of Automated Systems. Springer, Cham (2020). https://doi.org/10.1007/978-3-030-14628-3
10. Pegasus Research Project: PEGASUS symposium, federal ministry for economic affairs and energy (2019)
11. Verification and validation methods for automated vehicles in urban environments, safety standards for automated driving, VDA leitinitiative automated and connected driving, Pegasus Family (2019)
12. Menzel, T., Bagschik, G., Maurer, M.: Scenarios for development, test and validation of automated vehicles. In: 2018 IEEE Intelligent Vehicles Symposium (IV), pp. 1821–1827. IEEE (2018)

13. Frings, A.: Scenario generation for virtual test driving on the basis of accident databases. In: Automatisiertes Fahren 2021. P, pp. 159–168. Springer, Wiesbaden (2021). https://doi.org/10.1007/978-3-658-34754-3_12

14. Khatun, M., Glaß, M., Jung, R.: A systematic approach of reduced scenario-based safety analysis for highly automated driving function. In: 7th International Conference on Vehicle Technology and Intelligent Transport Systems (VEHITS), SciTePress (2021). https://doi.org/10.5220/0010397403010308

15. Khatun, M., Caldeira, G.B., Jung, R., Glaß, M.: An optimization and validation method to detect the collision scenarios and identifying the safety specification of highly automated driving vehicle. In: 21st International Conference on Control, Automation and Systems (ICCAS), IEEE (2021)

16. Khatun, M., Glaß, M., Jung, R.: Scenario-based extended HARA incorporating functional safety & SOTIF for autonomous driving. In: 30th European Safety and Reliability Conference and 15th Probabilistic Safety Assessment and Management Conference (ESREL2020 PSAM15) (2020)

17. Opgenoord, M.M., Allaire, D.L., Willcox, K.E.: Variance-based sensitivity analysis to support simulation-based design under uncertainty. J. Mech. Des. **138**(11), 111410 (2016)

18. Batsch, F., Daneshkhah, A., Palade, V., Cheah, M.: Scenario optimisation and sensitivity analysis for safe automated driving using gaussian processes. Appl. Sci. **11**(2), 775 (2021). https://doi.org/10.3390/app11020775

19. Ali, R.: Scenario analysis explained. https://www.netsuite.com/portal/resource/articles/financial-management/scenario-analysis.shtml. ORACLE netsuite. Posted 28 Oct 2020

20. Menzel, T., Bagschik, G., Isensee, L., Schomburg, A., Maurer, M.: From functional to logical scenarios: detailing a keyword-based scenario description for execution in a simulation environment. In: 2019 IEEE Intelligent Vehicles Symposium (IV), pp. 2383–2390. IEEE (2019)

21. Weber, H., et al.: A framework for definition of logical scenarios for safety assurance of automated driving. Traffic Inj. Prev. **20**(sup1), S65–S70 (2019)

22. Unfalltypen-Katalog, Leitfaden zur Bestimmung des Unfalltyps, Gesamtverband der Deutschen Versicherungswirtschaft e. V., Unfallforschung der Versicherer (2016)

State of the Art Study of the Safety Argumentation Frameworks for Automated Driving System

Ilona Cieslik[1] [ID], Víctor J. Expósito Jiménez[1] [ID], Helmut Martin[1(✉)], Heiko Scharke[2], and Hannes Schneider[2]

[1] Virtual Vehicle Research GmbH, 8010 Graz, Austria
{ilona.cieslik,victor.expositojimenez,helmut.martin}@v2c2.at
[2] AVL List GmbH, 8020 Graz, Austria
{heiko.scharke,hannes.schneider}@avl.com

Abstract. The automotive industry is experiencing a transition from assisted to highly automated driving. New concepts for validation of Automated Driving System (ADS) include amongst other a shift from a "technology based" approach to a "scenario based" assessment. The safety validation and vehicle type approval process of ADS are seen as the biggest challenges for the automotive stakeholders today. Considering a variety of existing white papers, standardization activities and regulatory approaches, manufacturers still struggle with selecting best practices that stay aligned with their Safety Management System and Safety Culture. A step forward would be to implement a harmonized and global safety assurance scheme that is compliant with relevant regulations, standards, and reflects locally accepted behavioural laws. This will ensure a common understanding of the safety and build needed trust around ADS.

Today many communities (regulatory bodies, local authorities, industrial stakeholders, and academia) work on proof-of-concept framework for the Safety Argumentation as an answer to this problem. Unfortunately, there is still no consensus on one definitive methodology and a set of safety metrics to measure ADS safety. An objective of this summary paper is to fill existing gaps in the literature reviews, concerning available methods and approaches for engineering frameworks, processes of scenario-based evaluation and a vendor- and technology-neutral Safety Argumentation approaches and tools. A particular focus is placed on safety metrics and emerging quantitative approaches.

Keywords: Safety metrics · Safety Argumentation · Automated Driving System (ADS) · Statistical approaches · Safety of the Intended Function (SOTIF)

1 The Need for a Safety Argumentation Framework

The automotive industry is experiencing a transition from assisted to highly automated driving. The regulatory Framework Document on Automated/Autonomous Vehicles under the United Nations Economic Commission of Europe (UNECE) WP.29 underlines that the certification process of the Automated Driving System (ADS) should prove

M. Trapp et al. (Eds.): SAFECOMP 2022 Workshops, LNCS 13415, pp. 178–191, 2022.
https://doi.org/10.1007/978-3-031-14862-0_14

that "a vehicle shall not cause any non-tolerable risk" [1]. Therefore, one of the biggest challenges to be solved before the release of ADS (i.e., Level 3 and higher according to ISO/SAE 22736 [2]) is their safety validation. One of the research questions is: "How can we argue the absence of unreasonable risk of ADS in its defined Operational Design domain (ODD)", without knowing an exact interpretation of "reasonable foreseeable", "preventable" or "tolerable" accidents?

The concepts of "WHAT" to audit and assess when introducing ADS on the public roads reached mature consensus [3, 4], comparing to the proof-of-concept frameworks for a Safety Argumentation (i.e., provisions on "HOW" to rational that the ADS is safe enough). Even though many industrial initiatives and research groups are active in this field, the latter still opens enormous room for stakeholders' discussions. Currently there is no agreement on one definitive methodology with qualitative and quantitative metrics to measure safety, related risks, and social acceptance.

The automotive community agrees that the introduction of ADS requires new assessment and test methods. New approaches for certification and standardization are arising to cover the growing needs of such complex systems. New concepts for validation of ADS include amongst other a shift from a "technology based" approach to a "scenario based" assessment that would allow various types of interventions. Scenario-based testing is already a known and established test approach within the industry for development, certification, and rating purposes [5] but needs to be adopted to the ADS validation purposes to foster public trust in this disruptive technology.

Finally, a step forward would be to implement a safety assurance framework that is embedded in the Safety Management System and aligned with the Safety Culture of the manufacturer. It will help not only to organize safety Verification & Validation (V&V) in an efficient, objective, transparent, and scalable manner but ensure dense coverage of traffic situations. Additionally, the manufacturer should demonstrate the compliance with relevant regulations, laws, standards, and good practices [6].

The project MASA (Methodology for KPI based ADAS/AD Safety Assessment and Argumentation) is a 2-year long project that started in 2021. Its main objective is to better understand and enhance existing methodologies and numerical approaches for V&V Safety Argumentation frameworks of ADS. The rest of the paper is structured as follows. The safety and engineering frameworks for ADS considering the regulatory regime, stakeholders' know-how and market demand are summarised in the Sect. 2. In the Sect. 3 attention is given to the elaboration of the Safety Case approach which is considered by many stakeholders at the center of the Safety Argumentation. The Sect. 4 covers the overview of novel performance models and state-of-the-art safety metrics that support the evidence creation process. This covers metrics proposed by the Contracting Parties to the UNECE and research and industrial projects. Section 5 summarises recommendations on existing Safety Argumentation frameworks and next steps for MASA project. The latest processes prescribed by the ISO 21448 - the Safety of The Intended Functionality (SOTIF) [7] on the risk/hazards and triggering conditions analysis are at the future research focus.

The collection of materials and access to the latest communities' updates were threefold, through i) list of publications, reports, and industry white papers selected according to the MASA key words ii) (online) attendance at sectorial conferences and webinars

organized by recognized and eligible organizations in area of ADAS/ADS and iii) participation and memberships of both project partners in the Working Groups (WGs) and regu-
latory/standardization committees. This methodology for identifying the state-of-the-art
(SOTA) resulted in more than one hundred short listed publications that provide a valuable and robust overview over current safety framework challenges for ADS. Moreover,
participation in around 60 webinars, workshops, community online meetings, including
mid-terms reviews and project showcases with dissemination networking opportunities
took place (e.g., event platforms like ScaleUp 360°, IEEE Mobility Practice, PAVE Virtual Panel, ITU-T Focus Group events, V&V Methoden, Set4to5, CertiCAV, VeriCAV
Final Showcases, ERTRAC/EUCAR/ERTICO workshops, among others). Additionally,
the experts from both partnering organizations, namely AVL and Virtual Vehicle participated in the discussions of relevant WGs, exchanged views and channeled feedback to
shape the regulatory and standardization landscape. In some of the WGs and projects,
the partners have very active roles (e.g., UNECE GRVA VMAD/FRAV, the JRC EC, ISO
FuSa/SOTIF/co-engineering national mirror groups, ASAM, IAMTS Alliance, PEGA-
SUS project family, etc.). In other groups the partners acted as observers to find some
convergent points (IEEE, SAE, etc.).

This paper provides the expert-driven selection of relevant groups, standards, and
projects. The complete report with an extensive SOTA list was reported to the board of
the COMET K2 Competence Centers for Excellent Technologies in Austria. Nominal
safety and hazard/risk analysis and emerging topics of SOTIF were in the main scope of
the MASA project. Functional safety, the presence of artificial intelligence (AI)/Human
Machine Interaction (HMI)/V2X communication components, security-informed safety,
cybersecurity, or software updates, indeed pose additional challenges for the safety
argumentation, nevertheless they were not in the project scope.

To sum up, it could be argued that the safety assurance approaches are lagging the
technology development. V&V of AD/ADAS brings novel challenges that try to be
tackled by new standards and regulatory draft documents capturing best practices. The
paper goal is to fill existing gaps in the literature reviews with a particular focus on safety
metrics.

2   A New Safety Assurance Scheme and Global Initiatives

In the literature there are defined different qualitative and quantitative ways to categorize
ADS safety: i) safety as a process/framework, ii) safety as a measurement, and iii)
safety as a threshold [8]. In the first stage, MASA focused on understanding assurance
frameworks and good practices that consist of interacting methods and tools.

The Safety Argumentation supports the process of gaining knowledge and trust on
the operating conditions of ADS. Its main objective is to deliver in a structured way the
right evidence to prove safety of the vehicle. Decomposition of the safety requirements
prescribed by the regulators and standardization bodies (see Sect. 2.1 and 2.2) and
implementation of methods for deriving test requirements (see Sect. 2.3) help to arrive to
credible evidence (Sect. 4). A well-structured framework could accelerate the exchange
of information and requirements between stakeholders and optimize the tests amount to
a manageable minimum [9].

The current automotive and transport communities that dialogue on enablers for industrialization of ADS could be split into i) regulatory Informal Working Groups (IWG), ii) standardization activities, and iii) research and industry initiatives.

2.1 Regulatory Informal Working Groups for ADS Safety Topics

In 2019 a new Working Party on Automated/Autonomous and Connected Vehicles (GRVA) of the UNECE was created. The WP was tasked with defining provisions for a "safe vehicle" and its approval. Its two IWGs play a significant role in the ADS Safety Argumentation, namely Functional Requirements for Automated and Autonomous Vehicles (FRAV) and Validation Method for Automated Driving (VMAD).

The starting point of the FRAV discussion was a "guardrails approach", where the regulatory bodies decided to not prescribe driving manoeuvres or values. The stakeholders recognise that more than one behaviour could be safe and do not want to hamper the technology development at so early stage of regulatory process. As an outcome of the FRAV sessions, a robust list of "General Safety Requirements" was concluded and reported to the GRVA committee [10]. The novelty of this list is that it does not focus on each technology and features separately but addresses the diversity of ADS applications. Moreover, it reflects a global and consolidated view provided by the Member States and the industry representatives covering the full range of anticipated safety needs. Nowadays, the FRAV members supersede where appropriate the list with technical specifications (limits, criteria, formulas, etc.).

On the other hand, the VMAD tackled the certification and audit/assessment process of ADS. The outcome of the discussions is the master document "New Assessment and Test Methods" (NATM) which describes existing test platforms and their interactions. Moreover, the group works on the documentation requirements needed during the audit and assessment phase. The goal is to demonstrate a combination of validation, engineering rigor, post-deployment feedback, and safety culture [5].

2.2 Global Standardization Activities

There are many standards that support the Safety Argumentation in different product development phases following known V-cycle: from the specification, design, integration, to V&V, product release and monitoring. The purpose of those documents is threefold: i) providing the terms, definition, and summarising existing state of the art of scenario-based validation, ii) defining processes, methods, and tools, and iii) sharing check lists or taxonomy/ontology trees. It is relevant to understand their scope and possible contributions to a global safety argumentation framework.

The following standards addressing existing ADS-equipped vehicle safety approaches were considered in MASA roadmap (Table 1). Their content is intended to be applied to ADS Level 3 and higher according to [2]. Currently, many discussions are taking place between standardization organizations like ISO, IEEE, SAE, BSI to align the terminology and look for a common vision for ADS deployment (e.g., the alignment activities for ODD specification under the umbrella of new ISO 3450x series). The dialogue between many member states, who express different perspectives and safety goals, should be seen as a long-lasting process, during which conflicting cases require further elaboration (e.g., mentioned in Sect. 4 safety targets and measurable criteria which strongly depend on local rules and societal acceptance). It is evident that a lot of effort was done towards standardization, nevertheless the ADS ecosystem stakeholders still need to invest further resources to speak a common language.

Table 1. Global standardization activities relevant for the Safety Argumentation framework.

Name of the standard, year of publication	Relevance for the ADS Safety Argumentation	Goal: Terms & Definitions (TD)/Process & methods (PM), Check list (CL)
ISO/PAS 21448:2019 Safety of the intended functionality (SOTIF), rev. in 2022	Limitations and shortcomings of the technology and the misuse of the function, iterative process of improving the acceptance criteria by triggering conditions and risk/hazards evaluation	TD, PM
ISO/SAE PAS 22736:2021 Taxonomy and definitions for terms related to driving automation systems for on-road motor vehicles	Definitions, taxonomies, and best practices for six levels of driving automation, inc. Terms for the dynamic driving task (DDT), DDT fallback, minimal risk conditions, etc. (aligned with SAE J 3016-2021)	TD
ISO 26262:2018 Functional safety (12 parts)	E/E faults and failures as a source of safety problems and calls for a safety case	TD, PM
ISO 3450x series inc. ISO 34501-34505 (u. development)	Terminology and definition of test scenarios for ADS, the overall scenario-based safety evaluation process, a hierarchical taxonomy for ODD, tags for scenarios categorization	TD, PM, CL
ISO/AWI TS 5083 Safety for ADS - Design, verification, and validation (u. development)	Safety by design, V&V methods based on safety goals and principles, safety case, def. of positive risk balance and avoidance of unreasonable risk (proceed from an ISO/TR 4804)	PM
SAE J3131:2022 Automated Driving Reference Architecture	ADS reference software architecture that contains functional modules (does not dictate configuration, neither design requirements)	TD

(continued)

Table 1. (*continued*)

Name of the standard, year of publication	Relevance for the ADS Safety Argumentation	Goal: Terms & Definitions (TD)/Process & methods (PM), Check list (CL)
IEEE P2846:2022 Formal Model for Safety Considerations in Automated Vehicle Decision Making	Set of assumptions and foreseeable scenarios for the development of safety-related models, an extension of the safety envelope violation concept (RSS)	PM
ASAM OpenX standards (concept/implementation)	Foundation of definitions, language, formats, and interfaces for V&V in simulation platforms	TD, PM, CL
ANSI/UL 4600: 2022 Standard for Safety for the Evaluation of Autonomous Products	Safety case approach goal-based and technology-agnostic, a catalogue of good practices in the whole ADS cycle, inc. safety metrics strategy	CL

2.3 Research and Industry Communities, Initiatives, and Projects

The R&D projects, industrial consortia and local initiatives try to discuss varied approaches related to ADS performance. The task of the MASA was to analyse their unique concepts and what new they bring to the Safety Argumentation. These initiatives not only contribute with the publications and white papers, besides provide valuable input to the regulatory/standardization landscape (see Sect. 2.1 and 2.2):

V&V Methods (Germany), a part of PEGASUS project family[1] supported by The Federal Ministry for Economic Affairs and Climate Action (BMWK). The project develops a method, called criticality analysis, which analyzes the open context of urban traffic. It introduces definitions and concepts that support the Safety Argumentation (criticality analysis, criticality phenomenon, criticality metric) [11].

The CertiCAV Safety Assurance Framework for CAVs (UK) executed by the Connected Places Catapult on behalf of the Department for Transport. The projects developed a framework that has number of novel ideas like a Highly Automated SuperSystem (HASS), the concept of Deployment Risk Classifications, and a foundation for developing requirements with performance indicators [12].

The SAKURA Safety Assurance KUdos for Reliable Autonomous Vehicles (Japan) funded by the Ministry of Economy, Trade, and Industry (METI). The project proposed a very robust framework that goes further than the nominal driving conditions. It elaborates

---

[1] PEGASUS, Set Level 4 to 5, V&V Methods are projects developed by the VDA Leitinitiative autonomous and connected driving, https://www.vvm-projekt.de/en/.

on safety-relevant disturbances that an ADS may face in a real traffic (called traffic, perception, and vehicle motion disturbance scenarios) [13].

AURORA/UBER Argumentation Concept (USA), a commercial initiative. Till now the stakeholders were reluctant to openly share safety cases and reveal the format. Aurora shared their version of the self-driving Safety Case Framework [14].

3 Safety Case as a Core Approach to Argue the Safety of ADS

The safety case could be seen as a starting point, as an easy and understandable tool to support the Safety Argumentation. A safety case approach is not a new tool, and many communities refer to it. There are available manuals and standards (e.g., IEC 61508, U.K. Defence Standard 00-55, HSE Railway Safety Case Regulations) which center on a safety case. The good practices from aeronautics, railway, marine or healthcare could have a value in the automotive sector [15]. Literature from R&D projects (see Sect. 2.3), University of York community [16] and Edge Case Research studies [17] bring additional input towards the safety case and its format.

3.1 Safety Case Content and Format

In the literature exist many complementary definitions for the safety case. ISO 26262:2018 for example defines a safety case in the context of the functional safety as "an argument that functional safety is achieved for items, or elements, and satisfied by evidence compiled from work products of activities during development." [18].

The elements of the safety case are i) goal, ii) argumentation, and iii) evidence. When it comes to the argument, it may be deterministic, probabilistic, or qualitative; the evidence may be design, process, or historic experience (with a proof of completeness for coverage of test cases). In the Safety Argumentation it is essential to decompose each goal (claim) further into tangible and measurable performance indicators (results and records). (Safety) metrics are a measurement used to evaluate and track safety performance [19] (see Sect. 4.1). Finally, as an outcome of V&V activities on different test platforms, relevant amount of supporting data should be collected to produce quantitative evidence of safety case credibility.

A format for structuring argumentation should be notation agnostic (i.e., textual, tabular, graphical). Some manuals like widely used the Goal Structuring Notation (GSN) [16], MISRA Safety Case Guideline [20], Structured Assurance Case Metamodel (SACM™) [21] or Claims, Arguments and Evidence (CAE) notation [22] support the arguments creation and documentation process. Using an agreed format enables a consistent and traceable decomposition from claims down to V&V methods and keeping the safety case evolving over the life cycle (a living document).

3.2 Safety Goals

At the beginning of the safety argumentation the manufacturer needs to define the Safety Goals. The current data bases of crashes and statistics often provide basic data on a high and aggregated level, without diving into the cause of the crash. For ADS there should be different types of the safety goals that are included in the argumentation process [23] and that support accident investigation and decomposition tasks:

Functional Safety Goals - according to ISO 26262 compliance - behavior in case of system or component failure (hazards) that may arise by the functionality in the E/E system within its ODD are identified and assigned to the required ASIL level [18],

SOTIF Goals - according to ISO 21448 compliance - triggering conditions (including foreseeable misuses) and obtained test results purpose is to reduce the residual risk to an acceptable level and to improve ADS nominal performance [7],

Ethics Goals and Societal Expectations - according to ethical standards (e.g., ISO 39003 u. development), human errors and intentions, that could endanger other actors lives or damage properties, discriminate road users by age, gender, clothes, handicap,

Laws and Regulations Goals - according to UNECE regulations, national and traffic law under Road Traffic Code and locally accepted behavioural laws respectively,

Cybersecurity/Software updates Goals - according to ISO/SAE 21434, SAE J3061, UN Regulation No. 155/UN Regulation No. 156 respectively.

The MASA project focuses mainly on prescriptive requirements coming from laws, regulations, and standards (see Sect. 4.1), and investigation of novel approaches to support SOTIF processes argumentation (see Sect. 4.2).

3.3 Acceptance Criteria

Acceptance criteria for ADS are based on a statement that "safe enough" is not just a number, it is an argument. In literature there are many strategies and accompanying argumentation patterns, e.g., PAS 1881 [24] includes references to ALARP (Reducing risk as low as reasonably practicable), safety case architecture as in UL 4600 [25] or ISO 21448 [7] (under revision) additionally refer to GAMAB ("generally at least as good as") and MEM (Minimum Endogenous Mortality), among others. Some of acceptance criteria widely used in other sectors are summarized in [26]. Those are mentioned ALARP, GAMAB, MEM criteria and other like MISRI (Minimum Industry Safety Return on Investment) or RAPEX (Rapid Exchange of Information).

Currently, "a positive risk balance" criteria gain more attention. In this context, ADS should generate a "statistical positive risk balance" such that ADS demonstrate superior performance when compared statistically against human driving performance. One of the objectives of a new ISO 5083 standard (under development) [27] is to structure a holistic safety approach with the safety case pattern for ADS. The recommendations are based on the German Ethics Commission report [28].

4 Safety Evidence: An Attempt to "Quantify" the ADS Safety

It is recognized that the safety case is one of elements to a complete safety assurance framework for ADS. Particularly challenging is to collect enough valid evidence to support the safety goals and arguments (Sect. 3.2) and to claim the safety case completeness and sufficient V&V coverage. The safety metrics with data collection strategy should be introduced to result in an acceptable and strong safety case.

4.1 Requirements-Based Testing with Numerical Approaches

The Sect. 2 explains the need to quantify the product safety, its social acceptance and liability. Indeed, the introduction of ADS requires new type of i) performance models and ii) safety metrics. Consolidation of safety related metrics was the main objective of MASA, for ADS none-safety related metrics (network efficiency, energy emission, drive quality, costs and public health or comfort), the reader could consult [29].

Performance Models are based on "roadmanship" concept, which means the ability to drive on the road safely without creating hazards and responding correctly to hazards created by others. They reflect the ADS's situational awareness, time to response, speed adjustment, the vehicle's physics, driving culture and laws and diverse driving scenarios [8]. In the literature, ADS performance models are named as mathematical models for trajectory planning, safety envelope or escape path. Some prominent models that are part of the ADS regulations and standards are:

Competent and Careful Human Driver's Performance Model (C&C) proposed by the Japanese delegation to the UNECE. The model is included in the UN Regulation No. 157 - Automated Lane Keeping Systems (ALKS), Annex 3. Its main assumption is that traffic accidents are split into rationally foreseeable and preventable [30].

The Responsibility-Sensitive Safety Model (RSS) by Intel (US). It is a white-box mathematical model. It formalizes the "duty of care", which means that a road actor should exercise "reasonable care" while performing acts that could harm others [31]. The safety envelope concepts are reflected in IEEE 2846 standard [32].

Fuzzy Safety Model (FSM) of the Joint Research Centre of the European Commission. This model builds on RSS findings. Its characteristics are based on fuzzy logic that would not require the vehicle to decelerate very sharply or very often. The model is considered next to the C&C model in the draft of ALKS extension (Annex 3) under the leadership of SIG UNR157 Task Force of UNECE [33].

The reader should be aware of other models existing in the literature, that were analysed under MASA but currently are rather in the concept phase: Safety Force Field (SFF), Instantaneous Safety Metric (ISM), Criticality Metric using Model Predictive Trajectory Optimization [19], among others.

Safety Metrics and Their Thresholds - till today the universal metrics for road safety were historical crash data like frequency and severity. The existing test procedures and protocols for assisted functions (ADAS) like Euro NCAP consumer tests or regulatory documents (e.g., UN No. 79, UN No. 131) introduce simple but comprehensive metrics to select situations out of traffic events to reduce the amount of test effort.

The need for harmonization and standardization of terms and techniques for ADS safety measures has been recognized over the last decade [34]. The metrics that refer to testing in nominal conditions are used under exchangeable terminologies: Behavioral Safety Measures [35], Safety Performance Assessment Metrics [36], Proximal Surrogate Indicators, Temporal/Spatial-based Conflict Indicators [37], Criticality/Risk Metrics [11]. They evaluate the criticality of the traffic situation.

Mentioned above references define important properties of each metric: definition, taxonomy, data source from off or onboard sources, observable variables, formulation: mathematical model, assumptions/thresholds when applicable, origin, limitations and advantages, reason for inclusion, research examples, type of scenario, manoeuvre colli- sion type suitability. The section "16. Metrics and Safety Performance Indicators (SPls)" of [25] gives additional guidelines on metrics as a part of the Safety Culture. The man- ufacturer should present a metric strategy with collection, evaluation, and improvement processes. Further, the safety metrics could be categorized into [8]:

Prior/Predictive (Leading Metrics) - including general performance characteristics, associated with vehicle kinematics (longitudinal and lateral distance), perception and assessment of Object and Event detection specification (OEDR) [38], safe motion control metrics etc. Leading metrics are particularly important for ADS because their events happen more frequently than lagging measures.

An Outcome (Lagging Metrics) - covering post deployment, longer term metrics like for driver disengagement [39], ODD metrics [40], violation of road rules and crash severity and frequency. Assessing a correlation of leading metrics to safety outcomes should be used to drive improvement of the metrics and thresholds [19].

The metrics could only be implemented successfully considering the threshold and the pass-fail criteria definition. Their definition is not an easy task, neither standardized (e.g., ADAS systems use fixed rules of thumb like the two-second rule for establishing safety envelope [41]). Additionally, [25] states that the thresholds could be a desired value, limit, or incident frequency. The authors recommend varied approaches for con- solidating claims of different stakeholders when selecting values/targets: i) technology aspects (the state-of-the-art technology limitations), ii) human driver aspects (response to traffic events: perception, recognition, decision), iii) social aspects (socially acceptable behaviours) iv) legal aspects (historical decisions of the court jurisdiction). Moreover, to allow ADS deployment, the thresholds should support federal, state, and local laws and could be a function of several parameters such as vehicle capabilities, road user type, and speed of the ego vehicle [19].

4.2 Quantitative Hazard and Risk Analysis as a Part of the SOTIF Processes

The safety metrics and performance models could support argumentation for known and nominal conditions. When it comes to edge and rare traffic scenarios, the probabilistic methods with the use of virtual testing environment could play a crucial role. A chal- lenge for ADS today is a sound and systematic methodology for the identification and quantification of scenarios that are likely to exhibit hazardous behaviour.

SOTIF standard focuses on the limitations of the technology and the misuse of the function. One of its work products is to discover "potential triggering events" with the purpose of improving the defined acceptance criteria and minimizing the known/unknown hazard scenarios with each iteration [7]. The MASA established exem- plary Triggering Conditions (TC) database and categorized them into 5 groups: i) Envi- ronmental TC (weather state, illumination, quality of the road surface), ii) Infrastruc- tural TC (geometry of the road, road furniture, objects on the road/surroundings), iii) Communication and interferences, iv) Other road actors (adverse traffic behaviour, non-standard actors, surrounding vehicles), v) Ego vehicle behaviour (perception, operation/maneuverers). What is novel in MASA, selected triggering events will be parametrized, aligned with ASAM OpenXOntology standard, and demonstrated in industrial settings with AVL SCENIUS™ V&V Toolchain.

Parametrization process of the SOTIF Triggering Conditions is a robust task as it requires a new type of statistics (unit/scale, boundary values, ground truth measurement process, source of potential statistics, etc.). Real world occurrence likelihoods of today's data (traffic and crash data, labelled data sets from the naturalistic driving, weather forecast records, or infrastructure maintenance reports) require a totally new way of looking at them. The triggering conditions dependencies and dependencies between triggering events and the scenarios constitute another challenge [42].

Currently, the authors investigate and compare preliminary statistical approaches for SOTIF safety argumentation, and the outcome will be reported in the second year of the project. Some of the prominent approaches taken into consideration include [35, 42, 43]. The main objective of the MASA project in the next phase is to enhance the existing workflow of the SOTIF standard with novel numerical approaches.

5   Conclusions and Outlook

The MASA project examined concepts for safety metrics, formal performance models, taxonomies, and process approaches for measuring the safety of ADS-equipped vehicles. The analysis of the available safety frameworks revealed the current research needs and existing gaps between regulatory and industrial pace. Today's regulatory documents on ADS V&V type approval leave a lot open to interpretation.

Determining metrics may help to demonstrate safety as a part of holistic approach for assessing/evaluating aspects of ADS safety. Unfortunately, no one has presented a fully suitable set of metrics for arguing safety of ADS across the range of its functions and features, use cases, and ODDs. The manufacturer could follow many available safety practices to decide which fit the best in their safety case, but still depend on the Type Approval Authority opinion of whether it complies with requirements.

On the other hand, the global consensus was reached on the need to develop ADS strategy for safety metrics. It is seen as a joint work of stakeholders from industry, academia, authorities, and consultation with the civil society. The members of the working groups and research projects recognize both quantitative (product-oriented test results and records) and qualitative approaches (the Safety Culture and Management Systems oriented on processes) as valid to understand the level of safety and duty of care. It still needs to be explored how to leverage a mix of those approaches.

Further, it is suggested that for level 3 ADS-equipped vehicles, the current practices coming from the "technology based" regulatory and standardization documents should be extended with novel standards, such as ISO 26262, ISO 21448, ISO/SAE 21434. In this paper, we only give an overview of the state of the art around statistical approaches for hazard and risk analysis to identify rare and unknown cases.

The goal of the next period of the MASA project is to combine and extend established techniques for hazard analysis and risk assessment. The challenge is to supersede traffic scenario databases and test case frameworks with low probability but high consequence events (in literature so called triggering conditions [7], disturbance scenarios [13], or criticality phenomena [11]) that are not captured in the existing database of global functional scenarios [5]. Unfortunately, there is still lack of publicly acceptable and systematic identification method for triggering events.

To conclude, the development of reliable safety measures will be a significant achievement that expands the current V&V methods. Extending nominal and well-known scenarios with SOTIF approach creates an additional trust in ADS technology.

Acknowledgement. The publication was written at Virtual Vehicle Research GmbH in Graz, Austria. The authors would like to acknowledge the financial support within the COMET K2 Competence Centers for Excellent Technologies from the Austrian Federal Ministry for Climate Action (BMK), the Austrian Federal Ministry for Digital and Economic Affairs (BMDW), the Province of Styria (Dept. 12) and the Styrian Business Promotion Agency (SFG). The Austrian Research Promotion Agency (FFG) has been authorised for the programme management. They would furthermore like to express their thanks to their supporting industrial project partner, namely AVL List GmbH.

References

1. WP.29 UNECE: ECE/TRANS/WP.29/2019/34/Rev.1. Revised Framework Document on Automated/Autonomous Vehicles (2019)
2. ISO: ISO/SAE PAS 22736:2021 - Taxonomy and definitions for terms related to driving automation systems for on-road motor vehicles (2021)
3. UNECE IWG VMAD, Subgroup 3 - Audit and in-service monitoring: VMAD-SG3-22-02 Audit Pillar (2022)
4. The EC: Draft regulations of the EC laying down rules for the application of Regulation (EU) 2019/2144 as regards uniform procedures and technical specifications for the type-approval of the automated driving system (ADS) of fully automated motor vehicles (2022)
5. UNECE IWG VMAD: ECE/TRANS/WP.29/GRVA/2022/2, the New Assessment/Test Method for Automated Driving (NATM) - Master Document (2022)
6. California PATH Program, University of Berkeley: Safety Assurance to earn public trust - Formalizing the Safety Case for ADS. In: V&V Methods Mid-term meeting (2022). https://www.vvm-projekt.de/midterm-docs. Accessed 02 June 2022
7. ISO: ISO/PAS 21448: 2022 - Road vehicles - Safety of the intended functionality (2022)
8. Blumenthal, M.S., Fraade-Blanar, L., Best, R., Irwin, J.L.: Safe Enough: Approaches to Assessing Acceptable Safety for AVs. RAND Corporation, Santa Monica, CA (2020)
9. Galbas, R.: How to systematically release AD systems? In: V&V Methods Mid-term Meeting (2022). https://www.vvm-projekt.de/midterm-docs. Accessed 02 June 2022
10. UNECE IWG FRAV: GRVA-12-23, Guidelines and Recommendations concerning Safety Requirements for ADS (2022)
11. Neurohr, C., Westhofen, L., Butz, M., Bollmann, M.H., Eberle, U., Galbas, R.: Criticality analysis for the verification and validation of automated vehicles. IEEE Access **9**, 18016–18041 (2021). https://doi.org/10.1109/ACCESS.2021.3053159
12. CATAPULT, CertiCAV Paper: A framework approach for assuring the behaviour of highly automated vehicles (2021)
13. Japan Automobile Manufacturers Association: Automated Driving Safety Evaluation Framework Ver 2.0 (2021)
14. Aurora: Aurora unveils first-ever Safety Case Framework that addresses the safety of both autonomous trucks and passenger vehicles. https://aurora.tech/blog/aurora-unveils-first-ever-safety-case-framework. Accessed 28 Apr 2022
15. Bishop, P., Bloomfield, R.: A methodology for safety case development. In: Redmill, F., Anderson, T. (eds) Industrial Perspectives of Safety-Critical Systems. Springer, London (1998). https://doi.org/10.1007/978-1-4471-1534-2_14

16. Kelly, T., Weaver, R.: The goal structuring notation–a safety argument notation. In: Proceedings of the Dependable Systems and Networks 2004 Workshop on Assurance Cases (2004)
17. Koopman, P., Osyk, B.: Safety argument considerations for public road testing of AVs. In: WCX SAE World Congress Experience (2019). https://doi.org/10.4271/2019-01-0123
18. ISO: ISO 26262:2018 - Road vehicles - Functional safety (2018)
19. Automated Vehicle Safety Consortium™: AVSC Best Practice for Metrics and Methods for Assessing Safety Performance of ADS (2021)
20. The MISRA Guidelines for automotive safety arguments. https://www.misra.org.uk/misra-safety-argument/. Accessed 28 Apr 2022
21. Structured Assurance Case Metamodel (SACM^{TM}). https://www.omg.org/spec/SACM/2.2/About-SACM/. Accessed 03 June 2022
22. Claims, Arguments and Evidence (CAE) notation. https://www.adelard.com/asce/choosing-asce/cae.html. Accessed 03 June 2022
23. Schittenhelm, H.: How to ensure a safe operation of an automated driving system by a methodological approach? In: V&V Methods Mid-term Meeting (2022). https://www.vvm-projekt.de/midterm-docs. Accessed 02 June 2022
24. BSI: PAS 1881:2022 Assuring the operational safety of automated vehicles - Specification (2022)
25. ANSI/UL 4600 Standard for Safety for the Evaluation of Autonomous Products (2021)
26. Rae, A.: Acceptable Residual Risk - Principles, Philosophies and Practicalities. pp. 26–31 (2007). https://doi.org/10.1049/cp:20070436
27. ISO: ISO/AWI TS 5083 Safety for automated driving systems - Design, verification and validation (under development)
28. BMVI: Ethics Commission - Automated and Connected Driving, Report extract (2017)
29. VTT: Key performance indicators for assessing the impacts of automation in road transportation Results of the Trilateral key performance indicator survey (2018)
30. ECE/TRANS/WP.29/2020/81: A new UN Regulation on uniform provisions concerning the approval of vehicles with regards to Automated Lane Keeping System (2020)
31. Shalev-Shwartz, S., Shammah, S., Shashua, A.: On a formal model of safe and scalable self-driving cars. arXiv preprint arXiv:1708.06374 (2017)
32. IEEE: IEEE 2846-2022, Standard for Assumptions in Safety-Related Models for Automated Driving Systems (2022)
33. SIG UNR157 TF: UNR157-09-03r1 Performance models of ALKS, Annex 3 (2021)
34. NIST Workshop: Consensus Safety Measurement Methodologies for ADS-Equipped Vehicles. www.nist.gov/news-events/events/2019/06/consensus-safety-measurement-methodologies-ads-equipped-vehicles. Accessed 28 Apr 2022
35. Kramer, B., Neurohr, C., Büker, M., Böde, E., Fränzle, M., Damm, W.: Identification and quantification of hazardous scenarios for automated driving. In: Zeller, M., Höfig, K. (eds.) IMBSA 2020. LNCS, vol. 12297, pp. 163–178. Springer, Cham (2020). https://doi.org/10.1007/978-3-030-58920-2_11
36. Wishart, J., et al.: Driving safety performance assessment metrics for ads-equipped vehicles. SAE Technical Paper 2, 2020-01-1206 (2020)
37. Mahmud, S.S., Ferreira, L., Hoque, M.S., Tavassoli, A.: Application of proximal surrogate indicators for safety evaluation. IATSS Res. 41(4), 153–163 (2017)
38. Hoss, M., Scholtes, M., Eckstein, L.: A review of testing object-based environment perception for safe automated driving. Automot. Innov. 5, 223–250 (2022). https://doi.org/10.1007/s42154-021-00172-y
39. Dixit, V.V., Chand, S., Nair, D.J.: Autonomous vehicles: disengagements, accidents and reaction times. PLoS ONE 11(12), e0168054 (2016)

40. ASAM OpenODD: Concept Paper. www.asam.net/index.php?eID=dumpFile&t = f&f = 4544&token=1260ce1c4f0afdbe18261f7137c689b1d9c27576. Accessed 28 Apr 2022

41. Koopman, P., Osyk, B., Weast, J.: Autonomous vehicles meet the physical world: RSS, variability, uncertainty, and proving safety. In: Romanovsky, A., Troubitsyna, E., Bitsch, F. (eds.) SAFECOMP 2019. LNCS, vol. 11698, pp. 245–253. Springer, Cham (2019). https://doi.org/10.1007/978-3-030-26601-1_17

42. De Gelder, E., Elrofai, H., Saberi, A.K., Paardekooper, J.P., Den Camp, O.O., De Schutter, B.: Risk quantification for automated driving systems in real-world driving scenarios. IEEE Access **9**, 168953–168970 (2021)

43. Karunakaran, D., Worrall, S., Nebot, E.: Efficient statistical validation with edge cases to evaluate highly automated vehicles. In: 2020 IEEE 23rd International Conference on Intelligent Transportation Systems (ITSC), pp. 1–8. IEEE (2020)

1st International Workshop on Security and Safety Interaction (SENSEI 2022)

1st International Workshop on Safety-Security Interaction (SENSEI 2022)

Christina Kolb[1], Milan Lopuhaä-Zwakenberg[2], and Elena Troubitsyna[3]

[1] Independent scholar, Enschede, the Netherlands
christina.kolb2022@gmail.com
[2] Department of Computer Science, University of Twente, Enschede,
the Netherlands
m.a.lopuhaa@utwente.nl
[3] Division of Theoretical Computer Science, KTH Royal Institute
of Technology, Stockholm, Sweden
elenatro@kth.se

1 Introduction

Two important criteria in designing hightech systems are safety (the absence of risk of harm due to technological malfunctioning) and security (the ability to withstand attacks by malicious parties). Safety and security are heavily intertwined, and measures to improve one may have a positive or negative effect on the other. For instance, passwords can secure patients' medical data, but are a hindrance during emergencies. On the other hand, cyberattacks can purposely cause a system to fail, and improving cybersecurity leads to increased safety. To ensure safety and security, it is vital to understand how safety and security interact.

The aim of SENSEI 2022 is to further our understanding of safety-security interaction. For example, two important topics are the co-engineering of safety and security, and integrated safety and security risk assessment. To foster the exchange of concepts, experiences, research ideas, and novel results, we bring together a wide range of researchers in safety and security, from theoretical to practical research. There will be room to present and publish the latest findings in the field, but also for discussion to share experiences and novel ideas.

As chairpersons of SENSEI 2022, we want to thank all authors and contributors who submitted their work, Friedemann Bitsch, the SAFECOMP Publication Chair, Jérémie Guiochet and Erwin Schoitsch, the SAFECOMP Workshop Chairs, the members of the International Program Committee who enabled a fair evaluation through reviews and considerable improvements in many cases, and Mariëlle Stoelinga for guidance and advice. We want to express our thanks to the SAFECOMP organizers, who provided us the opportunity to organize the workshop at SAFECOMP 2022.

We hope that all participants will benefit from the workshop, enjoy the conference and will join us again in the future!

Acknowledgements. This workshop is partially funded by ERC Consolidator grant 864075 CAESAR.

International Program Committee 2022

Barbara Gallina	Mälardalen University, Sweden
Brahim Hamid	Institut de Recherche en Informatique de Toulouse, France
Carlos E. Budde	University of Trento, Italy
Christoph Schmittner	Austrian Institute of Technology, Austria
Gabriel Pedroza	Commisariat à I'Energie Atomique, France
Georg Macher	Graz University of Technology, Austria
Rajesh Kumar	BITS Pilani, India

Increasing IoT Security by Supply Power Measurement

Uwe Becker[(✉)] (iD)

Draegerwerk AG&Co KGaA, Moislinger Allee 53-55, 23552 Luebeck, Germany
uwe.becker@draeger.com

Abstract. IoT devices are pervasive and provide helpful data in many aspects of life. People very often rely on the information provided by these devices. In contrast to this, IoT devices often are not designed with the right degree of security. Sometimes the assumptions made during development regarding their environment become invalid soon after roll-out. In addition, new threats arise, and new vulnerabilities are discovered frequently. Therefore, IoT devices are of great interest to attackers and often easily fall victim to them. This paper will describe a method to detect whether a medical IoT device is under attack and whether it runs any unexpected tasks. The method uses supply current monitoring and is both easy to implement and only requires very few resources (both in CPU performance and in memory). It can be used as an inexpensive early warning system.

Keywords: Medical IoT devices · Current measurement · Power measurement · Supply monitoring · IoT security · IDS · Malware detection · Sensor attack

1 Introduction

IoT devices are pervasive and we see a steep increase in their numbers. From the security point of view, this means a dramatic increase of devices at risk. Many of the devices were developed with the mind that they will operate in a secured network. This main assumption regarding security becomes more and more invalid by the way the devices are connected. Other devices are fielded largely ignoring security issues. The growing number of devices and the lack of security make them interesting targets for attackers.

Attacks on medical IoT devices can pose serious threats to patients. Therefore, it is important to decrease the attack surface as far as possible. If attacks cannot be avoided, they should at least be detected. In this paper, we describe a way to reliably detect an attack on a medical IoT device. For such devices, it is not feasible to use external equipment to detect an attack on them. Therefore, the device itself should detect any anomalies. The detection should only require low power and processing overhead. We use monitoring of supply current and power consumption of the devices for attack and intrusion detection. The paper is organized as follows: In the next section, we will define the attack scenarios to evaluate the approach against. This will be followed by a section describing the state of the art and a section on medical IoT devices. The approach will be described in Sect. 3. The results given in Sect. 4 will show that our approach is able to detect all relevant attacks. The paper will conclude with a short summary.

© The Author(s), under exclusive license to Springer Nature Switzerland AG 2022
M. Trapp et al. (Eds.): SAFECOMP 2022 Workshops, LNCS 13415, pp. 197–210, 2022.
https://doi.org/10.1007/978-3-031-14862-0_15

1.1 Attack Scenarios

In this paper we mainly focus on the following attack scenarios: a) the attack is performed using a (wireless) connection to retrieve information. b) the attacker makes the IoT device execute an additional task. This task can either be periodic or non-periodic. Attackers may use such tasks for personal gain. Consider for example mining, sending spam messages, or sending data packages to perform a DDoS attack on some other device. c) the attacker makes the IoT device change the measured values or the values transmitted, respectively. The attacker runs a task that changes the values before transmission. This scenario is often used to attack the system the IoT device is part of. Such attacks are commonly used either to perform damage or to request a ransom.

1.2 Pre-requisites and Assumptions

Our approach increases security of existing designs but should not be the only measure against attacks. It should be used as a supplement to increase security of the device. We assume that an attacker tries to hide the attack and thus any additional task will either have the name of a legitimate task or will not appear in the task list at all. This will prevent triggering the usual defenses where the number of running tasks is checked or the name of running tasks is checked. We assume that good security design practice is used, and additional security measures are in place. We give a short (incomplete) list of them below. A) Values are transmitted including a hash value (or something similar) to ensure correctness of transmissions. The receiving device must be able to detect (larger) delays and whether the values it receives are unchanged. B) There is a timestamp in the transmissions to detect whether the same values are transmitted again and again (replay attack). C) The devices check whether they run the expected tasks and the correct number of tasks (list of expected tasks). D) During boot time it is ensured that only tasks and processes are started that are signed or have a correct hash value (identical to a value in a secure storage). E) During run-time, it is checked whether all tasks are unchanged e.g. by again checking their signatures to avoid arbitrary code being executed. All these requirements are either already implemented in modern processors or can be implemented with low overhead. Implementation of basic cybersecurity measures is an essential part of good design practice. If devices can execute arbitrary code without any check neither safety nor correct function can be guaranteed. This security issue is also a safety issue as the attacker can deactivate any safety measures. Certification authorities nowadays are very sensitive to cybersecurity issues. Decent documentation is required to demonstrate usage of good design practice. Threat analysis documentation has to be filed to adequately address the relevant attack scenarios.

The values medical devices display often are used to derive therapy decisions from them. If the values are wrong, then very likely the therapy will be wrong as well. This can put patients at risk and is the reason why tampering of values should be detected.

1.3 Other Approaches/State of the Art

Ngo et al. [1] describe a similar approach, but their approach has different drawbacks. The approach depends on a single task system. It uses models that are too computing-intensive for most IoT devices. It requires large amounts of storage as a huge number of measured values is stored prior to evaluation. It is not suited for online evaluation due to the significant delay in the evaluation, as only complete junks of data are evaluated. Measurements are collected and then fed to a neural network for evaluation. Our approach strives to overcome all these limitations. Clark et al. showed that malware can be detected by the collection of power consumption [17]. It showed feasibility even only in a constraint scenario. Other approaches compare the measurements against predicted amounts of power. Many of them use (S)ARIMA models [13] [(Seasoned) Auto-Regression Integrating Moving Average]. In contrast to ARIMA models, SARIMA models can cope well with periodic demands of power. The predicted value is based on a moving average of the last values and on the auto-regression of the current and the previous measurements. The error between the prediction and the actual values is considered using an integration function. SARIMA models often are used to predict power consumption in a power grid but can be transferred to the power consumption of an IoT device. Pham et al. showed that by monitoring the electromagnetic signals malware running on an IoT device is detectable [16]. External equipment is required to perform the monitoring. Our approach provides online analysis without additional equipment.

In semiconductor manufacturing, IDD measurement is used for binning [5, 6] and to prove the correct functioning of the devices. Our approach is similar in that we compare the measured IDD value against some expected values stored in memory. Some attacks use supply current monitoring in order to find out which part of the program or even which data the system processes [7, 8, 11]. Thus, supply current monitoring is also suited to determine whether a system runs tasks that it is not expected to run [2, 3, 17].

2 Medical IoT Devices

In this paper, we consider two different types of medical IoT devices. The first type is small patches that measure a vital parameter of the patient. They are applied as patches on the patient's skin. Some of the devices even perform energy harvesting to increase battery life. The patches are used to measure e.g. skin temperature, skin resistance, or the like. We call these patches sensor patches as they only have sensors but no actuators. The other type is devices that both have sensors and actuators. Some devices may implement a closed-loop control to perform their function. Values are measured at a first interval and the actuators are controlled based on those measurements. After that, values are transmitted at a second interval to larger nodes for documentation or further processing. The first and the second interval may or may not be equal. Patches that measure ECG and breathing frequency control the auxiliary patient current in a faster control loop but provide their measurements in a slower update interval. Measurement of SpO2 (oxygen saturation of the blood) on the other hand typically controls their LED current based on the measurement values they also transmit. Similar devices can be found in other domains too. Environmental sensors or sensors that count cars on a highway like the sensor patches just sense values and transmit the results to another system. Larger devices with both sensors and actuators e.g. control heating in smart homes.

Sensor patches often use fixed scheduling of their tasks. The schedule of the tasks may be that first the results of the last measurements are transmitted. After that new measurement values are taken and processed. In the next step, the system goes to a sleep state to either save battery power or to harvest enough energy for the next cycle. If the devices harvest energy, they often are equipped with some circuitry to measure the amount of charge stored in or taken from a capacitor. This circuitry can be used for the attack detection proposed. Otherwise, additional hardware is required. The additional overhead will be small though. Fixed task scheduling makes attack detection very easy because energy consumption will largely be identical for all cycles. This can easily be checked, and changes can be detected. The total energy consumed will be higher when additional tasks are executed, or additional information is transferred.

3   Current Measurement for Security

In this paper, we will concentrate on simple power analysis (SPA) only [9, 10]. Most IoT devices will not have the infrastructure to use other power analysis methods that use statistical analysis methods and/or require sophisticated measurement equipment. We strive to keep both the hardware and software overhead as small as possible.

3.1   Description of the Expected Power Consumption

Modern systems often have multiple power rails. Even a single processor may have e.g. 5 different power rails at different voltage levels. If the system contains an FPGA additional power rails may be present. It is often infeasible to monitor every single power rail as this will increase cost and effort significantly. Depending on the attack model one may decide to monitor only a subset of the power rails and omit others (e.g. the power rail for the IO interface). We propose to monitor the main power rail the other power rails are derived from. The challenge is that the values obtained from the main power rail underwent some averaging and filtering. Smaller deviations from the expected values may no longer be detectable. The proposed monitoring of the main power rail also detects attacks that only increase currents flowing through the IO interfaces. Finding the optimal interval to monitor power consumption is an optimization problem. Shorter intervals lead to an increase in power consumption and the system might not be able to harvest enough energy between the intervals. If the interval is too large the additional power consumption of malicious tasks may get undetected. The higher the resolution of the measurement and the higher the measurement rate, the more information regarding the current system state can be gathered and smaller deviations from the expected values can be detected. In the best case, it can be detected that the system is processing data that at least are uncommon or unexpected. At the downside this comes at the expense of increased computational overhead and increased energy requirements.

We propose to use different sampling intervals in different operating states of the system. If a sensor with a high resolution is used one might use different resolutions of the samples in different operating states. If this is not possible, e.g. for economic reasons, we propose to change the sampling rate. A reduced sampling rate will reduce average computing load. A higher sampling rate will be able to provide more detailed information in situations where significant changes in the supply current are expected. Thus, the actual values can be closely compared to the expected values and differences will be detected easily. There is a trade-off between overhead and detection capabilities.

The likelihood of missing an unexpected change in the supply current increases with the decrease of sampling rate, processing overhead, and energy consumption.

From system design we know the typical time tasks will run. If an additional task causes a longer running time (larger than the typical time plus some tolerance) we will signal this during the next transmission. In addition, a counter is available that indicates how often we detected tasks running longer than expected. To reduce false positives an alarm is triggered based on a threshold. This is a trade-off between the number of false positive and false negative alarms. The larger the threshold the easier it is for a malicious task to hide by choosing a suitable long period for execution. We suggest that the threshold be determined for each specific device (within an allowed range of values). This will allow adjusting for the actual environment and will make it harder for an attacker as the attack will require fine-tuning for each device.

The number of tasks the system will execute is known in advance. For each task on that list, we specify the expected power consumption and its course. The list of tasks may depend on the state the system is in. For instance, a command shell may only be allowed in maintenance mode but not in normal operation mode. Any additional task will require extra power and such unexpected activity will be detectable. We expect the description of the expected power consumption to be such that an attacker will not be able to hide his activity in the normal noise of the measurements. If a fixed task schedule is used, the descriptions of the power consumptions are processed in sequence. If the task schedule is not fixed either processing and power consumption overlaps or there is a switching between tasks. The latter will make it harder to check whether the supply current is in the expected range. If the IoT device has enough processing power, one may use the outputs of several SARIMA models to predict the power consumption of the different tasks [13, 14]. The outputs of the different models are added to predict the power consumption of the whole system. The device can inform the predictor of the supply current about certain situations such as data transfers via radio. The model considers this to predict the next value. This increases flexibility and can account for jitter in the processing. It may require detecting whether the radio is active or measurement of the power it consumes to avoid that an attacker signals data transfers but does malicious actions instead. Our approach includes averaging of values but otherwise tries to minimize any delay in processing.

Small IoT devices need a memory-saving storage concept for comparison of current power consumption values against their expected values. Resource requirements for storage and comparison should be small. We started with storing the expected values as a pair of words describing a piecewise linearized function as depicted in Fig. 1. In the example, 18 words for the 9 different levels of power consumption are required. For each change in the power consumption, the expected time and the power at that time are stored. We use a table containing the P_i and the t_i. For instance, power is expected to increase from P_0 at time t_0 to P_1 at time t_1. The increase is expected to be stepwise. For linear increases, values are interpolated linearly in between. Time values are stored as relative time. That means if one expects that task 1 starts after 10 s of inactivity, the time at which task 1 starts becomes t_0. In some cases, the tables to describe the comparison values of different tasks can be combined. This is the case when the course of power consumption is very similar (tasks change power consumption at the same relative time) and only the amount of power consumed is different. In that case, the table would include a triple with time, power of task 1, and power of task 2.

Comparison of the values is done with some tolerance band around the expected values. In general, the tolerance below the expected value is larger than the tolerance above that value. Nevertheless, we want to check whether the rise of power consumption is as expected and detect if a task does not start as expected or a different task is started mimicking the expected task (but draws less power – at least for a certain amount of time). The upper limit of the tolerance is the detection threshold for the detection of unexpected tasks. This threshold should be large enough to avoid too many false positives but small enough to have a sufficient detection probability of such tasks.

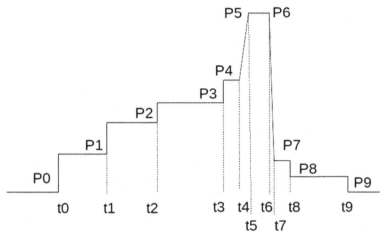

Fig. 1. An example of a piecewise linearized power consumption curve. The example curve would require 9 pairs of words for storage.

In our experiments we found that even with some averaging of the measurement values different parts of the course of the measurement may show noise levels that are too high to handle with a single average value. Different levels of noise need different strategies for comparison. A single value to compare against is not suited in segments with higher noise. Even if the noise at the end will average out, in between the deviation from the mean value might be high. In some measurements, we had 15% of noise on the signal. This is too high for a general tolerance band around the values as it will allow a malicious task to hide in that tolerance band. Therefore, it is beneficial to have different tolerances around the different segments of the proposed comparison curve. For signals with an expected higher degree of noise, we needed a special data type. The improved description of the power consumption uses the first byte to determine how to handle the respective segment of the curve. It either can be treated as a fixed value, as moving average, or to specify a tolerance band with the tolerance given in the bytes that follow. When a tolerance band is specified, the average value is specified too as it cannot be assumed that the average is in the center of the tolerance band. In contrast in our experiments, we found that the average is above the center of the tolerance band. The increased flexibility to specify the comparison values greatly justifies the investment in increased storage requirements. In addition, it does not increase computation requirements. The additional specification of the average value helps to detect whether a task tries to hide its energy requirements in the specified tolerance band.

We defined a flexible yet memory-saving format to describe the expected values. It can handle significantly changing amounts of noise on the measurements during the runtime of the tasks. It provides information for the different segments of the reference values. For segments with low expected noise, we provide an average value of the current. For other segments, we provide a tolerance band with or without an expected average value of the current. Our experiments showed that a tolerance band together with an average value yields the smallest number of false alarms. Approximation of the current by another function (higher-order polynomial function, periodic functions, etc.) did not result in better performance or lower number of false alarms. On the contrary, these approximations resulted in a higher processor load of the IoT devices. It was thus decided to continue with the linear approximation of the current. Even with the increased flexibility to describe the expected values, the overhead could be kept small while still providing good performance. A single byte to describe the format of the next value is used. In the example of Fig. 1, only 9 additional bytes of storage would be required.

The mean value of the supply current is multiplied by the mean value of the supply voltage to determine power consumption. This is compared against the value taken from the power accumulation register. If there are larger differences – due to an unexpected task – both the averaged current and the accumulated power will deviate from the expected value and thus the task will be detected. Selecting the size of the averaging window is a trade-off between the processing overhead and the time until an unexpected task is detected. The number of false positive alarms can be reduced if it is decided to only issue an alarm after a certain amount of unexpected current and/or power values. This on the other hand comes at the expense that it is easier for an unwanted task to hide just by lowering its process priority or by inserting some sleep commands.

Our approach just uses a coarse description of the energy consumption. On the other hand, it requires only a small amount of storage on the system and provides an easy-to-check upper limit of the values. Especially, when a low update rate of measurements is selected, the measured values only give a coarser description of the energy consumption. Nevertheless, it is sufficient to use such coarse descriptions because it is very probable that the unintended tasks will consume energy that is detectably above the given curve. In addition, it is very probable that the higher energy consumption will be present long enough to be detected even with a low update rate of the energy measurements. Our experiments show that the more powerful the system (processor of the system) is, the more memory is required to store the description of the expected power consumption. The rate at which actual power consumption is measured should be increased with increased computing power of the system. Otherwise, the probability that unintended tasks and their power consumption will remain undetected will increase.

3.2 Technical Realization with Off-the-Shelf Hardware

Commercially available ICs that measure supply current, supply voltage, and power consumption are ideally suited to fulfill the requirements of our approach. In many designs using such ICs saves additional hardware for signal conditioning such as amplifiers etc. even if the device already has its A/D converters. As shown in Fig. 2, it does not require any changes in the (proven) signal conditioning circuitry of existing designs. It is only required to insert a shunt resistor in the supply path of the device. The maximum power of the IoT device determines the shunt resistor. The monitoring IC is connected to the IoT device using either an I2C or an SPI interface. We used the I2C interface on the sensor patch and the SPI interface on the larger IoT device.

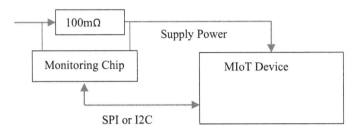

Fig. 2. Technical realization of the power monitoring

It is advantageous to use off-the-shelf current monitoring ICs that provide sophisti-cated features and settings to tune measurements according to the actual needs. To reduce the noise of the measurements either the number of bits used to represent measured val-ues, or the conversion time can be adjusted. Furthermore, it can be selected how many values are averaged before the result is output. In this case, the sampling rate remains constant but there are fewer updates of the data. The longer the averaging period the easier it is for an unexpected task to hide if it can keep the average current consumption constant. Some ICs calculate the power consumed based on the averaged current value. Others have a power accumulation register that calculates power consumption for each pair of current and supply voltage. The results are accumulated and provided together with the average values for current, voltage, and power. There is no loss of information even if a longer averaging time is selected. This makes it harder for unexpected tasks to hide. A stable power supply is essential when using the power accumulation register. If there are larger fluctuations in supply power, the values for consumed power will vary significantly and thus may be the cause of false positive alarms.

There is a trade-off between the exactness of the measurements and the costs the measurements introduce. The introduced costs both include the amount of hardware required to perform the measurements and the amount of computing power/processor time used. A coarse measurement with a comparatively long measurement period will likely miss some short spikes. Slight rises in the current consumed may also get unde-tected because of the tolerances required for comparison. On the other hand, if one expects that any additional task will consume a significant amount of power for a time much longer than the measurement period, cheaper hardware will do the job and detect all attacks according to the model of expected behavior. On more powerful machines the amount of power consumed by an additional task may only be small and it may only be drawn for a comparatively short amount of time. In this scenario, a more fine-grained measurement with both higher accuracy and shorter measurement periods is required.

3.3   Extension to Detect Replay Attacks

Attackers can record measurements of sensors and afterwards use the recorded information to perform replay attacks on the IoT devices. In general, it is hard to detect such replay attacks. In the literature, several approaches are proposed for their detection. One of them is performing some perturbations on the inputs of the system. It is assumed that the perturbations provoke reactions of the system the attacker cannot preview. Thus, it is harder to adjust the attack vector such that it still remains undetected. If perturbations are randomly introduced to the inputs, it is impossible for the attacker to anticipate when they are introduced. Therefore, it is impossible to change the replayed sensor information to avoid detection of the replay attack [1, 3, 12, 13, 15]. The perturbations, on one hand, have to be small enough to keep the control loop stable and on the other hand large enough to be distinguishable from the noise such that their presence can be detected. We propose to introduce similar perturbations on power monitoring by running a small task in a random schedule. We introduce a separate small task because we do not want to change the existing tasks and their programming. The task performs just a few calculations to increase detectability but to keep performance requirements low. The introduction of the small task can directly detect an attack on the current sensor. It might be difficult to detect a replay attack on other sensors just by monitoring power consumption. Replay attacks on other sensors can be detected if the time of measurement is used as a timestamp but not the time of transfer. The (small) delay introduced by the additional task will unpredictably change the timestamp. In addition, replay attacks can be detected if the system itself is unstable but the closed-loop control stabilizes the complete system. Other measures such as the introduction of additional perturbations on all sensors might be used to increase the detectability of attacks.

4   Results

To evaluate the effectiveness of our approach we used a small sensor patch with a fixed task schedule and a more powerful device running an operating system (Linux) with dynamic task scheduling. Both devices use MQTT to wirelessly transfer their data. Different attack scenarios were simulated on both devices and it was checked whether our approach was able to detect the simulated attacks. Attack scenario a) was simulated by both inserting data transmissions at the beginning or the end of a benign data transmission and by initiating a data transmission randomly between two benign data transmissions. In addition, its payload data was varied from one byte to 8 bytes. The sampling rate of the power monitoring IC has to be significantly shorter than the minimum transmission time to ensure reliable detection of an extra or prolonged transmission. In our setup, the power monitoring IC takes a sample every 28.5 μs and thus can reliably detect transmission that take 60 μs or more. The system draws additional power when a new connection is established, or additional data is transferred via an existing connection. For the smaller device, the radio consumes a significant amount of additional power. The simulation showed that our approach could detect all extra data transmissions.

Attack scenario b) was simulated by starting small shell scripts, shell commands, and small programs (a few lines of C code each). For the sensor patch, the tasks were inserted at a random position in the fixed task schedule. For the more powerful device, the tasks were started randomly and thus were executed in parallel to the normal tasks. We concentrated on non-periodic tasks as we consider them hard to be detected. In the fixed schedule scenario, it was very easy to detect the extra activity. We found that the description of the expected power consumption had to be extended such that the last entry was equal to the expected idle power. The additional tasks consumed more power than was expected and thus got detected. In the dynamic schedule scenario, the additional tasks were either executed during idle times or in parallel with other tasks. In a first test, we forgot to include a periodic housekeeping task of the operating system into the description of the expected power consumption. The housekeeping task and other activities of the operating system have to be described either in the same way the payload tasks are described, or a sequence of average values can be used. In that case, the averaging window has to be equal to the polling window of the power monitoring IC. The description of the operating system activities is added to the sum of the expected current of the active tasks. With this change, all additional tasks were detected reliably.

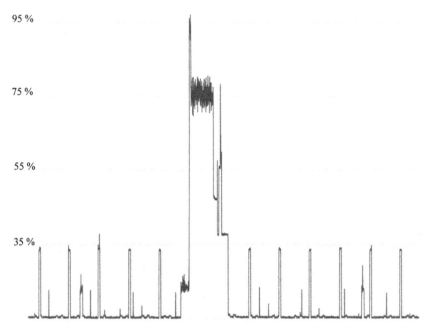

Fig. 3. Power consumption (and CPU utilization) of the IoT device running an unexpected task and using radio. The unexpected task runs in addition to the "normal" periodic tasks. Power consumptions add, as the device has enough computing power to process both its normal tasks and the additional task in parallel.

Figure 3 shows the power consumption of a system that runs tasks in a 10 ms schedule using about 35% CPU load. There is a single task that runs once for about 15 ms. It draws high processing power and power for the radio. The system is still able to run its "standard" tasks (although it nearly reaches maximum power) – see the small spikes atop the larger power demand. Therefore, the normal operation of the device is not compromised. This illustrates that attack scenario b) can be detected because the additional task requires additional energy and thus gets detected. In addition, the attack itself, when the attacker establishes a connection to the device and implements the additional task into the set of tasks will be detectable. The attacker either has to keep an already established connection open for a longer time or an additional connection is required. In both cases, additional power will be required. Therefore, this attack scenario can be detected reliably. We found that typical attacks and malware have distinct power signatures that can easily be detected. These patterns either overlap or replace the expected power consumption patterns. For scenario b) we simulated two additional variants and checked whether they could be detected. The first variant is changing the values for transmission using an additional task. This variant of the attack can reliably be detected as an additional task is used. It is also detectable when the change is in the task preparing the values for transmission. If changing of the values or preparation of the values takes longer than expected or the values get overwritten the measurement of current and power will be able to detect the change in the otherwise legitimate task.

The second variation of the attack is a change in the preparation of the values for transmission. If an offset is added to the values and the attack changes this offset, this will not cause an increase in power. It will also not cause an increase in the time needed to process the data or by checking for the names or number of running tasks. This variant of the attack will not be detectable by measurement of current or power alone.

There are different approaches to mitigate this attack. A first and very simple approach is to reset the system from time to time. After the reset, the system re-boots to a known state and the change to the task will be lost because the attacker can only change tasks in memory. Tasks on the boot device cannot be changed or their change will be detected because their signature will be different. Re-booting the system from time to time is not possible in every application. Therefore, we suggest running a special task to check the signature of all tasks in memory against predefined values. This explicitly includes the mentioned special task. Otherwise, an attacker could change this task and keep all attacks undetected. If a task in memory is detected to be compromised that task is killed and the system will restart the task. In addition, the connected system will be informed accordingly such that the last values can be discarded if required. Earlier we proposed to introduce perturbations by running a small task that just performs some calculations. This can be combined with the task to check all task signatures. Instead of just performing a few calculations, the signatures of the tasks in memory will be calculated. The calculation will be done for one task at a time to keep the delay short. In addition, the calculation will be done at random intervals to keep the perturbations unpredictable for a potential attacker. The combination of the two measures can reliably detect all attack scenarios and thus the most common attacks on IoT devices.

The power consumption curve of the sensor patch is shown in Fig. 4. Its power consumption is relatively constant. After measuring 1000 cycles, we noticed only minor deviations (+1.2% and −1.5%). The IoT device consumes more power during a simulated attack. At the end of the cycle, the power monitoring register significantly differs from the expected value (56721 instead of 46369). We store the expected value of the power accumulation register together with the description consisting of average, minimum, and maximum power consumption values for each phase as shown in Table 1.

Table 1. Description of the power consumption of the sensor patch (including real data)

Description	Length (Bytes)	Format	Value(s)
Type/bytes per entry	2	FD	0804
# of data	2	#	0004
Data	n	t1 av1 min1 max1 t2 av2 min2 max2 t3 av3 min3 max3 t4 av4 min4 max4	44, 290, 265, 320 22, 370, 355, 380 69, 260, 240, 275 115, 15, 5, 35

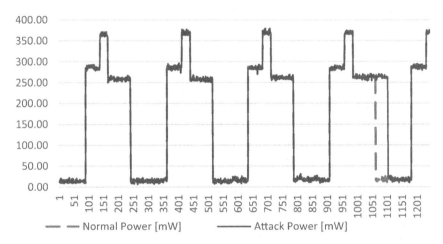

Fig. 4. Comparison of expected power consumption and power drawn during an attack

5   Conclusion

The growing number of IoT devices makes them increasingly becoming targets of attacks. Most IoT devices have limited hardware resources and thus do not allow the implementation of highly sophisticated but resource-intensive measures for attack detection and prevention. We presented a combination of two inexpensive measures capable of detecting the most frequent attack scenarios against IoT devices and malware running on them. Malware classification would require some delay in analysis and the power to perform AI-based analysis. We proposed to monitor supply power of the devices and to compare the actual value against expected values. In our experiments, we used inexpensive off-the-shelf power monitoring ICs to perform the measurements and a memory-saving description of the expected power consumption values. This is combined with a task running at random intervals, checking the signature of the tasks in the system. Both measures come with only modest resource requirements but detect attacks with high probability, low overhead, and in real-time. We can detect whether the system runs additional tasks, establishes additional network connections, and for known tasks it can be determined which data they process or which branch in the program is taken. Thus, the approach is also capable to determine whether the IoT device processes tampered data [4]. A few words of memory and a few calculations are required. Thus, it is well-suited for small IoT devices. One can adjust the required processing power by selecting an adequate averaging window for the measurement values. In general, the proposed defense only requires inexpensive additional hardware (with costs in the 1$ range). If the IoT device harvests energy and there is a measurement of the charge collected or drawn from a storage capacitor, even this measurement can be used. This measurement fulfills essentially the same function as the measurement of supply current and supply power. In this case no additional hardware costs will be generated. Supply current monitoring can be used as an Intrusion Detection System that can be adapted for a wide range of IoT systems with small effort. In addition, it can be combined with other measures such as AI-based behavioral monitoring [1, 2, 16]. Future investigations will extend the proposed approach to cover additional attack scenarios.

References

1. Ngo, D.-M., Temko, A., Murphy, C., Popovici, E.: FPGA hardware acceleration framework for anomaly based intrusion detection system in IoT. In: Proceedings of the 2021 31st International Conference on Field-Programmable Logic and Applications (FPL), pp. 69–75 (2021). https://doi.org/10.1109/FPL53798.2021.00020
2. Beasley, B.T., O'Mahony, G.D., Quintana, S.G., Temko, A., Popovici, E.: Lightweight anomaly detection framework for IoT. In: Proceedings of the 2020 31st Irish Signals and Systems Conference (ISSC), pp. 1–6 (2020). https://doi.org/10.1109/ISSC49989.2020.9180205
3. Shoukry, Y., Martin, P., Yona, Y., Diggavi, S., Srivastava, M.: Attack resilience and recovery using physical challenge response authentication for active sensors under integrity attacks. arXiv:1605.02062v2, May 2016
4. Roy, S., Sharmin, N., Acosta, J.C., Kiekintveld, C., Laszka, A.: Survey and taxonomy of adversarial reconnaissance techniques. arXiv:2105.04749v1, May 2021
5. Kaur, R., Jha, S., Roy, A., Park, S., Sokolsky, O., Lee, I.: Detecting OODs as datapoints with high uncertainty. arXiv:2108.06380v1, August 2021
6. Armengaud, E., et al.: DEIS: dependability engineering innovation for industrial CPS. In: Zachäus, C., Müller, B., Meyer, G. (eds.) Advanced Microsystems for Automotive Applications 2017. LNM, pp. 151–163. Springer, Cham (2018). https://doi.org/10.1007/978-3-319-66972-4_13
7. Ferré, A., Isern, E., Rius, J., Rodríguez-Montañé, R., Figueras, J.: I_{DDQ} testing: state of the art and future trends. Integr. VLSI J. **26**, 167–196 (1998)
8. Bar-El, H.: Known Attacks Against SmartCards. Discretix Technologies Ltd., WP (2021)
9. Kocher, P., Jaffe, J., Jun, B., Rohatgi, P.: Introduction to differential power analysis. J. Cryptogr. Eng. **1**, 5–27 (2011). https://doi.org/10.1007/s13389-011-0006-y
10. Kocher, P., Jaffe, J., Jun, B.: Differential power analysis. In: Wiener, M. (ed.) Advances in Cryptology—CRYPTO 1999, pp. 388–397. Springer, Heidelberg (1999). https://doi.org/10.1007/3-540-48405-1_25
11. Shoukry, Y., Martin, P., Yona, Y., Diggavi, S., Srivastava, M.: PyCRA: physical challenge-response authentication for active sensors under spoofing attacks. In: Proceedings of the 22nd ACM SIGSAC Conference on Computer and Communications Security. CCS, pp. 1004–1015 (2015). https://doi.org/10.1145/2810103.2813679

12. Morrow, K.L., Heine, E., Rogers, K.M., Bobba, R.B., Overbye, T.J.: Topology perturbation for detecting malicious data injection. In: Proceedings of the 2012 45th Hawaii International Conference on System Sciences. HICSS, pp. 2104–2113 (2012). https://doi.org/10.1109/HICSS.2012.594

13. Davis, K.R., Morrow, K.L., Bobba, R., Heine, E.: Power flow cyber attacks and perturbation-based defense. In: 2012 IEEE Third International Conference on Smart Grid Communications (SmartGridComm), pp. 342–347. IEEE (2012). https://doi.org/10.1109/SmartGridComm.2012.6486007

14. Badrinath Krishna, V., Iyer, R.K., Sanders, W.H.: ARIMA-based modeling and validation of consumption readings in power grids. In: Rome, E., Theocharidou, M., Wolthusen, S. (eds.) CRITIS 2015. LNCS, vol. 9578, pp. 199–210. Springer, Cham (2016). https://doi.org/10.1007/978-3-319-33331-1_16

15. Mo, Y., Weerakkody, S., Sinopoli, B.: Physical authentication of control systems – designing watermarked control inputs to detect counterfeit sensor outputs. IEEE Control Syst. Mag. 35(1), 93–109 (2015). https://doi.org/10.1109/MCS.2014.2364724

16. Pham, D.-P., Marion, D., Mastio, M., Heuser, A.: Obfuscation revealed: leveraging electromagnetic signals for obfuscated malware classification. In: ACSAC: Annual Computer Security Applications Conference, December 2021, pp. 706–719 (2021). https://doi.org/10.1145/3485832.3485894

17. Clark, S.S., et al.: WattsUpDoc: power side channels to Nonintrusively discover untargeted malware on embedded medical devices. In: 2013 USENIX Workshop on Health Information Technologies (HealthTech 13). USENIX Association, Washington, D.C. (2013). https://www.usenix.org/conference/healthtech13/workshop-program/presentation/clark

Towards Interdependent Safety Security Assessments Using Bowties

Luca Arnaboldi$^{(\boxtimes)}$ and David Aspinall

School of Informatics, University of Edinburgh, Edinburgh, UK
{luca.arnaboldi,david.aspinall}@ed.ac.uk

Abstract. We present a way to combine security and safety assessments using Bowtie Diagrams. Bowties model both the *causes* leading up to a central failure event and *consequences* which arise from that event, as well as *barriers* which impede events. Bowties have previously been used separately for security and safety assessments, but we suggest that a unified treatment in a single model can elegantly capture safety-security interdependencies of several kinds. We showcase our approach with the example of the October 2021 Facebook DNS shutdown, examining the chains of events and the interplay between the security and safety barriers which caused the outage.

Keywords: Safety and security · Bowtie diagrams · Risk analysis

1 Introduction

Structured graphical reasoning methods help the systematic discovery, assessment and mitigation of risks. A variety of methods have been used for security and for safety. While safety usually considers unintentional events and security deals with intentional malicious events, both safety and security assessments may consider causes and consequences of critical events. An early method is cause/consequence diagrams [23], commonly referred to as the "bowtie method" due to its graphical representation. A bowtie is formed of a tree of causes and a tree of consequences, fanning out to the left and right of a central critical (or *top*) event. Nodes in the tree represent causal or following events and *barriers* represent ways to prevent or mitigate events. Bowties have been used both for safety [27] and security [4] separately, and an initial investigation was even performed to inform a safety bowtie by an attack tree [1] in terms of risk quantification. They have many desirable properties, such as ease of visualisation [4] and the ability to quantify and calculate likelihoods of events, given a mathematical definition for a diagram's meaning.

In this paper we introduce a way to combine safety and security assessments together in a single bowtie, to enable reasoning about security and safety together. In particular we account for four different types of interplay between event types: safety and security can act independently, with conditional dependency, in concert, or in opposition [20]. An ideal structured reasoning approach should capture each of these.

© The Author(s), under exclusive license to Springer Nature Switzerland AG 2022
M. Trapp et al. (Eds.): SAFECOMP 2022 Workshops, LNCS 13415, pp. 211–229, 2022.
https://doi.org/10.1007/978-3-031-14862-0_16

2021 Facebook DNS outage. We use Facebook's recent global DNS outage as a running example, which nicely demonstrates some safety-security interplay [15, 16]. On October 4th 2021, there was a complete outage of all Facebook apps and services (including WhatsApp, messenger, Instagram, etc.), which lasted approximately 6 h. An initial small change to the DNS configuration triggered a complicated chain of events that made resolving a seemingly small issue overly complex and time consuming, and affected millions of people. This happened directly as an outcome of a security response disabling the ability for the safety engineers to patch the server remotely, forcing them to physically access the servers, which exacerbated the disruption.

A bowtie describing the sequence of events is presented in Fig. 1. In outline it shows that the DNS server-down event (the top event) could have a security cause or a safety cause. For example, a safety cause could be that a faulty update to the server configuration goes wrong; a barrier to stop this would be to check the patch doesn't cause the server to fail. A security cause might be that an attacker manages to access the DNS server and make a malicious update. If the DNS server does go down, we would like to find a path to a rapid fix to make the server operational again. But two fixes, a safety fix and a security fix, are *antagonistic* and act in opposition; only one of them should be undertaken. In the Facebook DNS incident, both fixes were implemented, disallowing remote access to the servers and delaying the response.

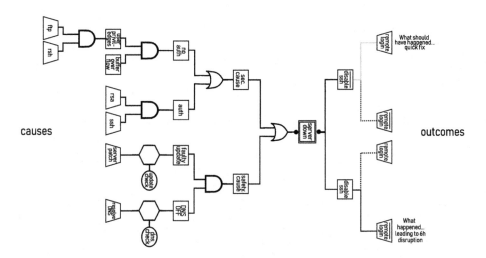

Fig. 1. High level bowtie diagram of the Facebook DNS outage (Table 2 expands the labels). The negative outcome is in black, whilst the grey path highlights the path that would avoid the negative outcome. Showing the antagonism between the security and safety responses.

Obviously this bowtie is not a complete safety-security assessment (and was constructed after-the-fact). A more complete model could cover the many bad consequences that can occur from a central DNS outage and ways those could be mitigated, as well as further ways such outages could occur. But this example serves to demonstrate how we can model some safety-security interdependences and we will give mathematical definitions which formalise this, returning to the example and variations of it in Sect. 4.

Outline. The rest of the paper is structured as follows: Sect. 2 contains background on diagrammatic representation of bowties, we note that further background is added as needed to the respective sections, Sect. 3 the formalisations of safety-security bowties, Sect. 4 the interdependence analysis and the formalisation of its operations, and in Sect. 5 we provide examples of related work, related assessment techniques, and discuss next steps for this work.

Contributions. The contributions of this work are the following:

1. A demonstration of security and safety interplay using bowtie diagrams and the Facebook DNS outage. Figure 1 highlights the need to treat safety and security together, before a critical event and afterwards.
2. Expanding on recent work on combining and formalising safety-security trees as *disruption trees* [29], we add barriers (safety) and mitigations (security), modelling both response forms in the same formalism.
3. We also add a corresponding mechanism for outcomes, to give a new definition for safety-security bowtie diagrams. This provides a solid underlying basis for the graphical notation, paving the way for further theoretical analysis and discussion, and ultimately towards trustworthy tools to reason about and manipulate such diagrams.

This paper is a first step and we want to investigate more complex case studies as well as studying properties of the definitions, see Sect. 5 for more discussion of next steps.

2   Diagrammatic Representations

Our bowtie diagrams use Boolean logic gate notation to show relationships between events tracking the passage of failures from "inputs" to "outputs". Boxes containing labels describe intermediate events.

Table 1. Symbols and relationships in a fault tree

Event Types	
▢	*Intermediate event* - an identity function labelling outgoing edges.
◯	*Prevention* - restrictive conditions, must fail to progress
△	*LEAF* - initiation event (BEs in Fault Trees) eventual outcome (in Event Trees)
Relationship Types	
⬡	INHIBIT - output occurs if the LH occurs and prevention does not
⟹	OR - output occurs if at least one of the inputs occurs
⟹	AND - output occurs if both of the inputs occur

Faults and attacks in the same diagram. Security analysis traditionally uses attack trees [26] whilst Safety analysis makes use of fault trees [30]. One shows the steps which an attacker can take to achieve a goal whilst the other shows the events leading to a fault. Stoelinga, however, has recently argued that fault trees and attack trees can be treated uniformly in a single structure [29]. Table 1 shows the symbols we use, following the Fault Tree Handbook notation [30].

Barriers and defences treated uniformly. We further propose to also treat barriers and defences in the same logic. To capture actions or conditions that impede fault conditions arising or defences in an attack tree, we use an INHIBIT gate drawn as a hexagon. The orthogonal side input is the inhibiting condition which prevents the flow of the fault or prevents the attack.

Safety Security Bowties. Now that we have a unified tree notation for attack trees and fault trees, we can use event tree tree notation for consequences as usual. This stays true to the essence of bowties as previously defined [25]. The focal point of the assessment is the critical risk event (or "top event", following fault tree parlance). To the left of the event are potential causes of the risk and ways to reduce them; this is the *prevention assessment*. On the right on the other hand we observe the outcomes of the risk event known as the *consequence assessment*.

An example unlabelled bowtie diagram is shown in Fig. 2. These diagrams are a Boolean network which are static and capture only logical dependencies: a bowtie itself is not quantitative, but it is a qualitative model that may be analysed quantitatively by adding additional annotations representing risk assessments. This has been done by various authors for fault and attack trees, for example [10,24]. For simplicity in the rest of this paper, we consider the basic logical interpretation only.

3   Formalisation of Safety-Security Bowties

Like typical bowties a safety-security bowtie will be composed of a *prevention assessment* and a *consequence assessment*. For the prevention assessment we use a *disruption prevention tree* which captures safety and security assessments, as well as attack and fault mitigations, which correspond to barriers in traditional bowties [25]. For the consequence assessment we use an event tree to show the consequences of the risk event and potential outcomes. The graphical representation from the figures includes intermediate events between gates, for enhanced understanding, but these are not part of the formalisation. We first showcase a general structure for trees we make use of for all subsequent formalisations in Sect. 3.1. We note that although, we are mostly concerned with trees, we adopt Directed Acyclic Graphs (DAGs) to allow input and outputs to be shared between gates.

3.1   Structure Trees

Our models are based on generalised n-ary trees with additional structure given by a node type labeling.

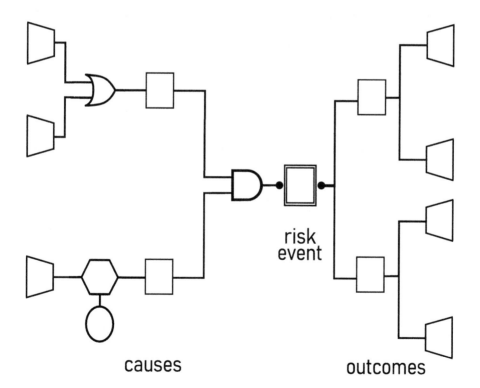

Fig. 2. Generic representation of Bowtie Diagram with causes on the left and outcomes on the right.

Definition 1 (Structure Tree). *A Structure Tree is a tuple* $T = \langle N, \mathbb{T}, t, ch \rangle$ *where:*

- *N is a finite set of nodes and $\mathbb{T}$ is a set of node types;*
- *$t : N \to \mathbb{T}$ gives the type of each node;*
- *$ch : N \to N^*$ gives the sequence of children of a node.*

Moreover, T satisfies the following constraints:

- *(N, E) is a connected DAG where $E = \{ (v, u) \in N^2 \mid u \in ch(v) \}$*
- *T has a unique root, denoted by $R_T : \exists! R_T \in N.\forall v \in N. R_T \notin ch(v)$ (where $\exists!$ stands for unique existence).*

Given a type $\texttt{LEAF} \in \mathbb{T}$, we write $\texttt{LEAF}_T = \{ v \in N \mid t(v) = \texttt{LEAF} \}$ for the nodes labelled with that type, and similarly for other types.

3.2   Disruption Trees

The notion of Disruption Trees (DTs) is introduced by Stoelinga as the uniform representation of static safety and security risk models [5,29]. Although extensions exists to each of these assessments which do result in key differences, in the simplest setting with only OR and AND nodes, they coincide.[1] Following Definition 1 we can interpret Stoelinga's DTs as:

Definition 2. (Disruption Tree [29]). *A Disruption Tree is a structure tree according to Definition 1 with $\mathbb{T} = \{ \texttt{LEAF}, \texttt{AND}, \texttt{OR} \}$ and such that $t(v) = \texttt{LEAF}$ iff $v \in LEAF_T$.*

Semantics pin down the mathematical meaning of models. The basic semantics of a disruption tree is given by its *structure function* over Booleans $\mathbb{B} = \{1, 0\}$, which defines a function from leaf events to the root in the obvious way. Structure Trees are more lax compared to models we usually want. Besides allowing useful DAG structure they include redundancies like nodes with repeated children. This is alright for AND and OR but would be confusing later on with gates that have some inputs (or outputs) being negated (or mutually exclusive). We call a structure tree (and later variants) *proper* if every child of a node is distinct, i.e., $|\{ ch(v) \mid v \in N \}| = length(ch(v))$. From now on we will restrict to models built on proper structure trees.

3.3   Prevention Assessments

We turn a Disruption Tree into a Disruption Prevention Tree by adding a new gate type for INHIBIT.

---

[1] There are subtleties in different ways to treat OR gates with quantified safety or security risks, which will not be considered here.

Definition 3 (Disruption Prevention Tree). *A Disruption Prevention Tree (DPT) is a Disruption Tree with an additional binary node type* INHIBIT, *i.e.,* $\mathbb{T} = \{\,$LEAF, AND, OR, INHIBIT $\}$ *and* $|ch(v)| = 2$ *whenever* $t(v) =$ INHIBIT. *The second child of an* INHIBIT *node corresponds to the inhibiting (prevention) condition.*

There is a similarity between Disruption Prevention Trees and Attack-Defence Trees. Formalisations of Attack-Defence Trees (see [18] for example) label nodes to represent their role in the model as a proponent (mitigating an attack or protecting against a fault event) or an opponent (actors causing damage leading to the root fault). It seems possible to recover this labelling from the root of DPT flipping the role when consider the prevention input of INHIBIT gates.

Structure of a DPT. The semantics of a DPT allows a proponent to block an opponent. These kind of barriers are called "avoid barriers" in fault trees [6,13] and "defences" in attack trees [18], but function in the same manner. Following from the DT semantics [29], we generalise the structure function to interpret the additional gate.

Definition 4 (Structure function for DPTs). *The structure function* $f_T :$ $N \times 2^{LEAF_T} \to \mathbb{B}$ *of a DPT* T *and* $A \subseteq LEAF$ *is defined by:*

$$
f_T(v, A) = \begin{cases} 1 & \begin{cases} \text{if } t(v) = \text{OR} & \text{and } \exists u \in ch(v).\ f_T(u, A) = 1 \\ \text{if } t(v) = \text{AND} & \text{and } \forall u \in ch(v).\ f_T(u, A) = 1 \\ \text{if } t(v) = \text{INHIBIT} & \text{and } f_T(u_1, A) = 1, f_T(u_2, A) = 0 \text{ where } ch(v) = [u_1, u_2] \\ \text{if } t(v) = \text{LEAF} & \text{and } v \in A \end{cases} \\ 0 & otherwise \end{cases}
$$

The interpretation for the overall tree is $f_T(A) = f_T(R_T, A)$.

We will sometimes use syntactic notation to construct DPTs using AND (written as $\cap$), OR ($\cup$) and INHIBIT ($\ocircle$) as term constructors and label names to stand for nodes in the graph. This can be made formal by defining interpretation functions on terms (for example, see [17]).

3.4   Consequence Assessments

A consequence assessment constitutes the right hand side of a safety-security bowtie and investigates potential ways to mitigate the central risk event or negative outcomes. As usually done with bowties, we make use of event trees to investigate each possible outcome of the central risk event. For the RHS of the bowtie, the leaf nodes in the DCT are potential final consequence events and each CHOOSE node represents a splitting point where a sub-event can have different outcomes (typically for a binary choice point, something happens or does not happen). This is captured by a *consequence function* C which selects the outcome event at each CHOOSE node, tracing a path through to a final outcome.

For the Boolean interpretation only a single choice can happen; for more general interpretations we might assign a possibility (Y/N/M) against each branch, probabilities or probability distributions, etc.

Definition 5 (Disruption Consequence Tree). *A Disruption Consequence Tree (DCT) is a structure tree with gate types* $\mathbb{T} = \{\text{LEAF}, \text{CHOOSE}\}$.

Definition 6 (Structure function for DCTs). *The structure function* f_T : $N \times (\text{CHOOSE}_T \to \mathbb{N}) \to N$ *of a DCT T is defined by:*

$$f_T(v, C) = \begin{cases} v & t(v) = \text{LEAF} \\ f_T(u_n, C) & \text{where } C(v) = n \text{ and } ch(v) = [u_1, \dots, u_n] \end{cases}$$

where C is a consequence function which selects an outcome for each CHOOSE *node, i.e.,* $1 \le C(v) \le length(ch(v))$ *for* $v \in \text{CHOOSE}_T$. *The interpretation for the overall tree is* $f_T(C) = f_T(R_T, C)$.

3.5   Bowties

A bowtie is just a pair of two structured trees. Intuitively, the top event corresponds to the two roots linked together, a realised disruption.

Definition 7 (Disruption Bowtie). *A Disruption Bowtie (DB) is a pair* $\langle T_P, T_c \rangle$ *of a disruption prevention tree and a disruption consequence tree.*

4   Interdependence Analysis

When assessing the interactions between security and safety we categorize them following the existing literature [9,20], they are:

1. *conditional dependency*, meaning the safety of the system depends on its security, and conversely,
2. *mutual reinforcement*, fulfilment of safety requirements or safety measures contributes to security, and conversely,
3. *antagonistic*, when considered jointly, safety and security requirements or measures lead to conflicting situations, and
4. *independence*, when the interactions are mutually exclusive or not in interference.

The interactions, obviously, have a great difference on the result of the assessment and in our case study we see dramatic differences in the same exact events inter-playing in different ways. We showcase in the scenarios the need for specific operations and describe their semantics in this section. We omit the right hand side of the bowtie for those interdependencies which do not strictly require it (*independence* and *conditional*). Whilst we find that both *reinforcing* and *antagonistic* require the recovery side of the bowtie. We note that each interdependency condition leads to trees joined in the usual fashion when combining to form a new tree.

4.1 Running Example: Safety Security Interplay

As main point of reference we use the reported chain of events by Facebook engineering [15, 16] as well as the external assessment conducted by CloudFlare [21]. We conducted a structured risk assessment of the Facebook DNS shutdown using security safety bowties focusing our analysis on how safety and security measures interacted to lead to the specific events. Our methodology of analysis was the following: i) we downloaded the analysis of the events released by the Facebook engineering team as well as an external examination by cloud hosting provider CloudFlare which witnessed the events externally. ii) we systematically labelled each brief to extract events, its causes and outcomes and the recovery/preventions that were in place (and failed in this case). For the sake of case study we choose to adapt an attack tree that reached the same risk event of the server outage, for this we borrow an existing example from [17]. For the sake of diagrammatic explainability edges are labelled by an identity function, which creates the intermediate events, a full table containing all edge labels is presented in Table 2.

Table 2. Explanations of edge and event labels.

Attack label	Explanation	Safety label	Explanation
Server Down	Once the attacker has gained access to the server he chooses to deny others access.	**Server Down**	Due to erros with DNS configuration and a faulty update with a failed check the server goes offline
auth	Breaching the authentication mechanism	**faulty update**	Due to unchecked issues in patch the faulty update when't through
no auth	Bypassing the authentication mechanism	**DNS OFF**	Due to safety procedure DNS hidden from internet
user privileges	Gain illegitimate privileges	**update check**	The safety checker for updates failed to spot the fault
buffer overflow	Exploit vulnerabilities to overflow	**dns check**	Internal safety procedure was that if the internal DNS resolver couldn't find its own address it removed the DNS from the internet
rsa	RSAREF2 library buffer overflow vulnerability	**server patch**	An engineer send an update to the backbone routers which was faulty
ssh	ssh deamon overflow vulnerability	**resolve dns**	DNS is unable to resolve its own addresss
rsh	Remotely executing shell commands	**remote login**	Remotely patch the server to remove failure
ftp	Exploit ftp vulnerability to upload files		
server disrupt	Once the attacker has gained access to the server he alters the DNS settings		
disable ssh	Remove ssh access to stop vulnerability		

The triggering of the initial Facebook blackout was caused by two independent events, firstly an engineer sent an update to the backbone routers which was faulty, this was not caught by the safety checker and was allowed to go through. An internal safety procedure was: that if the internal DNS resolver couldn't find its own address it removed the DNS from the internet, meaning they were invisible to the outside world. In the case of an attack we consider a generic server, offering ftp, ssh, and rsh services, as seen in previous work [17]. The attack tree in Fig. 1 shows how an attacker can disrupt a server in two ways: either without providing any user credentials (no-auth) or by breaching the authentication mechanism (auth). In the first case, the attacker must first gain user privileges and then perform a local buffer overflow attack. To gain user privileges, the attacker must exploit an FTP vulnerability to anonymously upload a list of trusted hosts as well as remotely executing shell commands using RSH. The second way is to abuse a buffer overflow in both the ssh daemon (SSH) and the RSAREF2 library (RSA) used for authentication.

Using the described notation we formalise the security and safety scenarios as DPT_S and DPT_A for safety and security respectively:

$$DPT_S = ((\texttt{server patch} \, \circ \, \texttt{update check}) \cap (\texttt{resolve DNS} \, \circ \, \texttt{dns check}))$$

$$DPT_A = ((\texttt{ftp} \cap \texttt{rsh}) \cap \texttt{buffer overflow}) \cup (\texttt{rsa} \cap \texttt{ssh})$$

4.2 Independence

The Independence relationship can simply be defined as an OR gate, whereby either the security scenario *or* the safety scenario lead to the eventual risk condition, an initial investigation of this has has been done before [28], and can be visualised in Fig. 3 for our case study.

For quantitative analysis there are, however, certain complications. Since now both a safety assessment is present as well as a security assessment, there needs to be a choice as to how the OR gate quantification is performed. Whilst this topic in itself warrants a deeper discussion orthogonal to the contributions of this work, a naive approach is to employ the approach from Steiner and Liggesmeyer and calculate a composition of risk-probability pairs leading to the OR gate outcome [28]. In the case study we simple see that the server outage may be caused by an active attacker (attack tree), or a failure of the update process and DNS misconfiguration (safety tree), or both.

Independence is modelled as two DPTs joining roots with an OR gate.

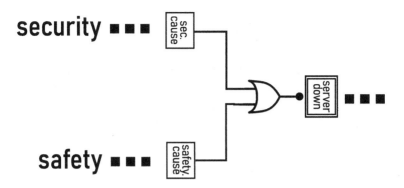

Fig. 3. Independence - when the two events do not interact to cause the final outcome. This is a sub-tree of the tree in Fig. 1, and as such details are omitted

Definition 8. *An independent joining of a security and a safety assessment (assuming both are modelled as disruption defence trees) is defined as: given two disruption defence trees DPT_A and DPT_F a new tree DPT_{AF} is formed as:*

- $DPT_{AF} := \langle N_A \uplus N_E \uplus \{R_{T_{AF}}\},\ \mathbb{T},\ t_a \uplus t_f \uplus \{R_{T_{AF}} \mapsto \text{OR}\},\ ch_A \uplus ch_F \uplus \{R_{T_{AF}} \mapsto [R_{T_A}, R_{T_F}]\}\rangle$

So for the example in Fig. 3, the independent joining would look like this:

$$FB_{IND} = (((\texttt{ftp} \cap \texttt{rsa}) \cap \texttt{buffer overflow}) \cup (\texttt{rsa} \cap \texttt{ssh})) \cup$$
$$((\texttt{server patch} \bigcirc \texttt{update check}) \cap (\texttt{resolve DNS} \bigcirc \texttt{dns check}))$$

4.3 Conditional Dependency

Given two disruption prevention trees a conditional dependence means that the vertex of one of the trees corresponds to a child node or intermediate event of the other. A conditional joining extends the tree to include all the children of the vertex being merged in, with the old vertex simply becoming an intermediate event to the other tree. The assessment now needs to include all the new nodes that lead to the risk event. In the example we can easily presume that the failure to resolve the DNS could be due to an attacker having gained access to the server (following the attack path from the attack tree) and changing the configuration. So by merging the attack tree to the fault tree on the resolve DNS node we get a conditional dependence, as seen in Fig. 4.

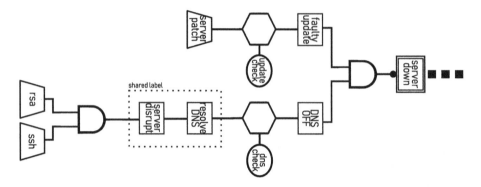

Fig. 4. Conditional - when the safety outcome is conditional on the security or vice versa. Scenario modelled by security outcomes (simplified) causing fault.

A conditional dependence may be viewed as the expansion of a previously unknown external event. Whilst previously we had a `LEAF` node that represented an input to an assessment, we now expand this node into a fully fledged disruption tree. This notion of external event is seen in previous literature [30], and this can be seen as an enhancement of knowledge of what lead to the input events. Semantically it means that a node at the bottom of a disruption tree simply gains as children all the nodes in another disruption tree, and the previous child leaf node is substituted.

Definition 9. *A conditional joining of a security and a safety assessment (assuming both are modelled as a disruption defence tree) is defined as: given a joining of two disruption defence trees DPT_A to DPT_F and a condition node n_c (of type* `INHIBIT`) *a new tree DPT_{AF} is formed as:*

- $DPT_{AF} := \langle N_A \uplus N_F \uplus \{n_c \mapsto R_{T_A}\}, \mathbb{T}, t_A \uplus t_F \uplus \{t_{AF}(n_c) := t_A(R_{T_A})\}, ch_A \uplus ch_F \rangle$

So for the example in Fig. 4, the conditional joining would look like this:

$FB_{COND} = ((\texttt{server patch} \ \circlearrowright \ \texttt{update check}) \ \cap \ ((\texttt{rsa} \ \cap \ \texttt{ssh}) \ \circlearrowright \ \texttt{dns check}))$

4.4 Reinforcing Dependency

The reinforcement dependency takes place when a DCT from one bowtie contains a response/outcome that leads to the resolution of the initial scenario of a separate DPT. This means that due to the response to an incident another incident is no longer plausible. If we take the same security response as previously, disabling ssh to stop the buffer overflow, we see that the patching of the server event which led to the faulty update cannot take place anymore, as per Fig. 5. This once again requires the right hand side of a bowtie. In this scenario the response outcome of one bowtie is chaining to the cause event of another tree.

Concretely, the response `disable ssh` negates the `server patch` event of the fault tree. This is modelled through a `INHIBIT` gate. Simply this is evaluated as the action no longer being possible (as the response is not negated it results to 0 in `INHIBIT` semantics).

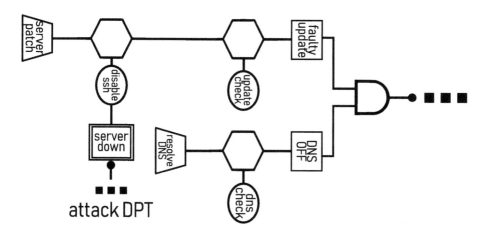

Fig. 5. Reinforcing - when a security or safety measure helps the other incident. This is modelled by the outcome of security (simplified) in this case, stopping the safety incident. Attack tree omitted as it is sub-tree of Fig. 1

Reinforcing dependence assumes that as an outcome of fixing a fault or mitigating an attack, another fault or attack is no longer possible. The approach taken in this scenario is to take the DCT on the right hand side of the bowtie, joining into the reinforced DPT, extending it, and creating a new DPT. This leads to the final risk event of the reinforced DPT being the new risk event of focus for the whole assessment. We make the assumption that if an event does not lead to any other disruptions in the DPT being reinforced it is not influencing the disruption and can be pruned (to preserver the tree structure and avoid back propagating branches). We infer that if an event is present in both trees there is an implied relationship, extensions could instead assign further labels to construct these relationships.

Definition 10. *A reinforcing joining of a disruption consequence assessment (implicitly joining any left most side DPT if a bowtie) DCT and any disruption defence tree DPT takes the form of a joining of the single reinforcing branch* $V_C = f_T(R_T \in DCT, C)$ *into a node* n_r *of type* `INHIBIT`:

- $DPT_{AF} := \langle N \uplus V_C, \mathbb{T}, t_P \uplus t_C, ch_P \uplus ch_C \uplus \{ch_{PC} : n_r \mapsto [u1, \overline{V_C}]\}$

We note that an inherent relationship between prevention and disruptions is assumed. This is not automatically inferred through formalisations. In this case a prevention, child two of the `INHIBIT` gate, is replaced by the branch of the DPT that reinforces the first child. We see that the previous child two $u2$ of the INHIBIT node is replaced by the branch V_C. One can observe that under this formalism some knowledge about the previous events are lost, as they are pruned in the joining. For clarity, an example joining between DCT_i and DPT_j:

$$DPT_i = (\text{X} \circ \text{Y}) \text{ and } DCT_j = ([j_i \cup \overline{j_i}, j_n \cup \overline{j_n}])$$

if j_n is reinforcing to X, their reinforcing joining DPT_{ij}, joins the path $V_j = \{j_i, j_n\}$ to DPT_i

$$DPT_{ij} = (\text{X} \circ \overline{V_j})$$

4.5   Antagonistic Dependency

When security and/or safety measures directly antagonise each other it means that a measure that attempts to make the system more secure has an adverse effect on its safety and conversely. We see that this antagonism is almost exclusively present in an outcome of an incident taking place (i.e. after the warning has gone off), and not visible in the bare DPT. For this specific scenario we need the use of the right hand side of a bowtie and event trees to represent the dependency. Going back to our case study, once the server has been taken down, engineers from the safety domain and the security domain investigate the incident. The first team (safety), sees that the incident is due to a faulty DNS configuration and patches the DNS remotely through SSH. The second team (security), sees that the incident is due to a vulnerability in the ssh library and therefore disables ssh (perhaps temporarily whilst the issue is being fixed by local engineers, as was the case for Facebook). As one can see, if the security response is put in place, there is no way the safety response can be put in place, this means that the fault or incident cannot be fixed if the security incident is fixed. We note this is exactly what took place during the Facebook outage, a security response disallowed the safety engineers to remote in and patch the fault, leading to physical access being required. In practice this means that the system can either be made safe or it can be made secure, but not both. This unlike the previous relationships is modelled through the consequence assessment and through the usage of event trees.

Definition 11. *An antagonistic joining of a security and a safety consequence is defined as: given a joining of two disruption consequence assessments DCT_A and DCT_F, and antagonistic event e, a new tree DCT_{AF} is formed as:*

- $DCT_{AF} := \langle N_a \uplus N_s, \mathbb{T}, t_a \uplus t_s, ch_s \uplus ch_a \uplus \{ch_{sa} : e \mapsto \textit{CHOOSE}\} \uplus \{ch_{sa} : \overline{e} \mapsto \textit{CHOOSE}\}\rangle,$

finally the Facebook DNS Disruption as a Bowtie can be defined in the following steps, given the DPT_S and DPT_A from Sect. 4.1 they can be *independently* joined following Definition 8 to form:

$$FB_{DPT} = (((\texttt{ftp} \cap \texttt{rsh}) \cap \texttt{buffer overflow}) \cup (\texttt{rsa} \cap \texttt{ssh})) \cup$$
$$((\texttt{server patch} \bigcirc \texttt{update check}) \cap (\texttt{resolve DNS} \bigcirc \texttt{dns check}))$$

and then given the two possible consequence trees, $[DCT_A, DCT_S]$:

$$DCT_S = (\texttt{remote login}) \; and \; DCT_A = (\texttt{disable ssh})$$

we can antagonistically join them following Definition 11 to form the FB case study situation of conflict:

$$FB_{DCT} = (\texttt{remote login} \cap \overline{\texttt{disable ssh}}) \cup (\overline{\texttt{remote login}} \cap \texttt{disable ssh})$$
$$\text{or more simply } (\texttt{remote login} \oplus \texttt{disable ssh}).$$

Putting the two together you can obtain the bowtie $FB_{Bowtie} = [FB_{DPT} \rightarrow [[\texttt{server outage}]] \rightarrow FB_{DCT}]$.

5   Conclusions

This work presented the first formalisation of safety security interdependence covering the full spectrum of dependencies through the use of bowtie diagrams. We notice some interesting outcomes: 1) for some of the dependencies dynamic gates are necessary i.e. INHIBIT gates (not typically used). 2) some dependencies make more sense on the outcome of the tree, are beyond the attack/fault tree, and need to be reflected in the recovery phase (showcasing the suitability of bowties as a way to explore interdependence). We also provide the first formalisation of DPTs alongside its semantics. Finally, this work is the first to provide formalisations of the safety security interdependence operations under a unified assessment.

5.1   Related Work

This work is by no means the first exploration of combining security and safety [1,12,14,19,20]. Existing work in the area also highlights that this is by no means an easy feat as there are several differences as an outcome of developing in completely different contexts [12]. Gould and Bieder [12] explore the initial development of the two fields and the contexts in which they coexist. Safety is originally developed as means to avoid systems failures guided by the increased understanding of hazards and inevitability of accidents. Conversely, security developed initially as an outcome of malicious parties wishing to harm systems, however has developed into a critical component of any system analysis. The authors cite the increase of emphasis on the reduction of risks associated with mitigating security threats as a key factor as to why security and safety should be integrated more. However security and safety fields diverge vastly on technology usages and quantification of risks. The two fields however are strongly interconnected and as such their integration is essential. The authors propose the need for new policies and shared practice as without the other neither field can be complete and neither safe nor secure [12]. This recent work highlights the need to unify the assessment techniques, although they do not provide intuition as to how to do so. Literature has already considered how these two fields may be considered under the same methodology [14], however, often this is done rather relying on expert analysis and without underlying formal foundations. However, there have also been some specific assessment techniques proposed to join the two assessments.

5.2   Assessment Techniques

An emerging field that has a deep integration between these two topics is that of industrial control systems (ICS) [20]. Industrial systems have always been focused on safety, however with the new integration of internet infrastructure and the IoT the avenues of attack greatly increase [2,3], leading to the need for better security evaluations to be in place. Work by Kriaa et al. [20], surveys a list of techniques used in this field for both safety and security. In this work the authors discuss the possibility for a safety case to be broken by security threats and discuss means to address this in the system assessment. The paper also discusses current standards for safety and security in the context of ICS, how they may integrate and assessments to decide which category needs to be considered. Using a different formalism of BMDPs previous work has similarly used the case study of a pipeline to observe security and safety interactions [19]. Their work was one of the first to evaluate the different interdependency types. In more recent work [11] address this same topic in the context of safety and security assurance. In this work the authors conduct an hazard analysis and risk assessment (HARA) a common safety assurance methodology alongside a threat analysis and risk assessment (TARA), which can be used to assess security risks. Combining these two techniques they are able to conduct a unified safety security assessment for their case study of an autonomous vehicle adhering to the safety standard ISO26262 and security standard ISO21434 for autonomous vehicles. Although we note that the unification of these techniques is not done formally under a single construct but more as an iterative manual process.

Having established the need for rigourous security assessment recent work experimented with the usage of bowties for this purpose [4]. In their work the authors apply the usage of bowties to security analysis in the maritime industry. They showcase the flexibility of the approach in quantified various threats and calculating the impact of the attacks. The paper proposes a formula for quantifying threat and consequence impact. The authors also ran a user study showed that people in the maritime industry thought Bowties for security were a very useful tool, showcasing the applicability of bowties to industry case studies. The first approach combining safety and security bowties [1], combines an attack tree with a safety bowtie, and whilst this proves to be a great first step, falls short of completely uniting the various interdependencies into a single assessment.

The literature showcases that there is already a wide use of these techniques across a wide range of fields and a formal representation allows to set the foundations for further expansions and reasoning. Formal descriptions allow to have a more rigorous way to analyse systems, they allow to establish what you can and can't do using the approach as well as reason about properties of a formalism. Previous work has applied this in the context of safety cases [7] and showcased it as a valuable way to create and assess system evaluations. Even more so, security researchers have applied formal representations to attack trees [17,22], showcasing its usefulness to reason about systems and performing structured analysis [10]. In more recent work [8] the authors formalise bowties in and causality sequences for usage of safety and avionics, their formalisation is similar to the one used in this work, although they omit the analysis of interdependency. As such they do not discuss joining operations and do not assess security and safety under the same construct, which lies at the foundation of our security and safety assessments. Our work begins to apply the same formal rigour to safety and security assessments using bowties to unify the assessment in a structured and formal manner, both drawing from clear semantic understanding as well as a clear visual representation.

5.3   Next Steps

In order to fully generalise this approach a larger case study should be adapted, in particular further analysis on how the two types of trees, event and disruption, can be chained to combine the analysis of several consequent risk events is desirable. We also see as desirable the investigation of further gate types to fully encapsulate the the full spectrum of analysis currently seen across the literature. The formal definition of joining operations we have provided for security and safety assessments presents a unique potential for automating the process of combining safety security analysis, future work into this area would have tremendous impact to more rigorously examine scenarios such as the Facebook DNS incident from both assessment angles. However there is also a need for further investigation into properties of these provided join operations. We also see the usefulness of hierarchicalisation as means to combine sequences of events into a single more readable structure. This has been explored in the past successfully for assurance cases [7] and as in this approach several assessments are joined together under the same formalism, an enhancement of this approach could be even more effective and desirable. We note that further to the formalisation of the structures and their semantics some distinctions exist in how the probabilities of risk are calculated, however this is orthogonal to the work presented here and we reserve this investigation to future work.

Acknowledgements. We're grateful to Ewen Denney for suggesting to us to investigate bowtie diagrams for safety-security assessments, as well as comments on an early draft. This work was funded by the AISEC grant under EPSRC number EP/T027037/1.

References

1. Abdo, H., Kaouk, M., Flaus, J.M., Masse, F.: A safety/security risk analysis approach of industrial control systems: a cyber bowtie-combining new version of attack tree with bowtie analysis. Comput. Secur. **72**, 175–195 (2018)
2. Arnaboldi, L., Czekster, R.M., Morisset, C., Metere, R.: Modelling load-changing attacks in cyber-physical systems. Electron. Notes Theor. Comput. Sci. **353**, 39–60 (2020)
3. Arnaboldi, L., Morisset, C.: Quantitative analysis of DoS attacks and client puzzles in IoT systems. In: Livraga, G., Mitchell, C. (eds.) STM 2017. LNCS, vol. 10547, pp. 224–233. Springer, Cham (2017). https://doi.org/10.1007/978-3-319-68063-7_16
4. Bernsmed, K., Frøystad, C., Meland, P.H., Nesheim, D.A., Rødseth, Ø.J.: Visualizing cyber security risks with bow-tie diagrams. In: Liu, P., Mauw, S., Stølen, K. (eds.) GraMSec 2017. LNCS, vol. 10744, pp. 38–56. Springer, Cham (2018). https://doi.org/10.1007/978-3-319-74860-3_3
5. Budde, C.E., Kolb, C., Stoelinga, M.: Attack trees vs. fault trees: two sides of the same coin from different currencies. In: Abate, A., Marin, A. (eds.) QEST 2021. LNCS, vol. 12846, pp. 457–467. Springer, Cham (2021). https://doi.org/10.1007/978-3-030-85172-9_24
6. De Dianous, V., Fievez, C.: Aramis project: a more explicit demonstration of risk control through the use of bow-tie diagrams and the evaluation of safety barrier performance. J. Hazard. Mater. **130**(3), 220–233 (2006)
7. Denney, E., Pai, G., Whiteside, I.: Formal foundations for hierarchical safety cases. In: 2015 IEEE 16th International Symposium on High Assurance Systems Engineering, pp. 52–59. IEEE (2015)
8. Denney, E., Pai, G., Whiteside, I.: The role of safety architectures in aviation safety cases. Reliab. Eng. Syst. Saf. **191**, 106502 (2019)
9. Eames, D.P., Moffett, J.: The integration of safety and security requirements. In: Felici, M., Kanoun, K. (eds.) SAFECOMP 1999. LNCS, vol. 1698, pp. 468–480. Springer, Heidelberg (1999). https://doi.org/10.1007/3-540-48249-0_40
10. Fila, B., Wideł, W.: Exploiting attack-defense trees to find an optimal set of countermeasures. In: 2020 IEEE 33rd Computer Security Foundations Symposium (CSF), pp. 395–410. IEEE (2020)
11. Gallina, B., Montecchi, L., de Oliveira, A.L., Bressan, L.P.: Multiconcern dependability-centered assurance via qualitative and quantitative coanalysis. IEEE Softw. **39**(4), 39–47 (2022)
12. Pettersen Gould, K., Bieder, C.: Safety and security: the challenges of bringing them together. In: Bieder, C., Pettersen Gould, K. (eds.) The Coupling of Safety and Security. SAST, pp. 1–8. Springer, Cham (2020). https://doi.org/10.1007/978-3-030-47229-0_1
13. Guldenmund, F., Hale, A., Goossens, L., Betten, J., Duijm, N.J.: The development of an audit technique to assess the quality of safety barrier management. J. Hazard. Mater. **130**(3), 234–241 (2006)
14. Haider, Z., Gallina, B., Carlsson, A., Mazzini, S., Puri, S.: ConcertoFLA-based multi-concern assurance for space systems. ADA USER **40**(1), 35 (2019)
15. Janardhan, S.: Update about the October 4th outage (2021). https://engineering.fb.com/2021/10/04/networking-traffic/outage/
16. Janardhan, S., Janardhan, S.: More details about the October 4 outage (2021). https://engineering.fb.com/2021/10/05/networking-traffic/outage-details/

17. Jhawar, R., Kordy, B., Mauw, S., Radomirović, S., Trujillo-Rasua, R.: Attack trees with sequential conjunction. In: Federrath, H., Gollmann, D. (eds.) SEC 2015. IAICT, vol. 455, pp. 339–353. Springer, Cham (2015). https://doi.org/10.1007/978-3-319-18467-8_23

18. Kordy, B., Mauw, S., Radomirović, S., Schweitzer, P.: Foundations of attack–defense trees. In: Degano, P., Etalle, S., Guttman, J. (eds.) FAST 2010. LNCS, vol. 6561, pp. 80–95. Springer, Heidelberg (2011). https://doi.org/10.1007/978-3-642-19751-2_6

19. Kriaa, S., Bouissou, M., Colin, F., Halgand, Y., Pietre-Cambacedes, L.: Safety and security interactions modeling using the BDMP formalism: case study of a pipeline. In: Bondavalli, A., Di Giandomenico, F. (eds.) SAFECOMP 2014. LNCS, vol. 8666, pp. 326–341. Springer, Cham (2014). https://doi.org/10.1007/978-3-319-10506-2_22

20. Kriaa, S., Pietre-Cambacedes, L., Bouissou, M., Halgand, Y.: A survey of approaches combining safety and security for industrial control systems. Reliab. Eng. Syst. Saf. **139**, 156–178 (2015)

21. Martinho, C.: Understanding how Facebook disappeared from the Internet (2021). https://blog.cloudflare.com/october-2021-facebook-outage/

22. Mauw, S., Oostdijk, M.: Foundations of attack trees. In: Won, D.H., Kim, S. (eds.) ICISC 2005. LNCS, vol. 3935, pp. 186–198. Springer, Heidelberg (2006). https://doi.org/10.1007/11734727_17

23. Nielsen, D.S.: The cause/consequence diagram method as a basis for quantitative accident analysis. Risø National Laboratory (1971)

24. Ren, H., Chen, X., Chen, Y.: Fault tree analysis for composite structural damage. In: Reliability Based Aircraft Maintenance Optimization Applications, pp. 115–131. Academic (2017)

25. de Ruijter, A., Guldenmund, F.: The bowtie method: a review. Saf. Sci. **88**, 211–218 (2016)

26. Schneier, B.: Attack trees. Dr. Dobb's J. **24**(12), 21–29 (1999)

27. Shahriar, A., Sadiq, R., Tesfamariam, S.: Risk analysis for oil & gas pipelines: a sustainability assessment approach using fuzzy based bow-tie analysis. J. Loss Prev. Process Ind. **25**(3), 505–523 (2012)

28. Steiner, M., Liggesmeyer, P.: Combination of safety and security analysis-finding security problems that threaten the safety of a system. In: DECS: ERCIM/EWICS Workshop on Dependable Embedded and Cyber-Physical Systems (2013)

29. Stoelinga, M., Kolb, C., Nicoletti, S.M., Budde, C.E., Hahn, E.M.: The marriage between safety and cybersecurity: still practicing. In: Laarman, A., Sokolova, A. (eds.) SPIN 2021. LNCS, vol. 12864, pp. 3–21. Springer, Cham (2021). https://doi.org/10.1007/978-3-030-84629-9_1

30. Vesely, W.E., Goldberg, F.F., Roberts, N.H., Haasl, D.F.: Fault Tree Handbook. Tech. Rep. NUREG-0492, Nuclear Regulatory Commission Washington DC (1981)

3rd International Workshop on Underpinnings for Safe Distributed Artificial Intelligence (USDAI 2022)

3rd International Workshop on Underpinnings for Safe Distributed AI

Merijn van Tooren[1], Morten Larsen[2], and Daniel Reti[3]

[1] Almende BV, Netherlands
merijn@almende.org
[2] AnyWi Technologies, Netherlands
morten.larsen@anywi.com
[3] German Research Center for Artificial Intelligence,
Kaiserslautern, Germany
daniel.reti@dfki.de

1   Introduction

Safe distributed Artificial Intelligence (AI) requires reliable and secure underpinnings, i.e. enabling technologies as well as legal and regulatory frameworks. These will be horizontal efforts, to be deployed in many and different application areas.

This workshop will discuss perspectives and approaches and frameworks for integrating cybersecurity in solutions and keeping those solutions explainable and understandable to the general public. More so than explaining concrete methods, the papers involved in this workshop explore ways of overseeing and managing these problems in general, and attempt to understand where these technologies stand in the present and may go in the future. This is sure to spark new ideas and conjure fantasies of novel approaches and understandings of security, safety and awareness.

The aim is to unite academic research, oriented towards applications in real-world settings, with industrial research and development to explore options for application-oriented uptake of new technologies in the field of safe distributed AI. The workshop will combine presentations of papers with panel discussions to explore the ideas presented and possible synergies that can lead to safer distributed systems.

2   This Year's Workshop

This year's workshop is set around two research papers: one about unresolved questions in the domain of SecDevOps for Small and Medium Enterprises and IoT solutions, and one about explainability in AI solutions. Talks will revolve around these papers and seek to generate new, interesting insights and avenues of exploration that build on the written material and related themes.

The first paper, "Research Questions in the Acceptance of Cybersecurity by SMEs in the EU", follows up on the SCRATCh research project funded by ITEA, which investigated SecDevOps: Secure DevOps, that is, integrating cybersecurity into a DevOps way of working. Specifically, the project investigated ways to make SecDevOps more viable and accessible for SMEs, especially when the complexity of IoT solutions is involved. The project bore interesting results, but highlighted certain larger questions that remained unanswered as they grew beyond the scope of the project itself. The paper contemplates these questions and possible ways to go forward.

The second paper, "On Explainability in AI-Solutions: A Cross-Domain Survey", surveys and studies ways of explaining algorithms and AI decisions to non-experts across a breadth of existing literature. It draws a map of currently relevant consider-ations and approaches in the domain of explaining AI algorithms and their decisions to stakeholders and end-users. While some relatively "simple" types of algorithms such as decision trees may be considered trivial or self-explanatory, there are multiple dimensions of increased complexity such as the complexity of the model itself or the complexity of the input or output, that necessitate and have encouraged novel approaches to this problem. For example, in image processing, there are ways to visually highlight the parts of the image that played the largest roles in the decision making.

We expect interesting commentary and ideas to arise from these two domains and the collisions between them, and heartily invite all to listen in!

Acknowledgement

We are grateful to the SAFECOMP organization committee and collaborators for their support in arranging USDAI, especially to Jérémie Guiochet and Erwin Schoitsch as Workshop Chairs, and to Friedemann Bitsch as Publication Chair. We also thank all the authors of the submitted papers for their interest in the workshop, and the program committee for its work. Finally, the workshop is supported by the projects SCRATCh (no. 17005, ITEA 3) and WaVE (19I21028R, German Federal Ministry of Education and Research (BMBF)).

Workshop Committees

Organization Committee

Morten Larsen	AnyWi Technologies
Merijn van Tooren	Almende

Programme Committee

Morten Larsen	AnyWi Technologies
Merijn van Tooren	Almende
Alan Sears	Leiden University
Anna Hristoskova	SIRRIS
Reda Nouacer	CEA
Morayo Adedjouma	CEA
Ricardo Reis	Embraer
Raúl Santos de la Cámara	Hi-Iberia

Raj Thilak Rajan   TU Delft
Tobias Koch   consider-it.de
George Dimitrakopoulos   Harokopio University
Ali Balador   Research Institutes of Sweden
Simon Duque Anton   comlet Verteilte Systeme GmbH
Daniel Reti   DFKI

On Explainability in AI-Solutions: A Cross-Domain Survey

Simon D Duque Anton[1]([envelope]) [iD], Daniel Schneider[2] [iD], and Hans D Schotten[2] [iD]

[1] Comlet Verteilte Systeme GmbH, 66482 Zweibruecken, Germany
simon.duque-anton@comlet.de
[2] DFKI, 67663 Kaiserslautern, Germany
{Daniel.Schneider,Hans_Dieter.Schotten}@dfki.de

Abstract. Artificial Intelligence (AI) increasingly shows its potential to outperform predicate logic algorithms and human control alike. In automatically deriving a system model, AI algorithms learn relations in data that are not detectable for humans. This great strength, however, also makes use of AI methods dubious. The more complex a model, the more difficult it is for a human to understand the reasoning for the decisions. As currently, fully automated AI algorithms are sparse, every algorithm has to provide a reasoning for human operators. For data engineers, metrics such as accuracy and sensitivity are sufficient. However, if models are interacting with non-experts, explanations have to be understandable.

This work provides an extensive survey of literature on this topic, which, to a large part, consists of other surveys. The findings are mapped to ways of explaining decisions and reasons for explaining decisions. It shows that the heterogeneity of reasons and methods of and for explainability lead to individual explanatory frameworks.

Keywords: Artificial intelligence · Explainability · Survey · Cross-domain

1 Introduction

Industrial revolutions provided humanity with novel technologies that fundamentally changed fields of work, mostly in manufacturing and processing industries. Currently, the fourth industrial revolution is said to introduce flexibility and ad-hoc connectivity to once inflexible industrial Operational Technology (OT) networks. This newly integrated means of connectivity in industrial networks, across physical factory boundaries, allows for new use cases and improved efficiency. Apart from the connectivity aspect, the introduction of Artificial Intelligence (AI) methods presents new paradigms. In industrial environments, AI methods are applied to production and resource planning [27], detection of anomalies in production processes [23–25], and improvement of processes [61]. Apart from industrial applications, AI methods lend themselves readily on other domains, such as finance and banking [14], medicine [32] and elderly care [51], autonomous

M. Trapp et al. (Eds.): SAFECOMP 2022 Workshops, LNCS 13415, pp. 235–246, 2022.
https://doi.org/10.1007/978-3-031-14862-0_17

driving [56,57] network management [22,39,40,58], and for control of unmanned vehicles [42,55], just to name a few. In all of these fields, automation and AI are intended to perform tedious and repetitive tasks to relieve workers. However, this autonomous performance of tasks requires trustworthy and understandable algorithms as an enabler. If a task is to be performed by an algorithm, the outcome must not deviate from expectations, jitters in the input data cannot change the outcome in an undesirable fashion. Especially regarding AI algorithms, understanding the reasoning behind a decision is complex and often hardly possible for human operators. This is an issue, especially regarding regulatory standards and acceptance issues of users. Consequently, AI algorithms need to be understandable and provide predictable outcomes in a reliable fashion to further their application. This need has created the term of Artificial Intelligence (XAI) that encompasses the need for AI methods to not only provide sound results, but also provide the reasoning in a useful and understandable manner.

This work aims at providing an overview of requirements as well as solutions for the explainability of AI algorithms. Works related to explainability in AI are discussed in Sect. 2. Methods and techniques for explaining outcomes of AI algorithms are introduced in Sect. 3. Common application scenarios that require explainable AI methods are presented in Sect. 4. This work is concluded in Sect. 5.

2 Related Work

This section captures an overview of related works discussing explainability of AI methods in different domains. A comprehensive overview is provided in Table 1.

This table lists the respective work, the domain which is discussed and the method used to explain the decision or recommendation made by the AI method. *Reddy* discusses the requirements formulated by stakeholders for acceptance of AI decisions in medical treatment and research while formulating the point that some argue in favour of higher accuracy algorithms instead of well-explainable ones [52]. *Neugebauer et al.* present a surrogate AI model, that addresses parameter changes of the base model and consequently highlights the relevant parameters in the decision, aiding its explainability [48]. *Vilone and Longo* survey scientific research addressing XAI and categorise findings in human-based explanations that aim at mimicking human reasoning, and objective metrics such as accuracy [64]. *Caro-Martínez et al.* introduce a conceptual model for e-commerce recommender systems that extends existing models with four ontological elements: User motivation and goals, required knowledge, the recommendation process itself, and the presentation to the user [15]. *Liang et al.* present a novel online Explainable Recommendation System (ERS) that, in contrast to commonly used offline ERSs, can be updated and instantly provides explanations with recommendations [44]. *Holzinger and Müller* discuss a mapping appraoch of explainability with causability [38]. That means creating links between the reasoning an AI algorithm implicitely makes and the intuitive conclusions humans

Table 1. Overview of related works

Year	Work	Domain	Topic of explainability
2022	[52]	Medicine	Accuracy vs. explainability
2021	[48]	Product & company success	Before and after model comparison
2021	[64]	Survey	Comparison of methods aimed at human-based understanding and objective metrics
2021	[15]	E-commerce	Ontological model
2021	[44]	Recommendation systems	Leverage of recommendation and explanation
2021	[38]	Medical domain	"Mapping of explainability with causability"
2021	[26]	Socio-economic decisions	Social transparency as guidelines for decision making
2021	[6]	Survey	Global vs. local, accuracy vs. explainability
2021	[47]	Survey	Multi-domain model
2021	[11]	Data science	Survey based on stakeholder use-case
2021	[59]	Product recommendation	Relationship of causability and explainability
2020	[60]	Medicine	Explainable image processing
2020	[9]	Survey	Fairness of the model
2020	[46]	Tree-based algorithms	Game theory-based approach
2020	[49]	Medicine	Contestability
2020	[7,8]	Data Science	Toolkit-framework combining state of the art methods
2020	[45]	Survey & Taxonomy	Survey
2020	[62]	Medicine	Survey
2020	[53]	Natural sciences	Survey
2020	[10]	Multidisciplinary	Three-step framework
2020	[19]	General	Responsibility of AI algorithms
2020	[13]	Survey	Stakeholder-driven explainability survey
2020	[5]	Mental health evaluation	Ontological agent
2020	[66]	Survey	Survey
2020	[20]	Survey	Survey
2020	[4]	Medicine	Multidisciplinary survey of requirements in explainability
2019	[18]	User product recommendation	Dynamic preference monitoring with neural networks
2019	[43]	Proof of Concept	Fault location in combinatorial testing
2019	[41]	Material sciences	Analogy creation and feature importance
2019	[63]	Medicine	Domain appropriate representation, potential accountability, and consistency
2019	[65]	General	Psychology-based theoretical cognitive framework
2019	[16]	Industrial planning	Contrastive explanations
2019	[34]	Human-centric decision making	Context-based
2019	[28]	Survey for industrial application	Survey
2019	[54]	Survey	Several
2019	[30]	Survey	Survey
2019	[37]	Medicine	Definition of causability and explainability
2018	[3]	Product recommendation	Knowledge-base embedding representation
2018	[12]	(Movie) recommendations	Knowledge graphs
2018	[33]	User acceptance	Survey
2018	[31]	Survey	Rule-based decisions & labels
2018	[2]	Survey	Survey
2018	[1]	Health, education, justice,	Survey
2018	[35]	Position paper	Context-adaptive procedures
2018	[29]	Position paper	Bridging cognitive valley with graph information
2018	[50]	Survey	Taxonomy for XAI
2017	[36]	Medicine	Hybrid distributional models

draw. This is applied to the area of image-based pattern recognition in medical treatment. *Ehsan et al.* present a concept for integrating social transparency into XAI solutions [26]. They present a framework based on expert-interviews. *Angelov et al.* discuss the relation of AI algorithms with high accuracy and high explainability factors [6]. A taxonomy is provided, global vs. local model explanation techniques for different domains and algorithms are surveyed and set in context with the remaining challenges. *Mohseni et al.* provide a survey of existing literature that clusters available methods and research approaches respective to their design goals as well as evaluation measures [47]. Their framework is founded on the distinction between the provided categories. *Belle and Papantonis* evaluate feasible methods of explainability on the use case of a data scientist that aims to convince stakeholders [11]. *Shin* discusses the relation of causability and explainability in XAI and the influence on trust and user behaviour [59]. *Singh et al.* evaluate methods to explain AI conclusions in the medical domain [60]. *Barredo Arrieta et al.* present an extensive survey on literature and solutions in XAI on which they base requirements and challenges yet to conquer [9]. Ultimately, they create the concept of fair AI that explains and accounts for decisions made. *Lundberg et al.* introduce a game-theoretic model for optimal explanations in tree-based algorithms [46]. Local explanations are combined to obtain a global explanation of the trained tree in a human-understandable format. *Ploug and Holm* present the concept of contestable AI decision making in a clinical context [49]. Contestability means that the decision algorithm has to provide information to the data used, any system biases, system performance in terms of algorithmic metrics, and the decision responsibility carried by humans or algorithms. If the decision is contested, the algorithm has to provide insight that the alternate solution was considered as well and has been adequately taken into account. *Arya et al.* introduce a collection of explainability tools that are combined into a framework to provide researchers and data scientists with the opportunity to exctract explanations for various algorithms [8]. *Linardatos et al.* introduce a survey and taxonomy, distinguishing between different types of interpretability in AI methods before presenting an exhaustive list of tools and methods [45]. *Tjoa and Guan* discuss challenges and risks of explainability in medical AI applications [62]. They survey existing solutions for different algorithm types while also introducing risks and challenges with existing solutions. *Roscher et al.* present an overview of methods to conserve scientific interpretability and explainability in natural sciences [53]. *Beaudoin et al.* introduce a framework for explainability that can be applied in multidisciplinary settings [10]. Three steps are required to obtain the suitable method of explainability: First, define the contextual factors regarding the explanation. Second, analyse the tools available for the technical problem at hand and third, chose the suitable global and local explanation tools that are compared to seven factors of cost created by lacking explanation. *Coeckelbergh* discusses the ethical and philosophical responsibility of decisions made by AI algorithms and evaluates the responsibility of agents for their decisions in time and conditional dependencies [19]. *Bhatt et al.* introduce a framework based on findings of a study that investigates the target audience of explainability in AI [13]. They find that most explainability approaches are created for machine learning engineers to adapt their model. Consequently, they propose a framework that allows the choice of a target audience and adapts the explainability accordingly. *Ammar and Shaban-Nejad* present a recommendation system for mental health analysis that is based on ontological knowledge of the domain [5]. *Zhang and Chen* survey ERS and their uses for end-users as well as developers [66]. *Confalonieri et al.* discuss the historical implications of XAI and propose criteria for explanations deemed necessary for human understanding of explanations [20]. *Amann et al.* evaluate the legal, ethical and organisational aspects of AI decisions in the medical domain [4]. *Chen et al.* develop a dynamic ERS that monitors user preferences and maps them to aspects of a product review to increase recommendation quality [18]. *Kuhn and Kacker* apply the well-established problem of fault location in combinatorial testing, where a software fails only after input of several bogus values that have to be identified, to the explainability problem in AI [43]. Based on feature combinations, the importance of any given feature for the decision is derived and thus used to explain the decision making process. *Kailkhura et al.* present a methodology for explaining classifications of AI algorithms in the domain of chemical material sciences [41]. Well-known and established algorithms, such as XGBoost [17], are extended with explanations regarding analogies in decisions to mimic human reasoning as well as feature importance to provide insight into the model design. According to their methodology, an AI model used for scientific research has to be transparent, the output should be interpretable, and the scientific result has to be explainable. Several methods are surveyed with respect to their dimensions of interpretability and the required integration of domain knowledge into the models. *Tonekaboni et al.* discuss requirements and conditions for AI in medical studies [63]. Explainability in this context describes the justifiability of results to stakeholders and colleagues, meaning explanations need to take stakeholder interests into account. The three metrics identified in their work contain domain appropriate representation, meaning that different disciplines in the medical field require different sets of information. Second, potential accountability describes a workflow for follow-up checking of the model outcome, meaning in the further treatment, the model decision should be validated with additional lab tests or checking in on patients. Third, consistency means that results provided by AI models should only be based on clinical variables and that any change in variable, and consequently outcome, should encompass a different but fitting explanation. *Wang et al.* apply psychology and cognitive sciences to obtain an understanding of human bias and interpretation [65]. Based on this information, they extract information from different decision algorithms and collect them in a framework where the individual data points are presented combined with their relevance for a decision. *Cashmore et al.* discuss explainability as a service [16]. In an industrial planning scenario, the user is asked to provide alternative plans with constraints from which an automated planner derives constraints that are the basis for an automated plan. These constraints are used to justify the automatatically generated plan. *Hois et al.* analyse the need for human-centric AI-based decision making and the subsequent context-dependant explanation [34]. Humans as users are the main focus of the explanation that has to be tailored to situation and context. *Gade et al.* introduce challenges and existing solutions for the application of explainability in various domains [28]. *Samek et al.* dedicate a book to an overview of challenges, solutions, and visualisation of XAI [54]. *Gunning et al.* summarise challenges and user expectations on XAI [30]. *Holzinger et al.* evaluate causability as the property of a person in terms of understanding automated reasoning and compare it to explainability as the property of a model to provide reasoning in histopatological examples [37]. *Ai et al.* present a deep learning approach on knowledge bases for recommender systems to improve the explainability aspects of recommendations [3]. *Bellini et al.* introduce a knowledge-graph-based method to explain user recommendations, thus increasing user satisfaction and acceptance [12]. *Hoffman et al.* present metrics regarding the acceptance and satisfaction of users regarding the explainability in different XAI methods [33]. *Hagras* discusses the challenges in XAI with a focus on dimensions of explainability as well as mapping of output to interpretation [31]. They discuss the necessity of rule-based mapping of decisions to explanations as well as labels and introduce fuzzy logic systems that can be used to explain class affiliation in a human-understandable fashion. *Adadi and Berrada* introduce a survey of concepts and challenges in XAI [2]. *Abdollahi and Nasraoui* evaluate the fairness of ERSs in the context of health, justice, education, and criminal investigations [1]. *Holzinger* provides a positional paper discussing the need for context-adaptive procedures in AI in order to make decisions understandable for humans [35]. *Goebel et al.* discuss the need for XAI in the context of increasingly complex AI systems [29]. Interactions between data points that can be represented in a graph can function as vectors of explainability, as these areas with high importance can be identified. *Preece* provides a survey and taxonomy of challenges and a possible solution of XAI [50]. *Holzinger et al.* present research on explainable AI in the medical domain [36]. They argue that benefits can be obtained from AI algorithms, but only in case the results are explainable and can be argumented. They summarise that hybrid distributional models which map sparse graph-based information to dense vectors of information are suitable to provide context by linking this information to lexical sources and knowledge bases.

3   What Is Explainability of AI

According to *Linardatos et al.*, explainability or interpretability of AI algorithms depends on four dimensions [45]:

- Local vs global,
- data types that are processed by the algorithm,
- the purpose of interpretability, i.e. when and how should the model be explained, and
- the generalisation of the interpretation, i.e. can the explanation be applied to individual models or to any model.

Furthermore, several works address the issue of target audience [66], which should also be taken into consideration. These dimensions are shown in Fig. 1.
  A trend that is observed by every work surveyed in this paper is the relationship between complexity of algorithms and difficulty of explainability. Models based on Decision Trees, such as Random Forests [21] and XGBoost [17] not only perform well in praxis [25], but also allow for a good understanding of global

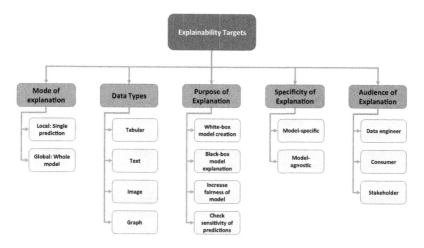

Fig. 1. Explainability goals according to *Linardatos et al.* [45], extended

explainability. That means the model provides information about the relevance of its learned features. Furthermore, the splits allow insight into the creation of output. In contrast, Deep Neural Networks (DNNs) create complex models that cannot easily be understood by humans. In case of image and video processing, methods are available to highlight the areas in an image that induce the highest neuron output and thus are most relevant for the algorithmic output [60]. This method cannot be applied as easily to abstract, high-dimensional information which is inherently difficult to interpret for humans. Several works use contextual information as well as knowledge bases that provide additional information and allow the generation and connection of the original algorithm with algorithms used to explain the outcome [15,26]. This can be closely combined with understanding of how humans explain decisions and understand explanations [65].

This question is closely coupled to the target audience of explanations: while data scientists and engineers are interested in model performance, users might be more interested in the base information that led to a certain outcome. In domain-specific applications, the explainability might be used to increase customer satisfaction and thus revenue [15], meaning the business operators need to understand not only what customers desire, but why. In medical applications, compliance and liability play important roles [38,60,62], meaning someone has to be responsible for a decision. Consequently, a medical professional has to be able to obtain information of the root cause of an automated decision. In social and judical applications, fairness independant of human-induced bias is relevant as well as argumentation regarding the reasons for conclusions [1,26].

This section shows that explainability is a broad and rather abstract concept, once one is trying to implement it. Not only does the data and algorithm have a strong influence on the methods of explainability that are possible in the first place, also the goal and audience of an explanation are relevant. The domains and consequentially the goals of explainability are discussed in the next section.

4   Domains for Expainability

It is noteworthy that there is distinction in related work, as discussed in Sect. 2, regarding the use cases discussed: The first part of papers present solutions, and sometimes challenges, to enhance explainability of certain algorithms or types of algorithms. At the same time, the second part of papers discusses requirements, challenges and solutions of certain fields or domains, without specific algorithms in mind. Furthermore, several papers address XAI as a means for improved outcomes and stakeholder or user acceptance, while others solely address technical challenges. For a holistic explainability architecture, those have to be merged. Generally, the two different ways of approaching explainability show in this survey. Domain experts have a concrete challenge that can be solved, or improved, with AI methods. Alternatively, an AI method is already solving the challenge and the domain expert needs reasoning for the model, be it to appease stakeholders or to increase customer satisfaction. Such approaches often use knowledge bases of methods to solve the issue without AI.

The other approach is from machine learning and AI experts who aim to make their models more transparent. Often, this is based in the need to understand the model in order to increase performance, resulting in explainability by accuracy and sensitivity metrics. Such information is difficult to interpret by non-experts and thus not suited for explainability for users. In summary, the different domains for explainability highlight the need for distinction in the solution. In recommender systems for e-commerce, a wrong recommendation will not have severe consequences, in stark contrast to recommendation systems for medical examination. Understanding models to fine-tune them is a valid task for data scientists and machine learning experts, while a ontological explanation similar to human reasoning is necessary for integration of AI models into socio-economic and organisational solutions. While it is a highly interesting concept, a holistic solution to explainability does not seem likely.

5   Conclusion

A large body of research regarding XAI has been presented in this work. This body of research spans several domains, including medicine and healthcare, commerce, criminal and social sciences, and recommender systems. While highlighting that all of these domains face similar challenges, the mass of surveys and taxonomies discussed in this work also show the wide span of requirements. Additionally, the technique of explainability strongly depends on the employed AI algorithm. Simpler algorithms, for example tree-based ones, can be understood by humans relatively easy as the information of the decision can be extracted directly from the model in a semantically understandable fashion. More complex algorithms, such as DNNs prove to be more difficult. If the data they analyse can be understood intuitively by humans, as is the case in image processing, the neuronal activity can be displayed. However, in complex and unstructured data, such as high dimensional tables, highlighting of the values does not provide humans with an understanding of the reasoning. Here, knowledge bases to map against or ontological translations of the results are required in order to provide an understanding.

AI-based recommender systems are bound to drastically increase performance and quality of services they provide. Due to the variety of said services, individual explanation frameworks will be applied. Furthermore, recipient and reason for wanting an explanation play an important role in chosing an explanation framework. In the future, AI systems might increasingly make decisions autonomously, i.e. without supervision and approval of a human operator. Such applications will require strict regulation and liability frameworks to ensure that AI methods perform in an expected and sound manner.

Acknowledgement. This work has been supported by the Federal Ministry of Education and Research (BMBF) of the Federal Republic of Germany (Foerderkennzeichen 19I21028R, WaVe) and the Investment and Structure Bank (ISB) Rhineland Palatinate (Foerderkennzeichen P1SZ26, InnoTop). The authors alone are responsible for the content of this paper.

References

1. Abdollahi, B., Nasraoui, O.: Transparency in fair machine learning: the case of explainable recommender systems. In: Zhou, J., Chen, F. (eds.) Human and Machine Learning. HIS, pp. 21–35. Springer, Cham (2018). https://doi.org/10.1007/978-3-319-90403-0_2
2. Adadi, A., Berrada, M.: Peeking inside the black-box: a survey on explainable artificial intelligence (XAI). IEEE Access **6**, 52138–52160 (2018)
3. Ai, Q., Azizi, V., Chen, X., Zhang, Y.: Learning heterogeneous knowledge base embeddings for explainable recommendation. Algorithms **11**(9), 137 (2018)
4. Amann, J., Blasimme, A., Vayena, E., Frey, D., Madai, V.I.: Explainability for artificial intelligence in healthcare: a multidisciplinary perspective. BMC Med. Inf. Decis. Making **20**(1), 1–9 (2020)
5. Ammar, N., Shaban-Nejad, A.: Explainable artificial intelligence recommendation system by leveraging the semantics of adverse childhood experiences: Proof-of-concept prototype development. JMIR Med. Inf. **8**(11), e18752 (2020)
6. Angelov, P.P., Soares, E.A., Jiang, R., Arnold, N.I., Atkinson, P.M.: Explainable artificial intelligence: an analytical review. Wiley Interdisc. Rev. Data Min. Knowl. Dis. **11**(5), e1424 (2021)
7. Arya, V., et al.: One explanation does not fit all: a toolkit and taxonomy of AI explainability techniques. arXiv preprint arXiv:1909.03012 (2019)
8. Arya, V., et al.: AI explainability 360: an extensible toolkit for understanding data and machine learning models. J. Mach. Learn. Res. **21**(130), 1–6 (2020)
9. Arrieta, A.B., et al.: Explainable artificial intelligence (XAI): concepts, taxonomies, opportunities and challenges toward responsible AI. Inf. Fusion **58**, 82–115 (2020)
10. Beaudouin, V., et al.: Flexible and context-specific AI explainability: a multidisciplinary approach. Available at SSRN 3559477 (2020)

11. Belle, V., Papantonis, I.: Principles and practice of explainable machine learning. Front. Big Data **39** (2021)
12. Bellini, V., Schiavone, A., Di Noia, T., Ragone, A., Di Sciascio, E.: Knowledge-aware autoencoders for explainable recommender systems. In: Proceedings of the 3rd Workshop on Deep Learning for Recommender Systems, pp. 24–31 (2018)
13. Bhatt, U., et al.: Explainable machine learning in deployment. In: Proceedings of the 2020 conference on fairness, accountability, and transparency, pp. 648–657 (2020)
14. Cao, L.: Ai in finance: challenges, techniques, and opportunities. ACM Comput. Surv. (CSUR) **55**(3), 1–38 (2022)
15. Caro-Martínez, M., Jiménez-Díaz, G., Recio-García, J.A.: Conceptual modeling of explainable recommender systems: an ontological formalization to guide their design and development. J. Artif. Intell. Res. **71**, 557–589 (2021)
16. Cashmore, M., Collins, A., Krarup, B., Krivic, S., Magazzeni, D., Smith, D.: Towards explainable AI planning as a service. arXiv preprint arXiv:1908.05059 (2019)
17. Chen, T., Guestrin, C.: Xgboost: a scalable tree boosting system. In: Proceedings of the 22nd ACM sigkdd International Conference on Knowledge Discovery and Data Mining, pp. 785–794 (2016)
18. Chen, X., Zhang, Y., Qin, Z.: Dynamic explainable recommendation based on neural attentive models. In: Proceedings of the AAAI Conference on Artificial Intelligence, vol. 33, pp. 53–60 (2019)
19. Coeckelbergh, M.: Artificial intelligence, responsibility attribution, and a relational justification of explainability. Sci. Eng. Ethics **26**(4), 2051–2068 (2020)
20. Confalonieri, R., Coba, L., Wagner, B., Besold, T.R.: A historical perspective of explainable artificial intelligence. Wiley Interdisc. Rev. Data Min. Knowl. Dis. **11**(1), e1391 (2020)
21. Cutler, A., Cutler, D.R., Stevens, J.R.: Random forests. In: Zhang, C., Ma, Y. (eds.) Ensemble Machine Learning, pp. 157–175. Springer, Boston (2012). https://doi.org/10.1007/978-1-4419-9326-7_5
22. Duque-Antón, M., Kunz, D., Ruber, B.: Channel assignment for cellular radio using simulated annealing. IEEE Trans. Veh. Technol. **42**(1), 14–21 (1993)
23. Anton, S.D., Kanoor, S., Fraunholz, D., Schotten, H.D.: Evaluation of machine learning-based anomaly detection algorithms on an industrial modbus/tcp data set. In: Proceedings of the 13th International Conference on Availability, Reliability and Security, pp. 1–9 (2018)
24. Anton, S.D.D.: Anomaly Detection in Industry. Verlag Dr, Hut (2021)
25. Anton, S.D.D., Sinha, S., Schotten, H.D.: Anomaly-based intrusion detection in industrial data with SVM and random forests. In: 2019 International Conference on Software, Telecommunications and Computer Networks (SoftCOM), pp. 1–6. IEEE (2019)
26. Ehsan, U., Liao, Q.V., Muller, M., Riedl, M.O., Weisz, J.D.: Expanding explainability: towards social transparency in AI systems. In: Proceedings of the 2021 CHI Conference on Human Factors in Computing Systems, pp. 1–19 (2021)
27. Elbasheer, M., Longo, F., Nicoletti, L., Padovano, A., Solina, V., Vetrano, M.: Applications of ML/AI for decision-intensive tasks in production planning and control. Procedia Comput. Sci. **200**, 1903–1912 (2022). https://www.sciencedirect.com/science/article/pii/S1877050922004008, 3rd International Conference on Industry 4.0 and Smart Manufacturing

28. Gade, K., Geyik, S.C., Kenthapadi, K., Mithal, V., Taly, A.: Explainable AI in industry. In: Proceedings of the 25th ACM SIGKDD International Conference on Knowledge Discovery & Data Mining, pp. 3203–3204 (2019)

29. Goebel, R., et al.: Explainable AI: the new 42? In: Holzinger, A., Kieseberg, P., Tjoa, A.M., Weippl, E. (eds.) CD-MAKE 2018. LNCS, vol. 11015, pp. 295–303. Springer, Cham (2018). https://doi.org/10.1007/978-3-319-99740-7_21

30. Gunning, D., Stefik, M., Choi, J., Miller, T., Stumpf, S., Yang, G.Z.: XAI-explainable artificial intelligence. Sci. Robot. 4(37), eaay7120 (2019)

31. Hagras, H.: Toward human-understandable, explainable AI. Computer 51(9), 28–36 (2018)

32. Hamet, P., Tremblay, J.: Artificial intelligence in medicine. Metabolism 69, S36–S40 (2017)

33. Hoffman, R.R., Mueller, S.T., Klein, G., Litman, J.: Metrics for explainable AI: challenges and prospects. arXiv preprint arXiv:1812.04608 (2018)

34. Hois, J., Theofanou-Fuelbier, D., Junk, A.J.: How to achieve explainability and transparency in human AI interaction. In: Stephanidis, C. (ed.) HCII 2019. CCIS, vol. 1033, pp. 177–183. Springer, Cham (2019). https://doi.org/10.1007/978-3-030-23528-4_25

35. Holzinger, A.: From machine learning to explainable AI. In: 2018 World Symposium on Digital Intelligence for Systems and Machines (DISA), pp. 55–66. IEEE (2018)

36. Holzinger, A., Biemann, C., Pattichis, C.S., Kell, D.B.: What do we need to build explainable AI systems for the medical domain? arXiv preprint arXiv:1712.09923 (2017)

37. Holzinger, A., Langs, G., Denk, H., Zatloukal, K., Müller, H.: Causability and explainability of artificial intelligence in medicine. Wiley Interdisc. Rev. Data Min. Knowl. Disc. 9(4), e1312 (2019)

38. Holzinger, A.T., Müller, H.: Toward human-AI interfaces to support explainability and causability in medical AI. Computer 54(10), 78–86 (2021)

39. Jiang, W., Anton, S.D., Schotten, H.D.: Intelligence slicing: a unified framework to integrate artificial intelligence into 5g networks. In: 2019 12th IFIP Wireless and Mobile Networking Conference (WMNC), pp. 227–232. IEEE (2019)

40. Jiang, W., Strufe, M., Schotten, H.D.: Intelligent network management for 5g systems: the selfnet approach. In: 2017 European Conference on Networks and Communications (EuCNC), pp. 1–5. IEEE (2017)

41. Kailkhura, B., Gallagher, B., Kim, S., Hiszpanski, A., Han, T.: Reliable and explainable machine-learning methods for accelerated material discovery. NPJ Comput. Mater. 5(1), 1–9 (2019)

42. Keneni, B.M., Kaur, D., Al Bataineh, A., Devabhaktuni, V.K., Javaid, A.Y., Zaientz, J.D., Marinier, R.P.: Evolving rule-based explainable artificial intelligence for unmanned aerial vehicles. IEEE Access 7, 17001–17016 (2019)

43. Kuhn, R., Kacker, R.: An application of combinatorial methods for explainability in artificial intelligence and machine learning (draft). Technical Report, National Institute of Standards and Technology (2019)

44. Liang, Q., Zheng, X., Wang, Y., Zhu, M.: O3ERS: an explainable recommendation system with online learning, online recommendation, and online explanation. Inf. Sci. 562, 94–115 (2021)

45. Linardatos, P., Papastefanopoulos, V., Kotsiantis, S.: Explainable AI: a review of machine learning interpretability methods. Entropy 23(1), 18 (2020)

46. Lundberg, S.M., et al.: From local explanations to global understanding with explainable AI for trees. Nat. Mach. Intell. 2(1), 56–67 (2020)

47. Mohseni, S., Zarei, N., Ragan, E.D.: A multidisciplinary survey and framework for design and evaluation of explainable AI systems. ACM Trans. Interact. Intell. Syst. (TiiS) **11**(3–4), 1–45 (2021)
48. Neugebauer, S., Rippitsch, L., Sobieczky, F., Geiβ, M.: Explainability of AI-predictions based on psychological profiling. Procedia Comput. Sci. **180**, 1003–1012 (2021)
49. Ploug, T., Holm, S.: The four dimensions of contestable AI diagnostics-a patient-centric approach to explainable AI. Artif. Intell. Med. **107**, 101901 (2020)
50. Preece, A.: Asking 'why'in ai: explainability of intelligent systems-perspectives and challenges. Intell. Syst. Account. Financ. Manag. **25**(2), 63–72 (2018)
51. Qian, K., Zhang, Z., Yamamoto, Y., Schuller, B.W.: Artificial intelligence internet of things for the elderly: from assisted living to health-care monitoring. IEEE Sig. Process. Mag. **38**(4), 78–88 (2021)
52. Reddy, S.: Explainability and artificial intelligence in medicine. Lancet Digit. Health **4**(4), e214–e215 (2022)
53. Roscher, R., Bohn, B., Duarte, M.F., Garcke, J.: Explainable machine learning for scientific insights and discoveries. IEEE Access **8**, 42200–42216 (2020)
54. Samek, W., Montavon, G., Vedaldi, A., Hansen, L.K., Müller, K.-R. (eds.): Explainable AI: Interpreting, Explaining and Visualizing Deep Learning. LNCS (LNAI), vol. 11700. Springer, Cham (2019). https://doi.org/10.1007/978-3-030-28954-6
55. Sands, T.: Development of deterministic artificial intelligence for unmanned underwater vehicles (UUV). J. Mar. Sci. Eng. **8**(8), 578 (2020)
56. Schutera, M., Goby, N., Neumann, D., Reischl, M.: Transfer learning versus multi-agent learning regarding distributed decision-making in highway traffic. arXiv preprint arXiv:1810.08515 (2018)
57. Schutera, M., Hussein, M., Abhau, J., Mikut, R., Reischl, M.: Night-to-day: online image-to-image translation for object detection within autonomous driving by night. IEEE Trans. Intell. Veh. **6**(3), 480–489 (2020)
58. Shen, X., et al.: Ai-assisted network-slicing based next-generation wireless networks. IEEE Open J. Veh. Technol. **1**, 45–66 (2020)
59. Shin, D.: The effects of explainability and causability on perception, trust, and acceptance: implications for explainable AI. Int. J. Hum. Comput. Stud. **146**, 102551 (2021)
60. Singh, A., Sengupta, S., Lakshminarayanan, V.: Explainable deep learning models in medical image analysis. J. Imaging **6**(6), 52 (2020)
61. Sun, W., Liu, J., Yue, Y.: Ai-enhanced offloading in edge computing: when machine learning meets industrial IoT. IEEE Network **33**(5), 68–74 (2019)
62. Tjoa, E., Guan, C.: A survey on explainable artificial intelligence (XAI): toward medical XAI. IEEE Trans. Neural Netw. Learn. Syst. **32**(11), 4793–4813 (2020)
63. Tonekaboni, S., Joshi, S., McCradden, M.D., Goldenberg, A.: What clinicians want: contextualizing explainable machine learning for clinical end use. In: Machine Learning for Healthcare Conference, pp. 359–380. PMLR (2019)
64. Vilone, G., Longo, L.: Notions of explainability and evaluation approaches for explainable artificial intelligence. Inf. Fusion **76**, 89–106 (2021). https://www.sciencedirect.com/science/article/pii/S1566253521001093
65. Wang, D., Yang, Q., Abdul, A., Lim, B.Y.: Designing theory-driven user-centric explainable AI. In: Proceedings of the 2019 CHI Conference on Human Factors in Computing Systems, pp. 1–15 (2019)
66. Zhang, Y., Chen, X.: Explainable recommendation: a survey and new perspectives. Found. Trends® Inf. Retrieval **14**(1), 1–101 (2020)

Research Questions in the Acceptance of Cybersecurity by SMEs in the EU

Merijn van Tooren[1(✉)], Daniel Reti[2], Daniel Schneider[2] (ORCID), Cédric Bassem[3],
Raúl Santos de la Cámara[4] (ORCID), and Hans Dieter Schotten[2] (ORCID)

[1] Almende BV, Rotterdam, Netherlands
merijn@almende.org
[2] German Research Center for Artificial Intelligence, Kaiserslautern, Germany
{daniel.reti,daniel.schneider,hans.schotten}@dfki.de
[3] NVISO BV, Bruxelles, Belgium
cbassem@nviso.eu
[4] HI Iberia Ingeniería y Proyectos S.L., Madrid, Spain
rsantos@hi-iberia.es

Abstract. Cybersecurity is a very challenging field that asks for a multitude of solutions to an even larger spread of threats and issues. Charting all the risks one is facing, and deciding what to do about each of them, is a task worthy of hiring one or several dedicated experts. It is difficult for large companies to organise, and essentially impossible for SMEs (Small and Medium Enterprises). Throughout the SCRATCh project research, these matters became quite visible. Based on the project findings, this paper discusses these problems and their nature, and establishes the need for a novel holistic solution to be found.

Keywords: Cyber · Security · DevOps · SME · IoT

1 Introduction

Cybersecurity is a sprawling, demanding field. It is the stage of a great arms race between those who would foster growth, and those who would try to piggyback on that for their own benefit or plainly just snuff it out. In this setting, pioneering projects and companies create various cybersecurity measures to provide layers of security to other companies, but certain fundamental issues stand in the way

This work has been supported by Centre for the Development of Industrial Technology (CDTI) of Spain (EXP 00111045/INNO-20181045, SCRATCh), the German Federal Ministry of Education and Research (BMBF, grant number 01IS18062E, 01IS18062C), the Netherlands Enterprise Agency (RVO, grant number ITEA181004), and the regional institute for research and innovation of Brussels Belgium, Innoviris. The SCRATCh project (no. 17005) is part of the ITEA 3 cluster of the European research program EUREKA. The authors alone are responsible for the contents of the paper.

M. Trapp et al. (Eds.): SAFECOMP 2022 Workshops, LNCS 13415, pp. 247–255, 2022.
https://doi.org/10.1007/978-3-031-14862-0_18

of the adaption of such measures, and become more pressing with every passing year.

In this whitepaper, we wish to share some insights that have been generated over the years of working together in the SCRATCh[1] project, which set out to systematically improve the security of applications in the Internet of Things (IoT) realm by focusing on the security of development and operations (DevOps). While SCRATCh resulted in a number of useful tools, it became clear that in order for Small and Medium Enterprises (SMEs) to be able to really benefit from newly developed security measures, a more holistic approach is needed. Since no such approach is in sight, after going over some of the relevant outcomes of the SCRATCh project, we seek to describe the main questions that such a holistic solution would need to address in order to be immediately useful for SMEs.

On the outset of the SCRATCh project, some of these problems were identified and heralded in preparation for work to diminish them[2]. In the IoT, ever a more relevant setting, many approaches fall flat, since these are distributed networks, with end nodes that are limited in hardware as well as their connection to headquarters. Devices may be left to do important work far away from the engineers that could identify security incidents, let alone resolve the matter if they were compromised.

Moreover, the participation of SMEs in the market for cybersecurity solutions is severely limited by the sheer complexity of the field. In a world where large companies must hire dedicated experts in the field of cybersecurity to attempt to earn certificates of trust, SMEs are all but powerless, as their company structure and budget often cannot afford a single such expert. Without one, it is plainly impossible to oversee the spectrum of cyber threats one faces, nevermind understand which security measures will address which parts of the threat landscape.

The SCRATCh project was able to identify and address some critical cybersecurity issues for the Internet of Things. However, over the course of the project, some rather more fundamental conundrums became visible, and the scope of the project was decidedly insufficient for an effective resolution thereof. There is no holistic method for threat analysis that is able to map all the cybersecurity requirements for a company without a cybersecurity expert. An SME, therefore, will lack the ability to do so; equally, it lacks the required terminology and awareness to understand what any particular cybersecurity product offers it.

In the world of cybersecurity, it is all about the weakest link, the avenue of attack that one forgot to protect entirely. Yet this world is so vast and complex, it is all but impossible for SMEs not to overlook certain threats and leave their flanks unnecessarily exposed. In order to foster, and to be able to regulate cybersecurity in SMEs in the EU, ground-breaking research into threat analysis, security requirements and the management thereof has become a severe necessity. This paper offers an examination of these quandaries, and suggestions for ways to seek solutions.

---

[1] https://scratch-itea3.eu/.

[2] https://arxiv.org/abs/2010.14865.

2   Status Quo for Security Practices in SMEs

But why do SMEs struggle with cybersecurity? There are multiple reasons that can be attributed. At their core, SMEs are often limited in resources, money and time, that they can dedicate to cybersecurity. With this limited budget, they have to balance many aspects of cybersecurity ranging over the security of their organisation and over the products, applications and services they provide to their customers. This is a lot of ground to cover.

With limited budget, investing in cybersecurity has to be high on the SME's agenda. Unfortunately, there is often a lack of awareness or importance and commitment by top management. Cybersecurity is still too often regarded as a cost and not seen as an investment into the future. When in truth, cybersecurity is an opportunity to invest in the trust that the customers of SMEs place into the SMEs' brand and product. This is an investment that will pay off in the future as customers are more and more aware of the cybersecurity risks and are starting to ask the tough questions. It's an investment that will prove to be a valuable sales differentiator in the future.

Due to the above, SMEs often lack in-house cybersecurity expertise. They have difficulties finding the right people with the right skill set and knowledge at a price that an SME can bear. And as they lack this expertise, they lack the cybersecurity terminology required to communicate their cybersecurity needs.

The EU regulates cybersecurity through certification systems, but as it stands, these certificates are practically outside the reach of SMEs. Not only are they quite complicated to read and understand, actually testing for them and deducing the necessary steps to reach compliance is a task so great that larger companies hire separate experts for all the certificates they wish to satisfy.

Generally speaking, bizarre as it is, the problem is not that great cyberse-curity solutions do not exist for SMEs. The problem is rather than there are too many such products, and the marketing for them is confusing, leaving SMEs unable to make good choices on what to invest in.

SMEs also seem not to realise that not every threat must be avoided - this is unreasonable even for the largest of companies. Modern security insights state that risks can be avoided, accepted, reduced or transferred. The key is to be aware of the risk and the options so a good choice can be made, and this can save incredible amounts of costs and even effort in the long run. Sadly, such a priority is not prolific at the time of writing.

2.1   Areas Addressed by SCRATCh Project

The SCRATCh project, rather then proposing a monolithic toolchain, developed a toolset to cater to the needs and necessities of SecDevOps. Since this can only be accomplished by providing flexibility and modularity, the requirements must match this approach and open up possibilities for process stage-specific handling. The requirements process is usually considered to consist of three phases: elici-tation and analysis, specification and validation. Injecting design constraints at the start of the requirements elicitation phase mostly impacts system requirements, while analyzing security features can be assumed to mainly impact system description and architecture, which are corrected or changed based on user or stakeholder needs.

Typically, an agile process feedback from early prototypes may require adaptation of security measurements from a usability perspective or technical limitations. It is these iterations that lead to a viable product, that is then as a last step validated against requirements and sector specific regulations. If due process is followed the system should pass the sector specific regulations as they were input in the early stage development, and deviation should be documented.

During SCRATCh it was found that it is best to start off with a set of generic good practices as a list of initial system requirements, e.g. through following the recommendations of ENISA[3], which offers architectural good practices regarding for example the authorization, cryptography, communications or network interfaces and services of a system. In addition to the architectural requirements, the process related requirements have to be established by identifying the relevant good practices, for example specifications of such guiding principles as "security by design" or "privacy by design". Since these requirements are generic in nature, they can be applied to virtually every project. Moving on from the generic set, the specific requirements must be identified. This should be done in an iterative manner as described above, during all stages of development, deployment and operation, to ensure that the product is indeed viable.

2.2 Developments Within the SCRATCh Project

We briefly describe in this subsection two particular elements of the overall design flow that were found relevant across Use Cases of SCRATCh.

Requirements. As mentioned before, requirements management is the starting point in engineering and for a DevOps operation it becomes a recurring theme. How to initially define the requirements, how to manage the implementation of components that comply to these requirements, how to ensure compliance with the well-established requirement proposals from standardizing bodies such as OWASP[4] and ENISA?

In SCRATCh we didn't look into one singular solution but rather explored a range of variations in this topic.

- Initially we proposed a quite integrated vision based on the usage of sphinx:needs[5] as the framework to specify the requirements. This is expressed in a simple yet expressive mark-up language that can easily be automatically processed by related tools in the DevOps spectrum (e.g., test suites, monitoring tools, update and customization mechanisms).

---

[3] https://www.enisa.europa.eu/.

[4] https://owasp.org/.

[5] https://sphinxcontrib-needs.readthedocs.io/en/latest/.

- We also started early in the project to collect the domain requirements proposed by relevant bodies in an easy-to-access Knowledge Base that is web-based and can be queried to get detailed contents.
- Finally we proposed tools such as OWASP ISVS[6] that enable even users without any knowledge of the above to get initial security requirements, validate the operation of a working system or customize it for any other means.

As in other areas of SCRATCh, we believe that the outcome of the project is that there is not one-size-fits-all solution. Many of the approaches we have followed may and can be applied in parallel. Critically, it would be important that any of these solutions combine an easy-to-understand paradigm even for novice users with some automation capability that enables connecting to further stages in the SecDevOps chain. As an example, we believe that such a combination of ISVS and sphinx:needs with some familiarity with the Knowledge Base would be an excellent starting point for SMEs interested in developing secure IoT.

Secure Storage. Providing Secure Storage for critical elements of data was one of the original goals of SCRATCh. Here, secure is to be understood as storage that is not accessible to unauthorized users or processes beyond the typical authentication mechanisms in regular operating systems. For that matter, we investigated hardware-based solutions that restrict access to data even if the physical device's integrity is compromised (e.g., an Internet of Things (IoT) device that is stolen and disassembled). The core goal was to ensure that at least for the most critical of data (such as private encryption keys) this can be ensured for all IoT applications built on the SCRATCh principles.

During the course of the project, it became apparent that such solutions present additional compromises such as requiring more, expensive and difficult to integrate hardware and posed extra strain on SMEs developing secure applications. A middle-of-the road solution was explored in more depth, leveraging the ARM TrustZone[7] extensions that are now widely deployed in most ARM SoCs. This proved to be a half success: while it is possible to do this, it still requires dedicated hardware and software, precise knowledge of the solutions and very tight integration, making the proposition of generalising such Secure Storage features quite difficult. Providing a standardized solution remains an open question for future efforts.

2.3   The Problems that SMEs Face Regarding Security

One of the key difficulties of SMEs when dealing with the application of security aspects in their products is very fundamental: how to describe the issues in security when you don't even have the experience or know-how to name things to be pointed at? In that regard, efforts such as SCRATCh are important because they can propose an integral approach to this that not only offers solutions, but

---

[6] https://github.com/OWASP/IoT-Security-Verification-Standard-ISVS.
[7] https://www.arm.com/technologies/trustzone-for-cortex-a.

a general framework to identify the problems themselves. In SCRATCh, we have done so by proposing our own methodology based on the Essence method and collapsing the whole DevOps cycle in a more fundamental one based around the three C's: *Constrain* to identify the applicable regulations and how they map to the developments in a product, *Comply*, which refers to testing the produced assets and see how they deal with the applied constraints and finally *Control* which deals with the Operations part of the cycle: how this situation works over time in a deployed state.

This 3C approach articulates on a fundamental level the SCRATCh offering and can be a necessary simplification for a company such as an SME that requires a very hands-on approach. Consequently, we clearly separated our produced tools and results according to this simplified model in the SCRATCh tool repository[8].

Another matter is the measuring of risks when compiling a cyber security report. A typical SMEs may be unable even to list and value all of its assets, let alone estimate chances and magnitudes of losses. Still, many of the threats they face are commonplace in their business world, and there is an opportunity for shared knowledge to greatly simplify these assessments.

One way for organizations to assess their level of security lies in the use of security maturity models. Such models commonly define policies, structures and implementations regarding security-related objectives. Based on a set of criteria, organizations can then find out their maturity level, with a higher level indicating correspondingly higher capability to deal with and learn from incidents. Maturity is achieved via a continuous process of improvement, rooted in an organization's structure and culture, rather then unsystematic implementation of technical solutions. While most maturity models are prescriptive in nature, usually based on recommended best practices, they can also be descriptive. An example for the latter is the BSIMM[9], which questions a variety of companies on their actual state of security practices, thus providing a model of the *de facto* industry standard in security. Even though organizations should optimally strive to follow recommended best practices, such an approach may serve as a good starting point for orientation, especially for SMEs without prior experience in continuous security improvement.

It is worth mentioning that even larger companies, which do not lack in resources or determination, struggle with cyber security thanks to the great complexity and chaos inherent. There is no definitive solution for threat assessment and security requirements in the same league as there are solutions for version management or online deployment. It is a field of work that is still more akin to a craftsmanship, a semi-absolute and semi-sentimental ability we can hardly grade, let alone teach.

---

[8] https://github.com/SCRATCh-ITEA3/SCRATCh-Tools-Repo.
[9] https://www.bsimm.com/about.html.

3   Holistic Angle

Desired is a complete, holistic methodology for the finding and managing of security requirements for a given product. Such a methodology must exhaustively list all relevant security threats, erring on the side of comprehensiveness rather than compactness. The methodology must then enable the user to find security requirements that will address the threats to a satisfactory level. It is acceptable if some threats cannot or will not be countered, due to cost concerns and the like, but they must at least be charted. In order to solve the problems of SMEs, such a methodology must also be usable by a team that lacks particular cybersecurity expertise beyond general IT training, and must be applicable within a limited budget of time and wages.

In our work as part of the SCRATCh project we have looked for such a holistic solution. There is not an available solution that combines the desired qualities of integral security management in all stages of the SecDevOps process that can readily be adopted by SMEs without massive monetary and staff investments. A minimum list of desired requirements for such as solution would be (1) to yield a complete list of security threats for a given product to be addressed, (2) to provide indications on how to deal with these security threats while (3) that could be the foundation of a cybersecurity approach (e.g., enforcing secure boot strategies) that does not impede growth but rather grows with the product and which is (4) applicable by a small team with general IT skills but perhaps lacking cybersecurity skills and also (5) applicable with a limited budget of time and resources.

3.1   Open Questions

Based on the general desired characteristics we built the solutions proposed for SCRATCh but as in any given research activity, resources were limited and we hit a number of walls that we could not solve. Thus, we highlight here a number of still open issues and approaches that remain relevant in the face of adoption of such security solutions by SMEs. The list is not exhaustive or prioritized by any means but serves as an indicator of current potential research and business lines to follow in the production of security solutions for this market:

– What will be the SME's **disruption of current practices**? This is one of the key aspects that should be kept in check for any solution. SMEs have typically a lean working force dedicated to a limited set of products, so the introduction of any charges is seen as a risk by their management. So, a potential solution should be flexible enough so that minimal disruption to current tool chains and processes is required. The discussed SCRATCh solution addresses this by its very form: a loosely connected set of tools that can be mixed and matched for adoption in most settings with minimal change to the underlying assets.

– What's the **learning curve** going to be for the company developers? This is very much connected with the point above: tool kits must be non-disruptive both at a technical level and as a tool to be operated by the current staff. This requires that any proposed solution comes well documented (e.g., including full comprehensive documentation but also quick tutorials and built-in recipes for common problems) and be as non-intimidating as possible. In order for this to happen, it would be advisable that it reuses known techniques of patterns from existing solutions.

– What's the impact going to be on the **staff** of the SME? Ideally, this should be kept to a minimum. It is also important to start from the assumption that the person tasked with implementing this solution in the SME's workflow might (a) not be fully aware of the security aspects and (b) not fully dedicated to managing the proposed solution.

– How does this impact the **automation** of the company's developments? This is also another of the key aspects that needs to be implemented in any solution. Most development teams now have adopted, or desire to adopt automated workflows such as the ones proposed in DevOps. Thus, any solution that tries to make a dent into the market needs to strongly propose its integration in these methodologies. Given the fragmentation of this market, compatibility with at least the major players (e.g., Maven, Jenkins, Travis) would be a good selling point and make the proposition more attractive for established software development teams.

– What's the visible commercial impact of the SME now complying to the new **certification/standards**? For SMEs, marketing is definitely part of the equation and sometime it's not just the alarm in your house that makes it secure, it's the 'Alarm in operation' sticker which deters thieves or changes your neighbors' attitude. Most SMEs are looking for ways to increase the perceived value of their products for their customers, so any solution that increases the security should reassure customers of this.

– Finally for this list, what's the monetary **cost** of this? Since for many of these SMEs' products security is a secondary consideration, it is essential that the cost associated to adopting any new tool is kept low. Since efforts such as the aforementioned SCRATCh toolkit are largely based on open source software, it can be argued that at least the initial cost is low. Total life cycle costs will nevertheless creep up since even for these open source solutions maintenance and customization costs apply, but the open source approach lowers the initial barrier to an acceptable level.

4   Conclusions

After the conclusion of the SCRATCh project, we have done a retrospective look on the achieved results and still open challenges on this front with particular focus on the role of SMEs in the domain of DevOps for IoT. In a world of growing cyberthreats, it is expected that even smaller companies that so far have delivered insecure products without major consequences will have to adapt and introduce security by design as a driving force into all of their outputs.

Thus during SCRATCh we have proposed a range of tools that enable companies without a dedicated budget or staff to quickly assess the security of their products and their compliance with standards. As a consequence of the varied background of partners in SCRATCh, we have also studied the drivers behind this lack of security and have tried to propose tools, methodologies and approaches that are adapted to these special characteristics of the European SME market. With this whitepaper and the rest of the results of the project, collected in an open library of results, we expect to contribute to a safer new generation of IoT and DevOps products.

5th International Workshop on Artificial Intelligence Safety Engineering (WAISE 2022)

Fifth International Workshop on Artificial Intelligence Safety Engineering (WAISE 2022)

Simos Gerasimou[1], Orlando Avila-García[2], Mauricio Castillo-Effen[3], Chih-Hong Cheng[4], and Zakaria Chihani[5]

[1] Department of Computer Science, University of York | Deramore Lane, YO10 5GH York, UK
simos.gerasimou@york.ac.uk
[2] Arquimea Reserch Center, Spain
oavila@arquimearesearchcenter.com
[3] Lockheed Martin, USA
mauricio.castillo-effen@lmco.com
[4] Fraunhofer IKS, Germany
chih-hong.cheng@iks.fraunhofer.de
[5] CEA LIST, CEA Saclay Nano-INNOV | Point Courrier 174, 91191 Gif-sur-Yvette, France
zakaria.chihani@cea.fr

1 Introduction

Realising the full potential of *Artificial Intelligence (AI)* entails guaranteeing expected levels of safety and resolving issues such as compliance with ethical standards and liability for accidents involving AI-enabled systems. Deploying AI-based systems that operate close to and/or in collaboration with humans necessitates revisiting current *safety engineering* and legal mechanisms to ensure that individuals –and their properties– are not harmed and that the desired benefits outweigh the potential unintended consequences. Researchers, engineers and policymakers with complementary expertise must join forces to tackle this challenge.

The increasing interest in developing approaches to enhance AI safety cover not only practical and engineering-focused aspects of autonomous systems and safety engineering but also pure theoretical concepts and topics, including ethical considerations and moral aspects. These two sides of AI safety cannot be considered in isolation. Instead, safe AI-enabled autonomous systems engineering mandates combining philosophy and theoretical science with applied science and engineering. Accordingly, a multidisciplinary approach is needed to encompass these seemingly disparate viewpoints and contribute to the engineering of safe AI-enabled systems underpinned by ethical and strategic decision-making capabilities.

Increasing levels of AI in "smart" sensory-motor loops allow intelligent systems to perform in increasingly dynamic, uncertain, complex environments with increasing degrees of *autonomy*, with the human being progressively taken out from the control loop. Adaptation to the environment is enabled by *Machine Learning (ML)* methods rather than more traditional engineering approaches, such as system modelling and programming. The enormous progress achieved by deep learning, reinforcement learning, and their combination in challenging real-world tasks such as image classification, natural language processing and speech recognition raises the expectation for their seamless incorporation into safety-critical applications. However, the *inscrutability* or opaqueness of their statistical models for perception and decision-making is a major challenge. Also, the combination of autonomy and inscrutability in these AI-based systems is particularly challenging in safety-critical applications, such as autonomous vehicles, personal care or assistive robots and collaborative industrial robots.

The Fifth *International Workshop on Artificial Intelligence Safety Engineering (WAISE)* explores new ideas on AI safety, ethically-aligned design, regulations, and standards for AI-based systems. WAISE aims to bring together experts, researchers, and practitioners from diverse communities, such as AI, safety engineering, ethics, standardisation, certification, robotics, cyber-physical systems, safety-critical systems, and application domain communities such as automotive, healthcare, manufacturing, agriculture, aerospace, critical infrastructures, and retail. The fifth WAISE edition was held on September 6, 2022, in Munich (Germany) as part of the 41st International Conference on Computer Safety, Reliability, & Security (SAFECOMP 2022).

2 Programme

The Programme Committee (PC) received 8 full research paper submissions. Each paper was peer-reviewed by at least three PC members, following a single-blind reviewing process. The committee decided to accept 7 papers (6 full research papers and 1as a position paper) for oral presentation.

The WAISE 2022 programme was organised into thematic sessions. In addition to the accepted papers, the workshop featured a keynote talk from Dr. Vahid Hashemi (Audi AG), 4 invited talks from research projects with a particular focus on safe AI, and a community debate.

The thematic sessions adopted a highly interactive format. They were structured into paper presentations and talks, with each presentation/talk followed by a discussion session. The theme of the community debate session was "Towards the last mile in engineering safe AI systems" and encouraged plenary discussion between participants.

The specific roles that were part of this format included session chairs, presenters and session discussants.

- *Session Chairs* introduced sessions and participants. The Chair moderated the session, took care of the time and gave the word to speakers in the audience during discussions.
- *Presenters* gave a paper presentation in 15 minutes and then participated in the discussion.
- *Session Discussants* prepared the discussion of individual papers and gave a critical review of the session papers.

The mixture of topics has been carefully balanced, as follows:

Session 1: AI Safety

- Safe Design of Stable Neural Networks for Fault Detection in Small UAVs, Kavya Gupta, Fateh Kaakai, Beatrice Pesquet-Popescu and Jean-Christophe Pesquet
- A Neural Criticality Metric for Object Detection Deep Neural Networks, Václav Diviš, Tobias Schuster and Marek Hrúz
- StaDRe and StaDRo: Reliability and Robustness Estimation of ML-based Forecasting using Statistical Distance Measures, Mohammed Naveed Akram, Akshatha Ambekar, Ioannis Sorokos, Koorosh Aslansefat and Daniel Schneider

Session 2: Advances in Safe AI (Invited Talks 1)

- FOCETA: FOundations for Continuous Engineering of Trustworthy Autonomy, Saddek Bens
- TAILOR: Trustworthy AI, Fredrik Heintz

Session 3: Advances in Safe AI (Invited Talks 2)

- Confiance.ai, Bertrand Braunschweig
- SESAME: Secure and Safe Multi-Robot Systems, Simos Gerasimou

Session 4: Assurances for Autonomous Systems

- A Safety Assurable Human-Inspired Perception Architecture, Rick Salay and Krzysztof Czarnecki
- Object Detection With Probabilistic Guarantees: a Conformal Prediction Approach, Florence de Grancey, Jean-Luc Adam, Lucian Alecu, Sébastien Gerchinovitz, Franck Mamalet and David Vigouroux
- A Novel Abstraction Framework for Neural Network Verification, Fateh Boudardara, Abderraouf Boussif, Pierre-Jean Meyer and Mohamed Ghazel
- Logically Sound Arguments for the Effectiveness of ML Safety Measures, Chih-Hong Cheng, Tobias Schuster and Simon Burton

3   Acknowledgements

As chairpersons of WAISE 2022, we want to thank all authors and contributors who submitted their work to the workshop. We also congratulate the authors whose papers were selected for inclusion in the programme and proceedings. We would also like to thank Friedemann Bitsch, the SAFECOMP Publication Chair, Erwin Schoitsch, the general workshop co-chair, and the SAFECOMP organisers, who provided us with the opportunity to organise the WAISE workshop at SAFECOMP 2022.

We would like to thank the Steering Committee (SC) for their support and advice to make WAISE 2022 a successful event:

Rob Alexander   University of York, UK
Huascar Espinoza   KDT JU, Belgium
Philip Koopman   Carnegie Mellon University, USA
Stuart Russell   UC Berkeley, USA
Raja Chatila   ISIR - Sorbonne University, France

We especially thank our distinguished PC members, for reviewing the submissions and providing useful feedback to the authors:

Rob Alexander   University of York, UK
Vincent Aravantinos   Autonomous Intelligent Driving GmbH, Germany
Alec Banks   Defence Science and Technology Laboratory, UK
Markus Borg   RISE SICS, Sweden
Simon Burton   IKS Fraunhofer, Germany
Radu Calinescu   University of York, UK
Carmen Carlan   Edge Case Research GmbH, Germany
Raja Chatila   ISIR - Sorbonne University, France
Huascar Espinoza   KDT JU, Belgium
John Favaro   INTECS, Italy
Jérémie Guiochet   LAAS-CNRS, France
Vahid Hashemi   Audi, Germany
Nico Hochgeschwende   Bonn-Rhein-Sieg University, Germany
Philip Koopman   Carnegie Mellon University, USA
Bettina Könighofer   Technical University of Graz, Austria
Timo Latvala   Space Systems Finland, Finland
Nicholas Matragkas   CEA LIST, France
Juliette Mattioli   Thales
Adedjouma Morayo   CEA LIST, France
Chokri Mraidha   CEA LIST, France
Philippa Ryan Conmy   Adelard LLP, UK
Mehrdad Saadatmand   RISE SICS, Sweden
Erwin Schoitsch   Austrian Institute of Technology, Austria
Hao Shen   Fortiss, Germany
Ioannis Sorokos   Fraunhofer IESE, Germany
Xingyu Zhao   University of Liverpool, UK

Safe Design of Stable Neural Networks for Fault Detection in Small UAVs

Kavya Gupta[1,2(✉)], Fateh Kaakai[2], Béatrice Pesquet-Popescu[2], and Jean-Christophe Pesquet[1]

[1] Université Paris - Saclay, CentraleSupélec, Inria Centre de Vision Numérique, Gif-sur-Yvette, France
`kavya.gupta100@gmail.com`
[2] Air Mobility Solutions BL, Thales LAS France, Rungis, France

Abstract. Stability of a machine learning model is the extent to which a model can continue to operate correctly despite small perturbations in its inputs. A formal method to measure stability is the Lipschitz constant of the model which allows to evaluate how small perturbations in the inputs impact the output variations. Variations in the outputs may lead to high errors for regression tasks or unintended changes in the classes for classification tasks. Verification of the stability of ML models is crucial in many industrial domains such as aeronautics, space, automotive etc. It has been recognized that data-driven models are intrinsically extremely sensitive to small perturbation of the inputs. Therefore, the need to design methods for verifying the stability of ML models is of importance for manufacturers developing safety critical products.

In this work, we focus on Small Unmanned Aerial Vehicles (UAVs) which are in the frontage of new technology solutions for intelligent systems. However, real-time fault detection/diagnosis in such UAVs remains a challenge from data collection to prediction tasks. This work presents application of neural networks to detect in real-time elevon positioning faults. We show the efficiency of a formal method based on the Lipschitz constant for quantifying the stability of neural network models. We also present how this method can be coupled with spectral normalization constraints at the design phase to control the internal parameters of the model and make it more stable while keeping a high level of performance (accuracy-stability trade-off).

Keywords: Safety · Stability · Lipschitz constant · Verification · Machine learning · Neural networks · UAV · Tabular data · Adversarial attacks

1 Introduction

Machine Learning (ML) methods and in particular neural networks are rapidly paving their way in various mission-critical and safety-critical domains such as aeronautics, aerospace, automotive, railways, and nuclear plants. In particular,

M. Trapp et al. (Eds.): SAFECOMP 2022 Workshops, LNCS 13415, pp. 263–275, 2022.
https://doi.org/10.1007/978-3-031-14862-0_19

UAVs are currently being used in various applications such as surveillance of critical infrastructures, delivery of goods in densely populated urban areas, disaster management, emergency services, etc. UAVs are capable of replacing humans in potentially dangerous situations, but also reduce the cost of operations in some businesses. But these kind of systems need to be continuously monitored to detect in real-time any problem ("fault") that could lead to a failure of the UAV and with a potential interruption of the mission, a potential collision with a manned aircraft (air risk), a potential collision with people on ground or with a critical infrastructure like a nuclear plant (ground risk). The need is to develop fault-tolerant systems. Formally, fault tolerance is the ability of a system to perform the intended function despite the presence or occurrence of faults, whether it is a physical damage to the hardware, software defects, or malicious attacks. In this paper, we deal with a Machine Learning based UAV fault detection (depicted in the red component of Fig. 1a) that implements a Deep Neural Network (DNN) to detect mechanical faults like an elevon stucked or locked in a given position. This real-time fault detection mechanism allows the remote pilot to take necessary actions (e.g. remote triggering of the drone emergency parachute) to avoid the loss of control of the UAV which could induce an air risk or a ground risk.

This Machine Learning based fault detection function should be safe to claim compliance with the applicable regulations. In particular, it should be stable with respect to noise perturbations in the input data coming from the inertial sensors and the autopilot i.e. the model continues to operate correctly despite small perturbations in its inputs within the Operational Design Domain (ODD). In other words, small perturbations that are considered as part of the real operating conditions should be considered in the designing phase of the model making the model 'stable-by-design'. However, the concept of adversarial attacks introduced in [21] shows that adding a designed imperceptible noise to the sample is able to fool a neural network even if the model is trained to achieve high accuracy and performance. There have been studies that design different attacks [10,16] on different model architectures and applications. Such design weakness in DNNs questions the desired stability property of neural networks and hence its deployment in mission-critical or safety-critical products like UAVs. Many works providing counter measures to adversarial attacks such as adversarial training [7] and defensive distillation have appeared in literature. But it is hard to demonstrate the completeness of these counter measures, i.e. their ability to address all types of foreseeable perturbations in the given operational context.

An example of formal measure of stability of neural network is the Lipschitz constant of the model which allows to evaluate how small perturbations in the inputs impact the output variations as illustrated in Fig. 1b. A sensitivity analysis of inputs using Lipschitz constant for neural networks in presented in [9]. The contributions of this work is to demonstrate the efficiency of formal guarantees based on the Lipschitz constant for checking the stability of DNNs. We present a stability control loop grounded on spectral normalisation constraints to achieve an accuracy-stability trade-off. We show the results in various experimental designs on a small UAV dataset for classification tasks. We start with presenting generalisation capabilities of neural networks over other machine learning methods such as SVM and logistic regression, and then give Lipschitz constant estimates of different neural network configurations. We show that it is possible to train a neural network satisfying both Lipschitz and accuracy targets using our stability control loop. We also demonstrate the effectiveness of spectral normalised models in handling adversarial tasks.

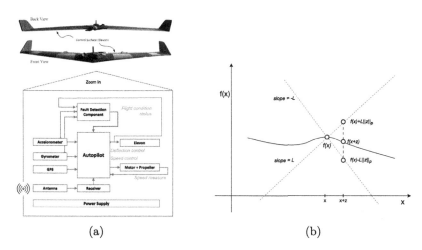

(a)	(b)

Fig. 1. (a) Fault detection in drones/UAVs: the component called "Fault Detection Component" computes a flight condition status (nominal or faulty) using the outputs of the inertial sensors and the elevon deflection control variable produced by the autopilot. (b) Intuition of using Lipschitz constant as a stability property of neural network [24].

The next section discusses related work in the field of fault detection using neural networks and stability analysis of these architectures. Following this, a spectral normalisation based stability control loop is described. Then the real flight data used to evaluate the fault detection model is presented. In the following section, results and observations for various scenarios related to binary and multi-class classification tasks are presented. The last section summarizes the main contributions of this work.

2   Related Works

2.1   Fault Detection and Diagnosis(FDD)

FDD strategies can be primarily divided into two categories model-based and data-driven. Model-based approaches require an accurate model of the aircraft for successful diagnosis of the faults. But a small UAV system is susceptible to various perturbations and lacks an accurate model. Hence, model based approaches fail in such scenarios and studies are then concentrated on using data-driven methods.

AI based data-driven techniques are gaining more and more interest in the field of fault detection. Fault detection in UAVs has been studied by using different sensors and/or for detecting faults in different fault prone parts of the vehicle. Freeman et al. [6] compares model-based and data-driven fault detection methods by using data from small, low-cost UAVs. Both approaches were shown to be capable of detecting different elevon faults in real data during maneuvers and in the presence of environmental variations. Guo et al. [8] proposed a hybrid feature model and deep learning-based fault diagnosis for UAV sensors. The model detects different sensor faults, such as GPS, IMU and ADS. The authors of [25] modelled fault detection using Generalized Regression Neural Network with a particle swarm optimization algorithm. Eroglu et al. [4] proposed a data-driven fault estimation method for estimating actuator faults from aircraft state trajectories. The authors propose to use an architecture with 1-D CNN followed by LSTM layers for learning state trajectories on simulated data of fault injected aircraft. Sadhu et al. [19] proposed a deep learning based real-time fault detection and identification on UAV IMU sensor data using CNN and Bi-LSTM. Iannace et al. [12] presented a single layered neural network for detecting unbalanced blades in a UAV propeller. Bronz et al. [1] uses an SVM classifier with RBF kernel to classify the different faults for small fixed-wing UAVs. We use the same real flight dataset for our analysis and make comparisons with the reported results for SVM classifier.

2.2   Stability Quantification Through Lipschitz Constant

The number of works studying the stability issue of neural networks has increased in manifolds with those defining and handling the stability of these networks in various manners. A way of quantifying the stability of a trained neural network model consists of studying the Lipschitz properties of the neural network. A Lipschitz constant of a multi-input multi-output function f is an upper bound on the ratio between the variations in the outputs and the variations in inputs of f, and thus it constitutes a measure of sensitivity of the function with respect to input perturbations.

For a feed-forward neural network represented by f where m is the number of hidden layers, N_i the number of neurons in layer $i \in \{1, \ldots, m\}$, let $x \in \mathbb{R}^{N_0}$ be the input and $f(x) \in \mathbb{R}^{N_m}$ be the associated output. If $L \in [0, +\infty[$ is such that, for every input $x \in \mathbb{R}^{N_0}$ and perturbation $z \in \mathbb{R}^{N_0}$, we have

$$\|f(x+z) - f(x)\| \leq L\|z\|, \tag{1}$$

then L is a Lipschitz constant of the neural network f. The smaller this constant value, the more stable the neural network.

A *trivial upper bound* on the Lipschitz constant of a neural network was defined in [7] as the product of spectral norms (S) of each layer independently. Mathematically it can be written as

$$\overline{L}_m = \|W_m\|_S \|W_{m-1}\|_S \cdots \|W_1\|_S. \tag{2}$$

where W_i are the weights/kernels at each layer $i \in \{1, \ldots, m\}$. This bound was found to be too loose for some practical applications.

In [23], it was proved that the problem of computing the exact Lipschitz constant of a neural network with differentiable activation functions is NP-hard. In [3], the authors proposed various bounds on the Lipschitz constant of a feedforward network under the assumption that the activation operator at each layer is α_i-averaged with $\alpha_i \in]0,1]$. This assumption is satisfied by most of the widely used activation functions, which are $1/2$-averaged [2]. If the activation function at each layer is separable, a general Lipschitz constant estimate, CPLip, is defined as

$$L_m = \sup_{\Lambda_1 \in \mathcal{D}_1, \ldots, \Lambda_{m-1} \in \mathcal{D}_{m-1}} \|W_m \Lambda_{m-1} \cdots \Lambda_1 W_1\|_{\mathrm{S}}, \qquad (3)$$

where, for every $i \in \{1, \ldots, m-1\}$, $\mathcal{D}_i$ is the set of diagonal matrices of size $N_i \times N_i$ with diagonal elements equal to $2\alpha_i - 1$ or 1. This estimate remains true even with other norms than the Euclidean, applied to the input and output perturbation spaces. In [13] authors proposed a polynomial constrained optimization (LipOpt) based technique for estimating Lipschitz constant. This estimate can be used for any ℓ_p norm for input and output perturbations, but it is valid for neural network with single output. Solving such an optimization problem can be achieved by solving a hierarchy of convex problems such as Lasserre's hierarchy.

SDP based Lipschitz Constant estimates were explored in [5]. This work focuses on neural networks using separable activation operators. It assumes that the activation functions at all layers are slope-bounded. By using the non-expansiveness property of the activation function, the optimization problem of estimating a Lipschitz constant is recast as solving a semi-definite positive programming (SDP) problem. This estimation can only be used when the Euclidean norm is employed at both input and output spaces. Also, the most optimized technique for estimating the Lipschitz constant in [5] is erroneous, as mentioned and proved in [18]. Hence, for all our results we use the valid version LipSDP-neuron for all our Lipschitz constant estimates.

3 Spectral Normalization Control of the Model Stability

For safety critical tasks, Lipschitz constant and performance targets can be specified as engineering requirements, prior to network training. A Lipschitz constant target can be defined by a safety analysis of the acceptable perturbations for each output knowing the input ranges and it constitutes a current practice in many industrial processes. The Lipschitz constant of a neural network can be arbitrarily high when unconstrained, making it sensitive to adversarial attacks. Imposing this Lipschitz target can be done either by controlling the Lipschitz constant for each layer or for the whole network, depending on the application at hand. Such a work for controlling the Lipschitz constant has been presented in [20] using Hinge regularization. Spectral normalization techniques [15,17] have been proved to be very effective in controlling stability properties of DNNs and counter adversarial attacks. But they require an exact computation of the spectral norm in (3), which is computationally expensive, and therefore it becomes intractable for deep neural networks. On the other hand, it has been shown that constraining the Lipschitz constant of DNNs enhances their stability, but it makes the minimization of the loss function harder. Hence, a trade-off between stability and prediction performance needs to be reached [26]. We subsequently propose an iterative procedure allowing us to find the best trade-off.

Given an m-layer fully connected NN architecture (FCN) denoted by T with a Lipschitz constant L_{target} and an accuracy target $\text{acc}_{\text{target}}$. We can constrain the spectral norm of each layer to be less than $\sqrt[m]{L_{\text{target}}}$. According to (2), this ensures that the upper bound on the global Lipschitz constant is less than L_{target}. This bound is however overpessimistic, which means that, by monitoring accurately the value of the actual Lipschitz constant of the network, we can relax the bound on individual linear layers so as to get an improved accuracy. In our proposed approach, this process is done in a closed loop with two targets : good performance ($\text{acc}_{\text{target}}$) and desired stability L_{target}.

The approach is summarized in Algorithm 1. Module $\text{Train}_{\text{SN}}(L, \ldots)$ is spectral normalisation training module which trains the defined neural network model with the Lipschitz constant constraint, i.e. each weight matrices W_i with $i \in \{1, \ldots, m\}$ of the neural network is divided by $(\sigma_i / \sqrt[n]{L})$, where σ_i is the largest singular value of W_i. Module LipEst estimates accurately the Lipschitz constant of the trained neural network using LipSDP-Neuron [5]. Module Predict checks the performance (here classification performance) of the trained model on the validation dataset. If L is small, training will be over-constrained and the accuracy of the model will suffer. To relax this constraint we iteratively increase the value of L through small α factor to find the best value of L_{opt} which would be less than L_{target} and ensure an increase in the performance on the validation dataset to achieve acc_{opt} greater than acc_{target}. We stop the iterations when both conditions are met i.e. accuracy of the trained model is greater than acc_{target} and Lipschitz constant is less than L_{target}.

4   Validation on Drone Flights Data

4.1   Dataset Description

For our fault detection and stability analysis, we use the real-flight dataset provided in [1]. The authors use Paparazzi Autopilot system [11] for possible flight trajectories. The flight test data is captured in outdoor setting on different days with varying environments especially wind speeds and also imperfections in the geometry due to manufacturing of the UAV.

The actuator fault model (F) as proposed in [22] is given by

$$u_{\text{app}} = F u_{\text{com}} + E \tag{4}$$

where u_{com} is the commanded control deflection from the autopilot to the actuators and u_{app} is the applied control deflection (i.e. final movement of the elevon)

Algorithm 1. Spectral Normalisation-based Stability Control Loop

---

1: **Inputs** : training dataset $(X_{\text{train}}, Y_{\text{train}})$, validation dataset $(X_{\text{valid}}, Y_{\text{valid}})$, target Lipschitz constant L_{target}, target accurcay $\text{acc}_{\text{target}}$, neural network T, multiplicative factor $\alpha > 1$, maximum iteration number $n_{\max}$

2: **Output** : optimal neural network T_{opt}, Lipschitz constant L_{opt}, and accuracy acc_{opt}

3: **Algo** :

4: $L \leftarrow L_{\text{target}}$, $n \leftarrow 0$

5: $T \leftarrow \text{Train}_{\text{SN}}(L, X_{\text{train}}, Y_{\text{train}})$

6: $L_{\text{est}} \leftarrow \text{LipEst}(T)$

7: $\text{acc} \leftarrow \text{Predict}(T, X_{\text{valid}}, Y_{\text{valid}})$

8: **while** $(n < n_{\max})$ and $(L_{\text{est}} < L_{\text{target}})$ and $(\text{acc} < \text{acc}_{\text{target}})$ **do**

9: $\qquad L \leftarrow \alpha L$

10: $\qquad T \leftarrow \text{Train}_{\text{SN}}(L, X_{\text{train}}, Y_{\text{train}})$

11: $\qquad L_{\text{est}} \leftarrow \text{LipEst}(T)$

12: $\qquad \text{acc} \leftarrow \text{Predict}(T, X_{\text{valid}}, Y_{\text{valid}})$

13: $\qquad n \leftarrow n + 1$

14: **end while**

15: $T_{\text{opt}} \leftarrow T$

16: $L_{\text{opt}} \leftarrow L_{\text{est}}$

17: $\text{acc}_{\text{opt}} \leftarrow \text{acc}$

18: **if** $n = n_{,\max}$ **then**

19: $\qquad$ Notification: No trade-off found between Stability and Accuracy

20: **else**

21: $\qquad$ Notification: Trade-off found between Stability and Accuracy

22: **end if**

---

and E is the offset. In vector form, it can be expressed as

$$\begin{bmatrix} u_{\text{app}_r} \\ u_{\text{app}_l} \end{bmatrix} = \begin{bmatrix} f_r & 0 \\ 0 & f_l \end{bmatrix} \begin{bmatrix} u_{\text{com}_r} \\ u_{\text{com}_l} \end{bmatrix} + \begin{bmatrix} e_r \\ e_l \end{bmatrix}, \tag{5}$$

where $()_r$ and and $()_l$ stands for the right and left elevon respectively. The feature set is a vector of length 8 consisting of linear accelerations at three coordinates (a_x, a_y, a_z), angular rates $(\omega_x, \omega_y, \omega_z)$, and auto-pilot commanded controls $(u_{\text{com}_r}, u_{\text{com}_l})$ for the two aerodynamic actuators. Depending on the values of f_r and f_l, the fault detection problem can be translated into two kinds of classification problems: 1) Binary Class Classification and 2) Multi-class Classification.

We use three performance measures: classification accuracy (%), F1 score, and Matthews Correlation coefficient (MCC). For stability measure we use Lipschitz constant estimate as calculated using LipSDP-Neuron [5]. We recall that we do not use LipSDP most tight bound LipSDP-Network since it is erroneous as mentioned in the Sect. 2.2.

4.2   Binary Classification Results

We train the data on 12th July and test the trained model on 12th july unseen and 13th July data. It is interesting to use 12th July flight data for training and predict fault for the next day, i.e. 13th July since 12th and 13th July had different atmospheric conditions at the time of data collection. For further checking the efficacy and generalization capabilities of the methods, we checked the trained models on flight data for 21st July. The faults were injected in the right elevon $f_r = 0.3$. Fault code 0 implies 'Nominal fault' and fault code 1 implies fault in the right elevon.

Table 1. Binary classification : comparison between SVM, logistic regression, and best NN trained with baseline training on 12th July.

Model	12th July			13th July			21st July		
	Acc. (%)	F1	MCC	Acc. (%)	F1	MCC	Acc. (%)	F1	MCC
SVM	**98.7**	**0.99**	**0.98**	60.5	0.59	0.38	85.3	0.85	0.72
LogReg	89.8	0.90	0.79	58.0	0.59	0.31	56.6	0.45	0.18
Baseline	98.6	0.99	0.97	**73.3**	**0.74**	**0.52**	**93.1**	**0.93**	**0.86**

Implementation Details: We propose to use fully connected feed-forward networks (FCN) for solving the problem. We train such neural networks of varying depth and width. We use ReLU as the activation function except for the last layer where it is employed with sigmoid for binary and softmax for multi-class classification. We use the cross entropy losses as the loss function for training the model. The feature set is standardized by removing the mean and scaling to unit variance. While training, the dataset is split into 4:1 ratio for train and validation sets. The models are trained using Keras with Tensorflow backend. The initializers are set to Glorot uniform and we use Adam as the optimizer. To capture the temporal dynamics of the system, feature set of length 8 $(a_x, a_y, a_z, \omega_x, \omega_y, \omega_z, u_{com_r}, u_{com_l})$ is concatenated T times. Therefore, the input feature vector to the model is of length $8T$. We observe a general increasing trend in the testing performance as we increase the value of T, which suggests that concatenating more feature lists from the time history of the flight data improves the performance of the real-time prediction. Hence, we found the value $T = 20$ as optimal for our experiments, adding time history beyond this level did not contribute to the learning and the neural network starts to overfit.

In the **first** set of experiments for binary classification, we train on 12th July flight data and test on of 12th July, 13th, and 21st July and directly compare our NN best models to SVM and logistic regression. SVM classifier is trained with a RBF kernel and is optimized using grid-search. The results are given in Table 1. The results obtained using SVM classifier are satisfactory, better than for logistic regression, but they fail to generalize on the unseen data from 13th and 21st July. We remark it is possible to train neural networks with much better generalization performance on different days with varying weather conditions.

In **second** set of experiments we discuss the stability performance of neural networks which is our primary concern pertaining to stable model design. The

Table 2. Binary classification : results on 12th and 13th July using NN trained with baseline training on 12th July for various configurations of FCN.

Model	12th July			13th July			L
	Acc. (%)	F1	MCC	Acc. (%)	F1	MCC	
(10)	98.3	0.983	0.967	66.4	0.67	0.41	**12.26**
(10,6)	98.4	0.985	0.969	71.0	0.71	0.47	27.56
(50,10,6)	**98.7**	**0.987**	**0.974**	**73.3**	**0.74**	**0.52**	37.76

Table 3. Comparison between models trained with baseline and spectral normalization constraint ($L_{target} = 4$).

Model	Baseline		Spectral	
	Acc. (%)	L	Acc. (%)	L
(10)	66.4	12.26	75.1	3.7
(10,6)	71.0	27.56	75.3	3.8
(50,10,6)	73.3	37.76	**76.7**	**3.7**

(a) Binary Classification: Results on 13th July trained on 12th July data.

Model	Baseline		Spectral	
	Acc. (%)	L	Acc. (%)	L
(50,10)	69.7	31.44	**72.65**	3.8
(100,10)	69.54	34.17	71.07	**3.6**
(100,75,10)	68.9	69.06	71.93	3.7

(b) Multi-class Classification: Results on 23rd July trained on 21st July data.

comparison of the classification task accuracy as well as the stability performance in terms of Lipschitz constant for a varying number of hidden layers and hidden neurons is shown in Table 2. Notation (10,6) in Table 2 implies that the FCN has two hidden layers with 10 and 6 hidden neurons and so on. In the baseline training, no constraints are employed while training the NN. Lipschitz constant (L) is computed using LipSDP-neuron [5] on the trained network.

Third, we show the performance and stability effect of constraining the training of the neural network by spectral normalization, as introduced in Sect. 3 with Algorithm 1. We chose the same configuration for the neural networks as baseline and introduced constraints, by setting $L_{target} = 4$ and $acc_{target} = 75\%$. Table 3a shows a comparison of the classification accuracy and Lipschitz constant value for baseline training and the new training procedure described in Algorithm 1. We remark that the proposed approach improves both accuracy and stability of neural network models.

We also test and compare the results of the trained neural networks when they are attacked with widely known adversarial attacks such as FGSM [7] and

Table 4. Binary classification: results on 12th July clean data, FGSM and PGD attacks using model trained on 12th July.

Model	Training	No attack		FGSM ($\epsilon = 0.2$)		PGD ($\epsilon = 0.2$)	
		Acc. (%)	MCC	Acc. (%)	MCC	Acc. (%)	MCC
(50,10,6)	**Baseline**	98.6	0.97	77.6	0.62	76.0	0.59
	Spectral	98.7	0.97	**81.0**	**0.66**	**79.2**	**0.62**

PGD [14]. The attacks are generated using ART toolbox[1]. An adversarial attack is a special case of addition of noise to the input samples. It is useful to test robustness of the neural network since the adversarial noise is crafted in a manner to generate misclassification errors. We show the results on 12th July test dataset in Table 4[2]. We remark that spectral normalised training is better in handling the adversarial attacks, leading to more stable models.

4.3   Multi-class Classification Results

We use the flight data captured on the days of 21st and 23rd July for detecting the faults in right and left elevon. For injecting the faults, efficiency of the right elevon is reduced ($f_r = 0.3$) and similarly for the left control elevon ($f_l = 0.9/0.3$). Fault codes:'0' - nominal ,'1' - $f_r = 0.3$,'2' - $f_l = 0.9$ and'3' - $f_l = 0.3$, making a 4-class classification problem. The emphasis has been put on detecting faults on the left elevon which has the effect of a geometric twist. Identical faults are injected in the flight data for both days. For capturing the temporal dynamics in the prediction performance, the optimal value of T is taken to be 20 as in the previous section.

Table 5. Multi-class classification: comparison between SVM, logistic regression and best NN trained with baseline training on 21st July and tested on 21st and 23rd July .

Model	21st July			23rd July		
	Acc. (%)	F1	MCC	Acc. (%)	F1	MCC
SVM	94.1	0.94	0.91	60.3	0.60	0.51
LogReg	89.0	0.88	0.84	57.8	0.55	0.43
Baseline	**95.2**	**0.95**	**0.93**	**69.7**	**0.68**	**0.58**

Table 6. Multi-class classification : results on 21st July and 23rd July using NN trained with baseline training on 21st July for various configurations of FCN.

Model	21st July			23rd July			L
	Acc. (%)	F1	MCC	Acc. (%)	F1	MCC	
(50,10)	95.2	0.95	0.93	**69.7**	**0.68**	**0.58**	**31.44**
(100,10)	95.3	0.95	0.93	69.5	0.68	0.57	34.17
(100,75,10)	**95.4**	**0.95**	**0.93**	68.9	0.67	0.57	69.06

---

[1] https://github.com/Trusted-AI/adversarial-robustness-toolbox.

[2] In case of SVM model, classification metric MCC had negative values for FGSM and PGD attacks implying model performs very poorly against adversarial attacks, hence we discard them from comparison.

For the experiments, we train a FCN with ReLU activation function for all layers, except the last one for which softmax is used. We train the neural network on the flight data of 21st July and test on data of 21st July not seen by the model at the time of training, and also on the flight data of 23rd July. We show the prediction and generalization capabilities of the neural networks over state-of-the-art SVM and logistic regression. We tabulate the classification metrics in Table 5. Varying configurations of model layers and neurons classification metrics along with the stability metric (L) have been considered in Table 6. We consider acc$_{target}$ = 70% and L_{target} = 4 as the model performance and stability requirements. The results are shown in Table 3b.

Observations of the performance and stability analysis:

- Neural networks perform better than SVM classifier and logistic regression in terms of prediction performance indicating better generalization capabilities of neural network models, when trained and tested on different days.
- We observe the trend of increased Lipschitz constant as the number of layers and neurons in the neural network increases.
- There is a steep decrease in the Lipschitz constant value when the models are trained with a Lipschitz target which satisfies the performance target as well Table 3. We also observe an increase of classification performance with spectral normalization constraint.
- Spectral normalised trained models are better against adversarial attacks implying since they are designed to be more stable.

5   Conclusion

Our work provides a formal method by means of estimating Lipschitz constant to evaluate and control the stability of a neural network, which is necessary for many mission-critical and safety-critical systems. This work analyses a real flight data collected on a small fixed-wing UAV in varying flight conditions to design a fully connected feed-forward neural networks that implements a fault detection function embedded in the UAV. The task is to detect mechanical faults like an elevon stucked or locked in a given position even in the presence of noise in the input data coming from the inertial sensors and the autopilot and to allow the remote pilot to take necessary actions to ensure the safety. The main contributions of this work are the following: Through the evaluation of classification performance we have shown that our approach based on DNN compares favorably with SVM and logistic regression techniques. Unlike many works related to the use of neural networks in industrial applications, we address the stability of our trained neural networks using a formal verification method based on the quantification of the Lipschitz constant of the model. We show the effectiveness of spectral normalization techniques in controlling the Lipschitz constant of the network to reach a Lipschitz safety target which can be defined at system level. Following the insights presented in the paper, we show that it is possible to build neural networks which are "Stable-by-Design" and verified through Lipschitz certificates. Such designed models are more robust to adversarial attacks and present a good accuracy. These results regarding stability are strong developments toward learning assurance artefacts in ML models.

References

1. Bronz, M., Baskaya, E., Delahaye, D., Puechmore, S.: Real-time fault detection on small fixed-wing UAVs using machine learning. In: DASC, pp. 1–10 (2020)
2. Combettes, P.L., Pesquet, J.C.: Deep neural network structures solving variational inequalities. In: Set-Valued and Variational Analysis, pp. 1–28 (2020)
3. Combettes, P.L., Pesquet, J.C.: Lipschitz certificates for neural network structures driven by averaged activation operators. SIAM J. Math. Data Sci. **2**, 529–557 (2020)
4. Eroglu, B., Sahin, M.C., Ure, N.K.: Autolanding control system design with deep learning based fault estimation. Aerosp. Sci. Technol. **102**, 105855 (2020)
5. Fazlyab, M., Robey, A., Hassani, H., Morari, M., Pappas, G.J.: Efficient and accurate estimation of lipschitz constants for deep neural networks. In: NeurIPS (2019)
6. Freeman, P., Pandita, R., Srivastava, N., Balas, G.J.: Model-based and data-driven fault detection performance for a small UAV. IEEE/ASME Trans. Mechatron. **18**(4), 1300–1309 (2013)
7. Goodfellow, I.J., Shlens, J., Szegedy, C.: Explaining and harnessing adversarial examples. arXiv preprint arXiv:1412.6572 (2014)
8. Guo, D., Zhong, M., Ji, H., Liu, Y., Yang, R.: A hybrid feature model and deep learning based fault diagnosis for unmanned aerial vehicle sensors. Neurocomputing **319**, 155–163 (2018)
9. Gupta, K., Kaakai, F., Pesquet-Popescu, B., Pesquet, J.C., Malliaros, F.: Multivariate lipschitz analysis of the stability of neural networks. Front. Sig. Process., 9 (2022)
10. Gupta, K., Pesquet, J.C., Pesquet-Popescu, B., Kaakai, F., Malliaros, F.: An adversarial attacker for neural networks in regression problems. In: IJCAI AI Safety Workshop (2021)
11. Hattenberger, G., Bronz, M., Gorraz, M.: Using the paparazzi UAV system for scientific research. In: IMAV, pp. pp 247–252, August 2014
12. Iannace, G., Ciaburro, G., Trematerra, A.: Fault diagnosis for UAV blades using artificial neural network. Robotics **8**(3), 59 (2019)
13. Latorre, F., Rolland, P., Cevher, V.: Lipschitz constant estimation of neural networks via sparse polynomial optimization. arXiv preprint arXiv:2004.08688 (2020)
14. Madry, A., Makelov, A., Schmidt, L., Tsipras, D., Vladu, A.: Towards deep learning models resistant to adversarial attacks. arXiv preprint arXiv:1706.06083 (2017)
15. Miyato, T., Kataoka, T., Koyama, M., Yoshida, Y.: Spectral normalization for generative adversarial networks. arXiv preprint arXiv:1802.05957 (2018)
16. Moosavi-Dezfooli, S.M., Fawzi, A., Frossard, P.: Deepfool: a simple and accurate method to fool deep neural networks. In: CVPR, pp. 2574–2582 (2016)
17. Pan, Z., Mishra, P.: Fast approximate spectral normalization for robust deep neural networks. arXiv preprint arXiv:2103.13815 (2021)
18. Pauli, P., Koch, A., Berberich, J., Allgöwer, F.: Training robust neural networks using lipschitz bounds. arXiv preprint arXiv:2005.02929 (2020)
19. Sadhu, V., Zonouz, S., Pompili, D.: On-board deep-learning-based unmanned aerial vehicle fault cause detection and identification. In: ICRA, pp. 5255–5261. IEEE (2020)

20. Serrurier, M., Mamalet, F., González-Sanz, A., Boissin, T., Loubes, J.M., del Barrio, E.: Achieving robustness in classification using optimal transport with hinge regularization. In: CVPR, pp. 505–514 (2021)
21. Szegedy, C., et al.: Intriguing properties of neural networks. arXiv preprint arXiv:1312.6199 (2013)
22. Tandale, M.D., Valasek, J.: Fault-tolerant structured adaptive model inversion control. J. Guidance Control Dyn. **29**(3), 635–642 (2006)
23. Virmaux, A., Scaman, K.: Lipschitz regularity of deep neural networks: analysis and efficient estimation. In: NeurIPS, pp. 3835–3844 (2018)
24. Weng, T.W., et al.: Evaluating the robustness of neural networks: an extreme value theory approach. arXiv preprint arXiv:1801.10578 (2018)
25. Xie, X., Xu, L., Zhou, L., Tan, Y.: GRNN model for fault diagnosis of unmanned helicopter rotor's unbalance. In: Huang, B., Yao, Y. (eds.) Proceedings of the 5th International Conference on Electrical Engineering and Automatic Control. LNEE, vol. 367, pp. 539–547. Springer, Heidelberg (2016). https://doi.org/10.1007/978-3-662-48768-6_61
26. Zhang, H., Yu, Y., Jiao, J., Xing, E., El Ghaoui, L., Jordan, M.: Theoretically principled trade-off between robustness and accuracy. In: ICML, pp. 7472–7482. PMLR (2019)

Neural Criticality Metric for Object Detection Deep Neural Networks

Václav Diviš[1]([✉]), Tobias Schuster[2], and Marek Hrúz[3]

[1] ARRK Engineering GmbH, Munich, Germany
vaclav.divis@arrk-engineering.com
[2] Fraunhofer IKS, Munich, Germany
[3] Faculty of Applied Sciences, Department of Cybernetics and
New Technologies for the Information Society,
University of West Bohemia, Pilsen, Czechia
mhruz@ntis.zcu.cz

Abstract. The complexity of state-of-the-art Deep Neural Network (DNN) architectures exacerbates the search for safety relevant metrics and methods that could be used for functional safety assessments. In this article, we investigate Neurons' Criticality (the ability to affect the decision process) for several object detection DNN architectures. As a first step, we introduce the Neural Criticality metric for object detection DNNs and set a theoretical background. Subsequently, by conducting experiments, we verify that removing one neuron from the computational graph of a DNN can have a significant (positive, as well as negative) influence on the prediction's precision (object classification and localization). Finally, we build statistics for each neuron from pre-trained networks on the COCO object detection validation dataset and examine the network stability for the most critical neurons in order to prove our metric's validity.

Keywords: DNN safety · Object detection · Neural criticality

1 Introduction and Motivation

The uncertainty [21] of DNNs is given by the nature of datasets collection, models' architecture and optimization process. As long as this uncertainty remains unresolved, the evaluation of DNN, in the context of functional safety, is only possible by fulfilling carefully-formulated safety requirements related to the Operational Design Domain (ODD) [2]. The outcome of the evaluation can be used during hazard and risk assessments [17] and the final road release process for

---

This work is partly funded by the ARRK Engineering GmbH as well as by the Bavarian Ministry for Economic Affairs, Regional Development and Energy as part of a project to support the thematic development of the Fraunhofer Institute for Cognitive Systems. This research was also supported by the Technology Agency of the Czech Republic, project No. TN01000024.

M. Trapp et al. (Eds.): SAFECOMP 2022 Workshops, LNCS 13415, pp. 276–288, 2022.
https://doi.org/10.1007/978-3-031-14862-0_20

Level 3 and higher functions of automated driving systems [34]. Since ODD is defined by the electronic control unit as well, it is important to be able to mitigate the potential influence of bit-flips or similar malfunctions. An Automotive Safety Integrity Level D (ASIL-D) [17] certified hardware is required for safety critical system, with which many functions of autonomous cars comply. Via a decomposition and freedom of interference mechanism [16,20] a higher ASIL requirement can be divided into two lower components (one D into two Bs), but it never reaches the lowest level ("Quality Management"). The same analogy applies to software. In order to identify and verify the ASIL level of a certain component, a method called SoftWare Criticality Analysis (SWCA) [17] is used for manually written code. To the best of our knowledge, there is no method, in the field of computer vision, that would evaluate and quantify the contribution of a neuron to the decision process of an arbitrary object detection DNN.

In our approach, we simulate a neuron's blackout and its class-related influence on the classification and localization performance. It is in general not desired to have neurons which, when removed e.g. due to malfunctioning hardware, cause a drop in the model's performance. Therefore, in order to prevent a possible malfunction, any neuron with a significant feature extraction ability should be distributed over several layers. Dropout layers [37] and other regularization methods [23,41] partially ensure such an independence and protect the network from over-fitting, but a quantified value was never part of any definition nor a concrete point of interest. As defined in this article, the Neural Criticality (NC) can be incorporated within the optimization loop or during the evaluation, where the critical and anti-critical neurons can be further investigated.

2   Background and Related Work

Our work connects approaches and methodologies from several domains such as functional safety, verification and validation, optimization and understanding of Machine Learning (ML) models' architectures.

2.1   Overview of Object Detection Approaches

The task of object detection consists of localizing and classifying. The brute-force localization by sliding window and classification of Histogram of Oriented Gradients [5] was outstripped in 2015 by the fast [10] and later the faster region-based approach (Faster-RCNN) [33]. In the latter, a chosen backbone performs the preliminary feature extraction, provides it to the region proposal network and classifier, the outputs of which go further into the Softmax layer and bounding box (BB) regressors. A compacter solution was introduced by Single Shot Detector [26] (SSD) and You Only Look Once [32] (YOLO), where a deterministic inference is ensured by applying a set of default BBs to the input image, and Non-Maximum Suppression (NMS) is used in order to merge the multiple stage predictions. The feature extraction task is commonly performed by a pre-trained backbone such as the ResNet architecture [14] (with various number of layers), or a smaller, scalable architecture that uses depth-wise convolution and inverse bottle necks (MobileNet [35], EfficientNet [38]).

The Attention mechanism [39] brought a new approach in object classification [4,40] and detection [3], which interrupted the trend of the Convolution Neural Networks' (CNNs) accuracy getting saturated. So far the prior knowledge of the object detection task was encoded in the design of the model (region proposals, default BBs). This need became unnecessary in DEtection TRansformer (DETR) [3], where the set of detections with absolute boxes is directly predicted. It seems that the Attention is the key mechanism in order to model the feature relations in the global context of an image. Recently, a work from Facebook [27] summarized the last decade of network-hyperparameters optimization journey and achieved state-of-the-art (SOTA) results on ImageNet [6] with a model called ResNeXt.

2.2 Functional Safety, Verification and Validation

Apart from the official standards ISO 26262 [17] and ISO/PAS 21448 SOTIF [18], the "Assurance of machine learning in autonomous systems" [12] as well as "Safety First for Automated Driving" [1] illustrate the challenges of deploying a ML system in the automotive industry. Their contents direct the reader to a safety requirements process definition, several trainings, validation techniques, and formal argumentation about the results. However, the lack of validation-unambiguity of these documents forced the community to investigate various methods in order to quantify the prediction uncertainty [11,29,36] of DNNs.

The majority of ML metrics were designed to quantify the distance between the prediction and its target (e.g. Accuracy, F1 Score and Averaged Precision), hence are used dominantly during training and validation. They can arguably contain safety relevant information but are in fact used as a metric of the model's ability to generalize. It became a standard [25] to calculate the Average Precision (AP) from a set of ten Intersection-over-Union (IoU) thresholds [0.50 : 0.05 : 0.95]. By doing so, the user can decide if the model's precision satisfies the requirements.

The current approach in deep learning testing led us to the background for coverage criteria and was therefore a starting point of our research. The focus of [22] was mainly laid on debugging and training of the network. In this work a combination of importance selection, based on two metrics (activation-output correlation and activation precision of a batch of data) and deconvolution mechanism, identifies and visualizes corresponding patches for top-x important neurons in the input space. DeepXplore [31] verifies a number of neurons' outputs which activation exceeded a certain threshold value. They incorporated this condition into a joint optimization to maximize the neuron coverage and compared the accuracy with SOTA results. Deep Importance [9] quantifies a characteristic of a neuron as a relevance distribution to a previous layer. Within this approach the DNN graph is traverse, using layer-wise relevance propagation, in order to get a proportional value of the contribution made by each neuron within a layer.

They pointed out that the redistribution rules can be applied also for other layers [28]. Even though their approach should allow it, they show no class related neuron's importance, but dataset related.

Overall all the above mentioned approaches focus on explaining network predictions in relation to the input features, or quantify a coverage based on neurons values or layer-wise relevance. Our method is inspired by an approach which uses Monte Carlo dropout during inference in order to sample a subset of networks, build statistics and calculate the thereof resulting uncertainty [8]. But rather than randomly sample a subset of neurons, we investigate the contribution of every single neuron and link the neuron's importance directly to the output by quantifying the predictions with and without every neuron.

3 From Classification to Object Detection Neural Criticality

The recent work by Divis et al. [7] defined a Neural Criticality Analysis (NCA) for classification and tested it on several CNN architectures in order to identify critical neurons. They proposed concrete measures on how to decrease the mean and standard deviation of the criticality and demonstrated that masking neurons with negative criticality has a positive influence on the model's decision confidence and call these neurons *anti-critical*. In the following section, we build upon this work and present the key contribution of the paper, namely the definition of the NC metric for DNN-based object detection models.

3.1 Formal Definition of the NC Metric

As described in Sect. 2, the task of object detection lies in localizing and classifying an object, and is therefore the focus of the NC metric. In the dataset, a ground-truth (GT) object y_{GT} is characterized by a BB R_{GT} enclosing the object and its class c_{GT}. An example prediction y_{PR} from a DNN consists of a BB R_{PR} and an object class c_{PR} with the corresponding confidence/probability $conf_{PR}$ for the predicted class.

In order to determine which object has been detected and which has not, the predictions need to be matched with the corresponding ground-truths. The commonly known IoU metric is used for this matter:

Definition 1. *Let a GT and predicted 2D bounding box be R_{GT} and R_{PR}, and let A_{GT} and A_{PR} be their area on the 2D plane. Then the IoU is defined as the ratio of overlap between A_{GT} and A_{PR} and the union area of A_{GT} and A_{PR} as depicted in Eq. 1.*

$$IoU(R_{GT}, R_{PR}) = \frac{A_{GT} \cap A_{PR}}{A_{GT} \cup A_{PR}} \tag{1}$$

The matching is done as follows: each predicted BB R_{PR} is counted as a true positive (TP) when having an IoU larger than threshold α with a GT BB R_{GT}

and when the predicted class c_{PR} is of the same class as the GT object c_{GT}. If more than one prediction is matched with a GT object, the prediction with the highest confidence for this class is counted; the remaining predictions are counted as false positives (FP). Any prediction that could not be matched is counted as a FP as well. In case a GT BB could not be matched with any prediction, the GT object is counted as false negative (FN). All matching possibilities are summarized in Table 1.

Table 1. The matching possibilities for object detection.

	True positive (TP)	False negative (FN)	False positive (FP)
Reality	Object present	Object present	No object present
Prediction	Object detected	No object detected	Object detected

Now we define the Neural Criticality, building upon the introduced supplement metrics and matching-methodology. Let $\mathcal{D}$ be an image dataset, containing images with a varying amount of objects of the classes c_j, $j \in [1, z]$, where z is total number of classes. We further define an input image as $d \in \mathcal{D}$, the unmasked neural network as DNN and the masked (m) network as DNN_m. For an image d, both networks predict a set of BBs $\mathcal{R}_{PR}$, $\mathcal{R}_{PR,m}$, a set of corresponding classes $\mathcal{C}_{PR}$, $\mathcal{C}_{PR,m}$ and a set of corresponding class confidences $\mathcal{CONF}_{PR}$, $\mathcal{CONF}_{PR,m}$.

Matching these predictions with the set of GT BBs $\mathcal{R}_{GT}$ and classes $\mathcal{C}_{GT}$ of the objects in image d for each class c_j leads to lists of confidence values $CONF_{c_j} = \{conf_1, ..., conf_{n_{c_j}}\}$, $CONF_{c_j,m} = \{conf_{1,m}, ..., conf_{n_{c_j},m}\}$ as well as IOU values $IOU_{c_j} = \{iou_1, ..., iou_{n_{c_j}}\}$, $IOU_{c_j,m} = \{iou_{1,m}, ..., iou_{n_{c_j},m}\}$ for the GT objects of class c_j. Here, n_{c_j} denotes the number of GT objects for each class c_j within the image d. If a GT object is identified as a TP, the respective confidence value and IoU value are recorded. For FN objects, the confidence as well as IoU values are set to zero. Additionally, the number of FP detections per class n_{FP,c_j}, $n_{FP,c_j,m}$ is counted for each image.

Subsequently, for each image d and each class c_j of objects, the NC metric compares the detection performance of the unmasked and masked DNN. The summed NC $f_{cri,total,c_j}$ per class and image is calculated according to Eq. 2. It takes into account the criticality of TPs and FNs $f_{cri,TP-FN,c_j}$, defined in Eq. 3 as well as the criticality for the FPs f_{cri,FP,c_j}, depicted in Eq. 4. The NC for TP and FN objects $f_{cri,TP-FN,c_j}$ is calculated as the sum of the confidence and IoU differences. The NC for FPs f_{cri,FP,c_j} is calculated according to the number of FPs per image of the class c_j and is limited to an upper value of 2.0 to avoid excessive values. In order to avoid division by zero in case of Eq. 4, we add a variable ϵ and set it to 10^{-6}.

$$f_{cri,total,c_j} = f_{cri,TP-FN,c_j} + f_{cri,FP,c_j} \tag{2}$$

$$f_{cri,TP-FN,c_j}(CONF_{c_j}, IOU_{c_j}, CONF_{c_j,m}, IOU_{c_j,m})$$

$$= \frac{\sum_{i=1}^{n_{c_j}}((conf_i - conf_{i,m}) + (iou_i - iou_{i,m}))}{n_{c_j}} \quad (3)$$

$$f_{cri,FP,c_j}(n_{FP,c_j}, n_{FP,c_j,m}) = min\left(\frac{n_{FP,c_j,m} - n_{FP,c_j}}{n_{FP,c_j} + \epsilon}, 2\right) \quad (4)$$

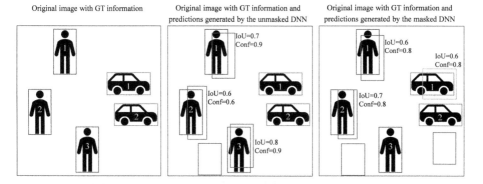

Fig. 1. An example showing the calculation of the NC metric. The left image depicts the original image with GT information, whereas the middle and right image additionally contain the predictions generated by the unmasked and masked DNN.

To illustrate the calculation of the NC metric for a single image, we show an example based on Fig. 1. The image contains three objects of class 'person' and two objects of class 'car'. The blue and green colored rectangles depict the GT BBs $\mathcal{R}_{GT}$ of the objects 'person' and 'car'. The red and orange colored rectangles depict the predicted BBs $\mathcal{R}_{PR}$ for both classes, respectively. For the TP objects, the IoU values as well as the class confidences are displayed. The matching decision between GT objects and predictions was done based on the IoU threshold $\alpha > 0.5$. The NC for the class 'person' is calculated as follows:

$$f_{cri,TP-FN,person} = \Big\{[(0.9 - 0.8) + (0.7 - 0.6)] + [(0.6 - 0.8) + (0.6 - 0.7)]$$

$$+ [(0.9 - 0.0) + (0.8 - 0.0)]\Big\}/3$$

$$= \{0.2 + [-0.3] + 1.7\}/3 = 0.533$$

$$f_{cri,FP,person} = min\left(\frac{2-1}{1+\epsilon}, 2\right) \approx 1$$

$$f_{cri,total,person} = f_{cri,TP-FN,person} + f_{cri,FP,person} \approx 1.533$$

As visible from the calculation above, the resulting criticality for person-1 and person-3 becomes positive as the localization and classification accuracy decrease by masking. It is especially severe for person-3, which does not get detected anymore by the masked DNN. The detection of person-2 is anti-critical since the localization and classification accuracy increase by masking. However, in this example, the overall criticality remains above zero, due to an increasing number of FPs. Similarly, the NC for the class 'car' is calculated:

$$f_{cri,TP-FN,car} = \left\{ [(0 - 0.8) + (0 - 0.6)] + [(0 - 0) + (0 - 0)] \right\}/2$$
$$= \{-1.4 + 0.0\}/2 = -0.7$$
$$f_{cri,FP,car} = min\,(0, 2) = 0$$
$$f_{cri,total,car} = f_{cri,TP-FN,car} + f_{cri,FP,car} = -0.7$$

In this example, it is obvious that the total criticality for the class 'car' is negative, as car-1 only gets detected when masking the DNN, whereas the unmasked DNN was not able to detect any of the cars.

4   Evaluation

In this section, we begin with the experimental setup and the conducted experiments, before showing the main results of applying the NC metric to the several SOTA object detection DNNs.

4.1   Experiment Setup

The COCO Validation Dataset 2017 [25] was chosen for the experiments and all images were batched and normalized according to their aspect ratio. PyTorch [30] was chosen as ML framework, as well as the following networks, pre-trained on the COCO training dataset: **Faster R-CNN** [33] with ResNet50 [14] backbone, **SSDlite** [26] with MobileNetV3 [15] backbone, **YoloV5** [19] and **DETR** [3] with ResNet50 backbone. For all models, only objects with confidence $\delta > 0.5$ and NMS threshold $\tau > 0.5$ were further examined. Due to the higher computational effort and for the sake of clarity we only focused on classes related to the automotive domain; analyzed labels = ['person', 'car', 'bicycle', 'motorcycle', 'bus', 'train', 'truck', 'traffic light', 'street-sign', 'stop sign']. With this setup, all inputs were analyzed according to Algorithm 1. Here, $unmask\_neuron()$ and $mask\_neuron()$ denote the functions that switches on and off any chosen neuron in the DNN. The functions $predict()$ and $match()$ respectively denote generating predictions on a given image and the matching between predictions and GT information. $CONF, CONF_m, IOU,$ $IOU_m, N_{FP}, N_{FP,m}$ denote the lists of confidence and IoU values of TPs and FNs as well as number of FPs per image for all classes in $\mathcal{C}$ for both the unmasked and masked DNN.

Algorithm 1: NCA algorithm

Input: DNN, criticality, NMS threshold τ, confidence threshold δ and IoU
threshold α, dataset $\mathcal{D}$, GT BBs $\mathcal{R}_{GT}$ and classes $\mathcal{C}_{GT}$
Output: Neural Criticality for $d \in \mathcal{D}$ and network DNN
Data: Given a testing set $\mathcal{D}$, a set of classes $\mathcal{C}$, the analyzed network DNN, the
number of neurons connection k in a layer L and $f_{cri,total,c_j}$, the
criticality function per image d and per class c_j

for *image $d \in \mathcal{D}$* do
  $\mathcal{R}_{PR}, \mathcal{C}_{PR}, \mathcal{CONF}_{PR} = predict(DNN, d, \tau, \delta)$
  for *every L in DNN* do
    for *every k in layer L* do
      $DNN_{masked} = mask\_neuron(k)$
      $\mathcal{R}_{PR,m}, \mathcal{C}_{PR,m}, \mathcal{CONF}_{PR,m} = predict(DNN_{masked}, d, \tau, \delta)$
      $CONF, IOU, N_{FP} = match(\mathcal{R}_{PR}, \mathcal{C}_{PR}, \mathcal{CONF}_{PR}, \mathcal{R}_{GT}, \mathcal{C}_{GT}, \alpha)$
      $CONF_m, IOU_m, N_{FP,m} =$
      $match(\mathcal{R}_{PR,m}, \mathcal{C}_{PR,m}, \mathcal{CONF}_{PR,m}, \mathcal{R}_{GT}, \mathcal{C}_{GT}, \alpha)$
      for *every c_j in $\mathcal{C}$* do
        $f_{cri,total,c_j} =$
        $f_{cri,TP-FN,c_j}(CONF_{c_j}, IOU_{c_j}, CONF_{c_j,m}, IOU_{c_j,m}) +$
        $f_{cri,FP,c}(n_{FP,c_j}, n_{FP,c_j,m})$
      $DNN_{masked} = unmask\_neuron(k)$

4.2   Results and Discussion

Due to the logical dependency of each step of the analysis we present results
for only one model (Faster R-CNN with ResNet50 backbone) and summarize
the architectural differences of the other models in the conclusion of this work
- we highly encourage the reader to visit our GitHub[1] and explore the topic of
Criticality Analysis for other models.

The execution of our experiment is divided into several steps:

1. As a first step we analyze all layers according to the defined Algorithm 1.
   Figure 2 presents the normalized MEAN of layers' criticalities.
2. In a second step we look closely at the most anti-critical and critical layers.
   Figure 3 shows an example of neurons' criticalities of the most and the least
   critical layers of the model. At this point, the position of the layer as well as
   the purpose were taken into account.
3. In order to prove our definition of the criticality, we conduct a stability experiment in the next step. The higher the SD of neurons' criticality is, the higher
   the fluctuation of masked predicted IoU and confidence will be. Considering
   this aspect, we have chosen a set of 10 extreme neurons (both critical and
   anti-critical) and for each masking iteration, we calculated the AP according
   to the COCO dataset definition. The results are visualized in Fig. 4.

---

[1] https://gitlab.com/arrk-fi/ObjectDetectionCriticality.

4. During the verification of the NCA outputs, we discovered several model-related phenomena. In the conclusion, we compare the differences between each architecture and present their distilled form in Table 2.

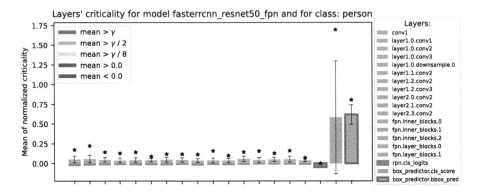

Fig. 2. In this figure only the critical and anti-critical layers exceeding a level of 0.05 and –0.05 are visualized. The criticality threshold γ was empirically set to 0.5, but it can be related to IoU and confidence deviation. As can be seen, the ResNet50 backbone preserves low criticality distribution throughout the layers. The last BB prediction layer (rpn.bbox_pred), is part of the "region proposal network" and contains some highly critical neurons. On the other hand, one of the layers (rpn.cls_logits) shows signs of anti-criticality as well as several layers in the backbone network.

Table 2. The results within this table reflects the discussion about architectural details in this section. The extreme values are highlighted.

	Number of neurons	Number of neurons $cri > 1.0$	$\|cr\|$ 'person'	AP 'person'	AP_{anti} 'person'	AP_{cri} 'person'
Faster R-CNN	31382	2	0.0295	43.97%	44.54%	**0.07%**
SSD	40244	**33**	0.0411	21.10%	21.16%	9.04%
YOLOv5	30781	1	0.0150	**44.41%**	**45.07%**	27.49%
DETR	**80576**	3	**0.0490**	20.34%	23.97%	0.65%

4.3 Models' Architectural Details

Within the **SSD** model, the criticality of the backbone (MobileNetv3) was consistent, with an increasing amount of anti-critical neurons in deeper layers. The normalized layers' criticality (0.0411) boomed in the last classification layers **(0.59)**, which draw features from the cascade SSD head layers and consequently

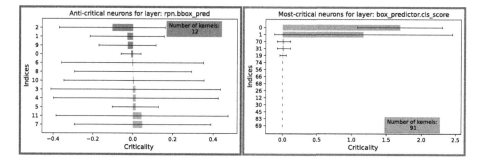

Fig. 3. On the left image, the criticality of the neurons from the least critical layer is visualized. The output of the region proposal network is not conditioned by any prior knowledge of the object and hence its layers should have a low criticality. A similar effect (but with opposite result) can be seen on the right image. As can be seen, some neurons within the prediction layer specialize to class 'person'. That behavior is comprehensible, since this layer predicts the final class score.

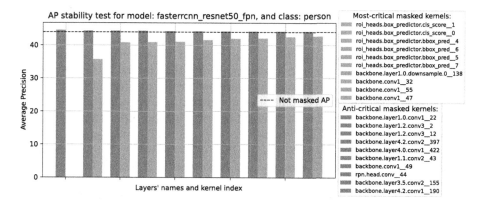

Fig. 4. As visible on this image, for the class 'person', the masking of the 10 neurons with the highest and lowest criticality leads to a significant decrease and increase of the AP, respectively.

ensure the increasing receptive field. Such a phenomenon was observed for all the analyzed classes even though a dropout was used on these layers during the training.

The **YOLOv5** architecture proved to be one of the most stable models in terms of criticality. The extracted features are well distributed over all layers. We've examined YOLOv5l6, which achieved 53.4% AP on the COCO validation set and holds one of the SOTA results. Those were achieved by several improvements on training (warm-up training, focal loss), architecture (Fast Spatial Pyramid Pooling) and data augmentation (HSV- hue, saturation, value variation, image mixup, segments copy-paste). The influence of these methods have been discussed in several articles [13, 24, 27, 39].

By choosing **DETR**, we aimed to analyze the criticality of the self-attention mechanism, which should extract features for objects in the global context of the image. Multihead Attention further ensures wider discrimination by combining several self-attention heads. Our analysis showed a slightly higher overall criticality than it was in the case of YOLOv5. However, due to much higher number of critical neurons, the average criticality was the highest out of all models.

5   Concluding Remarks

In this work, we defined a Neural Criticality metric for object detection DNNs and showed its potential to be used during assessments of safety critical systems, such as Advanced Driver Assistance Systems. It is important to mention, that while evaluating it only on an object detection task, our method can cope with any supervised learning model in any context. Algorithm 1 analyzes every single neuron in a very complex architecture for the whole dataset. By vectorizing all computational information, the bottleneck of the analysis speed is the DNN's inference time. That results in the complexity of $m\mathcal{O}(n)$, where m is the number of images and n the number of neurons.

Our experiments discovered that all analyzed models contain class-related critical neurons which can prohibit correct object detection. We assume that neurons with such a significantly higher criticality than layers' MEAN criticality are a by-product of an inefficient or non-present regularization during the training. From a functional safety point of view, the optimal criticality of the neurons within the layers should form a uniform distribution (in order to mitigate single point HW failure, ASIL-D failure rate $\lambda \leq 10^{-8}h^{-1}$), instead of which we observe a Gaussian distribution with a MEAN around zero. The explanation of anti-critical neurons is more complex and would require a deeper dive into cross-classes correlation. However, based on the principle of optimization we assume that anti-critical neurons of class 'A' can be critical neurons of classes 'B-C' (containing a feature predominantly related to classes 'B-C') and are therefore not positively contributing to the final decision.

With this article we opened a space for a potential future work such as: evaluation and explanation of anti-critical neurons, incorporation of the criticality into training loss and backpropagation mechanism, theoretical definition of a mapping to an ASIL, use of Neural Criticality as a potential network pruning metric, minimization of the computational costs and extending criticality by problem-specific parameters like distance to object or size of object.

References

1. BMW, et al.: Safety First for Automated Driving (SaFAD). https://www.daimler.com/innovation/case/autonomous/safety-first-for-automated-driving-2.html (2019). Accessed 08 June 2020
2. British Standards Institution: PAS 1883:2020 - Operational design domain (ODD) taxonomy for an automated driving system (ADS) - Specification. Technical Report, August 2020

3. Carion, N., Massa, F., Synnaeve, G., Usunier, N., Kirillov, A., Zagoruyko, S.: End-to-end object detection with transformers. In: Vedaldi, A., Bischof, H., Brox, T., Frahm, J.-M. (eds.) ECCV 2020. LNCS, vol. 12346, pp. 213–229. Springer, Cham (2020). https://doi.org/10.1007/978-3-030-58452-8_13

4. Chen, X., Hsieh, C., Gong, B.: When vision transformers outperform resnets without pretraining or strong data augmentations. CoRR (2021). https://arxiv.org/abs/2106.01548

5. Dalal, N., Triggs, B.: Histograms of oriented gradients for human detection. In: CVPR, vol. 1, pp. 886–893. IEEE (2005)

6. Deng, J., Dong, W., Socher, R., Li, L.J., Li, K., Fei-Fei, L.: Imagenet: a large-scale hierarchical image database. In: CVPR, pp. 248–255. IEEE (2009)

7. Divis, V., Hrúz, M.: Neural criticality: validation of convolutional neural networks. In: SafeAI 2021. CEUR Workshop Proceedings, vol. 2808. CEUR-WS.org (2021). http://ceur-ws.org/Vol-2808/Paper_36.pdf

8. Gal, Y., Ghahramani, Z.: Dropout as a bayesian approximation: representing model uncertainty in deep learning. In: ICML, pp. 1050–1059 (2016)

9. Gerasimou, S., Eniser, H.F., Sen, A., Çakan, A.: Importance-driven deep learning system testing. CoRR **abs/2002.03433**, https://arxiv.org/abs/2002.03433 (2020)

10. Girshick, R.: Fast r-cnn. In: Proceedings of the IEEE International Conference on Computer Vision, pp. 1440–1448 (2015)

11. Graves, A.: Practical variational inference for neural networks. In: Advances in Neural Information Processing Systems, vol. 24, pp. 2348–2356 (2011)

12. Hawkins, R., Paterson, C., Picardi, C., Jia, Y., Calinescu, R., Habli, I.: Guidance on the assurance of machine learning in autonomous systems (AMLAS). arXiv preprint arXiv:2102.01564 (2021)

13. He, K., Zhang, X., Ren, S., Sun, J.: Spatial pyramid pooling in deep convolutional networks for visual recognition. IEEE Trans. Pattern Anal. Mach. Intell. **37**(9), 1904–1916 (2015)

14. He, K., Zhang, X., Ren, S., Sun, J.: Deep residual learning for image recognition. In: CVPR, pp. 770–778 (2016)

15. Howard, A., et al.: Searching for mobilenetv3. In: ICCV, pp. 1314–1324 (2019)

16. IEC: IEC 61025:2006 - Fault tree analysis (FTA). Technical Report, December 2006

17. Road vehicles - functional safety (ISO 26262). Standard, International Organization for Standardization (2018)

18. Road vehicles - safety of the intended functionality. Standard, international organization for standardization (2019)

19. Jocher, G., et al.: ultralytics/yolov5: v4.0 - nn.SiLU() activations, weights& biases logging, PyTorch hub integration.https://zenodo.org/record/4418161

20. Grebe, J.C., Goble, W.M.: FMEDA - accurate product failure metrics. FMEDA Development Paper 1.6, 10 (2018)

21. Kendall, A., Gal, Y.: What uncertainties do we need in bayesian deep learning for computer vision? In: NIPS, pp. 5574–5584 (2017)

22. Lengerich, B.J., Konam, S., Xing, E.P., Rosenthal, S., Veloso, M.M.: Visual explanations for convolutional neural networks via input resampling. CoRR **abs/1707.09641**, http://arxiv.org/abs/1707.09641 (2017)

23. Li, F.F., et al.: Data preprocessing - cs231n convolutional neural networks.https://cs231n.github.io/neural-networks-2/ (2021). Accessed 31 Jan 2022

24. Lin, T.Y., Goyal, P., Girshick, R., He, K., Dollár, P.: Focal loss for dense object detection. In: Proceedings of the IEEE International Conference on Computer Vision, pp. 2980–2988 (2017)

25. Lin, T.-Y., et al.: Microsoft COCO: common objects in context. In: Fleet, D., Pajdla, T., Schiele, B., Tuytelaars, T. (eds.) ECCV 2014. LNCS, vol. 8693, pp. 740–755. Springer, Cham (2014). https://doi.org/10.1007/978-3-319-10602-1_48

26. Liu, W., et al.: SSD: single shot multibox detector. In: Leibe, B., Matas, J., Sebe, N., Welling, M. (eds.) ECCV 2016. LNCS, vol. 9905, pp. 21–37. Springer, Cham (2016). https://doi.org/10.1007/978-3-319-46448-0_2

27. Liu, Z., Mao, H., Wu, C.Y., Feichtenhofer, C., Darrell, T., Xie, S.: A convnet for the 2020s. arXiv preprint arXiv:2201.03545 (2022)

28. Montavon, G., Bach, S., Binder, A., Samek, W., Müller, K.: Explaining nonlinear classification decisions with deep taylor decomposition. CoRR **abs/1512.02479**, http://arxiv.org/abs/1512.02479 (2015)

29. Neal, R.M.: Bayesian Learning for Neural Networks, vol. 118. Springer, New York (2012). https://doi.org/10.1007/978-1-4612-0745-0

30. Paszke, e.a.: Pytorch: an imperative style, high-performance deep learning library. In: NEURIPS, pp. 8024–8035. Curran Associates, Inc. (2019)

31. Pei, K., Cao, Y., Yang, J., Jana, S.: Deepxplore: automated hitebox testing of deep learning systems. CoRR **abs/1705.06640**, http://arxiv.org/abs/1705.06640 (2017)

32. Redmon, J., Divvala, S., Girshick, R., Farhadi, A.: You only look once: unified, real-time object detection. In: CVPR, pp. 779–788 (2016)

33. Ren, S., He, K., Girshick, R., Sun, J.: Faster r-cnn: towards real-time object detection with region proposal networks. In: NIPS, vol. 28 (2015)

34. SAE international: taxonomy and definitions for terms related to on-road motor vehicle automated driving systems, vol. J3016 (2014)

35. Sandler, M., Howard, A., Zhu, M., Zhmoginov, A., Chen, L.C.: Mobilenetv 2: Inverted residuals and linear bottlenecks. In: CVPR, pp. 4510–4520 (2018)

36. Shridhar, K., Laumann, F., Liwicki, M.: A comprehensive guide to bayesian convolutional neural network with variational inference. arXiv preprint arXiv:1901.02731 (2019)

37. Srivastava, N., Hinton, G., Krizhevsky, A., Sutskever, I., Salakhutdinov, R.: Dropout: a simple way to prevent neural networks from overfitting. JMLR **15**(56), 1929–1958 (2014)

38. Tan, M., Le, Q.: Efficientnet: rethinking model scaling for convolutional neural networks. In: ICML, pp. 6105–6114. PMLR (2019)

39. Vaswani, A., et al.: Attention is all you need. NEURIPS **30** (2017)

40. Wu, B., et al.: Visual transformers: token-based image representation and processing for computer vision. arXiv preprint arXiv:2006.03677 (2020)

41. Zou, H., Hastie, T.: Regularization and variable selection via the elastic net. J. R. Stat. Soc. Ser. B (Stat. Methodol.) **67**(2), 301–320 (2005)

StaDRe and StaDRo: Reliability and Robustness Estimation of ML-Based Forecasting Using Statistical Distance Measures

Mohammed Naveed Akram[2(✉)] [ID], Akshatha Ambekar[3] [ID],
Ioannis Sorokos[2(✉)] [ID], Koorosh Aslansefat[1] [ID], and Daniel Schneider[2] [ID]

[1] University of Hull, Hull, UK
k.aslansefat@hull.ac.uk
[2] Fraunhofer IESE, Kaiserslautern, Germany
{naveed.akram,ioannis.sorokos,daniel.schneider}@iese.fraunhofer.de
[3] Technical University of Kaiserslautern, Kaiserslautern, Germany
ambekar@rhrk.uni-kl.de

Abstract. Reliability estimation of Machine Learning (ML) models is becoming a crucial subject. This is particularly the case when such models are deployed in safety-critical applications, as the decisions based on model predictions can result in hazardous situations. In this regard, recent research has proposed methods to achieve safe, dependable, and reliable ML systems. One such method consists of detecting and analyzing distributional shift, and then measuring how such systems respond to these shifts. This was proposed in earlier work in SafeML. This work focuses on the use of SafeML for time series data, and on reliability and robustness estimation of ML-forecasting methods using statistical distance measures. To this end, distance measures based on the Empirical Cumulative Distribution Function (ECDF) proposed in SafeML are explored to measure Statistical-Distance Dissimilarity (SDD) across time series. We then propose SDD-based Reliability Estimate (StaDRe) and SDD-based Robustness (StaDRo) measures. With the help of a clustering technique, the similarity between the statistical properties of data seen during training and the forecasts is identified. The proposed method is capable of providing a link between dataset SDD and Key Performance Indicators (KPIs) of the ML models.

Keywords: SafeAI · Safe machine learning · Machine learning reliability · Artificial intelligence safety · Statistical method

1 Introduction

The improved capabilities of hardware have triggered increased use of ML-based components in many applications. This also includes many safety-critical application domains such as medical, industrial, transportation, aviation, etc. This in

M. Trapp et al. (Eds.): SAFECOMP 2022 Workshops, LNCS 13415, pp. 289–301, 2022.
https://doi.org/10.1007/978-3-031-14862-0_21

turn requires new methods for increasing and assuring the reliability of ML-based components in safety-critical applications. One way to achieve this increase is by detecting dataset shift [32]. In previous work, SafeML has been introduced by the authors in [4], where statistical distance measures based on the Empirical Cumulative Distribution Function (ECDF) are used to detect distributional shift at runtime. Furthermore, the approach estimates the performance degradation of a classifier based on those measures. The results showed that there is a correlation between performance and Statistical Distance Dissimilarity (SDD). The proposed method was, however, limited to only tabular data and classification tasks. In [3], SafeML was improved to handle image classification tasks. Also, the authors proposed using bootstrap-based p-value calculation to improve the reliability of statistical distance measures. In this work, we extend these measures for time series data and use SDD to estimate the reliability (StaDRe) and robustness (StaDRo) of an ML component.

The remainder of this paper is divided as follows. Section 2 describes related literature, followed by a discussion of the problem statement in Sect. 3. Section 4 details the proposed methodology, and Sect. 5 describes the experiments conducted. Section 6 discusses the results, and the paper concludes in Sect. 7.

2   Related Work

For ML-based systems to be used in safety-critical systems, certain qualities of ML solutions such as reliability, fairness, robustness, transparency, and security are important. Several methods have been proposed to quantify and qualify these properties. For this work, the properties of an ML-based system resulting from dataset distribution and shifts are considered.

This section is divided into several subsections. In Sect. 2.1, we discuss the methods available for detecting dataset shift and distributional shift. In Sect. 2.2, we discuss the existing reliability metrics available in the literature, and in Sect. 2.3, the existing robustness evaluation methods.

2.1   Dataset Shift

The term dataset shift was introduced for the first time in the book [32]. There exist several names for the concept of dataset shift in the literature, including concept shift, contrast mining (in classification learning, fracture between data and fracture points and changing environments [23]). To overcome these inconsistencies, the authors in [23] defined dataset shift as the difference in the joint distribution in training and test datasets. Additionally, they identified three types of dataset shift: covariate shift, prior probability shift, and concept shift.

Several techniques for dataset shift detection are proposed in the literature for forecasting and classification problems. The work in [6] proposes measures that are applicable only to linear and multiple linear regression models; work on exponentially weighted moving average (EWMA) charts [29] is limited by analysis power in the presence of larger shifts; the technique proposed in [26] for image classification problems is restricted by the lack of support for online dataset shift detection; and the technique based on Particle Swarm Optimization (PSO) [25] obscures its usefulness due to the overhead of retraining every time a concept drift occurs. In addition to these limitations, the existing methods do not consider statistical distance measures for computing distributional shift in time series.

2.2 Reliability

In [5], a well-known work in the area of dependable systems, the authors define reliability as continuity of correct service. In classical systems, quality measures such as Mean Time Between Failures (MTBF) are usually used for reliability measurement. For an ML system, the authors in [9] define reliability by any qualitative attribute related to a "vital performance indicator" of that system. They include measures such as accuracy or inaccuracy, availability, downtime rate, responsiveness, etc. In the context of ML-model-driven systems, we consider continuity of correct service, or ML performance evaluation, to not only encompass service provision, but also the correctness of the ML model response itself.

Existing approaches proposed in the literature for reliability estimation can be classified into two classes: model-agnostic or model-specific approaches. While model-specific techniques [16, 24] are based on specific model designs and learning algorithms, they utilize probabilistic interpretations for reliability, in terms of confidence measurement. In our work, we focus on model-agnostic techniques.

Model-agnostic approaches are generic and provide distributional or indicator-based reliability estimates that are less probabilistically interpretable. Some examples of model-agnostic reliability estimation techniques are sensitivity analysis [8], local cross-validation [13], confidence estimation based on neighbors' errors and variance in the environment [11], bootstrapping [15], and an ML-based approach [1].

The work in [38] obtains a reliability assessment model (RAM) for 'Deep learning classifiers' using Operation Profiles information and robustness. Robustness is considered as misclassification error for Lp-norm perturbation, and relibaility is obtained as the probability of misclassification per input (pmi). In contrast, the work in this paper focuses on reliability assessment using the dissimilarity of the distribution of the input observed at runtime compared to the distribution at design time.

The authors in [11] propose the *"CONFINE"* metric for measuring reliability. In contrast to previous heuristic-based techniques, the CONFINE measure incorporates actual model prediction errors for reliability estimation, and estimations are based on the error of the test instance's nearest neighbors. However, this metric does not cover the effect of distributional shift on reliability. Hence, we propose extending the CONFINE metric with the rate of change of dissimilarity.

2.3 Robustness

In the machine learning literature, different aspects of model robustness such as robustness against adversarial attacks and robustness against dataset shift are evaluated. Adversarial robustness is used to measure the robustness of an ML model against adversarial attacks. The authors of [28] describe model robustness as the average size of the minimum adversarial perturbation over many samples. The majority of work in this field focuses on various kinds of adversarial attacks and building ML models that are robust against these.

However, in this work, we focus on robustness against dataset shift. A well-generalized network should be robust to data subpopulations it has not yet encountered [31]. A measure termed *relative accuracy* for computing a model's performance is presented in [31], with a focus on image classification problems. The authors in [17] argue that accuracy can suffer when the training and test distributions are dissimilar, so they implemented a data augmentation technique during training to improve the robustness of image classifiers. In addition, this work measures perturbation robustness by computing *flip probability*, which is essentially the probability that two adjacent frames with different perturbation levels contain mismatched predictions. The authors of [33] introduced a measure called *effective robustness*, which is the model's accuracy difference in the presence of distributional shift, taking into consideration an accuracy baseline determined using available standard models (without robustness interventions). The authors of [4] examined the use of statistical distance measures to evaluate the robustness of ML models. The work in [19] proposes verification of ML models in safety-critical applications by verifying generalized model performance using Neuron Region Distance (NRD) as an aid for measuring dissimilarity.

The author in [37] proposes an adversarial training method called TRADES. While this can be generalized further for dataset shift robustness, the focus of the work is mainly on improving robustness against adversarial attacks. Similarly, the work in [35] focuses on adversarial training to improve robustness against adversarial examples. The work in [34] presents statistical robustness; however, it focuses on adversarial robustness. The author in [36] presents a method for assessing the robustness of neural networks by measuring the proportion of inputs that violate certain properties. These require explicit definition of the properties and the input model at design time.

An ML model that is robust should be able to deliver acceptable performance under conditions like dataset shift. This notion of robustness is also closely related to the definition of robustness presented in [5,20] for classical systems. Though the existing methods cover a plethora of robustness measures, currently there are not many that use statistical distance measures to account for robustness against dataset shift. In our work, we propose using a performance vs. dissimilarity curve for evaluating robustness.

3   Problem Definition

When an ML model encounters input that differs from its training data, out-of-distribution (OOD) uncertainty emerges. This can be taken into account by estimating the SDD with which reliability and robustness can be estimated. Hence, in this work, the following research questions are established:

RQ1: SDD-Accuracy Correlation. How does SDD relate to the performance of a model specifically for time series application?

RQ2: SDD-based Reliability and Robustness. How can SDD be incorporated into the reliability and robustness measures of a model?

4   Proposed Method

In this section, we use the SDD measure to obtain the StaDRe and StaDRo. We also describe the experimental design for our evaluation of the proposed approaches on a univariate time series dataset.

In the remainder of this paper, we will use the following terms. Let us assume $X_{all} \in \mathbb{R}$ to be the overall univariate time series dataset, $X \in \mathbb{R}$ the training portion of it, and $Y \in \mathbb{R}$ the validation part. At runtime, we use X^* for available data. Let f be any ECDF-based distance measure such as Wasserstein, Kolmogorov-Smirnov, etc. Let M be the ML model function, and $Y' \in \mathbb{R}$ the prediction for a given input x. Due to its unbounded nature, geometry considerations, and a method that is essentially the area measured between two ECDFs, this work primarily uses Wasserstein distance as the ECDF function for estimating reliability and robustness [7].

4.1   SDD Vs. Performance

First, let us consider the behavior of the ML model performance with its SDD against the data observed during training. To observe this behavior, the performance of the validation data Y is compared against its SDD from the training set ($f(X, Y)$). The performance can be measured either in terms of root mean square error (RMSE) or mean absolute percentage error (MAPE). To obtain a sequence of observations, the validation set Y is divided into several subsets $Y^* \subset Y$ of length l. The performance of the model M can be obtained by getting the prediction $M(Y^*)$ over each subset Y^*. The corresponding SDD of subset Y^* is obtained using $f(X, Y^*)$. From these, a curve of the performance vs. SDD can be plotted. In Sect. 5, we will discuss the detailed experiments.

4.2   Statistical-Distance-Based Reliability Estimate - StaDRe

In [11], the reliability of an ML model is given in terms of confidence, by "CONFidence estimation based on the Neighbors' Errors" (CONFINE), as in Eq. 1.

$$cs_{CONFINE}(X^*) = 1 - \frac{1}{m} \sum_{i=1}^{m} \epsilon_i^2 \qquad (1)$$

where X^* is a data instance for which reliability is needed, ϵ_i is the error of a nearest neighbor i, and m are the total nearest neighbors. However, this does not take into account the SDD of the instance. Moreover, CONFINE uses Euclidean distance to obtain the nearest neighbors.

We extend this approach by taking into account the SDD and using DTW-based clustering for computing the nearest neighbors of X^*. Clustering is a technique commonly used to group together similar patterns in time series using distance measures like DTW, Fréchet, or Kullback-Leibler divergence [2,14,22]. Among these, K-Means clustering [10] with a DTW distance metric [27,30] was found to be adequate for univariate time series. Due to space limitations, the explanation of the DTW-based clustering technique used is omitted here, but is available on GitHub (see Sect. 7). Instead of using Euclidean distance, we use the DTW-based clustering technique to identify the appropriate cluster c for the input instance X^* obtained from Y'. Then the mean squared error (MSE) is obtained for the m members of the identified cluster c. Finally, the ECDF-based distance is computed between the cluster c and X^*, and the cluster c and the reference O. The StaDRe is then given by Eq. 2. The algorithm 1 describes the general procedure for StaDRe computation using statistical distance measures. For this work, the following assumptions are made:

1. The members of the cluster c to which X^* gets assigned are the nearest neighbors of X^*, where X^* is a data instance.
2. To compute d_{origin} in Algorithm 1 initialized for Wasserstein distance, the origin is a time series containing 0 at every time step and whose shape is the same as the cluster's center.

$$StaDRe(X^*) = \frac{2 - \frac{1}{m}\sum_{i=1}^{m}\epsilon_i^2 - \frac{f(c,X^*)}{f(c,O)}}{2} \tag{2}$$

where ϵ_i is the error of a given neighbor i.

4.3   Statistical-Distance-Based Robustness - StaDRo

In this section, we introduce a method for obtaining an evaluation of robustness against distributional shift using statistical distance measures. For this, the performance vs. SDD curve obtained in Sect. 4.1 is used. For a required minimum performance P_{min}, using the performance vs. SDD curve, the corresponding SDD distance for the P_{min} is obtained. For a given data instance X^* for which robustness is required, the ECDF distance measure is obtained against the instance X^* and the training set X. StaDRo for an instance X^* at a given P_{min} is given by Eq. 3.

$$StaDRo(X^*, P_{min}) = \begin{cases} True & \frac{f(X,X^*)}{d_{Pmin}} \leq 1 \\ \\ False & \frac{f(X,X^*)}{d_{Pmin}} > 1 \end{cases} \tag{3}$$

where $StaDRo(X^*, P_{min})$ gives the robustness of the model for the instance X^* at a given minimum required performance P_{min}. The Algorithm 2 shows a general procedure for StaDRo estimation using statistical distance measures.

Algorithm 1: Algorithm for StaDRe

Result: Reliability
X = GetTrainingSet();
X^* = GetDataInstance();
clusters = GetClusters(X);
for *c in clusters* **do**
    comparison = CompareClusters(c, X^*);
    if *comparison==True* **then**
        d = getStatisticalDistance(c, X^*);
        d_origin = getStatisticalDistance(c,O);
        break;
    end
end
MeanSquaredError = GetClusterMeanSquareError(c);
$$\text{Reliability} = \frac{(2 - MeanSquaredError - \frac{d}{d\_origin})}{2};$$
return Reliability;

Algorithm 2: Algorithm for StaDRo

Result: Robust
X = GetTrainingSubSet();
Y = GetValidationSet();
for *Sequence in Y* **do**
    P = GetPerformance(Sequence);
    d = getStatisticalDistance(X, Sequence);
    Performance.append(P);
    SDD.append(d);
end
Curved = FitCurve(plot(SDD, Performance));
X^* = GetDataInstance();
d_instance = getStatisticalDistance(X, X^*);
MINIMUM_REQUIRED_PERFORMANCE_LIMIT = CONSTANT;
d_from_curve = getDistanceForPerformance(Curved,
  MINIMUM_REQUIRED_PERFORMANCE_LIMIT);
Ratio = d_instance / d_from_curve;
if *Ratio <= 1* **then**
    Robust = True;
else
    Robust =False;
end
return Robust;

5 Experiments

We performed experiments on a stock price prediction application (an example of regression applications) and used several companies' stock price data. We considered the closing price of these stocks, which we extracted via the National Stock Exchange (NSE) library and Yahoo Finance. We excluded datasets that did not exhibit any kind of shift between data during training and validation. The data was divided into 80% for training and 20% for validation. We predicted the stock closing price for the next day at a given point when the model was used. All data was normalized to between -1 and 1. The two forecasting models we implemented were Long Short-Term Memory (LSTM) [18] and Gated Recurrent Unit (GRU) [12]. The choice of hyperparameters and other information is given in Table 1. All models were trained using the Adam optimizer [21] with a learning rate of 0.01 over 100 epochs for LSTM and 50 epochs for GRU.

To obtain StaDRo as described in Algorithm 2, the experiments were divided into three phases. In the first phase, we measured how the accuracy acc of the model M changed with a shift in the subset of the validation set Y. In the second phase, $f(X, Y)$ was computed for the same subsets of Y as in the first phase. For this work, we instantiated Wasserstein distance as an ECDF measure f. In the third phase, we fit a polynomial curve of degree 2 to derive the relationship between the dataset SDD and the forecasting model's performance. We then obtain a statistical distance for a desired minimum performance from the fitted curve. For a desired sequence X^*, we computed the SDD between X^* and X, then calculated the ratio and estimated the robustness.

For reliability estimation using the general procedure described in Algorithm 1, we applied clustering on the training data of several companies and then selected some validation points randomly at different time steps to compute StadRe for these points. When computing MSE, we chose the number of nearest neighbors (m) to equal the number of samples of X that get assigned to the smallest cluster c'. We applied random sampling for selecting m neighbors when the assigned cluster c was not c'.

Table 1. Details of several stocks and hyperparameters of LSTM and GRU model.

Characteristic	Dataset				
	Reliance	Google	Airtel	JP Morgan	MRF
Start date (dd.mm.yyyy)	04.01.2010	03.01.2005	04.01.2010	02.01.2003	03.01.2005
No. of data points	2,895	4,300	3,008	4,803	4,214
Window size	20	50	20	20	20
No. of clusters	7	5	6	5	5
LSTM (# layers; hidden size)	2; 32	2; 40	2; 32	2; 64	2; 32
GRU (# layers; hidden size)	2; 32				

6   Results and Discussion

This section presents the results of the experiments performed. Figure 1 shows how model performance (as MAPE, RMSE) deteriorates as SDD increases. Each performance measure is fit to a curve using second-degree curve fitting. When the ground truth is available (for example at design time), metrics like RMSE and MAPE are used for performance evaluation, while StaDRe and StaDRo could be used as performance indicators when no ground truth is available (runtime evaluation). In the validation experiments, we compared the behavior of StaDRe and StaDRo vs. design-time metrics such as RMSE and MAPE, thus validating the behavior of StaDRo and StaDRe and thereby enabling their use at runtime.

As can be clearly seen in Figs. 1(a) and 1(b), there is an increase in performance error with increasing SDD. Figure 2 displays the reliability measure against model performance. As with Fig. 1, the plots are fitted with a second-degree curve. The figures clearly show increasing performance with increasing reliability (StaDRe), which validates the measure.

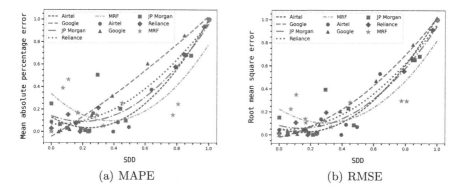

(a) MAPE   (b) RMSE

Fig. 1. Curve displaying performance vs. SDD for several stocks normalized to 0–1 range.

Table 2 shows the results of the StaDRo computation on some example stocks. The table consists of a sequence of validation sets across two stocks, corresponding performance metric (RMSE), and the StaDRo robustness results. It can be seen from the table that for a validation subset that StaDRo identified as not robust against SDD (listed as 'FALSE'), a higher error is observed. This indicates that StaDRo is a useful measure for robustness against statistical dissimilarity in datasets. We have only provided results for RMSE in this table and the rest is available on our GitHub.

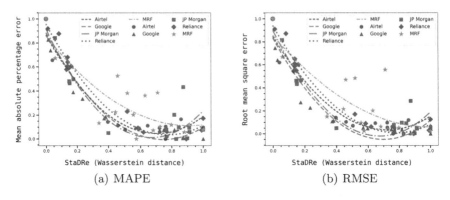

(a) MAPE   (b) RMSE

Fig. 2. Curve displaying performance vs. StaDRe for several stocks normalized to 0–1 range.

Table 2. Results displaying StaDRo estimates on some stocks

Data instance	Google (P_{min} (RMSE) = 500.0)				JP Morgan (P_{min} (RMSE) = 8.5)			
	RMSE	WD	Rate of change of SDD	Robust	RMSE	WD	Rate of change of SDD	Robust
0:70	24.85	634.73	0.39	TRUE	2.23	61.25	0.63	TRUE
70 : 140	31.12	740.50	0.45	TRUE	2.32	62.63	0.64	TRUE
140 : 210	26.35	717.43	0.44	TRUE	2.53	53.44	0.55	TRUE
210 : 280	36.73	842.07	0.52	TRUE	2.41	59.38	0.61	TRUE
280 : 350	82.03	910.24	0.56	TRUE	2.43	63.12	0.65	TRUE
350 : 420	82.46	945.59	0.58	TRUE	3.28	78.90	0.81	TRUE
420 : 490	133.10	1094.77	0.67	TRUE	7.16	66.65	0.68	TRUE
490 : 560	284.06	1330.72	0.82	TRUE	4.12	46.56	0.48	TRUE
560 : 630	620.01	1739.06	1.07	FALSE	2.43	50.30	0.52	TRUE
630 : 700	1014.97	2153.03	1.32	FALSE	5.11	76.55	0.78	TRUE
700 : 770	1287.46	2430.59	1.49	FALSE	10.40	105.03	1.08	FALSE
770 : 840	-	-	-	-	10.76	107.21	1.1	FALSE
840 : 910	-	-	-	-	14.77	114.84	1.18	FALSE

7 Conclusion and Future Works

In this paper, we described the use of SafeML for SDD-based assessment of ML models for time series applications. We investigated the performance behavior against SDD and found that performance is likely correlated to SDD. We proposed SDD-based metrics for reliability (StaDRe) and robustness (StaDRo).

The results on example applications show the effectiveness of these measures on univariate time series.

We considered a finance-critical example in this paper. However, in the future, we aim to focus on safety-critical examples such as ECG monitoring. In addition, we plan to experiment with the proposed measures on multivariate time series for both classification and regression tasks. Adversarial attacks could also be used to consider StaDRo for robustness against adversarial examples. However, this was out of scope for the work presented in this paper. The idea of this paper could be extended for videos (image-time-series-based inputs) and tested for autonomous vehicles in CARLA[1] simulation. Moreover, the proposed idea could be used as a foundation for enhancing the explainability and interpretability of ML-based systems, focusing on time-series applications.

All results, code, additional results, additional experiments, and exhaustive explanations will be made available in a GitHub[2] repository.

Acknowledgments. This work was supported by the Building Trust in Ecosystems and Ecosystem Component (BIECO) Horizon 2020 project under grant agreement no. 952702.

References

1. Adomavicius, G., Wang, Y.: Improving reliability estimation for individual numeric predictions: a machine learning approach. INFORMS J. Comput. **34**, 1–669 (2021)
2. Anh, D.T., Thanh, L.H.: An efficient implementation of k-means clustering for time series data with DTW distance. Int. J. Bus. Intell. Data Min. **10**(3), 213–232 (2015)
3. Aslansefat, K., Kabir, S., Abdullatif, A., Vasudevan, V., Papadopoulos, Y.: Toward improving confidence in autonomous vehicle software: a study on traffic sign recognition systems. Computer **54**(8), 66–76 (2021)
4. Aslansefat, K., Sorokos, I., Whiting, D., Tavakoli Kolagari, R., Papadopoulos, Y.: SafeML: safety monitoring of machine learning classifiers through statistical difference measures. In: Zeller, M., Höfig, K. (eds.) IMBSA 2020. LNCS, vol. 12297, pp. 197–211. Springer, Cham (2020). https://doi.org/10.1007/978-3-030-58920-2_13
5. Avizienis, A., Laprie, J.C., Randell, B., Landwehr, C.: Basic concepts and taxonomy of dependable and secure computing. IEEE Trans. Dependable Secure Comput. **1**(1), 11–33 (2004)
6. Becker, A., Becker, J.: Dataset shift assessment measures in monitoring predictive models. Procedia Comput. Sci. **192**, 3391–3402 (2021). https://doi.org/10.1016/j.procs.2021.09.112. https://www.sciencedirect.com/science/article/pii/S1877050921018512. Knowledge-Based and Intelligent Information & Engineering Systems: Proceedings of the 25th International Conference KES2021
7. Bellemare, M.G., et al.: The Cramer distance as a solution to biased Wasserstein gradients. arXiv preprint arXiv:1705.10743 (2017)
8. Bosnić, Z., Kononenko, I.: Estimation of individual prediction reliability using the local sensitivity analysis. Appl. Intell. **29**(3), 187–203 (2008)

---

[1] www.carla.org.

[2] https://github.com/n-akram/TimeSeriesSafeML.

9. Bosnić, Z., Kononenko, I.: An overview of advances in reliability estimation of individual predictions in machine learning. Intell. Data Anal. **13**(2), 385–401 (2009)
10. Bradley, P.S., Fayyad, U.M.: Refining initial points for K-Means clustering. In: Proceedings 15th International Conference on Machine Learning, pp. 91–99. Morgan Kaufmann, San Francisco (1998)
11. Briesemeister, S., Rahnenführer, J., Kohlbacher, O.: No longer confidential: estimating the confidence of individual regression predictions. PLoS ONE **7**(11), e48723 (2012)
12. Cho, K., van Merriënboer, B., Bahdanau, D., Bengio, Y.: On the properties of neural machine translation: encoder–decoder approaches. In: Proceedings of SSST-8, Eighth Workshop on Syntax, Semantics and Structure in Statistical Translation, pp. 103–111. Association for Computational Linguistics, Doha, October 2014. https://doi.org/10.3115/v1/W14-4012. https://aclanthology.org/W14-4012
13. Demut, I.R.: Reliability of predictions in regression models. Doktorandske dny 2010 (2010)
14. Driemel, A., Krivošija, A., Sohler, C.: Clustering time series under the Fréchet distance. In: Proceedings of the Twenty-Seventh Annual ACM-SIAM Symposium on Discrete Algorithms, pp. 766–785. SIAM (2016)
15. Efron, B.: Bootstrap methods: another look at the jackknife. In: Kotz, S., Johnson, N.L. (eds.) Breakthroughs in Statistics, pp. 569–593. Springer, New York (1992). https://doi.org/10.1007/978-1-4612-4380-9_41
16. Gammerman, A., Vovk, V., Vapnik, V.: Learning by transduction. In: Cooper, G.F., Moral, S. (eds.) UAI 1998: Proceedings of the Fourteenth Conference on Uncertainty in Artificial Intelligence, University of Wisconsin Business School, Madison, Wisconsin, USA, 24–26 July 1998, pp. 148–155. Morgan Kaufmann (1998). https://dslpitt.org/uai/displayArticleDetails.jsp?mmnu=1&smnu=2&article_id=243&proceeding_id=14
17. Hendrycks, D., Mu, N., Cubuk, E.D., Zoph, B., Gilmer, J., Lakshminarayanan, B.: AugMix: a simple data processing method to improve robustness and uncertainty. In: Proceedings of the International Conference on Learning Representations (ICLR) (2020)
18. Hochreiter, S., Schmidhuber, J.: Long short-term memory. Neural Comput. **9**(8), 1735–1780 (1997). https://doi.org/10.1162/neco.1997.9.8.1735
19. Hond, D., Asgari, H., Jeffery, D., Newman, M.: An integrated process for verifying deep learning classifiers using dataset dissimilarity measures. Int. J. Artif. Intell. Mach. Learn. (IJAIML) **11**(2), 1–21 (2021)
20. IEEE: Standard glossary of software engineering terminology. IEEE Std 610.12-1990, pp. 1–84 (1990). https://doi.org/10.1109/IEEESTD.1990.101064
21. Kingma, D.P., Ba, J.: Adam: a method for stochastic optimization. CoRR abs/1412.6980 (2015)
22. Lee, T., Xiao, Y., Meng, X., Duling, D.: Clustering time series based on forecast distributions using Kullback-Leibler divergence. In: International Institute of Forecasters (IIF). Web (2014)
23. Moreno-Torres, J.G., Raeder, T., Alaiz-Rodríguez, R., Chawla, N.V., Herrera, F.: A unifying view on dataset shift in classification. Pattern Recogn. **45**(1), 521–530 (2012)
24. Nouretdinov, I., Melluish, T., Vovk, V.: Ridge regression confidence machine. In: Brodley, C.E., Danyluk, A.P. (eds.) Proceedings of the Eighteenth International Conference on Machine Learning, pp. 385–392. Morgan Kaufmann, San Francisco (2001)

25. Oliveira, G.H., Cavalcante, R.C., Cabral, G.G., Minku, L.L., Oliveira, A.L.: Time series forecasting in the presence of concept drift: a PSO-based approach. In: 2017 IEEE 29th International Conference on Tools with Artificial Intelligence (ICTAI), pp. 239–246. IEEE (2017)

26. Rabanser, S., Günnemann, S., Lipton, Z.: Failing loudly: an empirical study of methods for detecting dataset shift. In: Advances in Neural Information Processing Systems, vol. 32 (2019)

27. Ratanamahatana, C.A., Keogh, E.: Everything you know about dynamic time warping is wrong. In: Third Workshop on Mining Temporal and Sequential Data, vol. 32. Citeseer (2004)

28. Rauber, J., Zimmermann, R., Bethge, M., Brendel, W.: Foolbox native: fast adversarial attacks to benchmark the robustness of machine learning models in PyTorch, TensorFlow, and JAX. J. Open Source Softw. 5(53), 2607 (2020). https://doi.org/10.21105/joss.02607

29. Raza, H., Prasad, G., Li, Y.: EWMA model based shift-detection methods for detecting covariate shifts in non-stationary environments. Pattern Recogn. 48(3), 659–669 (2015)

30. Sakoe, H., Chiba, S.: Dynamic programming algorithm optimization for spoken word recognition. IEEE Trans. Acoust. Speech Sig. Process. 26(1), 43–49 (1978). https://doi.org/10.1109/TASSP.1978.1163055

31. Santurkar, S., Tsipras, D., Madry, A.: BREEDS: benchmarks for subpopulation shift. arXiv preprint arXiv:2008.04859 (2020)

32. Storkey, A.: When training and test sets are different: characterizing learning transfer. In: Dataset Shift in Machine Learning, vol. 30, pp. 3–28 (2009)

33. Taori, R., Dave, A., Shankar, V., Carlini, N., Recht, B., Schmidt, L.: Measuring robustness to natural distribution shifts in image classification. Adv. Neural. Inf. Process. Syst. 33, 18583–18599 (2020)

34. Wang, B., Webb, S., Rainforth, T.: Statistically robust neural network classification. In: de Campos, C., Maathuis, M.H. (eds.) Proceedings of the Thirty-Seventh Conference on Uncertainty in Artificial Intelligence. Proceedings of Machine Learning Research, vol. 161, pp. 1735–1745. PMLR, 27–30 July 2021. https://proceedings.mlr.press/v161/wang21b.html

35. Wang, Y., Ma, X., Bailey, J., Yi, J., Zhou, B., Gu, Q.: On the convergence and robustness of adversarial training. In: Chaudhuri, K., Salakhutdinov, R. (eds.) Proceedings of the 36th International Conference on Machine Learning. Proceedings of Machine Learning Research, vol. 97, pp. 6586–6595. PMLR, 09–15 June 2019. https://proceedings.mlr.press/v97/wang19i.html

36. Webb, S., Rainforth, T., Teh, Y.W., Kumar, M.P.: A statistical approach to assessing neural network robustness. In: 7th International Conference on Learning Representations, ICLR 2019, New Orleans, LA, USA, 6–9 May 2019. OpenReview.net (2019). https://openreview.net/forum?id=S1xcx3C5FX

37. Zhang, H., Yu, Y., Jiao, J., Xing, E., Ghaoui, L.E., Jordan, M.: Theoretically principled trade-off between robustness and accuracy. In: Chaudhuri, K., Salakhutdinov, R. (eds.) Proceedings of the 36th International Conference on Machine Learning. Proceedings of Machine Learning Research, vol. 97, pp. 7472–7482. PMLR, 09–15 June 2019. https://proceedings.mlr.press/v97/zhang19p.html

38. Zhao, X., et al.: Assessing the reliability of deep learning classifiers through robustness evaluation and operational profiles. In: AISafety 2021 Workshop at IJCAI 2021, vol. 2916 (2021). ceur-ws.org

A Safety Assurable Human-Inspired Perception Architecture

Rick Salay and Krzysztof Czarnecki[(✉)] [iD]

University of Waterloo, Waterloo, Canada
rsalay@gsd.uwaterloo.ca, k2czarne@uwaterloo.ca

Abstract. Although artificial intelligence-based perception (AIP) using deep neural networks (DNN) has achieved near human level performance, its well-known limitations are obstacles to the safety assurance needed in autonomous applications. These include vulnerability to adversarial inputs, inability to handle novel inputs and non-interpretability. While research in addressing these limitations is active, in this paper, we argue that a fundamentally different approach is needed to address them. Inspired by dual process models of human cognition, where Type 1 thinking is fast and non-conscious while Type 2 thinking is slow and based on conscious reasoning, we propose a dual process architecture for safe AIP. We review research on how humans address the simplest non-trivial perception problem, image classification, and sketch a corresponding AIP architecture for this task. We argue that this architecture can provide a systematic way of addressing the limitations of AIP using DNNs and an approach to assurance of human-level performance and beyond. We conclude by discussing what components of the architecture may already be addressed by existing work and what remains future work.

Keywords: Safety assurance · Perception · Automated driving

1 Introduction

Artificial intelligence-based perception (AIP) using deep neural networks (DNN) has achieved remarkable performance. Yet as news reports can attest, AIP can fail in surprising and catastrophic ways. This highlights the fact that, currently, the level of safety assurance possible for AIP is insufficient to support the high levels of autonomy required for fully automated driving systems (ADS). In contrast, although human perception is imperfect, a status quo assumption by society is that the perception performance of a mature, unimpaired human is sufficient for the safe operation of a vehicle. Thus, achieving and assuring AIP performance against a human baseline would be necessary for a societally acceptable ADS and therefore a worthy goal.

In this paper, we take the position that this goal can be approached by studying how humans do perception and using this to construct a corresponding

M. Trapp et al. (Eds.): SAFECOMP 2022 Workshops, LNCS 13415, pp. 302–315, 2022.
https://doi.org/10.1007/978-3-031-14862-0_22

human-inspired AIP architecture. The idea of using humans as inspiration for AIP is not new. Many of the techniques of AI are based on human psychology or neurophysiology and this trend has accelerated in recent times (e.g., [27,37]). Instead, our focus is specifically on how to use the connection to humans to support the goal of *safety and its assurance*.

To investigate this concretely, we consider the basic perception task of *object image classification*: does an image X depict a member of a given class C? We show that a human-inspired AIP architecture for this task can assuredly address key limitations of current DNN-based AIP approaches while still leveraging the strengths of DNNs.

The remainder of the paper is structured according the following contributions: 1) we review research from the cognitive sciences on human object image classification; 2) we present a safe AIP architecture aligned with this work; and 3) we provide justification for the architecture from various perspectives including feasibility and assurability. Finally, we give conclusions.

2   How Humans (Probably) Do Classification

Dual Process Models. In the cognitive sciences, a *dual process* model of cognition is the dominant view [9,10,23]. Type 1 thinking is fast, non-conscious holistic, intuitive, and the same across different individuals. Type 2 thinking is slow, conscious, sequential conceptual reasoning that varies across individuals and is correlated with intelligence measures.

The dominant view on how the two types interact is *default-interventionism* [10,23]: the Type 1 process always produces some default response quickly, and the Type 2 process intervenes to produce a potentially different response only if "difficulty, novelty, and motivation combine to command the resources of working memory" [10]. The Type 1 default response may be wrong—humans often act as "cognitive misers" by substituting a less accurate easy-to-evaluate characteristic for a harder one, leading to biases (e.g., stereotyping). An important metacognitive factor is the level of "confidence" in the default response. When people are confident, they are less likely to invoke the Type 2 process [39]. Thus, low confidence is a key triggering factor for Type 2 intervention.

Time and risk play important roles. For fast (Type 1) binary perceptual decisions (less than 1,500 ms), research supports the idea that evidence accumulates over time until a threshold is reached and a decision is made. In addition, there is a speed/accuracy tradeoff. If speed is a priority then accuracy may be lower, while a focus on high accuracy slows the decision (e.g., [32]).

A natural criterion for choosing the priority is the perceived risk associated with the decision. Safety-critical decisions that must be made quickly, e.g., an object appears suddenly in front of the vehicle, prioritize speed. In this case, accuracy may suffer, and Type 2 intervention is not an option, because it is slow. This suggests that even inaccurate Type 1 decisions should be appropriately conservative to manage risk. For example, if there is not enough time to determine whether the object that suddenly appeared is a pedestrian or a cyclist, a safe response may be to assume that it is a pedestrian, since this suggests a more conservative behaviour.

Object Image Classification. Specific to the object image classification task, two prominent lines of research from different perspectives are *object recognition*, studied in the neuropsychology of vision [8], and *object categorization*, studied predominately in cognitive psychology and cognitive linguistics [14]. Object recognition concerns the ability to assign labels to particular objects sensed by the retina, including precise identifying labels and coarser category labels. Object categorization is the more general cognitive process of grouping objects based on similar or shared features [14]. Note that the term "categorization" used in the cognitive sciences is synonymous with "classification" as used in AI.

Vision processing in the brain has two major streams: the ventral stream is responsible for object recognition, whereas the dorsal stream is responsible for visually guided action. Recent research provides strong evidence that some Type 1 representation of a category is already in the ventral stream, expressed in terms of visual features, even though it is ultimately coded using more abstract (i.e., conceptual) features (Type 2) in downstream parts of the brain [4]. The categorization in the ventral stream is fast, with a response time as little as 250–290 ms for some categories, confirmed by multiple studies [11].

Humans are effective at recognizing objects under different confounding visual conditions, such as varying positions to the object, lighting, context, occlusion, etc. A key function of the ventral stream is to facilitate this ability by *transforming object images into representations invariant to these conditions* before further processing to categorize the object [8]. We refer to this transformation as *object normalization*. Two theories dominate regarding the form of the invariant object representation. The structural description theory [3] proposes a 3D parts-based representation, while in the view-based theory [31], objects are represented as a combination of a small set of particular 2D views that can be transformed to represent any other view.

Although object categorization can be seen to be part of object recognition, the research tradition in this area is focused on theories about *concepts*—the mental representation of a category. As such it is applicable to both Type 1 and Type 2 processes. The classical *rule-based* theory of concepts extending back to Greek philosophers is that they consist of the necessary and sufficient conditions for membership in the category. This view has been much critiqued. For example, Wittgenstein observed that the requirement for a set of necessary conditions often does not hold due to presence of exceptions and famously illustrated this by attempting to find the necessary conditions for the category "game". It is also inconsistent with empirical evidence obtained by Rosch [33] that categories are graded, with some members more central or typical than others, having more of the common features. This led Rosch to propose that concepts are *prototype-based* with membership determined by degree of similarity [15] to the prototype. Another dominant proposal supported by empirical evidence is that concepts are *exemplar-based* [28], where exemplars are specifically remembered examples of the category and membership is determined by collective similarity to all exemplars. Each approach has its strengths and weakness, and the current view is that all of these approaches may be used in some combination [29].

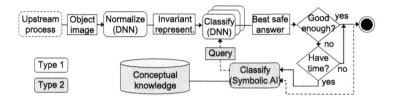

Fig. 1. Human inspired classification activity diagram.

3   An Assurable Human-Inspired Classification Architecture

Inspired by the research on object classification by humans presented above, in this section, we propose the high-level dual process architecture for classification shown in Fig. 1. Here, we assume that the fast Type 1 processes are carried out by DNNs, while slower Type 2 processes use reasoning with symbolic AI. The input is an object image from an upstream process (e.g., the first stage of an object detector). In alignment with the ventral stream processing, the first step is object normalization to eliminate the confounding effects of visual conditions. Then, a DNN-based classifier of the invariant object representation generates a classification based on visual features. We assume that these classifiers use prototype/exemplar methods to align with the human representations of concepts. Furthermore, we assume they measure confidence in their classification decision.

If the result produced by fast classifiers is inadequate (e.g., too low confidence) and if there is available time, then a reasoning process can intervene to attempt to improve the result by exploiting conceptual knowledge about object classes. The reasoning process considers alternative classification hypotheses, then generates perceptual queries of the invariant object representation that could provide evidence to affirm or refute a hypothesis; thus, we ground the Type 2 reasoning process in the Type 1 perceptual process [17]. Note that the a query is a recursive invocation (as indicated by the dashed arrows), since if the Type 1 process does not adequately answer a query, a Type 2 reasoning process can be invoked to intervene on it, and so on. Overall, the more time spent reasoning, the more this process can improve the quality of the classification by generating more potential hypotheses and by obtaining more evidence for hypotheses.

The Necessity of Dual Processes. We may reasonably ask whether the additional complexity of a dual process approach to classification is really necessary.

After all, a DNN is a universal approximator and with sufficient training examples, it should get arbitrarily accurate. However, we argue that a pure DNN approach is intrinsically limited.

The classes of objects, such as, pedestrian, cyclist and car, that are relevant for perception by an ADS have the crucial characteristic that they are not primarily determined by visual features but rather by conceptual features. For example, something is a cyclist not because of how it looks (visual features), but because it exhibits conceptual features such as having one or more wheels, carrying human rider(s), being propelled by rider effort, etc. Assessing the presence of these features definitively may require arbitrary amounts of reasoning. This suggests that visual features are insufficient to correctly characterize these classes, and thus, a DNN trained on object images alone *cannot ever achieve perfect accuracy, regardless of how many training examples are provided.*

However, having a similar visual appearance for certain subsets of class instances is a common occurrence. This could be due to genetics (for "natural kinds"), design or fashion. For example, cyclists on bicycles have visual similarity but look different from cyclists on recumbent cycles who are visually similar to each other. When such clustering according to visual similarity is available, visual feature-based classifiers are useful approximators for these subclasses of instances. But even here, their performance is intrinsically limited as illustrated in Fig. 2. It is always possible to find false negatives (FN)—unusual cyclists that fit the conceptual description but not the visual. On the other hand, we can also always find images that look like cyclists, but on careful inspection, do not satisfy the conceptual description, yielding false positives (FP).

Despite the inaccuracies of visual-feature based classifiers, the benefit is that they may be fast in comparison to a classifier based on reasoning about conceptual features. Thus, when a safety critical decision must be made quickly, a visual-feature based classifier is preferable. This suggests that an optimal classifier strategy should follow a dual approach, leveraging visual features for speed and conceptual features for accuracy when the time is available.

To further refine this conclusion, we must address an apparent paradox. The architecture in Fig. 1 shows that conceptual reasoning must ultimately be grounded in visual features (or, more generally, in features of available sense modalities). This is because evidence to support conceptual hypotheses about objects in the world can only be obtained through visual means—there is no way to directly access knowledge about these objects. Thus, all reasoning about conceptual features must be reducible to reasoning about visual features. However, if this is the case, then it would seem that *visual features alone must be enough* to characterize these classes, even if they are internally encoded in terms of conceptual features.

The way out of this apparent paradox is to acknowledge that, while individual queries about the object image issued by a Type 2 classifier are ultimately answered using visual features, each such query appeals to potentially different visual features and the scope of such queries is limited only by the size of the knowledge base. In contrast, the set of visual features used by a Type 1 classifier for a specific class is much smaller, focused on that class only. For example, if a bicycle is decorated with flowers attached to the frame, these may create enough of a visual distortion to cause an FP in a Type 1 cyclist classifier. However, the Type 2 conceptual reasoning process can potentially identify the presence of flowers (using a Type 1 flower classifier) and conclude that these do not affect the satisfaction of the conceptual definition of cyclist.

In this case, it is unlikely that the Type 1 cyclist classifier could ever learn to draw this conclusion because it would need to develop sensitivity to visual features about flowers. More generally, it would need to handle the visual features for every class in the knowledge base that could ever co-occur with a cyclist, which is likely to include most of the knowledge base. The dual process approach solves this scalability problem by delegating the job of ranging over the full span of world knowledge needed in the many varied, but rarer cases, to Type 2 classification and keeping Type 1 classification focused on typical class features.

Fig. 2. Visual feature based classifiers are intrinsically limited.

Addressing Safety. We assume that the safety requirements of an object classification subsystem are refined from system level (e.g., ADS) safety requirements (see [36] for a schema of such a refinement). This refinement identifies specific performance requirements of the subsystem needed to address different potential hazard scenarios. Since these requirements are system specific, for our proposed high-level architecture we instead consider the general implications of the high-level requirement that the subsystem provides performance at least as good as humans. In particular, the following three requirements are relevant and follow from the review of human classification.

Requirement 1. *The classification subsystem shall support accurate classification for both typical and atypical inputs.* Humans are able to effectively address both these types of inputs, and while it is well-known that DNN-based classifiers can achieve high accuracy on typical cases, they can often fail on unusual cases. As argued in the previous section, this is because DNN classifiers use visual features and these are only sufficient for characterizing subsets of class instances that cluster on visual similarity. These clusters identify visually prototypical class instances. However these only approximate the true class described by conceptual features, leading to both FNs and FPs for atypical cases. To correct these inevitable misperceptions by Type 1 classifiers, the architecture uses a Type 2 classifier based on conceptual reasoning.

The decision on when to invoke the Type 2 classifier is a crucial part of the architecture (i.e., the "good enough" decision in Fig. 1). One relevant signal is a measure of the uncertainty (or conversely, confidence) in the Type 1 classifier result. Assume the Type 1 classification process produces a categorical distribution $P(c)$ across classes and that this is *calibrated*— i.e., the value $P(c)$ for an input image accurately reflects the actual probability that c is the correct class.

A true positive (TP) classification corresponds to sharp distribution with one class having high probability and the others low. A distribution close to uniform probability indicates high uncertainty and a potential FN representing a visually atypical instance (Fig. 2, left). A distribution in which a few classes dominate also represents higher uncertainty indicating atypical visual ambiguity and could signal a potential FP. For example, the most right example in Fig. 2 could have highest probability for Cyclist (causing an FP) but with the probability of Pedestrian a close second. A limitation of this approach for detecting FPs is that it may require a large number of classes. For example, the third from the left example in Fig. 2 would only be caught if there was a class BicycleRide.

Requirement 2. *The classification subsystem shall support classification for both fast and slow safety-critical decisions.* This requirement acknowledges that safety-critical decisions may occur over different time-frames. For example, an object appearing suddenly ahead of the ADS requires a fast response, whereas an object causing a traffic slowdown ahead allows for a slower response. When fast classification is required, the architecture assumes that this is provided by the Type 1 process alone, since Type 2 processes are too slow. For typical cases, this can provide assuredly high levels of accuracy. A limitation of the architecture is that atypical cases may be misclassified by the Type 1 classifier and this can be a safety hazard in some situations. Uncertainty measurement of the Type 1 result, as discussed above, may play a mitigating role here by signaling to the driving policy when the classification may be incorrect and a conservative action should be taken to minimize risk.

In [35], a systematic way to approach this with a quantifiable safety guarantee is proposed. A *credible set* of $P(c)$ with confidence α, is a smallest subset of classes such that their cumulative probability is not less than α. Because the classifier is calibrated, the true class is in the credible set with probability at least α. Thus, if the Type 1 classifier sends the credible set as its result to the driving policy, any action it produces that is safe for all the classes in the set will be safe at least $\alpha \times 100\%$ of the time.

Requirement 3. *The classification subsystem shall support accurate classification in the presence of confounding visual conditions within the range tolerated by humans.* Humans are effective at ignoring conditions such as varying positions to the object, lighting, context, occlusion, etc. However, these kinds of variations have proven to be challenging for DNN-based classifiers and are the basis for many kinds of adversarial attacks. The architecture addresses this issue by introducing the object normalizer. The Type 1 classifiers operate on the invariant representation in which the confounding effects are mostly removed.

Type 1/Type 2 Consistency. We should expect that some *consistency* relation holds between the Type 1 and Type 2 classifications, but what should it be? As discussed above, the Type 1 classification based on visual features is inherently limited—it may achieve high accuracy for typical cases but often produces FNs and FPs for atypical cases. Furthermore, recall that for humans, the interaction between the Type 1 and Type 2 processes is not a decision fusion of redundant perceptual processes, but rather that the Type 2 process intervenes to improve on the Type 1 result when necessary and possible. This relationship is inherited by the proposed architecture. Thus, the Type 2 classification is considered both to be *authoritative* and it must be *no worse* than the Type 1 classification. The latter condition, which we term *classification consistency*, suggests that when Type 1 is TP, then so must Type 2, but when Type 1 is FN or FP, Type 2 may be the same or TP.

Note that we do not assume the Type 2 classification is necessarily always TP even though it is considered authoritative, since its accuracy is still limited when excessive aleatoric uncertainty is present. Furthermore, the degree of improvement over the Type 1 classification is limited by the reasoning time available, richness and correctness of the conceptual knowledge base and accuracy of the Type 1 classifiers used to answer queries.

Another kind of consistency is *risk consistency*—how is the safety of the classifications related? If we assume that a correct classification is always at least as safe (i.e., leads to a driving policy action that is not more hazardous) as a misclassification, then our classification consistency requirement implies that, when time is not a safety-critical factor, the Type 2 classification is always at least as safe as the Type 1 classification.

However, not all misclassifications are unsafe. For example, misclassifying a pedestrian as a cyclist, when it is still far ahead, may not lead to different behaviour by an ADS. Thus, the hazardousness of a given misclassification is situation-dependent. Can this fact be exploited to produce a stronger risk consistency requirement? In an assurance case, a fine-grained analysis of hazardous patterns of misperceptions relevant in different driving scenarios can provide a correspondingly fine-grained and risk-aware set of performance requirements for the Type 1 classifiers [36]. Such a set of requirements identify the kinds of images that are more likely to cause hazardous actions if misclassified, thus the training of Type 1 classifiers can focus more on these.

Related Work. Dual-processing architectures have been proposed for robotics and AI (e.g., [16]) but rarely discussed from the assurance perspective. The closest work is by Jha et al. [22], who also advocate for such architectures to support assurance. They propose that autonomous systems use (i) Type 1 processing to construct their world models and predict future observations and (ii) Type 2 processing to refine or revise the models when the prediction errors (aka surprise) become high. They target fusing observations from multiple sensors over time (sequential Bayesian filtering) and propose that an assurance argument focuses on (i) guarding against systematic misperceptions by Type 1 processing that fail to generate surprise and (ii) the safe handling of surprise by Type 2 processing. Our contribution is complementary: we explore image classification in depth, emphasizing the distinction between visual and conceptual features, the importance of normalization, and the role of time available to make a decision. Whereas surprise is an important trigger for Type 2 processing, so are other types of uncertainty, including ambiguity and novelty [2].

4   Validation

Although the proposed architecture is human-inspired, this alone is not sufficient to justify it. In this section, we validate the architecture by analyzing the feasibility and assurability of the components.

Feasibility of Architecture Components. We briefly review existing work that could address the requirements of architecture components.

Object Normalization. The field of computer graphics studies how to render object and image-taking specifications (e.g., 3D mesh, light sources, textures, camera position, etc.) into an object image. The problem of *inverse graphics* is how to produce such a specification from an object image; thus, it performs the task of object normalization. Solving the inverse graphics problem is active research and various recent approaches using neural networks have been proposed (e.g., [7,40,41]). The idea of *capsule networks* is a prominent approach [19] where the network learns an object class by decomposing into object parts and their structural relationships.

Type 1 Classification. An emerging trend for DNNs is *dynamic* inference where the DNN can exit early if needed [38]. This can implement the speed/accuracy tradeoff observed in the ventral stream. Classifiers that use DNNs are typically structured as a series of convolutional layers followed by fully connected layers. The lack of interpretability of these approaches limits their applicability as a Type 1 classifier when safety assurance is required. Alternative and interpretable DNN architectures based on prototype or exemplar approaches have recently been investigated and have shown positive results (e.g., [18,24,30]). The paper "This looks like that: deep learning for interpretable image recognition" [5] is good example of such architectures. Here, a classifier for different bird species is developed by learning for each class a set of prototypical image fragments taken from training images. Inference is done by judging similarity of the prototypes to an input image and assigning the image to the class with the best fit.

Type 2 Classification. In the absence of general AI, assurance can benefit from a wide range of classical AI approaches, which need to focus on *explaining* what the object image is. Thus, approaches to abductive reasoning are applicable. As the classes used by ADSs often do not possess a common set of necessary conditions, traditional monotonic logics may be inappropriate. Non-monotonic logics (e.g., default logic) have been developed to express class membership rules which allow exceptions. Case-based reasoning aligns well with exemplar-based categorization. Description logics have concepts as first class entities and have been extended to support prototype-based reasoning (e.g., [1]). Other formal executable models of conceptual categorization that incorporates both prototype- and exemplar-based reasoning also exist [25]. Reasoning using formalized "commonsense" theories provides a way to use human conceptual knowledge about various domains (e.g., physics of objects) [6,37]. Integration with Type 1 classification DNNs can use neuro-symbolic [20] or information fusion frameworks [37].

Safety Assurance. We also review the assurability of the architecture.

Performance Comparison. An assurance argument regarding a human baseline must rely on some performance metrics for comparing component performance to the baseline. A naive way to proceed is to use one of the many performance metrics that have been proposed to compare the performance of different classifiers (e.g., accuracy, precision, F1-score). Such "generic" metrics are problematic for several reasons. First, such comparisons should be "species-fair" and not be biased by operational differences [12]. For example, the retina is high resolution in the fovea but loses resolution and is color blind at the periphery. Thus, it sees an image differently than a DNN that gets an image as a uniform pixel grid. This difference can result in different classification accuracy of an image even if this has nothing to do with classification knowledge.

Second, comparisons should be *risk-aware*—performance differences in a context that is not safety relevant are not important. One way to achieve this is to define specialized perception performance metrics for different hazardous driving scenarios [36]. Finally, because generic metrics average performance over many trials, an AIP may obtain the same value as a human on the metric but still make, what to humans seem like unjustifiable errors (e.g., adversarial examples), undermining the assurance argument. To address this, performance measurements should be made for different difficulty categories for humans. In particular, cases that are easy for humans (e.g., variations due to confounding visual conditions) should also be easy for the AIP—adversarial examples violate this condition. Furthermore, the use of an *error consistency* metric is needed here, which measures the degree to which the AIP is making the same decision as a human on individual trials [13]. A high error consistency provides evidence that the AIP is following a similar strategy as the human in its classification decision. Note however that we are only interested in preserving strategies where humans make correct decisions and do not want to replicate their weaknesses.

Object Normalization. The object normalizer identifies where the confounding effects of visual conditions are explicitly addressed in the architecture. Thus, the assurance argument regarding robustness to adversarial cases focuses here. Furthermore, since we take human performance as a baseline, the performance of the normalizer needs only to be assured up to human tolerable bounds on these conditions (e.g., maximum level of fog after which human performance is inadequate). Methods for eliciting formal requirements representing such bounds, as well as corresponding testing criteria, have been recently proposed [21].

A generic DNN-based object normalizer would be reusable for different classification tasks allowing any assurance effort to be amortized over all its applications. Thus, although not-interpretable, it could be subjected to increased and extensive testing scrutiny. In addition, this testing effort would be robust because it is not subject to distributional shift or dependencies on community-specific norms since "objecthood" is such a basic concept.

Techniques for formally verifying DNNs are being developed (e.g., [26]). Thus, formal verification may be a possible solution for invariances that can be expressed formally as object image transformations (e.g., affine transformations or injected Gaussian noise). Formalizable aspects of object normalization may also allow non-data-driven implementation amenable to traditional assurance.

Type 1 Classification. A significant positive impact of object normalization is to simplify the classification problem since the classifier needs only to learn the visual features of the class instances in an idealized setting. This reduces the size and diversity needed in the dataset to assure adequate sample coverage of the input distribution. It also improves generalization by reducing the likelihood of spurious correlations with noncausal features of the input.

Prototype/exemplar-based classifier approaches using DNNs provide interpretability by allowing human inspection of the prototypes/exemplars to determine whether they are meaningful. For example, in "This looks like that" discussed above, the prototype fragments of bird images can be inspected by birding experts to determine whether they are indicative of the classes they correspond to. This expert assessment provides evidence for correctness in the safety argument. Unlike the many post hoc explainability mechanisms that have been proposed for DNNs, such as saliency maps, interpretability provides the faithful explanations needed for assurance [34].

Type 2 Classification. The knowledge base used by reasoning here is expressed in terms of human understandable concepts; therefore, it is interpretable and inspectable. This allows verification of alignment with community-specific consensus knowledge about object classes. Additionally, since reasoning is formal and based on a logic, evidence of internal consistency (i.e., soundness) and areas of (in)completeness of the knowledge base can be facilitated using formal methods.

The requirement of classification consistency imposes an important constraint between the knowledge at the Type 1 and Type 2 levels that must be verified as part of an assurance argument. Automatic cross-validation methods between the levels could facilitate this. For example, Type 2 reasoning could be used to label images with semantic information that is then used to train or test the Type 1 classifiers. Reasoning about the scope of conceptual knowledge used by Type 2 could form the basis for completeness claims about the Type 1 classifiers and the datasets used to train and test them.

5   Conclusion

Although imperfect, human perception performance is often assumed to serve as a minimum baseline for safety that a societally acceptable AIP must meet.

However, it is widely known that while current state-of-the-art AIP has achieved high levels of performance using DNNs, they still fall short of this baseline. In this paper, we review research on how humans do the basic perception task of object classification. Then we propose a dual process architecture for a safety assurable object classification AIP aligned with the findings of this research. We discuss how such an architecture is both potentially feasible and assurable.

We plan on investigating several issues as part of future work. First, while this paper explores a dual processing architecture for classification, the ideas must be further developed for more general perception and decision making, potentially in a unified way. This should also go beyond a single modality like vision. When a fast and critical decision needs to be made, one may need to introduce additional sensing modalities. For example, tailpipe fumes on a cold day may appear in LiDAR like a potentially solid object, but a camera image can easily remove this ambiguity. Second, an interesting next step would be to develop a safety argument template that could be evolved and drive the development of concrete AIP architectures in a safety-first manner. Finally, a key limitation is still the challenge to be robust to and detect out-of-distribution (OOD) samples at the Type 1 level when it needs to be fast and we intend to explore this further (plus validating the hypothesis that Type 2 can refute Type 1 for OOD samples in the long run with sufficient accuracy). Perhaps neuroscience can be helpful here too by providing insights into how the brain deals with uncertainty and novelty. Ultimately, the lessons we can learn from the human brain may be the key to achieving assurable and societally acceptable AIP.

References

1. Baader, F., Ecke, A.: Reasoning with prototypes in the description logic $\mathcal{ALC}$ using weighted tree automata. In: Dediu, A.-H., Janoušek, J., Martín-Vide, C., Truthe, B. (eds.) LATA 2016. LNCS, vol. 9618, pp. 63–75. Springer, Cham (2016). https://doi.org/10.1007/978-3-319-30000-9_5
2. Barto, A., Mirolli, M., Baldassarre, G.: Novelty or surprise? Front. Psychol. **4**, 907 (2013)
3. Biederman, I.: Recognition-by-components: a theory of human image understanding. Psychol. Rev. **94**(2), 115 (1987)
4. Bracci, S., Ritchie, J.B., de Beeck, H.O.: On the partnership between neural representations of object categories and visual features in the ventral visual pathway. Neuropsychologia **105**, 153–164 (2017)
5. Chen, C., Li, O., Tao, C., Barnett, A.J., Su, J., Rudin, C.: This looks like that: deep learning for interpretable image recognition. Preprint arXiv:1806.10574 (2018)
6. Davis, E.: Logical formalizations of commonsense reasoning: a survey. J. Artif. Intell. Res. **59**, 651–723 (2017)
7. Deng, B., Kornblith, S., Hinton, G.: Cerberus: a multi-headed derenderer. Preprint arXiv:1905.11940 (2019)
8. DiCarlo, J.J., Zoccolan, D., Rust, N.C.: How does the brain solve visual object recognition? Neuron **73**(3), 415–434 (2012)
9. Epstein, S.: Integration of the cognitive and the psychodynamic unconscious. Am. Psychol. **49**(8), 709 (1994)

10. Evans, J.S.B., Stanovich, K.E.: Dual-process theories of higher cognition: advancing the debate. Perspect. Psychol. Sci. **8**(3), 223–241 (2013)
11. Fabre-Thorpe, M.: The characteristics and limits of rapid visual categorization. Front. Psychol. **2**, 243 (2011)
12. Firestone, C.: Performance vs. competence in human-machine comparisons. Proc. Nat. Acad. Sci. **117**(43), 26562–26571 (2020)
13. Geirhos, R., Meding, K., Wichmann, F.A.: Beyond accuracy: quantifying trial-by-trial behaviour of CNNs and humans by measuring error consistency. Preprint arXiv:2006.16736 (2020)
14. Goldstone, R.L., Kersten, A., Carvalho, P.F.: Categorization and concepts. In: Stevens' Handbook of Experimental Psychology and Cognitive Neuroscience, vol. 3, pp. 275–317 (2018)
15. Goldstone, R.L., Son, J.Y.: Similarity. Oxford University Press, Oxford (2012)
16. Gurney, K., Hussain, A., Chambers, J., Abdullah, R.: Controlled and automatic processing in animals and machines with application to autonomous vehicle control. In: Alippi, C., Polycarpou, M., Panayiotou, C., Ellinas, G. (eds.) ICANN 2009. LNCS, vol. 5768, pp. 198–207. Springer, Heidelberg (2009). https://doi.org/10.1007/978-3-642-04274-4_21
17. Harnad, S.: The symbol grounding problem. Physica D **42**(1–3), 335–346 (1990)
18. Hase, P., Chen, C., Li, O., Rudin, C.: Interpretable image recognition with hierarchical prototypes. In: HCOMP, vol. 7, pp. 32–40 (2019)
19. Hinton, G.E., Sabour, S., Frosst, N.: Matrix capsules with EM routing. In: ICLR (2018)
20. Hitzler, P., Sarker, M.: Neuro-Symbolic Artificial Intelligence: The State of the Art. IOS Press, Amsterdam (2021)
21. Hu, B.C., Marsso, L., Czarnecki, K., Salay, R., Shen, H., Chechik, M.: If a human can see it, so should your system: Reliability requirements for machine vision components. In: ICSE (2022)
22. Jha, S., Rushby, J., Shankar, N.: Model-centered assurance for autonomous systems. In: Casimiro, A., Ortmeier, F., Bitsch, F., Ferreira, P. (eds.) SAFECOMP 2020. LNCS, vol. 12234, pp. 228–243. Springer, Cham (2020). https://doi.org/10.1007/978-3-030-54549-9_15
23. Kahneman, D.: Thinking, Fast and Slow. Macmillan, London (2011)
24. Li, O., Liu, H., Chen, C., Rudin, C.: Deep learning for case-based reasoning through prototypes: a neural network that explains its predictions. In: AAAI, vol. 32 (2018)
25. Lieto, A., Radicioni, D.P., Rho, V.: Dual PECCS: a cognitive system for conceptual representation and categorization. JETAI **29**(2), 433–452 (2017)
26. Liu, C., Arnon, T., Lazarus, C., Strong, C., Barrett, C., Kochenderfer, M.J.: Algorithms for verifying deep neural networks. Preprint arXiv:1903.06758 (2019)
27. Malowany, D., Guterman, H.: Biologically inspired visual system architecture for object recognition in autonomous systems. Algorithms **13**(7), 167 (2020)
28. Medin, D.L., Schaffer, M.M.: Context theory of classification learning. Psychol. Rev. **85**(3), 207 (1978)
29. Murphy, G.L.: Is there an exemplar theory of concepts? Psychon. Bull. Rev. **23**(4), 1035–1042 (2015). https://doi.org/10.3758/s13423-015-0834-3
30. Papernot, N., McDaniel, P.: Deep k-nearest neighbors: towards confident, interpretable and robust deep learning. Preprint arXiv:1803.04765 (2018)
31. Poggio, T., Edelman, S.: A network that learns to recognize three-dimensional objects. Nature **343**(6255), 263–266 (1990)
32. Ratcliff, R., McKoon, G.: The diffusion decision model: theory and data for two-choice decision tasks. Neural Comput. **20**(4), 873–922 (2008)

33. Rosch, E.H.: Natural categories. Cogn. Psychol. **4**(3), 328–350 (1973)
34. Rudin, C.: Stop explaining black box machine learning models for high stakes decisions and use interpretable models instead. NMI **1**(5), 206–215 (2019)
35. Salay, R., Czarnecki, K., Elli, M.S., Alvarez, I.J., Sedwards, S., Weast, J.: PURSS: towards perceptual uncertainty aware responsibility sensitive safety with ML. In: SafeAI@AAAI, pp. 91–95 (2020)
36. Salay, R., et al.: The missing link: developing a safety case for perception components in automated driving 2022–01-0818. SAE (2022)
37. Suchan, J., Bhatt, M., Varadarajan, S.: Commonsense visual sensemaking for autonomous driving-on generalised neurosymbolic online abduction integrating vision and semantics. Artif. Intell. **299**, 103522 (2021)
38. Teerapittayanon, S., McDanel, B., Kung, H.T.: BranchyNet: fast inference via early exiting from deep neural networks. In: ICPR, pp. 2464–2469. IEEE (2016)
39. Thompson, V.A., Turner, J.A.P., Pennycook, G.: Intuition, reason, and metacognition. Cogn. Psychol. **63**(3), 107–140 (2011)
40. Yao, S., et al.: 3D-aware scene manipulation via inverse graphics. arXiv:1808.09351 (2018)
41. Yildirim, I., Belledonne, M., Freiwald, W., Tenenbaum, J.: Efficient inverse graphics in biological face processing. Sci. Adv. **6**(10), eaax5979 (2020)

Object Detection with Probabilistic Guarantees: A Conformal Prediction Approach

Florence de Grancey[1], Jean-Luc Adam[2], Lucian Alecu[3],
Sébastien Gerchinovitz[4,5(✉)], Franck Mamalet[4], and David Vigouroux[4]

[1] Thales AVS France SAS, Toulouse, France
`florence.de-grancey@fr.thalesgroup.com`
[2] Renault, Toulouse, France
`jean-luc.adam@renault.com`
[3] Continental, Toulouse, France
`Lucian.Alecu@continental-corporation.com`
[4] IRT Saint Exupéry, Toulouse, France
{`sebastien.gerchinovitz,franck.mamalet,`
`david.vigouroux`}`@irt-saintexupery.com`
[5] Institut de Mathématiques de Toulouse, Toulouse, France

Abstract. Providing reliable uncertainty quantification for complex visual tasks such as object detection is of utmost importance for safety-critical applications such as autonomous driving, tumor detection, etc. Conformal prediction methods offer simple yet practical means to build uncertainty estimations that come with probabilistic guarantees. In this paper we apply such methods to the task of object localization and illustrate our analysis on a pedestrian detection use-case. We highlight both theoretical and practical implications of our analysis.

Keywords: Object detection · Conformal prediction · Uncertainty quantification

1 Introduction

Recent works in object detection show a great variety of models and approaches. Among the most notable we can mention: RCNN [14], Fast-RCNN [13], RetinaNet [25], FPN [24], YOLO and its several versions [31–33], SSD [27], DETR [7].

Despite their impressive success observed on various benchmarks, many challenges remain ahead. For critical systems, several additional guarantees shall be provided to avoid catastrophic consequences: in an autonomous vehicle, a pedestrian mislocated by the system could be hurt or killed; in a cancer detection system, several cancer cells missed by the object detector might not be treated. To ensure the safety of the user, the uncertainty of the location of the object to be detected should be quantified, so as to create safeguards around the object.

M. Trapp et al. (Eds.): SAFECOMP 2022 Workshops, LNCS 13415, pp. 316–329, 2022.
https://doi.org/10.1007/978-3-031-14862-0_23

The main challenge consists in providing *reliable* uncertainty quantification of their prediction errors. While many object detection models compute so-called confidence scores which can be interpreted as basic estimators of uncertainty, they are often unreliable (i.e. over or under-estimating the true uncertainty). Another difficulty stems from the complex interplay between the classification-type errors and the localization-type errors of the object detectors. In addition, the risks associated with each type of error are application-dependent.

For safety-related applications, one may seek to obtain various guarantees. One such guarantee related to object localization, that will be addressed in this paper, may read: ensure that at least a significant portion (i.e. a user-specified fraction) of the objects recognized in visual images satisfy this property: their true bounding boxes are fully covered[1] by the boxes predicted by a given object detection model. This type of guarantee may be helpful, for example, to build reliable models for tumor discovery, obstacle detection or trajectory estimation.

Uncertainty Quantification for Object Detection. Several techniques such as Deep Ensembles methods [21,28] or Monte Carlo-Dropout methods [2,10,29,30] have been developed to provide epistemic uncertainty quantification. Other methods such as Direct Modeling add additional layers on top of the object detector to achieve such estimations [22]. More recent works introduce *probabilistic object detectors* which distinguish between the aleatoric and epistemic uncertainties and estimate their variances separately. Based on the work of [16], the authors extend Bayesian neural networks to object detectors [15,19]. A complete survey on uncertainty estimation for object detectors can be found in [12].

The cited methods have been applied to uncertainty quantification in object detection tasks with various success. Nevertheless, to the best of our knowledge, none of these works provide statistical guarantees about the estimated uncertainties, e.g., that the relevant objects are correctly classified with high probability, or that they are correctly localized in the image most of the time, or both.

Related Works in Safety Engineering. Safe Box localization for object detection has been investigated in the literature (without statistical guarantees). The works [8,36] propose a data-driven formulation and an analytic approach to compute safe enlarged boxes, which could be interpreted as a special case (worst case) of our methodology. The papers [17,18] provide uncertainty wrappers to enrich model predictions, with a similar model-agnostic approach.

Main Contributions and Outline of the Paper. In this work, we consider a relatively recent family of statistical methods called *Conformal Prediction*, which are post-processing methods to compute guaranteed "error margins" for various learning tasks, at a low computational cost. Our main contribution is the first application of such ideas to a practical object detection use-case, namely, pedestrian *localization* (i.e. correct prediction of the minimum area bounding box encompassing objects classified as pedestrians). This may be further used to

---

[1] All the coordinates of the true box will be found inside the rectangle defined by the predicted bounding box of the object.

increase the reliability of, e.g., collision avoidance or assisted braking functions. To that end, the paper is organized as follows:

- After presenting the main ingredients of conformal prediction in Sect. 2 we describe the experimental setting in Sect. 3.
- In Sects. 4 and 5 we show several ways to apply conformal prediction methods for object localization, with various statistical guarantees.
- In Sect. 6 we emphasize subtle pitfalls that a user may fall into, to help interpret conformal prediction guarantees when applied to object detection.

Fig. 1. Conformalization example (box-wise, risk level $\alpha = 0.1$) on a BDD100k image with Ground Truth, Inference and Conformalized boxes. (Color figure online)

2   Background: Conformal Prediction

Consider a supervised learning task (e.g. classification or regression), where we want to predict an unknown label y (e.g. a class or a real number) given an observed input x (e.g. an image). Typical ML models such as deep neural networks output predictions $\hat{f}(x)$ with little or no hint as to whether $\hat{f}(x)$ is close to the unknown label y. To that end, *Conformal Prediction* [1,23,37] is a family of post-processing methods that are useful to compute guaranteed "error margins", under some assumptions on the data (see Theorem 1 below for an example). The overall process from learning to inference typically unfolds as follows.[2]

1. **Data collection:** Two different datasets are collected: a *training set* and a *calibration set*, which will be used to learn and evaluate a ML model. (See below for independence and distribution requirements on the data.)

---

[2] More complex variants exist. The typical process outlined here is more precisely known as *split conformal prediction*.

2. **Training step:** a machine learning model $\hat{f}$ is learned on the *training set*. It can be of virtually any kind (a deep neural network, a random forest, etc.).
3. **Conformalization step:** the learned model $\hat{f}$ is evaluated on the *calibration set*. This step consists in measuring the errors of $\hat{f}$ on the calibration set, and in reporting a quantile q_α of these errors for some pre-specified risk level $\alpha \in (0,1)$. More precisely, given a *non-conformity score* $s(\hat{y}, y)$ to assess the "distance" between a prediction $\hat{y} = \hat{f}(x)$ and a ground truth y, we compute the errors of $\hat{f}$ on all data points (x_i, y_i) of the calibration set[3]:

$$R^i = s(\hat{y}_i, y_i), \quad i = 1, \ldots, n_c, \tag{1}$$

where n_c is the size of the calibration set. (For example, in regression, we can take the absolute difference $s(\hat{y}, y) = |y - \hat{y}|$.) Then, the quantile q_α is defined as the $\lceil (1 - \alpha)(n_c + 1) \rceil$-th largest value among the observed errors R^i.
4. **Inference step:** Given a new input x, instead of outputting a simple prediction $\hat{f}(x)$, we output a prediction set $C^\alpha(x)$, with the goal of containing the unknown ground truth y. It is defined as the set of all labels y' that are "close enough" to the prediction $\hat{y} = \hat{f}(x)$ of the ML model:

$$C^\alpha(x) = \left\{ y' : s(\hat{y}, y') \leq q_\alpha \right\}, \tag{2}$$

where the quantile q_α defined in Step 3 serves as an "error margin". For example, in the regression example mentioned above, the prediction set is given by $C^\alpha(x) = [\hat{y} - q_\alpha; \hat{y} + q_\alpha]$, which comes at no computational cost. Other non-conformity scores lead to other prediction sets, as shown later.

Dataset Requirements. In order to be able to prove that a prediction set $C^\alpha(x)$ contains the unknown label y "most of the time", the datasets must satisfy some requirements. Sufficient requirements are that:[4]

(i) data from all 3 datasets (training, calibration, inference) are independent;
(ii) data distributions at calibration and inference steps are identical.

Requirement (i) is useful to avoid overfitting issues. Requirement (ii) is useful to make sure that errors measured during the conformalization step are representative of errors at inference time. Interestingly though, training data can be distributed differently, which can be useful when computational resources or data for training are rather scarce, while an ML model carefully trained for a close distribution is already available. (Of course, a model that was pre-trained for a very different distribution will perform poorly at the conformalization step, and thus the error margin q_α will be large.)

Under the above dataset requirements, the conformal prediction process 1–4 outlined above satisfies the following probabilistic guarantee.

---

[3] The errors are sometimes called "residuals" (hence the R^i notation).
[4] Mathematically speaking, it is in fact sufficient that the calibration data and the data at inference time are exchangeable, conditionally on the training data.

Theorem 1 (see, e.g., [1,23,37]). *Assume the training, calibration, and inference datasets satisfy Requirements (i) and (ii) above. Then, on average over the choice of the calibration set and the new data point (X, Y),*

$$P\big(Y \in C^\alpha(X)\big) \geq 1 - \alpha\,.$$

We say in this case that the method has a *coverage* of $1-\alpha$. The above guarantee means that, for a fraction $1 - \alpha$ of all possible calibration sets in Step 3 and possible data points (x, y) in Step 4, the prediction set $C^\alpha(x)$ contains the true label y. In other words, if we repeated the overall conformal prediction process 1–4 many times independently, it would err a fraction at most α of the time. Details about dangers of interpretation are given in Sect. 6.

3   Experimental Setting and Goals

In the following sections we describe how conformal prediction methods can be applied to post-process (i.e. shrink or enlarge) the prediction boxes provided by a pedestrian detector. The goal is that the new boxes, called *conformalized boxes*, fully cover the true bounding boxes of the objects of interest, "most of the time". For example, in Fig. 1 we would like to cover all gold boxes with green boxes, which are obtained by adjusting the predicted boxes in cyan. The precise interpretation and limitations of the "most of the time" statement will be detailed shortly, when we apply conformalization procedures on different levels respectively: per coordinate, per bounding box or per image.

Both the level at which conformalization is conducted, and the design of non-conformity scores are *engineering choices*, as they depend on the actual usage of the model in real-world applications. For the pedestrian detection case considered here we may be interested in providing guarantees related to individual objects. In this case, a box-wise conformalization seems more appropriate. However, in other cases we may be interested in image-wise conformalization, as to ensure that a majority of images satisfy a desired property (e.g. all or most of the objects of interest in the image are "well" localized).

In all our experimental settings we consider the YOLOv3 object detector [33] pretrained on the COCO training dataset [26] (i.e. Step 2 described in Sect. 2 is fixed). As stated in Sect. 2 we can conformalize on a calibration dataset with a distribution that is different from that of the training set. Therefore we conduct all our experiments on the BDD100k dataset [38] by considering its training set as our calibration set (denoted by $\mathcal{D}_{\mathrm{BDD}}^{calib}$ thereafter) and its validation set as our test set (denoted by $\mathcal{D}_{\mathrm{BDD}}^{test}$). Since we focus on pedestrian detection, the original $70k + 10k$ images of training and validation sets reduce to 22213 and 3220 images with at least one person/pedestrian (we include riders), containing 91349 and 13262 annotated persons respectively.

In the following sections we propose non-conformity scores for each level of analysis (coordinate, box or image) and discuss practical implications of these choices. Finally, we emphasize some statistical aspects that are essential to any correct interpretation of the obtained guarantees.

4   Coordinate-Wise and Box-Wise Conformalization

As mentioned above, our goal is to post-process the boxes predicted by an object detector such that they cover the true bounding boxes of the objects of interest. In this section, we compute error margins at box level, by treating boxes as individual data points for the conformal prediction process of Sect. 2. We compute error margins for each coordinate $x_{min}, x_{max}, y_{min}, y_{max}$ separately (Sect. 4.2), and then show how to correct them to obtain guarantees at box level (Sect. 4.3).

4.1   Preliminary Assignment

On a given image, in order to compare predicted boxes with true boxes at box level (that is, compare box A with box B), we need to assign predicted boxes to true boxes. A preliminary pre-processing *assignment stage* is thus necessary. This step is performed with the Hungarian matching algorithm [20] based on the IoU metric. By applying it, we retain exclusively the true positive bounding boxes for calibration. Therefore, at inference time our probabilistic guarantee will only ensure that true positives are correctly covering the ground truth, while false negatives might still exist. In the following experiments, unless otherwise stated, a detection box must have a confidence score higher than 0.5 and an IoU with a ground truth object above 0.5 to assign the predicted box to a true box. Based on this assignment stage, the BDD100k calibration and test sets reduce to 42824 and 6138 assigned persons respectively.

4.2   Coordinate-Wise Conformalization

We explain in details how to instantiate Steps 3 and 4 of Sect. 2.

Conformalization Step. Assume that we have assigned predicted boxes to true boxes as in Sect. 4.1. In order to compare the i-th predicted box with the i-th true box, we compare each of the four predicted coordinates $\hat{x}^i_{min}, \hat{x}^i_{max}, \hat{y}^i_{min}, \hat{y}^i_{max}$ with the four true coordinates $x^i_{min}, x^i_{max}, y^i_{min}, y^i_{max}$, by counting errors positively when the truth lies outside the prediction (e.g. $\hat{x}^i_{min} > x^i_{min}$ or $\hat{x}^i_{max} < x^i_{max}$), and negatively otherwise. This choice is less conservative than considering absolute error values and leads to the following four errors (cf. Eq. (1)): for $i = 1, \ldots, n_c$,

$$
\begin{aligned}
R^i_{x_{min}} &= \hat{x}^i_{min} - x^i_{min} \\
R^i_{x_{max}} &= x^i_{max} - \hat{x}^i_{max}
\end{aligned}
\qquad
\begin{aligned}
R^i_{y_{min}} &= \hat{y}^i_{min} - y^i_{min} \\
R^i_{y_{max}} &= y^i_{max} - \hat{y}^i_{max}
\end{aligned}
\qquad (3)
$$

Note that n_c is given by the total number of predicted objects assigned to a true object, which is larger than the number of images in the calibration set.

Then, following Step 3 of Sect. 2, we compute a quantile q_α for each of the four errors above, defined as the $\lceil(1-\alpha)(n_c+1)\rceil$-th largest value among the observed errors R^i. These four quantiles will serve as error margins for each coordinate.

As an illustration, the errors $R^i_{y_{max}}$ on $\mathcal{D}^{calib}_{BDD}$ are represented on the histogram on the left side of Fig. 2 (in red: the quantile q_α for $\alpha = 0.1$, i.e., for a specified coverage of 0.9). The right side shows the evolution of the quantile q_α w.r.t. the parameter α. High guarantees ($\alpha < 0.05$) imply large margins, whereas low guarantees only require small modifications of the predicted coordinates.

Inference Step. We now instantiate Eq. (2) of Sect. 2 to compute a prediction set C^α for each coordinate $x_{min}, x_{max}, y_{min}, y_{max}$, given four predicted coordinates $\hat{x}_{min}, \hat{x}_{max}, \hat{y}_{min}, \hat{y}_{max}$ as inputs. These prediction sets are intervals and can be obtained at no computational cost (simple additions):

$$
\begin{aligned}
C^\alpha_{x_{min}} &= [\hat{x}_{min} - q^{x_{min}}_\alpha, +\infty) & C^\alpha_{y_{min}} &= [\hat{y}_{min} - q^{y_{min}}_\alpha, +\infty) \\
C^\alpha_{x_{max}} &= (-\infty, \hat{x}_{max} + q^{x_{max}}_\alpha] & C^\alpha_{y_{max}} &= (-\infty, \hat{y}_{max} + q^{y_{max}}_\alpha]
\end{aligned}
\tag{4}
$$

In Table 1, the first four lines (coordinate-wise) give the evaluation of the observed coverage on the $\mathcal{D}^{test}_{BDD}$ set, i.e., for each coordinate, the proportion of (true positive) boxes for which the true coordinate lies within the corresponding prediction set. We can see that Theorem 1 is verified whatever the specified coverage.

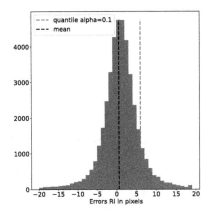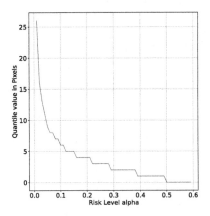

Fig. 2. Left: histogram of the errors R^i for the coordinate y_{max}, and the corresponding quantile q_α for $\alpha = 0.1$. Right: Evolution of the quantile value q_α with risk level α. (Color figure online)

Table 1. Evaluation of observed coverage on $\mathcal{D}_{\text{BDD}}^{test}$ using the quantile evaluated for three specified coverage values (in red when the specified coverage is not reached).

Method	Specified coverage $(1-\alpha)$	0.7	0.9	0.95
		Observed coverage		
Coordinate-Wise Sect. 4.2	$x_{\min}$	0.76	0.91	0.96
	$x_{\max}$	0.78	0.91	0.96
	$y_{\min}$	0.70	0.92	0.95
	$y_{\max}$	0.71	0.91	0.95
Box-Wise Sect. 4.3	w/o Bonferroni	0.35	0.73	0.86
Box-Wise Sect. 4.3	with Bonferroni	0.79	0.92	0.96

4.3 Bonferroni Correction for Box-Level Guarantees

In this section we seek the following guarantee: at inference time, among all true bounding (pedestrian) boxes that are detected, a fraction $1 - \alpha$ of them are correctly covered by conformalized boxes.[5] We explained in Eq. (4) how to compute error margins to locate unknown coordinates $x_{\min}, x_{\max}, y_{\min}, y_{\max}$ of a box, given predictions $\hat{x}_{\min}, \hat{x}_{\max}, \hat{y}_{\min}, \hat{y}_{\max}$. It might be tempting to define the *conformalized box* as the largest (worst-case) box whose coordinates are within the intervals C^α, i.e., the box with coordinates

$$\hat{x}_{\min} - q_\alpha^{x_{\min}} \qquad \hat{x}_{\max} + q_\alpha^{x_{\max}} \qquad \hat{y}_{\min} - q_\alpha^{y_{\min}} \qquad \hat{y}_{\max} + q_\alpha^{y_{\max}} .$$

However, looking at the experimental results of Table 1 (line w/o Bonferroni), we remark that for, e.g., a specified coverage of 95%, only 86% of true boxes are covered by conformalized boxes. The lower-than-expected coverage is a direct consequence of considering each coordinate of the bounding boxes independently, since errors on each coordinate can happen on different boxes.

One simple solution is to apply a so-called *Bonferroni correction* (e.g., [5]), a statistical adjustment to account for this $4 - way$ dependency. This is straightforward, as it amounts to perform the exact same procedure as described in the previous section, but replacing q_α with $q_{\alpha/4}$. With this slight change the new coverage on the test set becomes within the expected levels (see Table 1, line with Bonferroni). Note that since $q_{\alpha/4} \geq q_\alpha$, the conformalized boxes will be larger. For example, for the $y_{\max}$ coordinate and for a specified coverage of 0.9 ($\alpha = 0.1$), we obtain $q_\alpha = 6$ pixels and $q_{\alpha/4} = 14$ pixels.

5 Image-Wise Conformalization

The method of the previous section aimed at guaranteeing that, at inference time, among all true (pedestrian) bounding boxes that are detected, a fraction

---

[5] The $1 - \alpha$ guarantee only holds on average over all calibration sets, see Sect. 6.

$1 - \alpha$ of them are correctly covered by conformalized boxes. (see Footnote 5) This guarantee has two limitations: (i) false negatives (undetected pedestrians) are not taken into account, without any control on their occurrence rate; (ii) the fraction of detected true boxes that are covered on a given image might be much different from $1 - \alpha$ (the $1 - \alpha$ coverage is an average over all boxes across the test set). While the box-wise approach can still be useful for pedestrian detection (e.g., for tracking true positives), for medical applications such as cancer cell detection, (i) and (ii) imply that we might miss too many cancer cells on too many images.

Next we study another non-conformity score to pursue a guarantee at image level rather than at object level. We aim at the following guarantee: on average over the choice of the calibration set, a fraction $1 - \alpha$ of images at inference will be such that a fraction $1 - \beta$ of true boxes in the image will be correctly covered by conformalized boxes.

To that end, we consider a non-conformity score $s_\beta(\hat{B}, B)$ that is a close variant of the *partial (or quantile) directed Hausdorff distance* [34]. It compares two sets of boxes on a given image: the set $\hat{B}$ of all predicted boxes, and the set B of all true boxes. Our score $s_\beta(\hat{B}, B)$ is defined as the smallest margin $r \geq 0$ that it suffices to add to *all* predicted boxes in $\hat{B}$ (on *all* four coordinates) so that a fraction at least $1 - \beta$ of true boxes in B are correctly covered by the union of enlarged predicted boxes. We then follow the whole process of Sect. 2. In particular, the quantile q_α computed at conformalization is the margin that will be added to all predicted boxes at inference.

A BDD100k example is shown on Fig. 3 for $\alpha = 0.1$ and $\beta = 0.25$ (the aim is to correctly locate 75% of all pedestrians on each of 90% of all possible images). Interestingly, though only 5 pedestrians were detected (in cyan), 9 pedestrians (in gold) are located within conformalized boxes (in green). This positive effect

Fig. 3. Conformalization example (image-wise, risk level $\alpha = 0.1$, $\beta = 0.25$) on a BDD100k image with Ground Truth, Inference and Conformalized boxes. (Color figure online)

is due to the presence of multiple pedestrians nearby. Though this effect is not frequent in our use-case (pedestrians are often more isolated) and prevents the system from tracking pedestrians individually, it seems more useful for applications where objects of interest are often nearby, such as cancer cell detection.

6   Statistical Pitfalls

While very useful in practice, the probabilistic guarantees behind conformal prediction such as Theorem 1 should be interpreted with care. They rely on assumptions and have some limitations, which we outline below.

A Guarantee "on average" over the Box/Image Domain. As explained after Theorem 1, the inequality $P(Y \in C^\alpha(X)) \geq 1 - \alpha$ is a guarantee *on average* over calibration sets and test data points. In our use-case, this implies that the $1 - \alpha$ coverage is correct on average over all boxes/images at inference time, but might be incorrect in some subsets of the box/image domain. For example, for our box-wise conformalization experiment on the BDD100k dataset, when restricting the test set $\mathcal{D}_{\text{BDD}}^{test}$ to pedestrians that are close to the camera (height larger than 150 pixels), the coverage is smaller than 64% for a specified coverage of 70% ($\alpha = 0.3$), and smaller than 81% for a specified coverage of 90% ($\alpha = 0.1$).[6] Of course, a simple solution here is to apply conformal prediction for close pedestrians only (predicted height larger than 150 pixels). However, this solution cannot work in settings where a very large number of subdomains need to be distinguished (since calibration sets need to be large enough) or where these subdomains are not known a priori. In any case, due to the statistical nature of conformal prediction methods, one must keep in mind that there are some boxes or images on which these methods will fail at inference.

A Guarantee "on average" over Calibration Sets. Similarly, while the $1 - \alpha$ coverage is correct on average over all possible calibration sets, its value might be different for the single calibration set used in practice. The way the coverage varies from one calibration set to another was described in details in [1]. Next we illustrate this variability on BDD100k with box-wise conformalization (as in Sect. 4.3) and $\alpha = 0.1$, by re-sampling various calibration sets and reporting the associated test coverage values. The histogram on Fig. 4 (a) shows a large variability of coverage values, which means that different calibration sets lead to different coverage values at inference. Fortunately here, most values are above the specified coverage of 0.9 (since the margins are a little conservative due to the Bonferroni correction), but the tail probability on the left of 0.9 implies that the user has still a chance to use a calibration set that would result in a lower-than-expected coverage at inference. Recent works have proposed variants of conformal prediction (with more conservative margins) to deal with this variability (e.g., [4, 11]).

---

[6] These coverage values include statistical error margins at level 95%.

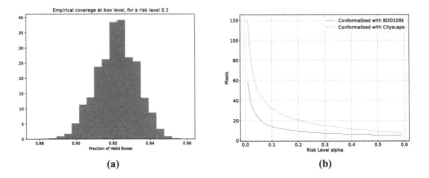

Fig. 4. (a) Empirical coverage distribution measured on same test set when sampling different calibration sets and applying box-wise conformalization as in Sect. 4.3. (b) Quantile curves $\alpha \mapsto q_\alpha^{y_{\max}}$ when calibrating with BDD100k or Cityscape training sets.

Datasets Requirements: Independence Assumption. As recalled in Sect. 2, several properties on the datasets are required for the probabilistic guarantee of Theorem 1 to be valid. This is not at all surprising due to the statistical nature of conformal prediction. The independence requirement (i) between all data involved (training, calibration, test) is to avoid overfitting issues. In particular, dependencies between training and calibration data could lead to measure artificially small errors R^i at conformalization, while dependencies within the calibration set may reduce statistical power in an uncontrolled manner.[7] In practice, the independence assumption seems difficult to guarantee or test, but data collection practices should aim at it. For the box-wise procedure of Sect. 4.3, it is not clear a priori that errors R^i are independent, because of possible intra-image dependencies between boxes. Dependencies seem a little easier to prevent in the image-wise setting of Sect. 5 (by, e.g., discarding neighboring images in a sequence). For our use-case however, our box-wise and image-wise test coverage values, which reach specified coverage, are really encouraging.

Distribution Shift Between Calibration and Test. We now investigate the importance of the dataset requirement (ii) of Sect. 2. To that end, we use our model calibrated on $\mathcal{D}_{\mathrm{BDD}}^{calib}$ for the box-wise criterion, as in Sect. 4.3, but we test its coverage on a new dataset, namely the Cityscape validation set [9]. This might be a reasonable thing to do, as both datasets are quite similar (they include urban scenes for autonomous driving scenarios). Yet the obtained coverage on this new dataset is 0.790 for $\alpha = 0.1$, i.e. significantly lower than expected. On the opposite, the coverage on $\mathcal{D}_{\mathrm{BDD}}^{test}$ is 0.924, which is consistent with the expected guarantee. In our haste to apply our methods on new data, we misinterpreted the offered guarantee: even if conceptually similar, the two datasets (the one used for calibration and test) probably do not share the same intrinsic data

---

[7] In fact, conformal guarantees work slightly beyond independence—under a so-called "exchangeability" assumption [1,23,37].

distribution, as confirmed by the two different quantile curves on Fig. 4 (b). This invalidates the data-related assumptions described in Sect. 2, and consequently the offered guarantee. While this is obviously a contrived example, in many practical situations it is quite easy to mislead oneself into believing that the data processed at inference time follows exactly the same distribution as the one used for the calibration of the model. Properly specifying the calibration set is a first important direction to address this issue. Another direction consists in explicitly taking *distribution shift* into account, and was recently addressed by conformal prediction methods such as [3,35]. In our future work, we aim to apply these results on our own experiments.

7   Discussions and Future Works

In this paper we present a practical guideline of how conformal prediction methods can be applied to object localization to provide uncertainty estimations with probabilistic guarantees. We illustrate the essential aspects on a pedestrian localization use case. We propose several variants of conformal prediction methods that provide guarantees at various levels (coordinate, bounding box or image) and with different non-conformity scores. Finally, we highlight several statistical aspects that one must take into account, and discuss the interpretation of the obtained guarantees.

An Engineering Choice. Conformal prediction methods rely on the choice of a non-conformity score that can be designed according to the targetted task and a priori knowledge. For example, if we wish to differentiate the level of uncertainties w.r.t. the size of the object we can normalize the scores of Eq. 3 by the width and height of the predicted box, i.e., $\tilde{R}^i_{x_{\min}} = R^i_{x_{\min}}/\Delta^i_x, \tilde{R}^i_{x_{\max}} = R^i_{x_{\max}}/\Delta^i_x$, where $\Delta^i_x = |\hat{x}^i_{\max} - \hat{x}^i_{\min}|$ (and similarly for the y coordinates). Such scores would lead to margins that scale multiplicatively with the size of the predicted object. Though this is undesirable for our pedestrian use-case (since pedestrians that are close to the camera correspond to the largest objects), this might be useful in applications where we are ready to pay larger margins for larger objects. Likewise, we can extend proposed scores as to compute simultaneously an inner and outer conformal bounding box covering most of the true boxes (by considering errors in absolute value). Note that the choice of the non-conformity score can also help to analyze the data quality in test or calibration sets: high scores can be indicative of 'extreme cases', such as suspicious inputs or anomalous annotations.

Future Work. This paper focused on the localization task. Next we will address the classification problem, and the interplay between the two—that is, the global detection problem. At a system level, it would also be important to build a link between such statistical guarantees and safety-related risks (e.g., fault rate). This task is however difficult, as this necessarily relies on additional assumptions and uncertainties [6]. All these aspects, together with the numerous potential statistical pitfalls, including a proper specification of the calibration set, open up very challenging research avenues.

Acknowledgements. This work has benefited from the AI Interdisciplinary Institute ANITI, which is funded by the French "Investing for the Future - PIA3" program under the Grant agreement ANR-19-P3IA-0004. The authors gratefully acknowledge the support of the DEEL project (https://www.deel.ai/).

References

1. Angelopoulos, A.N., Bates, S.: A gentle introduction to conformal prediction and distribution-free uncertainty quantification (2021). arXiv:2107.07511
2. Azevedo, T., de Jong, R., Maji, P.: Stochastic-YOLO: efficient probabilistic object detection under dataset shifts. In: ML4AD Workshop, NeurIPS 2020 (2020)
3. Barber, R.F., Candes, E.J., Ramdas, A., Tibshirani, R.J.: Conformal prediction beyond exchangeability (2022). arXiv:2202.13415
4. Bates, S., Angelopoulos, A., Lei, L., Malik, J., Jordan, M.I.: Distribution-free, risk-controlling prediction sets. J. ACM **68**(6), 1–34 (2021)
5. Bickel, P.J., Doksum, K.A.: Mathematical Statistics: Basic Ideas and Selected Topics, vol. 1. Chapman and Hall/CRC, London (2015)
6. Bonnin, H., et al.: Can we reconcile safety objectives with machine learning performances? In: ERTS 2022 (2022)
7. Carion, N., Massa, F., Synnaeve, G., Usunier, N., Kirillov, A., Zagoruyko, S.: End-to-end object detection with transformers. In: Vedaldi, A., Bischof, H., Brox, T., Frahm, J.-M. (eds.) ECCV 2020. LNCS, vol. 12346, pp. 213–229. Springer, Cham (2020). https://doi.org/10.1007/978-3-030-58452-8_13
8. Chih-Hong Cheng, T.S., Burton, S.: Logically sound arguments for the effectiveness of ML safety measures (2021). arXiv:2111.02649
9. Cordts, M., et al.: The cityscapes dataset for semantic urban scene understanding. In: CVPR 2016 (2016)
10. Deepshikha, K., Yelleni, S.H., Srijith, P.K., Mohan, C.K.: Monte Carlo DropBlock for modelling uncertainty in object detection (2021). arXiv:2108.03614
11. Ducoffe, M., Gerchinovitz, S., Sen Gupta, J.: A high-probability safety guarantee for shifted neural network surrogates. In: SafeAI 2020 (2020)
12. Feng, D., Harakeh, A., Waslander, S.L., Dietmayer, K.: A review and comparative study on probabilistic object detection in autonomous driving. IEEE T-ITS, 1–20 (2021)
13. Girshick, R.B.: Fast R-CNN. In: ICCV 2015 (2015)
14. Girshick, R.B., Donahue, J., Darrell, T., Malik, J.: Rich feature hierarchies for accurate object detection and semantic segmentation. In: CVPR 2014 (2014)
15. Harakeh, A., Smart, M., Waslander, S.L.: BayesOD: a Bayesian approach for uncertainty estimation in deep object detectors. In: ICRA 2020 (2020)
16. Kendall, A., Gal, Y.: What uncertainties do we need in Bayesian deep learning for computer vision? In: NeurIPS 2017 (2017)
17. Kläs, M., Jöckel, L.: A framework for building uncertainty wrappers for AI/ML-based data-driven components. In: Casimiro, A., Ortmeier, F., Schoitsch, E., Bitsch, F., Ferreira, P. (eds.) SAFECOMP 2020. LNCS, vol. 12235, pp. 315–327. Springer, Cham (2020). https://doi.org/10.1007/978-3-030-55583-2_23
18. Kläs, M., Sembach, L.: Uncertainty wrappers for data-driven models: increase the transparency of AI/ML-based models through enrichment with dependable situation-aware uncertainty estimates. In: WAISE 2019 (2019)
19. Kraus, F., Dietmayer, K.: Uncertainty estimation in one-stage object detection. In: ITSC 2019 (2019)

20. Kuhn, H.W.: The Hungarian method for the assignment problem. Naval Res. Logistics Q. **2**(1–2), 83–97 (1955)

21. Lakshminarayanan, B., Pritzel, A., Blundell, C.: Simple and scalable predictive uncertainty estimation using deep ensembles. In: NeurIPS 2017 (2017)

22. Le, M.T., Diehl, F., Brunner, T., Knol, A.: Uncertainty estimation for deep neural object detectors in safety-critical applications. In: ITSC 2018 (2018)

23. Lei, J., G'Sell, M., Rinaldo, A., Tibshirani, R.J., Wasserman, L.: Distribution-free predictive inference for regression. JASA **113**(523), 1094–1111 (2018)

24. Lin, T., Dollar, P., Girshick, R., He, K., Hariharan, B., Belongie, S.: Feature pyramid networks for object detection. In: CVPR 2017 (2017)

25. Lin, T., Goyal, P., Girshick, R., He, K., Dollar, P.: Focal loss for dense object detection. IEEE T-PAMI **42**(02), 318–327 (2020)

26. Lin, T.-Y., et al.: Microsoft COCO: common objects in context. In: Fleet, D., Pajdla, T., Schiele, B., Tuytelaars, T. (eds.) ECCV 2014. LNCS, vol. 8693, pp. 740–755. Springer, Cham (2014). https://doi.org/10.1007/978-3-319-10602-1_48

27. Liu, W., et al.: SSD: single shot MultiBox detector. In: Leibe, B., Matas, J., Sebe, N., Welling, M. (eds.) ECCV 2016. LNCS, vol. 9905, pp. 21–37. Springer, Cham (2016). https://doi.org/10.1007/978-3-319-46448-0_2

28. Lyu, Z., Gutierrez, N., Rajguru, A., Beksi, W.J.: Probabilistic object detection via deep ensembles. In: Bartoli, A., Fusiello, A. (eds.) ECCV 2020. LNCS, vol. 12540, pp. 67–75. Springer, Cham (2020). https://doi.org/10.1007/978-3-030-65414-6_7

29. Miller, D., Dayoub, F., Milford, M., Sunderhauf, N.: Evaluating merging strategies for sampling-based uncertainty techniques in object detection. In: ICRA 2019 (2019)

30. Miller, D., Nicholson, L., Dayoub, F., Sünderhauf, N.: Dropout sampling for robust object detection in open-set conditions. In: ICRA 2018 (2018)

31. Redmon, J., Divvala, S., Girshick, R., Farhadi, A.: You only look once: unified, real-time object detection. In: CVPR 2016 (2016)

32. Redmon, J., Farhadi, A.: YOLO9000: better, faster, stronger. In: CVPR 2017 (2017)

33. Redmon, J., Farhadi, A.: YOLOv3: an incremental improvement (2018). arXiv:1804.02767

34. Rucklidge, W.: Efficiently locating objects using the hausdorff distance. IJCV **24**, 251–270 (1997)

35. Tibshirani, R.J., Barber, R.F., Candes, E.J., Ramdas, A.: Conformal prediction under covariate shift. In: NeurIPS 2019 (2019)

36. Schuster, T., Seferis, E., Burton, S., Cheng, C.H.: Unaligned but safe - formally compensating performance limitations for imprecise 2D object detection (2022). arXiv:2202.05123

37. Vovk, V., Gammerman, A., Shafer, G.: Algorithmic Learning in a Random World. Springer, New York (2005). https://doi.org/10.1007/b106715

38. Yu, F., et al.: BDD100K: a diverse driving dataset for heterogeneous multitask learning (2018). arXiv:1805.04687

Interval Weight-Based Abstraction for Neural Network Verification

Fateh Boudardara[1]([✉]) [iD], Abderraouf Boussif[1], Pierre-Jean Meyer[2],
and Mohamed Ghazel[1,2]

[1] Technological Research Institute Railenium, 180 rue Joseph-Louis Lagrange,
59308 Valenciennes, France
{fateh.boudardara,abderraouf.boussif}@railenium.eu
[2] Univ Gustave Eiffel, COSYS-ESTAS, 20 rue Élisée Reclus,
59666 Villeneuve d'Ascq, France
{pierre-jean.meyer,mohamed.ghazel}@univ-eiffel.fr

Abstract. In recent years, neural networks (NNs) have gained much maturity and efficiency, and their applications have spread to various domains, including some modules of safety-critical systems. On the other hand, recent studies have demonstrated that NNs are vulnerable to adversarial attacks, thus a neural network model must be verified and certified before its deployment. Despite the number of existing formal verification methods of neural networks, verifying a large network remains a major challenge for these methods. This is mostly due to the scalability limitations of these approaches and the non-linearity introduced by the activation functions in the NNs. To help tackle this issue, we propose a novel abstraction method that allows the reduction of the NN size while preserving its behavioural features. The main idea of the approach is to reduce the size of the original neural network by merging neurons belonging to the same layer, and defining the new weights as intervals and sums of absolute values of those of the merged neurons. The approach allows for producing an abstract (i.e., reduced) model that is smaller and simpler to verify, while guaranteeing that this abstract model is an over-approximation of the original one. Our early experiments show that the approach enhances the scalability when performing verification operations, such as output range computation, on the abstract model.

Keywords: Neural network abstraction · Neural network verification · Over-approximation · Output range computation

1 Introduction

Neural networks (NNs) are a machine learning technique that is extensively integrated today in several domains, such as financial transactions and trading, image recognition and object detection [13]. Moreover, NNs are increasingly deployed in safety-critical systems such as autonomous vehicles and trains [3, 18]. The standard evaluation methods of neural networks, that rely on running

M. Trapp et al. (Eds.): SAFECOMP 2022 Workshops, LNCS 13415, pp. 330–342, 2022.
https://doi.org/10.1007/978-3-031-14862-0_24

a series of tests on a finite subset of sample input data, cannot provide any guarantee on the unseen samples. Indeed, these methods have proven to be sensitive and easy to fool by applying imperceptible perturbations. For instance, some undesired behaviours can be generated by applying small perturbations on the inputs [12,22]. This raises the issue about how these models can be verified and certified when it comes to deploy them in safety-critical systems.

Being given the accomplishments of formal methods in proving safety features in different software and hardware systems including in safety-critical applications [2,4], the idea of applying these methods on NNs has attracted a lot of attention; significant progress has been achieved in recent years and many NN verification methods and tools are developed [8,23]. In fact, NN verification methods can be classified into two main groups: complete and incomplete. Complete verification methods, also called exact methods, encode the exact behaviour of the model and the property to verify as linear programming (LP) problem, and then apply an adequate LP-solver to perform the verification. Mixed-Integer Linear Programming (MILP) and SAT/SMT based methods are the main techniques in this category of NN verification methods [5,6,9,11,15]. Because of the non-linearity of NNs (related to non-linear activation functions), these methods are able to verify only small networks. In contrast, incomplete methods construct an abstract model, generally by linearizing the activation function using abstract domains [20], linear functions [6] or some quadratic functions [25]. These methods are more scalable and can verify larger NNs, but since they actually investigate over-approximations of the model, they suffer from spurious counterexamples.

The main challenge of the aforementioned works lies in their scalability; indeed, the existing methods do not scale to verify large NNs [8,23]. To handle this issue, some model reduction methods are proposed [1,7,16,17,19,21]. The broad concept of these methods is to reduce the size of the neural network by merging some similar-behaving neurons while guaranteeing an over-approximation of the original network. This ensures that the property at hand holds on the original network whenever it holds on the reduced one.

In this work, we propose a novel NN reduction method to enhance the scalability of NN verification techniques. The method consists in merging nodes in the same layer based on formulas for calculating their incoming and outgoing weights. The obtained model $\overline{N}$ over-approximates[1] the behavior of the original one N, i.e., for every input x, the output y of N is included in the set of outputs $\overline{Y}$ of $\overline{N}$. The obtained network $\overline{N}$ is called an interval neural network since it may have interval weights [17]. To evaluate the efficiency of the proposed approach, we implemented it as a Python framework and used it to build the abstract model.

With regard to the related works, the closest approaches to our work are those proposed by Prabhakar and Afzal [17] and Elboher et al. [7]. The former is based on taking the interval hull of the incoming and the outgoing weights of the merged neurons. In our method, we replace the outgoing weights by the sum of the absolute value of the weights to enhance the precision. Elboher et al. [7]

[1] With a slight abuse of notation, we write $N \subseteq \overline{N}$.

abstract the outgoing weights by taking their sum after ensuring that they have all the same sign (positive or negative). In addition, the abstraction of incoming weights is done by either taking their *min* or *max* depending on the category of the merged neurons (only neurons belonging to the same category can be merged); hence an important preprossessing phase is required before applying the abstraction. In our approach, no preprossessing phase is required and, theoretically, all neurons of the same layer may be merged together. In addition, and unlike these approaches that support only NNs with *Relu*, our approach can abstract networks with *Tanh* and *Relu* activation functions; furthermore, it can be extended to cover a wide range of activation functions.

The remaining of this paper is structured as follows: in Sect. 2 we provide a technical background on NNs and their verification. Section 3 is devoted to presenting our abstraction approach. Section 4 is dedicated to the numerical evaluation of the approach based on the ACAS Xu benchmark. Finally, Sect. 5 provides some concluding remarks and future work directions.

2   Background

2.1   Neural Networks

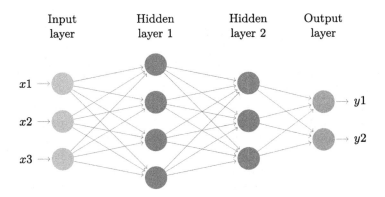

Fig. 1. Example of a neural network

A neural network N is a set of layers $L = \{l_0, l_1, ...l_n\}$ where l_0 and l_n are the input and the output layer, respectively, and $H_l = \{l_i : 1 \leq i \leq n-1\}$ is the set of hidden layers. Each layer l_i contains a set of nodes S_i, such that $\forall\, 1 \leq i \leq n$, a node $s_{ij} \in S_i$ is connected to all the nodes $s_{i-1,k}$ of the predecessor layer l_{i-1} with weighted edges $w^i_{jk} = w(s_{i-1,k}, s_{ij})$. Accordingly, the value $v(s_{ij})$ of a node $s_{ij} \in S_i : 1 \leq i \leq n$ can be calculated using Eq. 1.

$$\begin{cases} z(s_{ij}) = \sum_{s \in S_{i-1}} w(s, s_{ij}) \times v(s) + b_{s_{ij}} \\ v(s_{ij}) = \alpha(z(s_{ij})) \end{cases} \tag{1}$$

where $\alpha : \mathbb{R} \rightarrow \mathbb{R}$ is the activation function of node s_{ij}, and $b_{s_{ij}}$ is its bias. Calculating the output of N for a given value of the input x is performed by calculating $v(s_{nj}), \forall s_{nj} \in S_n$. This can be done by initializing S_0 with the given values of x (x is a vector and $|S_0| = |x|$), and then repeatedly applying Eq. 1 to each hidden node $s_{ij} \in S_i, i \in \{1, 2, ..., n\}$. In this paper, and for the sake of simplicity and readability, z_{ij} can be used to denote the value of a node $s_{ij} \in S_i$ before activation instead of $z(s_{ij})$, similarly, the value after activation can be denoted as v_{ij}. Besides, the value of a hidden layer l_i for a given input is represented by the column vector $V_i = [v_{i1}, v_{i2}, ..., v_{i|S_i|}]^T$.

Prabhalar and Afzal [17] introduced a new representation of neural networks called interval neural networks (INNs). The weights of edges in INNs are intervals $w = [w^l, w^u]$ instead of scalars as in classic NNs. It is worth noticing that the classic neural networks can be considered as a particular case of INNs where $w^l = w^u$. The general structure along with the operations on INNs are similar to those on NNs.

As mentioned before, α in Eq. 1 is an activation function. Recall that there are various types of activation functions which are used in NNs. Equations 2 and 3 represent *Relu* and *Tanh* activation functions, respectively.

$$relu(x) = max(0, x) ; \qquad x \in \mathbb{R} \qquad (2)$$

$$tanh(x) = \frac{e^x - e^{-x}}{e^x + e^{-x}} ; \qquad x \in \mathbb{R} \qquad (3)$$

A neural network can be seen as a function $\mathcal{N} : \mathbb{R}^{|S_0|} \rightarrow \mathbb{R}^{|S_n|}$, such that: $\mathcal{N}(x) = f_n(f_{n-1}(...(f_1(x))...))$, where f_i is the corresponding function of layer l_i, for $1 \leq i \leq n$. Figure 1 depicts a network of 3 inputs, 2 hidden layers and 2 outputs. Its associated function is: $\mathcal{N} : \mathbb{R}^3 \rightarrow \mathbb{R}^2$, s.t: $\mathcal{N}(x) = f_3(f_2(f_1(x)))$.

Remark 1. Notice that a neural network with α activation function (denoted as α-NN) means that the same function α is applied on all its hidden layers. For instance, a *Relu*-NN (resp. *Tanh*-NN) has only *Relu* (resp. *Tanh*) activation functions.

2.2 Verification of Neural Networks

Formal verification is the process of checking the correctness of a system model M with respect to a set of specifications, i.e., to check whether or not a model of a system satisfies a set of requirements (specifications) [4]. A formal verification method is used to prove that some property P holds on a system-model M (denoted as $M \models P$); otherwise, some counterexamples illustrating that P is not satisfied by M ($M \not\models P$) can be issued.

Similarly, NN verification consists of determining whether the NN model N satisfies some property P, which is generally defined by a set of constraints on its input and output. That is to say, the NN verification problem can be defined by the tuple $\langle N, Pre, Post \rangle$ where N is the NN model, Pre is the set of input

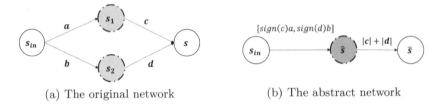

(a) The original network   (b) The abstract network

Fig. 2. An example explaining the main idea of the proposed approach.

constraints and **Post** is the set of output constraints [14]. Let us denote by $\mathcal{N} : \mathbb{R}^{|S_0|} \to \mathbb{R}^{|S_n|}$ the associated function of **N**, a verification property **P** on **N** can be formally expressed as:

$$\forall x \in \mathbb{R}^{|S_0|}, Pre(x) \implies Post(\mathcal{N}(x)) \tag{4}$$

3   Proposed Approach

3.1   Main Idea

In this paper, we propose a method to construct an over-approximation of NNs by merging neurons that belong to the same layer. To explain the general idea of the method, let us refer to Fig. 2 where the original network N is presented on Fig. 2a and its abstract network $\overline{N}$ after merging nodes s_1 and s_2 is presented on Fig. 2b. The challenge is how to determine the weights of the edges connecting the node $\hat{s}$ to the previous and the next layer, while ensuring that $y = v(s)$ is included in $\bar{y} = \hat{v}(\bar{s})$ for all possible values of s_{in} (keeping in mind that the values of nodes of the abstract network $\overline{N}$ are intervals). The value of s is $y = \alpha(c \times v(s_1) + d \times v(s_2))$, and the value of its associated abstract node $\bar{s}$ is $\bar{y} = \alpha(\hat{w}_2\hat{v}(\hat{s}))$, s.t: $\hat{v}(\hat{s}) = \alpha(\hat{w}_1 x)$, where $\hat{w}_2$ is the weight connecting $\hat{s}$ to $\bar{s}$ and $\hat{w}_1$ the weight $w(s_{in}, s)$. Our goal is to calculate $\bar{y}$ in such a way that $y \in \bar{y}$. We can define the abstract incoming weight of $\hat{s}$ as $\hat{w}_1 = [min(a, b), max(a, b)]$ to ensure that $v(s_1) \in \hat{v}(\hat{s})$ and $v(s_2) \in \hat{v}(\hat{s})$. The next step is to define $\hat{w}_2$. One way to do that is to sum c and d, i.e., $\hat{w}_2 = c + d$. However, in case of $c = -d$, the sum would be zero (which leads to always having $\bar{y} = 0$). To avoid that, we take the sum of the absolute value of c and d, and we transfer the signs of c and d backward to the previous layer's weights. The formula for calculating the interval weights will be provided in the sequel for $Tanh$ and $Relu$ activation functions.

For the sake of clarity, we firstly provide the abstraction formula for the case of merging two neurons. Then, we discuss the general formula when it comes to the case of merging a set of neurons.

Let us consider the example in Fig. 3 showing a sub-network that contains three hidden layers with the same activation function α, and we aim to merge neurons s_{ip} and s_{iq} of layer l_i. The incoming weights to s_{ip} and s_{iq} are denoted by a_k and b_k, respectively. Formally, $a_k = w(s_{i-1,k}, s_{ip})$ and $b_k = w(s_{i-1,k}, s_{iq})$

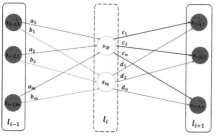
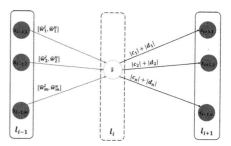
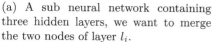

(a) A sub neural network containing three hidden layers, we want to merge the two nodes of layer l_i.

(b) The sub neural network after abstraction. Here $\hat{w}_k^l, \hat{w}_k^u : 1 \leq k \leq m$ are the weights calculated using formula (6)

Fig. 3. An illustration of our abstraction method applied on a hidden layer l_i. The model on the right is the abstraction of the one on the left, where the node $\hat{s}$ is obtained upon merging s_{ip} and s_{iq}.

for each $s_{i-1,k} \in S_{i-1}$. Analogously, we denote the outgoing weights by c_j and d_j such that $c_j = w(s_{ip}, s_{i+1,j})$ and $d_j = w(s_{iq}, s_{i+1,j})$, for all $s_{i+1,j} \in S_{i+1}$.

Definition 1. *We define the sign function in this paper as follows: sign :* $\mathbb{R} \rightarrow \{-1, 1\}$

$$sign(x) = \begin{cases} 1, & if \ x \geq 0 \\ -1, & otherwise \end{cases} \tag{5}$$

3.2 Abstraction for NNs with *Tanh*

In this part, we suppose that the used activation function $\alpha = tanh$. The abstraction of the two nodes of l_i is obtained by applying the steps presented in Procedure 1.

Procedure 1

1. *Create a new node $\hat{s}$*
2. *Calculate the incoming weights of $\hat{s}$:* $\forall s_{i-1,k} \in S_{i-1} : w(s_{i-1,k}, \hat{s}) = [\hat{w}_k^l, \hat{w}_k^u]$, *such that:*

$$\begin{cases} \hat{w}_k^l = \min_{1 \leq j \leq n} \{sign(c_j) \, a_k, sign(d_j) \, b_k\} \\ \hat{w}_k^u = \max_{1 \leq j \leq n} \{sign(c_j) \, a_k, sign(d_j) \, b_k\} \end{cases} \tag{6}$$

where $n = |S_{i+1}|$ is the the number of neurons of l_{i+1}.
3. *Calculate the outgoing weights of $\hat{s}$, namely* $\forall s_{i+1,j} \in S_{i+1}$:

$$\hat{w}(\hat{s}, s_{i+1,j}) = |c_j| + |d_j| \tag{7}$$

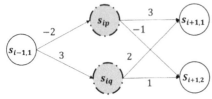
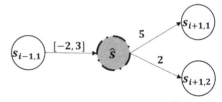

(a) The original model N: s_{ip} and s_{iq} of layer l_i are to be merged.

(b) The obtained model $\overline{N}$ after abstraction.

Fig. 4. An example of the abstraction method applied on two neurons of hidden layer l_i. Let us take $v(s_{i-1,1}) = 2$, then we have $v(s_{i+1,1}) = 0$ and $v(s_{i+1,2}) = 10$, $\hat{v}(s_{i+1,1}) = [-20, 30]$ and $\hat{v}(s_{i+1,2}) = [-8, 12]$. Hence, the over-approximation is fulfilled, since $v(s_{i+1,k}) \in \hat{v}(s_{i+1,k})$ for $k = 1, 2$.

4. *Calculate the biases of $\hat{s}$: $b_{\hat{s}} = [b_{\hat{s}}^l, b_{\hat{s}}^u]$, such that: $b_{\hat{s}}^l = \min\limits_{1 \le j \le n} \{sign(c_j)b_{s_{ip}},$*
   $sign(d_j)b_{s_{iq}}\}$ and $b_{\hat{s}}^u = \max\limits_{1 \le j \le n} \{sign(c_j)b_{s_{ip}}, sign(d_j)b_{s_{iq}}\}$, where $b_{s_{ip}}$ and $b_{s_{iq}}$
   are the biases of s_{ip} and s_{iq}, respectively.
5. *Remove s_{ip} and s_{iq} from S_i, add $\hat{s}$ to S_i and connect $\hat{s}$ to the nodes in l_{i-1} and l_{i+1} using the calculated weights.*

Procedure 1 can be applied repeatedly on the same layer to merge pairs of neurons, and can be iterated on multiple layers. An example depicting the execution of our abstraction method is given in Fig. 4.

Proposition 1. *Let N be a NN with Tanh activation function. The application of Procedure 1 on a hidden layer $l_i : i \in \{1, 2, \ldots, |N| - 1\}$, guarantees that for every possible value of $v_{i-1}(s), s \in S_{i-1}$: $v_{i+1} \in \hat{v}_{i+1}$.* ∎

Due to the limit on the number of pages, the proofs are omitted from this version of the paper.

Up to now, we have considered the procedure of abstraction through the successive merging of two neurons each time. Hereafter, we propose the generalized procedure to merge more than two nodes at the same time. This can be done by updating Eqs. 6 and 7, as follows:

Procedure 2
Lets denote by $\hat{S} \subseteq S_i$ the set of neurons to merged:

1. *Incoming weights of the abstract node $\hat{s}$:*

$$
\begin{cases}
\hat{w}_k^l = \min\limits_{s_i \in \hat{S}, s' \in S_{i+1}} \{sign(w(s_i, s')) \times w(s_{i-1,k}, s_i)\} \\
\hat{w}_k^u = \max\limits_{s_i \in \hat{S}, s' \in S_{i+1}} \{sign(w(s_i, s')) \times w(s_{i-1,k}, s_i)\}
\end{cases}
$$

2. *Outgoing weights for each $s' \in S_{i+1}$:*

$$
\hat{w}(\hat{s}, s') = \sum_{s_i \in \hat{S}} |w(s_i, s')|
$$

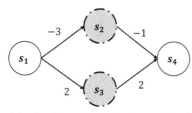

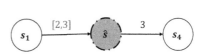

(a) A fragment of the original model N: we want to merge s_1 and s_2.

(b) The obtained partition after abstraction procedure defined by Equations 6 and 7.

Fig. 5. A counter-example of applying Procedure 1 on a *Relu* NNs.

Corollary 1. *Let N be a network with Tanh activation function, and $\overline{N}$ its abstract model obtained using Procedure 2 on one or multiple hidden layers. Then, the following holds: $N \subseteq \overline{N}$.* ∎

Remark 2. Applying the proposed abstraction method until saturation would result in a network with a single neuron in each hidden layer, which would be a massive reduction of the size of the original network. However, it is plain to state that there is a trade-off, between the size reduction of the original model and the precision of the obtained abstract model, to be considered.

In the previous section, we considered networks with *Tanh* activation function. In the next section, the approach will be adjusted to handle *Relu*-networks.

3.3   Abstraction for NNs with *Relu*

We present in this section an adaptation of Formula 6 in order to extend our abstraction technique to NNs with *Relu*. The *Relu* eliminates the negative values. Hence, when we shift the signs of c_j and d_j back to previous layer (see Fig. 3), the lower bound of the obtained output may be greater than the original output (as shown in Fig. 5); namely assume that $v(s_1) = 1$, then $v(s_4) = 4 \notin \hat{v}(s_4) = [6, 9]$. To tackle this issue, we propose the following procedure to calculate **the lower bound** of the incoming weights for NNs with *Relu* activation function.

Therefore, we update the main abstraction procedure, presented in Sect. 3.1, by adding a condition that checks whether the incoming and the outgoing weights have the same signs. Adding such a condition guarantees that the abstract model over-approximates the behaviour of the original one. For instance, let us apply the new abstraction procedure on the same sub-network presented in Fig. 5a. Assume again that $v(s_1) = 1$, then the value of s_4 is $v(s_4) = 4$. Its abstract sub-network is presented in Fig. 6; and for the same value of s_1 ($v(s_1) = 1$) $\hat{v}(s_4) = [0, 9]$; hence, $v(s_4) \in \hat{v}(s_4)$.

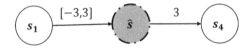

Fig. 6. An example illustrating the execution of Procedure 3 on a NN with *Relu*

Procedure 3

1. *Create a new node $\hat{s}$*
2. *Let c_j^* (resp. d_j^*) be the outgoing weight c_j (resp. d_j) such that $sign(c_j*)\,a_k = \min_{1 \leq j \leq n} \{sign(c_j)\,a_k\}$ (resp. $sign(d_j*)\,b_k = \min_{1 \leq j \leq n} \{sign(d_j)\,b_k\}$).*
   Calculate the incoming interval weights of $\hat{s}$ as follows: $\forall s_{i-1,k} \in S_{i-1}$, $w(s_{i-1,k}, \hat{s}) = [\hat{w}_k^l, \hat{w}_k^u]$, such that:
   (a) if $sign(a_k) \neq sign(c_j^*)$ or $sign(b_k) \neq sign(d_j^*)$, then:

$$\begin{cases} \hat{w}_k^l = \min_{1 \leq j \leq n} \{sign(c_j)\,a_k, sign(d_j)\,b_k\} \\ \hat{w}_k^u = \max_{1 \leq j \leq n} \{sign(c_j)\,a_k, sign(d_j)\,b_k\} \end{cases}$$

   (b) if $sign(a_k) = sign(c_j^*)$ and $sign(b_k) = sign(d_j^*)$ then:

$$\begin{cases} \hat{w}_k^l = \min\{a_k, b_k\} \\ \hat{w}_k^u = \max_{1 \leq j \leq n} \{sign(c_j)\,a_k, sign(d_j)\,b_k\} \end{cases}$$

3. *Calculate the outgoing weights of $\hat{s}$ as follows:*

$$\forall s_{i+1,j} \in S_{i+1}, \hat{w}(\hat{s}, s_{i+1,j}) = |c_j| + |d_j|$$

4. *Remove s_{ip} and s_{iq} from S_i, and add $\hat{s}$ to S_i. Connect $\hat{s}$ to the nodes in l_{i-1} and l_{i+1} using the calculated weights.*
5. *After applying the abstraction on all hidden layers, replace all the remaining scalar weights $w \in \mathbb{R}$ by an interval: $[min(w, 0), max(w, 0)]$.*

Proposition 2. *For a network N with the Relu activation function, applying the abstraction method defined in Procedure 3 on a layer $l_i : i \in \{1, \ldots, |N| - 1\}$ guarantees that for every possible value $v_{i-1}(s)$ of $s \in S_{i-1}$ and $\forall s_{i+1,j} \in S_{i+1}$: $v(s_{i+1,j}) \in v(\hat{s}_{i+1,j})$.* ∎

Notice that in Propositions 1 and 2, we assume that the layers l_{i-1}, l_i and l_{i+1} have the same activation function (either *Tanh* or *Relu*).

4   Early Experiments

We implemented our abstraction method as a Python framework while considering a NNET format reader [10]. The user can set the abstraction's parameters, such as the maximum number of nodes on each layer after abstraction and the strategy of nodes selection. In our analysis, we simply used random selection, but different nodes' selection strategies (using heuristics for instance) can be integrated. To evaluate the performance of our proposed method, we conducted a series of experiments on the ACAS Xu benchmark [10]. This benchmark is a set of 45 NNs pertaining to an airborne-collision avoidance system. Each network has 300 hidden nodes (6 hidden layers with 50 neurons each), 7 inputs and 5 outputs.

After uploading the model N from the NNET file[2], we generate 5 abstract models $\overline{N}_i$, $i \in \{1, 2, 3, 4, 5\}$ with 5, 15, 25, 35 and 45 nodes on all hidden layers, respectively. We also considered some constraints on the NN input, namely specified by property ϕ_5 as defined in [11]. Moreover, we used the Interval Bound Propagation (IBP) algorithm [24] for calculating the output range of N and abstract networks $\overline{N}_i$. Over 50 random runs, we calculated the average of the abstraction time for each abstract network $\overline{N}_i$ and we compared the average of the output ranges (upper bound) and the IBP computation time of abstract networks to those of the original network N. The obtained results are summarized in Figs. 7a, 7b, 8.

From Fig. 7a, we can observe that the precision of the abstract model highly depends on the number of the merged nodes, i.e., allowing for more abstract nodes leads to less precise abstract models. Contrarily, the output computation time is proportional to the number of nodes on each layer as shown in Fig. 7b. It is straightforward to notice that the fewer the number of nodes of each layer, the faster the computation is performed. Although IBP is among the fastest verification methods, its computation time is significantly higher than the abstraction time which can be neglected if a more costly verification method is applied.

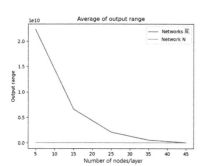 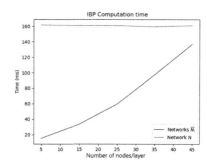

(a) Average of upper output range on dimension 1

(b) IBP computation time on the original and the reduced models

Fig. 7. Comparison between the output and computation time of the original and the abstract models

---

[2] The network $ACASXU\_experimental\_v2a\_1\_1.nnet$ is used in this work.

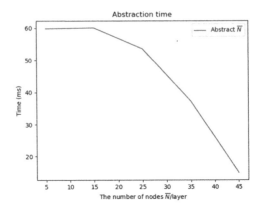

Fig. 8. Abstraction time for different size of abstract models.

5   Conclusion

In this paper, we proposed a novel NN reduction method for the sake of enhancing the efficiency of various analysis operation that can be performed on NNs, such as, for instance, the computation of the output range (for invariant's checking for instance) or any other verification operations. Our method can be applied on both feed-forward *Tanh*-NN and *Relu*-NN. Yet, the approach can be extended to further activation functions. The model reduction approach guarantees that the abstract model is an over-approximation of the original one. Therefore, once some property is satisfied on the abstract model $\overline{N}$, it necessarily holds on the original one N.

The approach is implemented using Python, and an experimental study was conducted to analyse the efficiency and the precision of the generated abstract model. The conducted experiments on the basis of a state-of-the-art benchmark show how the precision of the abstract model is impacted by the size of its hidden layers. Furthermore, we showed that the proposed method can effectively reduce the output range computation time.

In the present paper, we proved the over-approximation of the abstract model w.r.t. the original one in the case of *Tanh* and *Relu* activation functions. In future work, we aim to extend the proof to consider the *Sigmoid*, *Leaky Relu* and *SELU* activation functions. In addition, in the present work, the nodes to be merged were selected randomly; but we intend to develop some nodes' selection heuristics that can improve the precision of the abstract model.

Acknowledgements. This research work contributes to the french collaborative project TASV (autonomous passengers service train), with Railenium, SNCF, Alstom Crespin, Thales, Bosch, and SpirOps. It was carried out in the framework of IRT Railenium, Valenciennes, France, and therefore was granted public funds within the scope of the French Program "Investissements d'Avenir".

References

1. Ashok, P., Hashemi, V., Křetínský, J., Mohr, S.: DeepAbstract: neural network abstraction for accelerating verification. In: Hung, D.V., Sokolsky, O. (eds.) ATVA 2020. LNCS, vol. 12302, pp. 92–107. Springer, Cham (2020). https://doi.org/10.1007/978-3-030-59152-6_5
2. Biere, A., Heule, M., van Maaren, H.: Handbook of Satisfiability, vol. 185. IOS Press, Amsterdam (2009)
3. Bojarski, M., et al.: End to end learning for self-driving cars. arXiv preprint (2016)
4. Clarke, E.M., Henzinger, T.A., Veith, H., Bloem, R., et al.: Handbook of Model Checking, vol. 10. Springer, Cham (2018). https://doi.org/10.1007/978-3-319-10575-8
5. Dutta, S., Jha, S., Sankaranarayanan, S., Tiwari, A.: Output range analysis for deep feedforward neural networks. In: Proceedings 10th NASA Formal Methods, pp. 121–138 (2018)
6. Ehlers, R.: Formal verification of piece-wise linear feed-forward neural networks. In: D'Souza, D., Narayan Kumar, K. (eds.) ATVA 2017. LNCS, vol. 10482, pp. 269–286. Springer, Cham (2017). https://doi.org/10.1007/978-3-319-68167-2_19
7. Elboher, Y.Y., Gottschlich, J., Katz, G.: An abstraction-based framework for neural network verification. In: Lahiri, S.K., Wang, C. (eds.) CAV 2020. LNCS, vol. 12224, pp. 43–65. Springer, Cham (2020). https://doi.org/10.1007/978-3-030-53288-8_3
8. Huang, X., et al.: A survey of safety and trustworthiness of deep neural networks: verification, testing, adversarial attack and defence, and interpretability. Comput. Sci. Rev. **37**, 100270 (2020)
9. Huang, X., Kwiatkowska, M., Wang, S., Wu, M.: Safety verification of deep neural networks. In: Majumdar, R., Kunčak, V. (eds.) CAV 2017. LNCS, vol. 10426, pp. 3–29. Springer, Cham (2017). https://doi.org/10.1007/978-3-319-63387-9_1
10. Julian, K.D., Lopez, J., Brush, J.S., Owen, M.P., Kochenderfer, M.J.: Policy compression for aircraft collision avoidance systems. In: 2016 IEEE/AIAA 35th Digital Avionics Systems Conference (DASC), pp. 1–10. IEEE (2016)
11. Katz, G., Barrett, C., Dill, D.L., Julian, K., Kochenderfer, M.J.: Reluplex: an efficient SMT solver for verifying deep neural networks. In: Majumdar, R., Kunčak, V. (eds.) CAV 2017. LNCS, vol. 10426, pp. 97–117. Springer, Cham (2017). https://doi.org/10.1007/978-3-319-63387-9_5
12. Kurakin, A., Goodfellow, I.J., Bengio, S.: Adversarial examples in the physical world. In: Artificial Intelligence Safety and Security, pp. 99–112. Chapman and Hall/CRC (2018)
13. LeCun, Y., Bengio, Y., Hinton, G.: Deep learning. Nature **521**(7553), 436–444 (2015)
14. Leofante, F., Narodytska, N., Pulina, L., Tacchella, A.: Automated verification of neural networks: advances, challenges and perspectives. arXiv preprint arXiv:1805.09938 (2018)
15. Lomuscio, A., Maganti, L.: An approach to reachability analysis for feed-forward ReLU neural networks. arXiv preprint (2017)
16. Prabhakar, P.: Bisimulations for neural network reduction. In: Finkbeiner, B., Wies, T. (eds.) VMCAI 2022. LNCS, vol. 13182, pp. 285–300. Springer, Cham (2022). https://doi.org/10.1007/978-3-030-94583-1_14
17. Prabhakar, P., Rahimi Afzal, Z.: Abstraction based output range analysis for neural networks. Adv. Neural Inf. Process Syst. **32** (2019)

18. Ristić-Durrant, D., Franke, M., Michels, K.: A review of vision-based on-board obstacle detection and distance estimation in railways. Sensors **21**(10), 3452 (2021)
19. Shriver, D., Xu, D., Elbaum, S., Dwyer, M.B.: Refactoring neural networks for verification. arXiv preprint (2019)
20. Singh, G., Gehr, T., Püschel, M., Vechev, M.: An abstract domain for certifying neural networks. Proc. ACM Program. Lang. **3**(POPL), 1–30 (2019)
21. Sotoudeh, M., Thakur, A.V.: Abstract neural networks. In: Pichardie, D., Sighireanu, M. (eds.) SAS 2020. LNCS, vol. 12389, pp. 65–88. Springer, Cham (2020). https://doi.org/10.1007/978-3-030-65474-0_4
22. Szegedy, C., et al.: Intriguing properties of neural networks. arXiv preprint (2013)
23. Urban, C., Miné, A.: A review of formal methods applied to machine learning. arXiv preprint (2021)
24. Xiang, W., Tran, H.D., Yang, X., Johnson, T.T.: Reachable set estimation for neural network control systems: a simulation-guided approach. IEEE Trans. Neural Netw. Learn. Syst. **32**(5), 1821–1830 (2020)
25. Zhang, H., Weng, T.W., Chen, P.Y., Hsieh, C.J., Daniel, L.: Efficient neural network robustness certification with general activation functions. arXiv preprint (2018)

Logically Sound Arguments for the Effectiveness of ML Safety Measures

Chih-Hong Cheng$^{(\boxtimes)}$, Tobias Schuster, and Simon Burton

Fraunhofer IKS, Munich, Germany
{chih-hong.cheng,tobias.schuster,simon.burton}@iks.fraunhofer.de

Abstract. We investigate the issues of achieving sufficient rigor in the arguments for the safety of machine learning functions. By considering the known weaknesses of DNN-based 2D bounding box detection algorithms, we sharpen the metric of imprecise pedestrian localization by associating it with the safety goal. The sharpening leads to introducing a conservative post-processor after the standard non-max-suppression as a counter-measure. We then propose a semi-formal assurance case for arguing the effectiveness of the post-processor, which is further translated into formal proof obligations for demonstrating the soundness of the arguments. Applying theorem proving not only discovers the need to introduce missing claims and mathematical concepts but also reveals the limitation of Dempster-Shafer's rules used in semi-formal argumentation.

1 Introduction

Ensuring safety has been considered one of the critical barriers in realizing autonomous driving functionalities. While newly developed safety standards such as ISO 21448 SOTIF [1] address hazards directly caused by the intended functionality such as performance limitations of perception modules, it only provides a high-level methodology for safety assurance, and how one implements the process and the resulting evidence construction are left for interpretation.

In this paper, we study how to achieve sufficient rigor in the safety argumentation for *Deep Neural Networks* (DNN) [7] using an example of 2D object detection. In contrast to classical software, deep neural networks offer a more direct approach to quantify the risk associated with the software. Nevertheless, the first barrier towards scientific rigor occurs due to standard quality attributes for evaluating the performance of DNNs having very obscure connections to safety. We demonstrate with a simple example that the widely used Intersection-over-Union (IoU) metric may not be positively correlated to simple safety goals such as avoiding collisions. We then use a simple criterion to evaluate the DNN perception module against their impact on safety. For issues caused by localization

This work is funded by the Bavarian Ministry for Economic Affairs, Regional Development and Energy as part of a project to support the thematic development of the Fraunhofer Institute for Cognitive Systems.

M. Trapp et al. (Eds.): SAFECOMP 2022 Workshops, LNCS 13415, pp. 343–350, 2022.
https://doi.org/10.1007/978-3-031-14862-0_25

imprecision, the simple and direct criterion leads to an introduction of a safety post-processor whose configuration is determined after training is completed.

Subsequently, we utilize the semi-formal Goal Structuring Notation (GSN) [6] to detail arguments why introducing such a post-processor is sufficient to achieve the safety goal. Due to the clarity of the newly introduced safety metrics, we can *formulate all semi-formal specifications into logical formulae*, and try to formally deduce that the arguments are sufficient to derive the goal using interactive theorem proving [9]. This deduction step is critical to achieve the desired rigor for safety-critical ML systems - There exists a fundamental difference between claims (supported by a qualitative, semi-formal argument) and proven conjectures. In our example, the deduction fails unless we introduce (1) additional problem-specific claims and (2) mathematical concepts as lemmas. This initial result demonstrates the possibility of bringing mathematical rigor in the safety argumentation of DNNs, provided that the definition of safety and the associated evaluation function are made available.

Finally, moving towards quantitative argumentation, the failed logical deduction highlights the *limitation of existing semi-formal approaches in evidence combination* based on Dempster-Shafer's evidence theory [5,10]. Precisely, when using GSNs in the SOTIF context, the computed probability based on evidence combination shall be viewed as a claim or as an upper bound. The corollary is that quantitative safety assessment of machine learning functions is only valid when the connection between low-level arguments and high-level goals is sound through logical deduction.[1]

2   Addressing Insufficiencies in Object Detection

In this section, we consider an example of vision-based 2D object detection using deep neural networks. To ease understanding, some of the statements or assumptions are simplified to establish the formal proof. Readers may extrapolate the ideas stated in this section and integrate various corner cases that one should consider when encountering real-world scenarios.

(Background). Given an image, a 2D object detector generates *bounding boxes* around the area where it considers an existing object (e.g., pedestrian) with high probability. To train such an object detector, one provides a *data set*; each data point in the data set is an image together with its associated ground truth bounding boxes. Ideally, the data set should be a *good approximation* of the *operational design domain* (ODD) where the object detector is used.

(Understanding the Meaning of Safe Perception). For autonomous vehicles, one hazardous scenario occurs when an un-occluded pedestrian within a certain distance is not properly identified. It is necessary to precise the definition of "properly identifying a pedestrian", as in the SOTIF process, one needs to make

---

[1] Due to space limits, we refer readers to the extended version [2] for details including the formal proof.

sure that the probability of improper identification is sufficiently low. Very commonly, one then proceeds by associating "proper detection" with quality attributes/performance metrics widely used in machine learning.

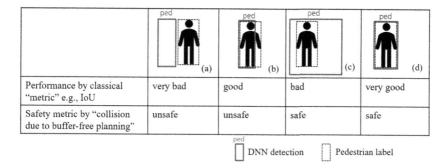

	(a)	(b)	(c)	(d)
Performance by classical "metric" e.g., IoU	very bad	good	bad	very good
Safety metric by "collision due to buffer-free planning"	unsafe	unsafe	safe	safe

Fig. 1. Standard performance metrics such as IoU may be incorrectly related to safety

Nevertheless, as this association step is commonly done informally, the ambiguity can lead to severe problems in safety. For example, consider the four sub-cases listed in Fig. 1, where we show the DNN prediction and the ground truth label, both as bounding boxes. Between a prediction bounding box and a label bounding box, the commonly used *Intersection-over-Union (IoU)* metric computes the area of overlap (of two bounding boxes) against the area over the union (of two bounding boxes). One can derive that the computed IoU values for Fig. 1(a) and Fig. 1(d) equal 0 and 1, respectively. For Fig. 1(b), the computed IoU is larger than 0.5; for Fig. 1(c), the computed IoU is smaller than 0.5. Subsequently, when one uses IoU as an evaluation metric, one needs to *argue how the computed IoU value is related to safety*. Consider a setup where there is no safety buffer associated with the motion planning algorithm, then the situation in Fig. 1(b) is not safe, as the vehicle may assume that the area outside the prediction corresponds to drivable free-space, thereby inducing the risk of collision. This contrasts with Fig. 1(c), where although the DNN-predicted bounding box is large, a buffer-free motion planner that never encroaches the prediction bounding box can never hit the pedestrian. Therefore, under specific assumptions on the capability of the motion planner, the IoU has no direct correlation with safety. In this example, one possible definition of safe detection can be informally stated using Definition 1.

Definition 1 (Safe DNN pedestrian detection). *A DNN pedestrian detection is safe, if the DNN-predicted bounding box strictly contains the labeled bounding box of the pedestrian.*

(Addressing Imprecise Detection as Functional Insufficiency). Based on Definition 1, one can take an object detector and understand if the generated prediction is safe. Unsafe predictions may further be categorized by their demonstrated

behaviors. For each category, one should design a corresponding counter-measure to inhibit the likelihood of occurrence. Here we focus on addressing the behavior of *imprecise localization*, i.e., a pedestrian is detected by the object recognition module, but the imprecision of the detector can not fully cover the bounding box, similar to the examples in Fig. 1(a) and (b). The consequence of using standard performance metrics such as mean-average precision (mAP) is that one needs to *perfect the performance to achieve safety*. Unfortunately, the state-of-the-art DNN-based object detectors as of 2021 [4] setting a benchmark for the COCO object detection dataset [8] only reaches an mAP of 78.5%, making it still far away from claiming the performance to be "perfect". However, we demonstrate in the below paragraph that we have a simpler way of improving the overall perception module.

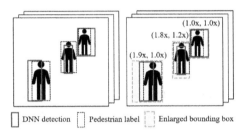

Fig. 2. Enlarging the bounding box to enable full containment

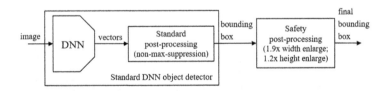

Fig. 3. Function modification by adding safe post-processing modules

(Conservative Safety-Aware Post-processing). Given that a DNN-based perception module is unable to generate bounding boxes that fully cover the pedestrian labels, instead of retraining the DNN module, we perform *function modification* as detailed below. The intuition is that by observing and measuring the degree of localization imprecision from the training data, one can conservatively compensate it in operation by enlarging the bounding box.

1. For each image collected in the training data set, and for each predicted bounding box that does not fully cover the pedestrian label, measure the

minimum enlargement ratio required to enclose the bounding box label. Consider the example in Fig. 2. For the bounding box prediction in the bottom left, to fully cover the label, one should enlarge the width of the bounding box by 1.9×. For the prediction in the center of the image, to fully cover the label, one should enlarge the width of the bounding box by 1.8× and enlarge the height by 1.2×.

2. Learn the required ratio from the previous step, in order to be larger than all previously computed ratios while considering variations in the training data distribution. Consider again the example in Fig. 2, a simple "mechanical learning" can be to memorize the maximum ratio for all images in the training data set (or a special "calibration set") and for all bounding boxes analyzed in the previous step. In Fig. 2, the maximum width expansion ratio equals $\mathsf{max}\{1.9, 1.8, 1.0\} = 1.9$, and the maximum height expansion ratio equals $\mathsf{max}\{1.0, 1.2, 1.0\} = 1.2$.

3. Finally, add another post-processing unit after the standard post-processing unit, as illustrated in Fig. 3. During runtime, whenever a bounding box is generated, the post-processor always enlarges the predicted bounding box by the ratio stored in the previous step. For the example in Fig. 2, for every bounding box predicted in run time, the additional post-processor enlarges its width by 1.9× and its height by 1.2× to create the final prediction.

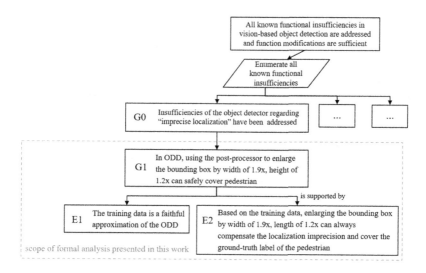

Fig. 4. Structuring the argument for safety, as a first attempt

3   From Structural to Logical Argumentation

For the approach presented in the previous section applied on the example in
Fig. 2, Fig. 4 shows an attempt to depict the structural argumentation connecting
the goal G1 with two supporting arguments E1 and E2. The underlying idea is
that the prediction can cover the pedestrian (G1), provided that

- enlarging bounding boxes demonstrates its sufficiency (E2) in-sample, and
- the training data is a good approximation of the ODD (E1), thereby creating
  a formal connection between in-sample and out-of-sample performance.

Subsequently, we perform a manual translation from informal specification to
logical specification. Table 1 shows the translated formula, and we refer readers
to the extended version [2] for formal specifications described using PVS [9]. The
meaning of each predicate and function should be self-explanatory; here we only
briefly explain its usage without giving a formal definition: $\mathsf{Training}(d)$ returns
true iff an image d is within the training data set; $\mathsf{ODD}(d)$ returns true iff an
image d is in the ODD. Given an image d, $\mathsf{DNN}(d)$, $\mathsf{label}(d)$ and $\mathsf{ground\_truth}(d)$
returns the predicted, labelled, and ground-truth bounding boxes of pedestrians.
Function $\mathsf{Enlarge}_{(1.9,1.2)}$ is the post-processor that enlarges each of the bounding
boxes generated by the DNN prediction. Finally, $\mathsf{Cover}(S1, S2)$ returns true iff
bounding boxes in $S1$ can cover bounding boxes in $S2$.

For E1, there can be multiple ways of interpreting "faithful approximation"
such as Probably Approximately Correct (PAC) learning with bounded generalization errors. Here for the ease of understanding, we use an extremely strong
condition on *behavior equivalence*, i.e., the behavior of the DNN demonstrated
in the ODD will be the same as the behavior demonstrated in the training
data set, applicable for every evaluation function $\mathsf{Behavior}$, under possible local
transformations over the output of the DNN (F_1) and the data point (F_2). By
translating E1, E2, and G1 into logical formulae, one can perform a deduction
and infer that *even under such a strong generalizability condition*, E1 and E2
alone are *not sufficient* to derive G1.

Table 1. Translating informal arguments in Fig. 4 into logical formula

Index	Informal description and the corresponding formal specification
E1	The training data is a faithful approximation of the ODD
	$\forall \mathsf{Behavior}, \mathsf{F}_1, \mathsf{F}_2 : (\forall d : \mathsf{Training}(d) \to \mathsf{Behavior}(\mathsf{F}_1(\mathsf{DNN}(d)), \mathsf{F}_2(d)))$ $\to (\forall d_{op} : \mathsf{ODD}(d_{op}) \to \mathsf{Behavior}(\mathsf{F}_1(\mathsf{DNN}(d_{op})), \mathsf{F}_2(d_{op})))$
E2	Based on the training data, enlarging the bounding box by width of 1.9×, height of 1.2× can always cover the ground-truth label of the pedestrian
	$\forall d : \mathsf{Training}(d) \to \mathsf{Cover}(\mathsf{Enlarge}_{(1.9,1.2)}(\mathsf{DNN}(d)), \mathsf{label}(d))$
G1	In ODD, enlarging the bounding box by width of 1.9×, height of 1.2× can safely cover the pedestrian
	$\forall d_{op} : \mathsf{ODD}(d_{op}) \to \mathsf{Cover}(\mathsf{Enlarge}_{(1.9,1.2)}(\mathsf{DNN}(d_{op})), \mathsf{ground\_truth}(d_{op}))$

Table 2. Additional arguments

E3	Based on the training data, ground-truth label of the pedestrian always strictly contains the pedestrian
	$\forall d : \mathsf{Training}(d) \rightarrow \mathsf{Cover}(\mathsf{label}(d), \mathsf{ground\_truth}(d))$
E4	If A covers B, and B covers C, then A covers C
	$\forall A, B, C : (\mathsf{Cover}(A, B) \wedge \mathsf{Cover}(B, C)) \rightarrow \mathsf{Cover}(A, C)$

– Within the training data, it is also important that the label of a pedestrian actually surrounds the corresponding pedestrian. This is characterized by E3 as stated in Table 2.
– To allow mechanical deduction, one needs to additionally add a *mathematical concept* (transitivity rule) for *area containment*, stating that if A covers B, and if B covers C, then A also covers C. This is characterized by E4 as stated in Table 2.

The formally stated specification in PVS [9] is checked mechanically using interactive theorem proving to derive that G1 can be deduced by arguments {E1, ..., E4}. Intuitively, the logical deduction of proving G1 proceeds by first creating a new lemma E5, stating that within the training data set, as every enlarged bounding box covers the label (E2), and as every label covers the ground truth location of the pedestrian (E3), the enlarged bounding box can (due to transitivity E4) cover the ground truth location of the pedestrian.

$$\forall d : \mathsf{Training}(d) \rightarrow \mathsf{Cover}(\mathsf{Enlarge}_{(1.9,1.2)}(\mathsf{DNN}(d)), \mathsf{ground\_truth}(d)) \qquad (E5)$$

Subsequently, use E1 by instantiating Behavior, F_1, and F_2 with Cover, $\mathsf{Enlarge}_{(1.9,1.2)}$, and ground_truth. Then together with E5, one derives G1.

(Towards Quantitative Argumentation). The example demonstrated in Fig. 4 also provides an example on the limitation of using semi-formal notations for quantitative argumentation suggested by earlier results. Even when E1 and E2 have 100% confidence of being correct, one may be tempted to use evidence combination theory such as Dempster's rule on structural argumentation [3,5, 11,12] and to conclude that G1 holds with 100% confidence. Nevertheless, based on the logical deduction, G1 does not hold without E3. This implies that the result of evidence combination can only be counted as an upper bound.

References

1. ISO/PAS 21448:2019 road vehicles - safety of the intended functionality (2019). https://www.iso.org/standard/70939.html
2. Cheng, C.-H., Schuster, T., Burton, S.: Logically sound arguments for the effectiveness of ml safety measures. arXiv preprint arXiv:2111.02649 (2021)
3. Cyra, L., Gorski, J.: Support for argument structures review and assessment. Reliab. Eng. Syst. Saf. **96**(1), 26–37 (2011)
4. Dai, X., et al.: Dynamic head: unifying object detection heads with attentions. In: Proceedings of the IEEE/CVF Conference on Computer Vision and Pattern Recognition (CVPR), pp. 7373–7382. IEEE (2021)
5. Idmessaoud, Y., Dubois, D., Guiochet, J.: Belief functions for safety arguments confidence estimation: a comparative study. In: Davis, J., Tabia, K. (eds.) SUM 2020. LNCS (LNAI), vol. 12322, pp. 141–155. Springer, Cham (2020). https://doi.org/10.1007/978-3-030-58449-8_10
6. Kelly, T., Weaver, R.: The goal structuring notation - a safety argument notation. In: Proceedings of the Dependable Systems and Networks Workshop on Assurance Cases, p. 6. Citeseer (2004)
7. LeCun, Y., Bengio, Y., Hinton, G.: Deep learning. Nature **521**(7553), 436–444 (2015)
8. Lin, T.-Y., et al.: Microsoft COCO: common objects in context. In: Fleet, D., Pajdla, T., Schiele, B., Tuytelaars, T. (eds.) ECCV 2014. LNCS, vol. 8693, pp. 740–755. Springer, Cham (2014). https://doi.org/10.1007/978-3-319-10602-1_48
9. Owre, S., Rushby, J.M., Shankar, N.: PVS: a prototype verification system. In: Kapur, D. (ed.) CADE 1992. LNCS, vol. 607, pp. 748–752. Springer, Heidelberg (1992). https://doi.org/10.1007/3-540-55602-8_217
10. Sentz, K., Ferson, S.: Combination of evidence in Dempster-Shafer theory, vol. 4015. Sandia National Laboratories (2002)
11. Wang, R.: Confidence in safety argument-an assessment framework based on belief function theory. Ph.D. thesis, INSA de Toulouse (2018)
12. Yuan, C., Wu, J., Liu, C., Yang, H.: A subjective logic-based approach for assessing confidence in assurance case. Int. J. Performability Eng. **13**(6), 807 (2017)

Author Index

Printed in the United States
by Baker & Taylor Publisher Services